Savage Exchange

HARVARD-YENCHING INSTITUTE MONOGRAPH SERIES 94

Savage Exchange

HAN IMPERIALISM, CHINESE LITERARY STYLE, AND THE ECONOMIC IMAGINATION

Tamara T. Chin

Published by the Harvard University Asia Center
Distributed by Harvard University Press
Cambridge (Massachusetts) and London 2014

Printed in the United States of America

The Harvard-Yenching Institute, founded in 1928, is an independent foundation dedicated to the advancement of higher education in the humanities and social sciences in Asia. Headquartered on the campus of Harvard University, the Institute provides fellowships for advanced research, training, and graduate studies at Harvard by competitively selected faculty and graduate students from Asia. The Institute also supports a range of academic activities at its fifty partner universities and research institutes across Asia. At Harvard, the Institute promotes East Asian studies through annual contributions to the Harvard-Yenching Library and publication of the *Harvard Journal of Asiatic Studies* and the Harvard-Yenching Institute Monograph Series.

Library of Congress Cataloging-in-Publication Data

Chin, Tamara T., 1975–
   Savage exchange : Han imperialism, Chinese literary style, and the economic imagination / Tamara T. Chin.
      pages cm. — (Harvard-Yenching Institute monograph series ; 94)
   Includes bibliographical references and index.
   ISBN 978-0-674-41719-9 (hardcover : acid-free paper); ISBN 978-0-674-24452-8 (paperback : alk. paper)   1. Chinese literature—Qin and Han dynasties, 221 B.C.-220 A.D.—History and criticism.   2. China—History—Han dynasty, 202 B.C.-220 A.D.   3. Imperialism—Social aspects—China—History—To 1500.   4. Imperialism—Economic aspects—China—History—To 1500.   5. Economics and literature—China—History—To 1500.   6. Politics and literature—China—History—To 1500.   7. Commerce in literature.   8. China—Commerce—History.   9. China—Economic conditions—To 1644.   10. China—Territorial expansion.   I. Title.
   PL2284.C547 2014
   895.109'0022—dc23

                                                                                        2014011090

Index by Cynthia Col, Jac Nelson, and Tamara Chin

♾ Printed on acid-free paper

Last figure below indicates year of this printing

29   28   27   26   25   24   23   22   21   20

*For my parents
and for Leslie Kurke*

Contents

Illustrations

Acknowledgments

My first debt is to my teachers, above all Leslie Kurke, as well as Michael Nylan and Jeffrey Riegel, who provided guidance, inspiration, and painstaking comments on my dissertation and on multiple drafts of this book.

Lydia Liu first introduced me to the possibilities of sinology and comparative literature, and I thank her, Donald Harper, Nicola di Cosmo, and Jim Chandler for their feedback and advice in developing my original project into this book. Richard Von Glahn provided helpful comments on my manuscript and shared his own unpublished work on Chinese economic history. I am grateful to him and to the following persons for their insightful readings of various chapters: Elaine Freedgood, Paola Iovene, Michael Loewe, Boris Maslov, Michael Murrin, Haun Saussy, John Tain, Wu Hung, Alice Yao, Anthony Yu, and Judith Zeitlin. I am especially grateful to Leela Gandhi, who read every chapter with care and provided invaluable suggestions at every stage.

I was generously invited to present portions of this book at various institutions: Columbia University, Cornell University, Harvard University, Indiana University, the Institute for Advanced Studies, New York University, NYU-Abu Dhabi, Penn State University, the Royal Geographical Society in association with the University of Nottingham, the University of Chicago, the University of Rochester, and Yale University, and Yale-NUS College. I am grateful to Andrea Bachner, Shadi Bartsch, Joanne Bernardi, Michael Bourdaghs, Nicola Di Cosmo, Valerie Hansen, Eric Hayot, Mike Heffernan, Wai-yee Li, Robin McNeal, Moss Roberts, Morris Rossabi, Carlos Rojas, Kevin Tsai, Shamoon Zamir, Judith Zeitlin, Xudong Zhang, Yiqun Zhou, and others for facilitating these visits and to those who took the time to listen and make suggestions and corrections. At these workshops and talks, as well as at the University of Chicago's China Before Print Workshop, I have been particularly grateful for the comments of Gardner Bovingdon, Erica Brindley, Jack Chen, Thomas Dipiero, Mark Elliott, Lothar Von Falkenhausen, Magnus Fiskesjö, Paul Goldin, Martin Kern, Esther Klein, Carla Nappi, Michael Puett, Christopher Nugent, Stephen Owen, Charles Sanft, Alan Thomas, Ping Wang, and Anthony Yu. Further thanks are due to Bill Brown, Jim Chandler, Judith Farquhar, Jim Hevia, Kenneth Pomeranz, and Victoria Kahn for their support of my work.

I am grateful to the Silk Road Foundation, the American Council of Learned Societies for supporting a year's leave in which to finish this book and to the University of Chicago's Franke Institute and NYU's Institute for the Study of the Ancient World for allowing me to participate as an honorary fellow in their respective workshops. The latter institution, in particular, helped to reshape the way I think about material culture and cross-cultural history and my analysis is indebted to the talks and casual conversations with fellow scholars there.

During early stages, the UC Berkeley Comparative Literature Department and the Designated Emphasis on Women, Gender, and Sexuality program provided a nurturing and intellectually exciting home. I greatly benefited from Ralph Hexter's advice on my dissertation and from graduate coursework at Berkeley and at Harvard with Anthony Appiah, Martin Backstrom, Wendy Brown, Judith Butler, Margaret Conkey, Wilt Idema, Barbara Johnson, Victoria Kahn, Leslie Kurke, Wai-yee Li, Lydia Liu, Anthony Long, Ian Morris, Michael Nylan, Jeffrey Riegel, and Stephen Owen. I am also grateful for early encouragement from Sandra Naddaff, Gregory Nagy, Anne Seaton, and Deborah Sze-lan Sang. Yukiko Hanawa, Kota Inoue, Rebecca Karl, Thomas Looser, Janet Poole, Moss Roberts, Keith Vincent, and Xudong Zhang provided a welcoming and stimulating home during a subsequent postdoctoral fellowship in NYU's East Asian Studies department, support for which I remain indebted.

My book has ventured into disciplines far from my intellectual home base. For their conversations, expertise, and indulgent encouragement, especially in the fields of archaeology, art history, and numismatics in the US, China, UK, and along the Silk Road, I thank the visiting scholars and Roger Bagnall at New York University's Institute for the Study of the Ancient World, as well as Wu Hung, Alice Yao, Wang Qingzhong, Ma Chengyuan, Roderick Whitfield, Youngsook Pak, and Albert Dien. Thanks also to Guo Wu of the Chinese Academy of Social Sciences for sharing his research on frontier archaeology, and to Li Jianmao of the Hunan Provincial Museum. My work on money was helped by discussions with numismatists at the "International Conference on Silk Road Coins" (hosted by the Shanghai Museum in 2006), who included Wang Yu, Osmund Bopearachchi, and François Thierry; as well as discussions with Helen Wang and Joe Cribb at the British Museum and Jiang Baolian and other numismatists in Xi'an. I am grateful to curators at the Gansu Provincial Museum, the Shanghai Museum, and the British Museum for showing me samples of coins. I would like to thank the archaeologist Li Yong and Li Guangning of the Anhui Bureau of Cultural Relics; Michael Alram of the Kunsthistorisches Museum–Wien; and Helen Wang, Christopher Sutherns, and the Trustees of the British Museum for their generous help and permission in reproducing their photographs of coins. I am grateful to Li Jianmao and the Hunan Provincial Museum, and to Li Yinde and the Xuzhou Museum for so graciously facilitating my reproduction of photographs. I also thank James Lin of the Fitzwilliam Museum, Cambridge.

Conversations with other colleagues, students, and friends have provided sustenance and stimulation over the years: Shi Tou, Ming Ming, Frances Ferguson, Jim Hevia, Judith Farquhar, Yü Chun-fang, Reggie Jackson, Jing Tsu, Robert Chi, Ping Foong, Deb Kamen, Agnes Lugo-Ortiz, Diane Miliotes, Boris Maslov, Lital Levy, Jacob Eyferth, Paola Iovene, Mae Ngai, Gao Fengfeng, Christiane Frey, Lina Steiner, Emanuel Mayer, Alan Thomas, Julia Thomas, Yiqun Zhou, Timothy Campbell, Tom Mitchell, Jen Scapettone, Michael Geyer, Miriam Hansen, Glen Weyl, Alain Bresson, Chris Faraone, Raju Pandey, Sanjay Seth, Michael Dutton, David Eng, Maud Ellman, John Wilkinson, Françoise Meltzer, Lauren Berlant, Alexander Beecroft, Tom Kelly, Adhira Mangaligiri, Nic Wong, Shengyu Wang, Ernest Caldwell, Smadar Winter, Lida Wu, Rivi Handler-Spitz, Bruce Rusk, David Halperin, Danielle Allen, Susie Jolly. Thanks also to Bronte Adams, Claire Murray, Santiago Moreno and Carl Kutsmode, Rita Balzotti, Michelle Sanford, Ruth Vanita and Mona and Arjun, Lucy Eyre, Judy Weatherhead, Oui Coulson, Anna Kaminski, Gisela Alvarez, Tanya Krohn, Huma Dar, John Hill, Sharon Marcus, Ellis Avery, Karen Tongson, Katrin Pahl, Alan Yu, Fifi Chu, Nick and Narween, Michael and Mimi Kan, Greg Kan, Doreen and Ajzyk Jagoda, Suzu Tokue, and Mahesh Rangarajan.

I am grateful to my editor at Harvard University Asia Center, Kristen Wanner, and to Robert Graham, for their guidance and efficiency, and to my wonderful copyeditors Alice Davenport and Ernst Schwintzer. I am also grateful to Scott Walker and Kathy Dempsey, for their talent in producing the original maps in this book; to Fan Guangxin and Ellen Herbert for their research assistance; and to Bea Malsky and Xindi Yan for their help with images. For their help in looking at rare materials I thank the curators of National Museum, Delhi, and the Government Museum, Chennai; and the librarians of the British Library, the National Library of China, the Shanghai Library, the Baotou County Library (Inner Mongolia), the Royal Geographical Society Library, and the University of Chicago Library. I am also grateful for the hospitality of Indu Gandhi and Veenapani Chawla.

Special thanks to John Tain, Josh Oppenheimer and Shu Harada, Shi Tou and Ming Ming, Larushka Ivan-Zadeh, Serena Yuan Volpp, Sophie Volpp, and Kyeong-Hee Choi, and to my two grandmothers, deeply missed.

Material for chapters 3 and 5 first appeared in "Defamiliarizing the foreigner: Sima Qian's ethnography and Han-Xiongnu marriage diplomacy," *Harvard Journal of Asiatic Studies* 70, no. 2 (Dec 2010): 311–54 and is reprinted here with permission of the editors.

Finally, Leela Gandhi has provided a more loving home than anyone could ask for and I thank her for bringing wonder, joy, and a bigger world into it.

—T.T.C.

Conventions

Translations are the author's unless otherwise noted. The original Chinese is generally included either in the main text or in the footnotes, depending on its relevance to the discussion at hand. The editions of texts used are noted in the bibliography. Where multiple editions have been consulted, the relevant edition is noted accordingly. In the case of the Standard Histories, references are, unless otherwise noted, to the punctuated editions of *Zhonghua shuju* that are recorded in the bibliography. To aid the non-specialist I have generally used conventional English translations of titles of early Chinese works (e.g., the *Classic of Odes*) except in the case of extensively discussed works such as the *Shiji*.

INTRODUCTION

Savage Exchange

The past half-century of archaeology has unearthed a Han dynasty (206 BCE–220 CE) world more urbanized, monetized, and connected to maritime and overland Silk Routes than previously understood. But what did these material changes of the Han period mean to its participants? How did early Chinese writers represent and reorganize the shifting world around them? Why did they introduce new genres and metaphors to do so? How, in other words, might literary analysis yield a fresh perspective on Han economic debates and sentiments?

To address such questions, this book pursues the relationship between literary form and social history. It gathers together a set of received and excavated Han dynasty texts and shows how the innovative forms of these texts are situated in the specific historical circumstances of China's emergence as an imperialist and commercial power in Eurasia. Bringing the scholarship on literary and visual representation into closer conversation with political and economic studies of early China, this book examines some poems, narratives, images, and symbolic practices through which certain fractions of Han society debated trade and territorial expansion. Aesthetic and cultural concerns shaped the canonical sources of Han economic history to a greater degree than has been previously appreciated. At the same time, novel Han dynasty ways of reconceiving the political economy inspired literary experiments that deserve greater attention in histories of Chinese literature.

This book focuses on the watershed reign of Han Emperor Wu 漢武帝 (r. 141–87 BCE), which marks China's earliest expansion of monetized markets and the largest-scale extension of frontiers in Chinese imperial history.

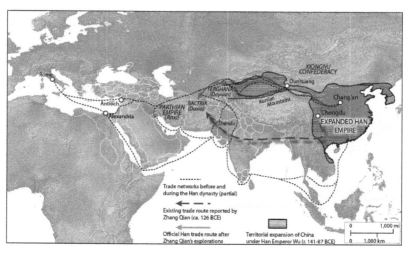

FIGURE 0.1. Map of the Former Han empire and the Silk Road, showing the territorial expansion of China during the reign of Emperor Wu and part of the official and unofficial trade network across Eurasia.

As shown in figure 0.1, Emperor Wu's armies forcibly extended the Former Han Empire into modern-day Inner and Outer Mongolia, Xinjiang, Yunnan, Guangzhou, Vietnam, Korea, and eastern Central Asia. As is also shown on this map, Emperor Wu's envoy Zhang Qian 張騫 (d. 113 BCE) helped to open up new official trade routes with Central Asia and to uncover some of the unofficial networks of trade with India and southeast Asia that were already flourishing. During this period some officials and scholars took the market as an inspiration for social and aesthetic reform. For the first time, they placed quantitative calculations, not ethics and ritual propriety, at the heart of the political economy. To promote the abstract laws of the market, these scholars and officials developed new forms of fiction, new genres, and new symbolic forms. In opposition to them, a group of traditionalists reasserted the authority of classical texts and promoted a return to the historical, ritual propriety-centered, agricultural economy that such texts described. These classically trained scholars (a group traditionally hostile to merchants) protested that market price was increasingly determining social values and that commerce was facilitating improper exchanges between Chinese and foreigners, between men and women, and between farmers, artisans, and traders.

The discussion of the new frontiers and markets was thus part of a larger debate over the relationship between the world and the written text. To foreground this politics of representation, my book approaches the political economy from the perspective of a history of literary and material practices. Three chapters focus on a textual tradition or genre (philosophical dialogue, prose-poetry, historiography); two explore symbolic or embodied practices (money, kinship). Together these describe the art and conventions of representation through which texts problematized frontiers and markets in relation to language, gender, cosmology, and history. In other studies, modern scholars have observed that the classical record of premodern Chinese market life has come down to us largely through the lens of its critics. By tracing a more implicit ideological battle over the very idiom of the political economy, this study will reconstruct both sides of this debate. Both positions were asserted in and through a set of symbolic practices, whose aesthetically encoded suggestions were sometimes at odds with their expressed content. In this way the political crisis at the frontiers transformed—and was transformed by—diverse debates over money, gender, kinship, and poetic labor.

I trace this disarticulated and ambivalent imagination of the political economy through a selection of transmitted and excavated Han dynasty texts. My treatment does not aim to be comprehensive, but rather to be selective and exemplary in modeling an interdisciplinary approach—one that brings together excavated and transmitted economic, political, legal, mathematical, visual, and literary texts that today are often read separately for reasons of academic specialization. I focus on the transmitted texts that modern historians have relied upon most to reconstruct Han economic history and thought. These texts comprise the two canonical histories of the Former Han dynasty—Sima Qian's 司馬遷 (?145–?86 BCE) *Shiji* 史記 (Records of the grand scribe) and Ban Gu's 班固 (32–92 CE) *Hanshu* 漢書 (History of the Former Han) —and the respective economic dialogues of Huan Kuan's 桓寬 (fl. 60 BCE) *Debate on Salt and Iron* (*Yantielun* 鹽鐵論) and the *Guanzi*'s 管子 "Qingzhong" 輕重 ("Light and heavy") chapters (compiled ca. 100 BCE). I bring these more overtly "economic" texts to bear on other prose and poetic texts, including the Han dynasty's most popular literary genre, the prose-poetic *fu*, whose rhythmic catalogs of exotica have long been associated with trade and empire by art historians and literary scholars.

The broader significance of this case study is, I suggest, twofold. First, the past half century of archaeological discovery has tended to affirm linear narratives of Chinese empire derived from traditional interpretations of Han literary texts. I question the longstanding appropriation of key texts for characterizing Emperor Wu's reign as that which consolidated the foundations of the Chinese tributary empire, China's cultural heritage, and Han ethnicity. I trace experiments in Han dynasty dissident thought and aesthetic practice that were radically at odds with what came before *and* after in China's history. These "dead ends" in cultural history—that is, the uses of genre and language, and the symbolic practices that failed to become hegemonic—are, I argue, worth recovering for less teleological reconstructions of China's past. The concluding coda will address this mode of historical inquiry in a comparative context.

Second, the Han archive showcases—more clearly than many other global contexts—the benefits of a literary and cultural approach to economic history. During the Han expansion of monetized markets, there was an unusual self-reflexiveness, creativity, and rhetorical playfulness with the very idiom of monetary exchange. For example, some Han scholars exploited historical shifts in Chinese terms for, and material forms of, money to mythologize monetary exchange. Others used new metaphors and new kinds of literary abstraction to introduce a more quantitative, "economic" logic of market price than one might expect of a premodern text. Since, as chapter 5 will explore further, some Han writers approached coinage as a form of writing, an account of Han dynasty economic thought demands the consideration of Han literary systems of value. A complete analysis of Han money is therefore contingent not only on the definition of money used in analyzing archival sources, but also on the modern reader's interpretive decisions about literary meaning in the basic sources.

The remainder of this introduction will elaborate this book's analytical methods and arguments, in the contexts both of existing scholarship and of the particular difficulties of working with early Chinese texts.

Cultural and Material Poetics

Han discussions about frontier and market were embedded in a larger debate over the relationship between the world and the written text.

Scholars and officials differed not only over their ideals of the political economy, but also over how to represent and reproduce those ideals. Did inherited classics represent the past that policy makers should reproduce? Or were new literary forms and metaphors needed? In 136 BCE Emperor Wu established the Five Classics (*Wu jing* 五經) as the basis of official learning (*guan xue* 官學) and in 124 BCE as the basis of the new Imperial Academy (*tai xue* 太學). However, it seems that the classical learning acquired its prestige largely after Emperor Wu, and partly as a backlash against his advisers who had transgressed classical ideals with their political and economic reforms. By the Later Han, scholars had become transformed from ritual experts into textual experts and the imperial examination system developed over subsequent centuries. In this context Han dynasty written texts served not simply as a reflection or product of social reality, but as one of many potentially antagonistic practices that included material and ritual practices.

The Han dynasty conflicts about the political economy helped to shape the ways we now define and appreciate early Chinese "literature" (*wenxue* 文學). Fifty years or so years after Emperor Wu's reign, the imperial librarians Liu Xiang 劉向 (79–8 BCE) and Liu Xin 劉歆 (46 BCE–23 CE) reorganized, edited, and rewrote the entire holdings of the imperial library to produce the copies upon which most of our received books from early China are based. Records of their interpretive choices (in selecting between multiple versions and in translating archaic into standardized Han dynasty characters) have been largely lost.[1] This bibliographic project was very much part of the politicized elevation of classical learning that occurred after Emperor Wu's demise. Gu Jiegang's 顧頡剛 (1895–1980) "doubting antiquity" (*yigu* 疑古) movement developed earlier arguments that the Liu librarians and other Han classicists tampered with texts to legitimate various imperial rulers. According to Gu and his collaborators, by inserting or perpetuating myths about China's longevity and historical personae into canonical classical texts, such scholars lengthened Chinese history from a mere 2,500 years to over 5,000 years (or to 2,276,000 years, according to apocryphal texts). Although recent

---

1. On Qin-Han orthographic reforms beginning with Li Si 李斯 (ca. 280–208 BCE) reforms to standardize the script after political unification in 221 BCE, see Boltz, *The Origin and Early Development of the Chinese Writing System*, 156–78 and Galambos, *Orthography of Early Chinese Writing*.

scholarship on excavated texts has overturned Gu's textual chronology, it has reaffirmed the collusion of classicism and imperial administration.

Rather than track the well-known rise of this classical "imperial ideology," my book explores political ambivalence and protest within the classical tradition.[2] Each chapter takes a key genre or practice (philosophy, *fu*-rhapsody, historiography, money, kinship) through which different groups sought to imagine the political economy. Together these chapters describe the art and conventions of representation through which texts problematized frontiers and markets in relation to kinship, language, and history. In contrast to existing English language studies of individual economic texts (e.g., Nancy Lee Swann, Allyn Rickett, Michael Loewe) and social groups such as artisans (Anthony Barbieri-Low), slaves (C. Martin Wilbur), and agriculturalists (Cho-yun Hsu), I focus on the politics of representation.[3] This cultural and material approach to poetics situates the meaning of literary innovations in the larger semiotic world of economic transactions and political/imperial rivalries. Two discernible shifts or ruptures crosscut discourses and genres. Crudely put, these ruptures straddle Emperor Wu's half-century reign, marking his reign out from what came before and after. The most radical or experimental early Chinese approaches to market and frontier (the *Guanzi*'s "Qingzhong" chapters, the *Shiji*, Sima Xiangru's *fu*) coincided with Emperor Wu's activist reign. And the most explicit strategies for containing the forms and ideology that these works provoked are exemplified in works that date to the post-Emperor Wu period (i.e., during the final decades of the Former Han and through the Later Han).[4]

---

2. For alternate approaches to intracultural conflict in the Han, see, for example, Puett, *The Ambivalence of Creation*, and Aihe Wang, "Correlative Cosmology." For studies of the role of writing, classical texts, and classical scholars in establishing the political authority during the Han dynasty, see Lewis, *Writing and Authority*; Connery, *The Empire of the Text*.

3. Swann, *Food and Money*; Rickett, *Guanzi*; Loewe, *Crisis and Conflict* (which includes an interpretive account of the *Debate on Salt and Iron* debate); Barbieri-Low, *Artisans*; Wilbur, *Slavery in China*; Hsu, *Han Agriculture*.

4. These shifts are far more limited than Michel Foucault's notion of epistemic ruptures. In the *Order of Things* these refer to wholesale transformations in the limits in what a historical culture could or could not think. This relatively slender selection of texts highlights emergent possibilities and tendencies, rather than defining outermost limits. See the coda for a further discussion.

TEXTS AND GENRES BEFORE "LITERATURE"

Han dynasty readers and writers had no fixed category of "literature." Although modern literary scholarship on Chinese texts generally focuses on poetry, early readers did not differentiate between literary and non-literary, or fictional and non-fictional genres. They appreciated the greater or lesser moral-aesthetic style or patterning (*wen* 文) of a text.[5] The general privileging of historiography over fiction was often articulated through the opposition of *xu* 虛 ("emptiness," understood as "fiction") and *shi* 實 ("fullness"; "historical reality," conflated with "truth"). The classicizing turn after Emperor Wu brought a more self-conscious discourse privileging *wen* and *wenzhang* 文章 as writing.[6] With the political rise of textual experts, *wenzhang*, which originally referred to ritual demeanor, political order, and ornament, increasingly became associated with classicist learning, official texts, and literature (*wenxue*). The belles-lettristic restriction of early Chinese literature to lyric poetry (*shi* 詩), rhapsody (*fu* 賦), and various other prose and poetic traditions, properly began only in the Six Dynasties period (220–589). The Later Han philosopher Wang Chong 王充 (27–ca. 100) had included in his "five classes of literature" (五文 *wu wen*) the Five Classics; the philosophical masters and commentaries; treatises and theories; letters and submitted presentations; and efficacious works, but not poetry per se.[7] It is only toward the end of the Later Han and over subsequent centuries, with Cao Pi's 曹丕 (187–226) "Discourse on Literature" (*Lun wen*), Lu Ji's 陸機 (261–303) "*Fu* on Literature" (*Wen fu*), Liu Xie's 劉勰 (fl. 6th c.) *The Literary Mind and the Carving of Dragons* (*Wenxin diaolong*), and Xiao Tong's 蕭統 (501–531) *Selections of Literature* (*Wen xuan*), that self-consciously belles-lettristic traditions began to divorce most types of texts from the proper purview of *wen*.

---

5. For example, apt quotation from the *Odes* (*shi*, one of the Five Classics) in political and diplomatic speech was a longstanding marker of eloquence and of moral-cultural belonging. See *Lunyu* 11.3 on *wenxue* as skill in cultural tradition.

6. See Kern, "Ritual, Text, and the Formation of the Canon," and Schaberg, *A Patterned Past*, 57–95. For the argument that Eastern Zhou uses of *wen* in *shi* poetry as a generalized positive epithet for ancestors (as part of ancestor cult and ritual) differed from the development of *wen* as "ornament," see von Falkenhausen, "The Concept of *Wen*."

7. *Lun heng*, 867. The following post-Han works varied in generic expansiveness.

To consider early notions of texts during this pre-"literature" epoch of Chinese writing, one might look to the "Treatise on Arts and Writing" (*Yiwen zhi* 藝文志). This chapter of the *Hanshu* (composed in the Later Han) provides a schema for bibliographical classification that lists a much wider range of texts than we might now associate with literature or the "literary" (*wen*). Based on an earlier outline by the imperial librarians Liu Xiang and Liu Xin, it catalogs several hundred works, under six major rubrics or tenets (*lüe* 略), listed by their authors or titles:

1) The Six Arts (*liu yi* 六藝), i.e., the Five Classics, which lay at the core of any person's classical education, and their commentarial and related traditions.
2) The Masters (*zhu zi* 諸子), i.e., philosophical texts.
3) Poetry and Rhapsody (*shi fu* 詩賦).
4) Military Books (*bing shu* 兵書).
5) Computations and Arts (*shushu* 術數), including astronomy and divination.
6) Remedies and Techniques (*fangji* 方技), including medical texts and arts of the bedchamber.

These six bibliographic categories and their various sub-categories (*zhong* 種) are not what we would call genres but nevertheless offer a glimpse at the kinds of formal and thematic expectations associated with genre. For example, the "Treatise on Arts and Writing" does not tell us that the *Shiji* introduced (what we now call) the "annals and traditions form" (*jizhuanti* 紀傳體) that influenced subsequent Chinese historiography, but it does classify it under the chronicle tradition that the *Shiji* effectively transformed, namely the *Spring and Autumn Annals* (*Chunqiu* 春秋) subsection of the "Six Arts" (*liu yi* 六藝).[8] Likewise, the classification of the *Guanzi* and the *Debate on Salt and Iron* under the "Various Masters" (*zhu zi* 諸子) tradition draws attention to the use of the philosophical dialogue form in these works. These two texts are now treated as political or economic texts, but this study explores the way each of them uses the medium of philosophical dialogue. The recurrence of names across bibliographic categories suggests that authors did not restrict themselves to a single tradition (or did not know of or use these classifications). For

---

8. The classics were generally understood to be works or edited anthologies of Confucius, and also included the *Changes* (*Yi*), *Odes* (*Shi*), *Documents* (*Shu*), *Rites*, and *Music*.

this reason, the terms *genre* or *discourse* serve as placeholders, and I pursue literary innovations across a number of traditions. Chapter 2, for example, examines the significance of the use of personification in both the *Guanzi*'s economic dialogues and Sima Xiangru's *fu*.[9]

Notions of authorship are further complicated by the composite nature of early Chinese texts. Transmitted and excavated Chinese texts were generally the work of multiple, often anonymous, composers and editors that were copied, edited, and interpreted by generations of scribes. The texts or chapters selected for analysis here are contingently dated, based on specialist studies. Names such as Guanzi, Sima Qian, and Ban Gu serve as the conventional author-functions, that is, these are the authoritative names that ancient and modern readers have assigned to the text or textual tradition.[10] Much of the transmitted text that is now called the *Guanzi* postdates its ascribed author Guanzi (Guan Zhong 管仲, d. 645 BCE). Thus, although there is consensus that the *Guanzi*'s "Qingzhong" section was composed around the Former Han period, I do not single it out as Pseudo-Guanzi, as others do. Instead, chapter 1 asks how the "Qingzhong" section in its introduction of economic theory drew on the rhetorical form of the earlier Guanzian dialogue. In the case of the (multi-author-function) *Hanshu* and *Shiji*, I use "Sima Qian" or "Ban Gu" as shorthand for the authorial persona. Thus any resonances that I argue between the autobiographical postface and the authorial end comments to individual chapters pertain not to the historical Sima Qian (or his co-author and father Sima Tan 司馬談 [d. 110 BCE]), but to the frustrated authorial *persona* "Sima Qian" constructed by the *Shiji*. The *Shiji* offers an extreme example of this problem of the unified work. Parts of the *Shiji* went missing as early as the first century BCE likely due to its political sensitivity. Our transmitted *Shiji* contains chapters explicitly composed by a Han scholar writing shortly after the time of Sima Qian (Chu Shaosun 褚少孫, fl. first c. BCE), and the *Hanshu* reported, "[The *Shiji*] lacks ten chapters; they have titles but no

---

9. One might note in this vein that Yang Xiong's 揚雄 (53 BCE–18 CE) various works appear under the "Six Arts," "The Masters," and "Poetry and Rhapsody," and that Sima Qian, Liu Xiang, the King of Huainan, Ban Gu, and Ban Zhao all composed (largely lost) *fu* in addition to their better known works. See Aihe Wang, "Correlative Cosmology."

10. See Foucault, "What Is an Author?"

texts."[11] Although the *Hanshu* ostensibly took its "annals and traditions" structure, as well as long passages, often verbatim, from the *Shiji*, comparisons of graphic variants and lexical or syntactic differences have led many modern scholars to conclude that post-Han scribes reconstructed certain sections of the *Shiji* from the chronologically later *Hanshu*. There is general consensus that these cases need to be evaluated on a chapter-by-chapter basis. In the cases at stake, the debates about chronology do not actually affect my argument. For example, it does not fundamentally matter to my analysis of Sima Xiangru's prose-poetic *fu* in chapter 2 whether the (nearly identical) *Shiji* or *Hanshu* "Account of Sima Xiangru" came first. We may be left with a Later Han rendition of Sima Xiangru's life and *da fu* 大賦 ("great *fu*" or epideictic *fu*), but we can follow the approach of other Han writers in attributing to Sima Xiangru 司馬相如 (179–117 BCE) the genre's controversial "excesses" in length and sound patterning.[12]

This focus on conflict within (as well as across) generic traditions aims to move beyond a tendency in modern scholarship either to conflate all Han texts with "Confucian imperial ideology," or to explain the syncretism of Han thought in terms of rival Warring States "schools of thought" (*jia* 家). Although the Han bibliography subcategorizes the *Debate on Salt and Iron* as "Ruist" and the *Guanzi* as "Daoist," these schools do not coherently organize listings outside the "Masters" category.[13]

Modern "histories of Chinese economic thought" (*Zhongguo jingji sixiang shi*) usefully draw attention to ideological differences between individual texts, especially during the Han. Ye Shichang, Hu Jichuang, Wu Baosan, Han Fuzhi and others have clarified how these Han period rivalries overshadow those of the Warring States, which usually take center stage in any account of Chinese thought. These authorities generally agree that the *Guanzi*'s Han dynasty "Qingzhong" chapters established

---

11. *Hanshu* 62.2724. 十篇缺，有錄無書.

12. Likewise, even if lexical variants between the *Shiji*'s "Account of the Xiongnu" and the first half of the *Hanshu* version suggest that portions of the latter predate the former, it is their radically different authorial end comments that matter to the argument of chapter 4.

13. One might note that the *Hanshu*'s ten *jia* include inconsequential materials or "Storytellers" (*xiaoshuo jia* 小説家).

the foundations of Chinese economic thought.[14] Their comparisons with modern economic ideas (e.g., *Guanzi*'s quantity theory of money, Sima Qian's laissez-faire) highlight for my own study not so much the "modernity" of the *Guanzi*'s or Sima Qian's economic jargon, as its strangeness within the Han idiom. Such histories build on the early efforts of Liang Qichao (1873–1929), Guo Moruo (1892–1978), and others to give China a place within what still remains a West-centric genealogy of economic thought. The problem is that in so doing these authors detach a preconceived rubric of "economic thought" from the synchronic political and literary contexts that my study precisely aims to reconstruct. In delimiting the "economic," they fail to explain why, for example, a quantity theory of money was both justified and rejected in terms of territorial expansionism or the breakdown of marital norms, and why economic debates entailed experiments in literary style. Cultural approaches to the economy offer ways to address these thicker, more occluded contexts.

TRIBUTARY, TRANSACTIONAL, AND CULTURAL-AESTHETIC ORDERS

Previous studies of economic thought that do address problems of representation tend to focus exclusively on the official classical (or "Confucian") tradition. This book, by contrast, historicizes the political rise of this classicist tradition based on (but not restricted to) the Five Classics during and after the first century BCE.[15]

It explores the innovations in literary genre and style through which traditional values were challenged or re-affirmed. My subject is thus not the Han dynasty frontier or the newly monetized market per se, but rather the unraveling and "re-raveling" of a classical matrix that organized frontier, market, agriculture, commerce, kinship, gender, sexuality, politics,

---

14. On this genre that most trace back to Liang Qichao, see Ye Shichang, *Gudai Zhongguo jingji*; and on Hu Jichuang's place in this tradition, see James Chang, "History of Chinese Economic Thought"; see also Spengler, "Ssu-Ma Ch'ien, Unsuccessful Exponent of Laissez Faire."

15. On the development of this state-sponsored tradition that drew freely on (what became known as) Confucian and non-Confucian texts, see Nylan, *The Five Confucian Classics*, 1–71.

culture, and literature in mutually constitutive relations. This matrix—or set of conflictual, evolving matrices—patterned social and aesthetic hierarchies of lord-subject, husband-wife, father-son, farmer-artisan-merchant, antiquity-present, and historiography-fiction (or *shi* 實 over *xu* 虛). These cultural-aesthetic orders or propositions were encoded in Han texts and were more complex, more historically dynamic, and more contested than earlier studies have shown.

The dominant cultural-aesthetic paradigm of China's premodern political economy was the tribute system or the Confucian tributary order. This model was drawn from the Five Classics tradition. Rather than conflate traditional China with this singular model, as some studies do, my book foregrounds the ways in which Han dynasty officials and scholars reformulated or contested it. Before introducing the tributary order further, it is worth mentioning several other cultural approaches to economic thought that also prioritize a singular Confucian literary-cultural order. Chen Huan-chang's *The Economic Principles of Confucius and his School* (1911) differentiated traditional China's Confucian "human economy" based on moral redistribution ("administering wealth," *li cai* 理財) from a Western-style economics of exchange.[16] To make Confucian texts representative of traditional China, however, Chen explicitly excluded the *Guanzi*'s "Qingzhong" chapters.[17] Lien-sheng Yang's analyses of the traditional economy placed equal emphasis on the Confucian tradition. He borrowed Marcel Mauss's universal principle of archaic reciprocity, arguing that the Confucian principle of *bao* 報 ("report," "repay," "revenge") formed the basis of Chinese social relations. This

---

16. Chen Huan-chang, *Economic Principles of Confucius*. Chen's book was positively reviewed by J. Maynard Keynes in *The Economic Journal*. Chen's book was one of the few works cited on Chinese thought in Joseph Schumpeter's *History of Economic Analysis*; and has been repeatedly republished, including in Chinese. See Chen Huanzhang, *Kongmen licai xue*, 1–3.

17. Chen, *The Economic Principle of Confucius*, 140–41: "The economic system of Confucius is not nationalism, but cosmopolitanism. Before Confucius, economic theories were mostly like the doctrines of the mercantile school and took the nation as the unit. The chief representative of this was Kuan Tzu [Guanzi], who was the most successful minister for the realization of mercantilism and of state socialism. He was the first one to have a complete economic system which we can see today. But we have no room to deal with his economy, and the only reason we mention him is to contrast him with Confucius." For a different interpretation of Guanzian economics see chapters 1 and 5.

logic of reciprocity included hospitality, sacrifices, and filial mourning as well as gifts and payments. David Schaberg extended this Confucian reciprocity to classical pre-Qin historiography, showing how *bao* governs the relation between the author and the reader.[18] He-Yin Zhen's 何殷震 (1884–ca. 1920) earlier theoretical work had similarly drawn attention to the role of Confucian texts in cultural production. She reframed Confucianism within an analysis of the general problem of "livelihood" *sheng ji* 生計, the system of gender and social inequality that resulted from the institution of private property.[19] In this analysis, Confucian teachings and practices are but one of the many global ideologies that sustain economic and gender oppression. At the same time she denaturalized the relation of classical texts to traditional China, showing how the political institutionalization of classical learning (*xue shu* 學術) and the writing system came to inscribe gender inequality into Chinese society.

The tribute system is a modern name for a model that was also grounded in canonical classical texts. It refers to a hierarchical and centrally organized agricultural world order that was symbolically reproduced through the annual submission of material tribute to the ruler. Its locus classicus is the *Book of Documents* (*Shang shu* 尚書), which Han classicists elevated as one of the Five Classics. Allegedly compiled by Confucius, these Classics held up certain idealized figures and actions from pre-imperial antiquity for emulation. For Han scholars and officials the "Tribute of Yu" (*Yu gong* 禹貢) chapter of the *Book of Documents* invoked a world order that had come under threat during the period of Emperor Wu's radical reforms. The "Tribute of Yu" describes how the ancient sage Yu dredged the world into nine provinces after a flood and determined the material tribute (*gong* 貢) due to the ruler from each region (according to its soil type). As reconstructed in figure 0.2b, this chapter further schematizes the world into five concentric "zones" (*fu* 服). These zones, which radiate outward from the central "Royal Domain," are simultaneously political, economic, military, and cultural.

---

18. Lien-sheng Yang, "The Concept of *pao*"; Yang Liansheng, *Zhongguo wenhua zhong 'bao,'* 5–10, 21–26; Schaberg, *A Patterned Past*, 207–21.

19. For a translation and critical introduction to He-Yin Zhen's "On the Question of Women's Labor" (女子勞動問題) "Economic Revolution and Women's Revolution" (經濟革命與女子革命), and "On the Revenge of Women" (女子復仇論), see Lydia Liu, *The Birth of Chinese Feminism*, 1–52, 72–169.

Within the Royal Domain (see figure 0.2a), the different concentric sub-regions differentiate tax regimes for different populations. The "Tribute of Yu" catalogs the locally produced tribute such as grain in husks or cleaned grain, which betokens political submission to the ruler. The outer zones shown in figure 0.2b differentiate foreign policy modes (such as "civilizing and instruction") and foreign groups (such as the Yi 夷 and Man 蠻).

This tribute system is essentially a fragment of the larger set of classically-derived complexes that Chen Huan-Chang, Lien-sheng Yang, David Schaberg, and He-Yin Zhen proposed. It focuses on the lord-subject and farmer-artisan hierarchies rather than on other classical hierarchies (e.g., husband over wife). For this reason the tribute system has served as a useful modern lens through which to explore frontiers and markets alone. Many modern scholars have argued that this text-based ethical paradigm reflected a historical reality as well as a dominant pre-twentieth-century Chinese worldview. For example, the economic historian Hu Jichuang argued that the tribute system was the "canonical classification for land and taxation" from the Zhou through the early twentieth century; and Ying-shih Yü identified the Han dynasty as the first to successfully institutionalize the *Book of Documents'* tributary ideal of foreign relations that shaped China's subsequent foreign relations through to the twentieth century.[20] More recent scholarship on frontiers and markets has, however, rightly reframed the tribute system as an ideological rather than historical phenomenon. Work on excavated materials has revealed a more symbiotic Inner Asian frontier, and more complex, price-setting markets than classicizing Han writers admitted.[21] Nicola Di Cosmo, in particular, has argued the need to use archaeologi-

---

20. See Hu Jichuang, *Concise History of Chinese Economic Thought*, 18–19 and Ying-shih Yü, *Trade and Expansion in Han China*. In John Fairbank's influential account, this "Chinese world order"—also known as "Sinocentrism"—was the normative traditional Chinese ideal of administering its foreign subjects according the hierarchical patterns laid down for China proper. For critiques of this model see Hevia, *Cherishing Men From Afar*; Crossley, "Thinking about Ethnicity"; Elliot, *The Eight Banners*. For a comparative model for thinking about the role of language and symbolic exchange in the context of competing imperial rivalries, see Liu, *The Clash of Empires*.

21. See Barbieri-Low, *Artisans in Early Imperial China* for an illuminating account of Han China's markets.

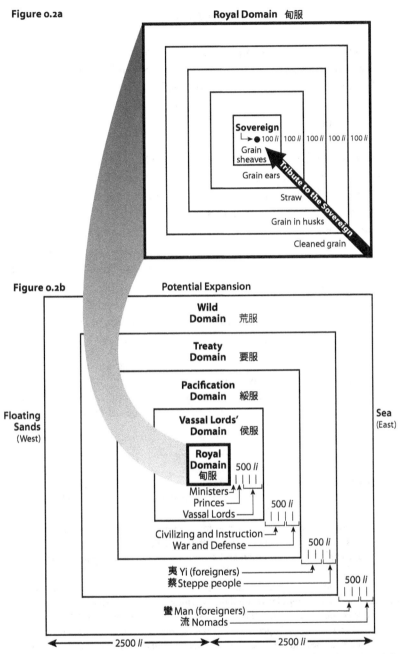

Figure 0.2a

Royal Domain 甸服

Sovereign
● 100 *li* | 100 *li* | 100 *li* | 100 *li* | 100 *li*
Grain sheaves
Grain ears
Straw
Grain in husks
Cleaned grain

Tribute to the Sovereign

Figure 0.2b

Potential Expansion

Wild Domain 荒服

Treaty Domain 要服

Pacification Domain 綏服

Vassal Lords' Domain 侯服

Royal Domain 甸服

Floating Sands (West)

Sea (East)

500 *li*
Ministers
Princes
Vassal Lords

500 *li*
Civilizing and Instruction
War and Defense

500 *li*
夷 Yi (foreigners)
蔡 Steppe people

500 *li*
蠻 Man (foreigners)
流 Nomads

◄— 2500 *li* —► ◄— 2500 *li* —►

FIGURE 0.2. Diagram of the geopolitical relations described in "The Tribute of Yu" (*Yu gong* 禹貢) chapter of the *Book of Documents* (*Shang shu* 尚書), which shows the types of tribute (figure 0.2a, top) and five zones (0.2b, bottom).

cal materials to move beyond the "claustrophobic narrowness of Chinese classical tradition (largely endorsed by the modern Western exegesis)."[22] To do so he and others have worked to sift the empirical data from the cosmological and historiographic "rationalizations" of that data within imperial ideology.[23]

This reinterpretation of the tribute system as the ideological product of classics-based scholarship raises two problems that this book addresses. The first concerns the reduction of official texts to a single cultural model; the second concerns the role of literary style in encoding intra-cultural differences. Even as newly excavated materials illumine vital new perspectives, work still remains to be done in reassessing what the transmitted classical tradition has already been assumed to say. In rereading well-known anecdotes, dialogues, and poems concerning frontiers and markets, my book finds several competing literary-cultural ideals, rather than a unitary cultural logic. Han classicists had to quash blatantly anti-tributary suggestions, such as that of the *Shiji*'s description of a market unregulated by the tributary state:

> Therefore [a society] awaits farmers for things to eat; for foresters to extract resources; for artisans to manufacture things; and for merchants to circulate them. Once [these categories of workers] exist, why should there be government regulations and instruction, summons [for labor duty], and

---

22. Di Cosmo, *Ancient China and Its Enemies*, 3.

23. Di Cosmo, *Ancient China and Its Enemies*, especially 1–12 and 255–312. Before this, Ying-shih Yü, Anatoly Khazanov, Thomas Barfield, and others, had argued that nomadic dependence on settled communities for agricultural products shaped frontier relations. However, against this dichotomy of nomadic and settled populations, Di Cosmo presents an interdependent, less differentiated, economic relationship between the two. He explains the formation and disintegration of the Xiongnu state in political terms: the formation as a response to Qin-Han appropriation of their land and aggressive construction of the Great Wall, the disintegration as a result of internal struggles among leaders and a popular revolt against Xiongnu elites. Crucially, it is the politics of *Chinese* economic interests that better explains the integration of China's political economy into that of the larger region—that is, there was an increased pressure to acquire foreign horses during the Qin-Han era because of the empire's adoption of mounted warfare. Ying-shih Yü had interpreted both the Han-Xiongnu peace treaty that followed the defeat of the Han imperial army in 200 BCE and the subsequent resumption of war under Emperor Wu in 133 BCE as different strategies of the same Han tribute system. By contrast, Di Cosmo interprets the terms of the peace treaty as China's submission of "tribute" to the Xiongnu.

regular assemblies? People are individually responsible for using their own abilities and for maximizing their own labor in obtaining what they desire. Therefore demand for cheap goods will make [such goods] expensive; [decreased] demand for expensive [goods] will make them cheap. When people are encouraged to individually pursue their occupation, they will delight in their own work and, like the downwards plunge of water, day and night without ceasing, they "will naturally come without having been summoned," and people will produce things without having been asked. Does this not complement the Way and attest to its accordance with nature?[24]

Since the late nineteenth century, commentators have cited this, and similar passages, to argue for the strange "modernity" of Sima Qian's economic thought. The division of labor, the individual's pursuit of material satisfaction, price fluctuation, and the "natural" supply and demand of commodities suggest an outlook closer to that of the laissez-faire (or bourgeois) economist than of the denizen of a primitive economy.[25] This book, however, approaches the strange familiarity of Sima Qian's work, not as proof of what Karl Polanyi called a "dis-embedded economy," but rather as a context in which to explore the stresses and anxieties produced by dis-embedding economic calculations from traditional political ones (and re-embedding economic calculations in other spheres).

The term tributary orders, as elaborated through this book, refer to the classical-cultural matrices of hierarchies in, through, and against which Han officials and scholars sought to competitively pattern this changing world. Especially during and after the reign of Emperor Wu

---

24. *Shiji* 129.3254.

25. Liang Qichao, "Shiji huozhi zhuan." The modernizer, Li Hongzhang 李鴻章, had, in 1893, already made a passing comparison in a speech (given by his secretary) during a banquet hosted by the Hong Kong Shanghai Bank of China: "The theory of political economy which treats of the circulation of wealth, or the banking system, the pivot on which the international commerce of the civilised nations turns, though a modern science in Europe, has been originated, we presume, from the principles of the law of administration of the *Chow* dynasty. The subsequent writings of the two most celebrated Chinese historians, *Tze Ma-chien* (司馬遷) [i.e., Sima Qian] and *Pan Ku* (班固) [i.e., Ban Gu] on the Balance of Trade (平準書) and commodities (食貨志) may be compared to those of Adam Smith on the 'Wealth of Nations'" (*North China Herald*, 17 March 1893, 393–94). For the claim that, via eighteenth-century sinophile French physiocrats, Sima Qian indirectly influenced Adam Smith, see Young, "The Tao of Markets"; for a critique of this claim, see McCormick, "Sima Qian and Adam Smith."

they did so through innovations in literary genre, language, and symbolic practice. Attempts to redefine the place of expanded markets and frontiers in the Zhou tributary order transformed (and were transformed by) ostensibly unrelated spheres such as kinship practice. Thus during the Han, the "Tribute of Yu" implicated a theory of literary as well as social reproduction: it was used to promote classical learning based on official texts, as well as the ideal Zhou world order described in such texts.

The expansion of monetized markets during the Han did not signal a shift from a gift economy to a money economy, nor from a precapitalist to capitalist system, nor from a credit to bullion culture. Monetization in this book loosely refers to the increased circulation of money (whether general-purpose or special-purpose money); market expansion broadly refers to the increase in local or long-distance trade (especially in which money was used as a method of payment), rather than to "self-regulating" markets or to the replacement of what remained a primarily agricultural economy. At stake here is the intersection of imagined and historical economic processes, within which the state was generally understood (Sima Qian aside) to play a central role. For this reason, the Han debate over the meaning of money might be understood, in part, by using the anthropological model of Maurice Bloch and Jonathan Parry. The tributary orders of Han classicists somewhat resemble the moral "long-term transactional order" that Bloch and Parry contrast with the "short-term transactional order." These long-term exchanges are understood to be moral because they promote the safe and divinely sanctioned passage of society from generation to generation. The short-term transactional order "is the legitimate domain of individual—often acquisitive—activity." This economic activity between individuals to facilitate quotidian life is generally morally neutral unless it threatens (rather than complements) the long-term order. For Han classicists, the long-term transactional order was grounded in moral principles of "ritual propriety" (*li yi* 禮儀) and "moderation" (*jie* 節).[26] Money, in Bloch and Parry's model, does necessarily transform society as it can be converted into the long-term order (e.g., through taxation). Since money

---

26. Since texts such as the *Guanzi*'s "Qingzhong" chapters reject the priority of such moral terms, my book will at times refer to the traditional ideals of Han classicists loosely as the "moral economy."

had circulated in China before the Han period, the transactional model offers one way of articulating the Han dynasty transformation of the Zhou tributary order in comparative terms.

Unlike Bloch and Parry's anthropological studies, however, this book pursues the aesthetic dimension of Han transactional orders, looking to literary and visual practices to reveal rival conceptions of the ideal long-term order. Leslie Kurke's literary study of the rise of Greek coinage models a more historically sensitive approach in its description of the contestation between aristocratic elites and "middling" citizens over the definition—and redefinition—of the long-term transactional order.[27] Important here is the role of literary genre (or the differentiation of genres) in encoding economic discourse. In the context of the Greek political economy, silver coinage became the controversial token of the civic state, but was just one of the many associated literary and symbolic practices in and through which poets and prose-writers contested civic ideology. In Han dynasty China, imperial tribute betokened a tributary empire but was also only one of the many metaphors (including coinage) through which generations of competing scholar-officials debated the political economy. Unlike in the Greek case, genre does not so easily correlate with ideological position. The new genres and the tokens supposedly invented to commemorate tributary empire explored in this volume— philosophical dialogue (the *Debate on Salt and Iron*, the *Guanzi*); Han historiography (the *Shiji* and *Hanshu*); the Han dynasty *fu* (of Sima Xiangru and Yang Xiong); the unified currency (the *wuzhu* 五銖 coin)—exploited ideological ambivalence in ways that were subsequently contained or revised to better fit the tributary order of later Han classicists. As but one part of a tangled set of cultural-aesthetic claims, any tributary order implicated a broader set of asymmetrical relations. Thus the proposition that tributary empire should promote commerce or delimit its frontiers was understood to be interlinked with the future of gender and sexual orders on the one hand, and with literary decorum on the other.

---

27. Kurke, *Coins, Bodies, Games, and Gold*; Kurke, "Money and Mythic History." Kurke draws in part from Pierre Bourdieu's analyses of symbolic and economic "fields" of competitive struggle. For another useful study of the relation of literary genre to economic discourse, see Poovey, *Genres of the Credit Economy*.

Outline of the Argument

This book comprises three chapters on discursive genres (philosophical dialogue, epideictic *fu*, and historiography) and two chapters on social practices (money, kinship). Together these chapters argue the significance of literary innovation within political economic debate, and map out two general tendencies. First, the literary and material experiments of the Former Han, especially under Emperor Wu, challenged the tributary order of Zhou texts. Second, to overcome such challenges, the classicists of the post-Emperor Wu period revised aspects of the Zhou tributary order, even as they reasserted its authority. To do so they modified earlier Han developments in genre and language.

Chapter 1 (on Masters dialogue) introduces the historical framework and literary stakes of the debate over frontiers and markets. To finance the unprecedented scale of imperial expansion Emperor Wu's advisers turned to commerce and industry, introducing state monopolies on iron, salt, and liquor, and new strategies of stimulating and regulating local and long-distance markets. Military campaigns and colonial settlement in the northwest alone cost over one hundred billion cash, or over eight times the entire annual revenue of earlier governments.[28] Chapter 1 begins with the politics and rhetoric of *qingzhong* economics that gained currency during this period. It asks how, and to what effect, the *Guanzi*'s "Qingzhong" chapters and the *Debate on Salt and Iron* appropriated the Masters tradition of philosophical dialogue to propose oppositional ideals. Modern scholars have generally treated these as two different types of non-literary text: that is, the former as an economic treatise (often identified as the foundations of Chinese economic thought); and the latter as a historical record of a court debate over Emperor Wu's reforms. *Qingzhong* economics departed from the classical tradition by placing economics before ethics, prioritizing the ruler's profit-seeking strategies over his ritual propriety (*li jie* 禮節). This radical revision of the classical tributary ideal taught its readers economic rules abstracted from cultural contexts, including the calculation of price in terms of quantitative relations between circulating money and commodities. As chapter 1 argues, the *Guanzi*'s provocation was literary as well as political. Guanzi,

---

28. Chang, *Frontier, Immigration, and Empire*, 175–76.

the eponymous Master, grounded his authority in literary abstractions (e.g., Mr. Calculate-y) rather than in the recorded deeds and sayings of traditional sages and Masters. By inventing new metaphors and personifications of abstract economic principles to explain fiat and international credit currencies, the *Guanzi* transgressed classical ideals of writing (*wen*).

Neither the *Guanzi* nor the *Debate on Salt and Iron* have garnered much attention in modern histories of Chinese literature. Despite widespread recognition of the political rise of classicism from the first century BCE onwards, the circumstances of that development are generally relegated to historical footnotes. The *Guanzi's* use of overtly fictive dialogue suggests a more complex discursive space in and through which classical habits of historical and literary citation became dominant. In the *Debate on Salt and Iron*, the Classical Scholars (*Wenxue*) have to actively defend the rhetorical authority as well as the traditional economic ideals of pre-Qin Masters against the attacks of Emperor Wu's former economic adviser, Sang Hongyang 桑弘羊 (152–80 BCE). The Classical Scholars emerge as the true Masters, despite the political seniority of their interlocutor, in part by recalling the economic metaphors *ben* 本 ("fundamental"; "agriculture") and *mo* 末 ("secondary"; "commercial") that were used in traditional Masters accounts of the moral agricultural order. The Classical Scholars see a fundamental split between antiquity and modernity brought about by the state-sponsored rise of the market and they lament the breakdown of the moral bonds of sodality and kinship organizing the agricultural order. For the Classical Scholars, the growth of the market signifies something as socially destructive as a Polanyian Great Transformation, but of another order. Representation lies at the heart of this social experience. The savagery of market exchange is, for the Classisists, a break from *wen*: from the fundamental patterns of the cultural order encoded in the Zhou texts that they, as scholars of *wen* (the *Wenxue*), must defend. The *Debate on Salt and Iron* thus furnishes a first-century BCE manifesto for classicism as well as an anti-imperialist, anti-market call for a return to traditional hierarchies.

Chapter 2 (on the epideictic *fu*) reconsiders the Han dynasty's most popular genre, the *fu*, in light of this enlarged politics of representation. Sima Xiangru's 司馬相如 "Fu on the Excursion Hunt of the Son of Heaven," the earliest *fu* to be formally presented to the imperial court (and probably the most famous and influential epideictic *fu*), was structured around an economic metaphor of linguistic expenditure. Ancient

and modern critics have traditionally used a classical ideal of moderation and thrift to evaluate the *fu*'s signature "excesses" in length and ornamentation. As argued in Chapter 1, this classical economic idiom did
not occupy a discursive vacuum in the Former Han, but elaborated itself
partly in opposition to the *Guanzi*'s quantitative approach to value.
Chapter 2 explores how Sima Xiangru patterned the *fu*'s generic innovations (self-reflexive dialogue, extended length, euphonic ornament) on
both classical and quantitative notions of expenditure. Lavish lifestyles
and profit-seeking *qingzhong* theories were at odds with the ethical promotion of moderation. Pre-Han and Han sections of the *Guanzi* debated a proposal that "lavish expenditure" (*chi mi* 侈靡) *creates* wealth,
i.e., that market consumption of luxuries stimulates production, thereby
increasing employment and revitalizing the general economy. Excavated
examples of such Han dynasty market luxuries, as chapter 2 notes, offer
an alternate resource to the classical poetic tradition for considering the
fu's innovations in imagery and style. At the beginning of an era of unprecedented military and public spending, Sima Xiangru exploited both
classical and non-classical forms, and the aesthetic encoding of this ideological tension influenced the subsequent development of the genre. During and after the first-century BCE backlash against Emperor Wu's expenditures, Yang Xiong, Ban Gu, Ban Zhao, Zuo Si, and others re-asserted
the tributary model of the political economy through later *fu*.

Like philosophical dialogue and the prose-poetic *fu*, historical narrative became a medium through which Han writers challenged or reformulated the ideal of agricultural tributary empire. Chapter 3 (on historiography) examines the *Shiji*'s new thematic and formal patterning of Chinese
historiography. Both at the frontiers and at the core of the Han empire,
material accumulation appears to have dissolved classical hierarchical
differences between Xiongnu and Chinese, and between persons of different social statuses. The *Shiji* heretically proposed the withdrawal of
the state from market activity, advocated the "natural" rise and fall of
market prices, and proposed to consider the businessperson ("commodity producer") as an ethical subject (*junzi* 君子). Through competing
narrative perspectives, ambiguous metaphors, and authorial comments,
the *Shiji* also draws attention to the politics of economic and cultural
ethnography. Although the *Hanshu* replicates long sections from the
Shiji, it determines for the reader the moral significance of these sections
through editing and reframing: for example, representing the Xiongnu

as morally deficient, unimprovable foreigners and showing businesspersons as socially destructive. The *Hanshu* thereby configures China's domestic and foreign markets—and the historiographic act itself—within the unified tributary order of classic texts.

The first half of this book on literary genres thus argues the symbiotic relation between the politics of genre and the politics of expansionist economics. How to *represent* the world order mattered precisely because literary innovation enabled and enacted diverse Former Han challenges to an archaizing agricultural ideal that was grounded in classical texts. Given this inseparability of practice from discourse, the shift to material and embodied practices in the second half of this book is primarily for heuristic purposes. Chapters 4 (on kinship) and 5 (on money) contextualize the canonical genres already encountered within a broader array of literary and visual/material forms. These two chapters explore the encoding of ideology through rival practices, and chart a more complex Han debate over the expanding reach of classical *wen* (writing, pattern, decorum, Chinese civilization) across gendered bodies and coins.

As historians have long pointed out, the conjugal household became the basic administrative and economic unit of Qin-Han society. The expansion of the Han empire is, from the (often conflicting) perspectives of administrative, taxation, and classical documents, generally understood to have enabled the replication of this household unit across space. However, chapter 4 (on kinship) brings the history of that household unit and the history of frontiers into closer conversation. It argues that two of the most important developments in Chinese frontier history—imperial interstate diplomacy (*heqin* 和親 "peace through kinship") and long-distance tributary trade across Eurasia (the so-called Silk Road)—originated in discourses and practices that departed from classical ideals of kinship. After China's northern neighbors, the Xiongnu confederacy, defeated the Han imperial army in 200 BCE, the *heqin* peace treaty demanded annual payments to the Xiongnu, along with the marriage of a Han princess to the Xiongnu leader. Before Emperor Wu ended the peace in 133 BCE, Han scholars and officials tied the aberrant kinship rituals of the *heqin* to kinship violations in the imperial court. During the post-*heqin* era of expansion, *qingzhong* economists offered an imagination of long-distance silk markets within which traditional social and marital bonds had no productive place.

In opposition (or in contrast) to this, the new classicizing texts written by or for women that emerged by the late Former Han emphasized women's kinship roles as good wives, mothers, and daughters-in-law. The female author Ban Zhao 班昭 (ca. 48–ca. 120) and other classicists contracted the world of women's work from the economic frontiers to the conjugal household. They taught women how to experience and to represent their actions in terms of classical aphorisms and tropes, without interpreting women's scholarship as political or economic work. This new literary tradition for women that became so influential over subsequent millennia might thus be better understood not simply as the (re-) gendering of the evolving classical tradition, but also as a historical reaction, in part, to profit-seeking visions of women's roles as industrial workers in a world system. One effect of the classical restoration of women to the moral household economy was thus to sever kinship from frontier history, thereby eclipsing a consideration of any productive role the weaver played in the historical Han expansion of the Silk Road.

Chapter 5 brings these two debates—about the imagined relation between China and the world, and about the discursiveness of social practice—to bear on Han money. Modern historians generally treat Emperor Wu's establishment of the bronze *wuzhu* coin as an enduring symbol of unified Chinese empire, and as the crucial signifying practice of China's expanding market. Chapter 5, by contrast, highlights the lack of unity in the competing meanings and pragmatics of Han dynasty money. It maps out four sets of competing social and symbolic "counter-practices" of money: burying money (for afterlife exchanges); experimental minting (including coin design); classicizing money (i.e., elaborating money's place in classical ethics and historiography); and quantifying money (according to a market logic). These four approaches variously embedded money within cosmological and ethical calculations, or sought to reduce money to its temporal market functions as a medium of exchange, method of payment, and standard of value. This enlarged field of monetary practice illumines an imaginary politics of foreign exchange that has been overlooked within economic history.

For example, burial money helped to mediate between two alien domains, the human and the spiritual. Like other "spirit articles" that accompanied and aided the deceased in their journey to the next world, this money was sometimes—but not always—of a different size or material (e.g., clay instead of bronze). Many understood the relation between the afterlife and temporal economies to be dynamic and interactive. By contrast, the *Guanzi*'s "Qingzhong" chapters theorized foreign exchange in a disenchanted, anti-cosmological vein. Since monetary value was established quantitatively, by the relative amounts of commodities and money in circulation, all world currencies could theoretically become exchangeable. It is with such dreams of temporal (and afterlife) commerce with foreign domains that we might reconsider Emperor Wu's experiments with Central Asian numismatic traditions and the startling excavations of Han coins with blundered Greek inscriptions shown in figures 5.8, 5.9, 5.10, and 5.11, and as described in the appendix.

Han dynasty historiographers and classical scholars tried to contain the threat of the market world by treating the monetary quantity inscribed on coins as a form of writing. A coin's inscription was commonly termed *wen* (文), also the term for culture, pattern, and writing. The question of *wen* (monetary inscription) had no place in the quantitative *qingzhong* theory of money. However, classicists represented money as a transgressive form of *wen* that generally failed to adequately represent the shared values that governed classical *wen*, especially as inscriptions of truth/reality and as patterns of Chinese civilization. In introducing monetary values into classical discourse (for example through etiologies of money or stories of debt), classicists simultaneously embedded market price into a broad array of social and ethical calculations, and asserted the superiority of text-based classicism over market values. Money thus became a new site for the political rise of classicism. In contrast to the *Guanzi*'s economically connected world of international fiat currencies that demand no translation, the classicizing imagination produced China-centered histories of money that remain influential to this day.

Together, these five chapters offer a counterhistory to the Han dynasty establishment of the expanded frontiers, unified script, classical texts, imperial bureaucracy, and cultural cohesion that has been commemorated over subsequent millennia of Chinese history.[29] By rereading canonical texts and introducing non-canonical and recently excavated texts, this book explores ambivalence and outright opposition to aspects of the

---

29. In Catherine Gallagher and Stephen Greenblatt's account, counterhistories aim to "make apparent the slippages, cracks, fault lines, and surprising absences in the monumental structures that dominated a more traditional historicism." See Gallagher, *Practicing New Historicism*, 17; 49–74, and my discussion in the coda.

expansionist project. It shows that for many the savagery of imperialism concerned modes and rituals of exchange, rather than the borders between the civilized and the barbarian. For some, the market appeared to be destroying society and social values; for others, the market enabled new ways of making commensurate the hierarchies of lord and subject, man and woman, cultural Self and Other. (The master-slave, convict-freeman hierarchies were not as extensively problematized, as they might well have been).[30] Representation was intrinsic to this experience of social transformation. For the Han classicists whose political rise was crucial to the ways in which we now define and appreciate Chinese literature, new accounts of expansionist economics threatened a break from the fundamental patterns of the cultural order (*wen*) encoded in their classical texts.

This book thus narrates the circumstances within which classical texts increasingly became used to restore literary decorum. It emphasizes—overemphasizes, some readers may feel—a historically specific tension between two oppositional tendencies: quantitative and qualitative; abstracting and classicizing; calculating and moralizing; globalizing and sinicizing. Each chapter follows a similar temporal arc spanning Emperor Wu's reign. Together they show that Han traditionalists had to reinvent the Zhou ideal of the agricultural tributary economy with more linguistic creativity—and in the context of a far more ideologically heterodox, culturally hybrid, and historically dynamic symbolic economy—than modern scholarship has thus far suggested. And the temporal arc of Emperor Wu's reign is important to this discussion. By the Later Han the expansion of cities, markets, and frontiers under Emperor Wu had ceased or even reversed. In juxtaposing canonical and non-canonical Han texts, this book argues that minor narratives or new uses of genre, language, and sign—even if they failed to become hegemonic—are worth recovering for a better understanding of both literary history and the history of the political economy.

The five core chapters contain the principal argument of my book. However, I have added a concluding coda on the comparative origins

---

30. Wang Bao's 王褒 (fl. 60 BCE) mock "The Contract for a Youth" is an important exception in the received tradition. See *Hanshu* 64B.2821. Excavated texts are yielding new insights into the lives of slaves and my book unfortunately does not address this topic in its own right. On debt and bondage, see chapter 5.

and stakes in this argument. I originally trained in classical Chinese, Greek, and Latin literatures, and although this book remains fully grounded in a short period of Chinese cultural history the topic and method used in this book were developed in relation to a set of problems that I perceived in comparative approaches to antiquity. Specialists should feel free to ignore this coda, but others, who desire more enticement to enter into Chinese antiquity, may like to head there next.

PART I

Genres

CHAPTER I

Abstraction:
Qingzhong *Economics, Literary Fiction,*
and Masters Dialogue

Only when granaries are filled up tight
Can one comprehend what's ritually right (*li jie*).
—The *Guanzi* ("Qingzhong A")

In his 1957 essay "Aristotle discovers the economy," Karl Polanyi used a discussion of the earliest economic theorist in the Western tradition to defamiliarize the modern term "economy." Writing at the dawn of the growth of the ancient Greek market, Aristotle asserted that economic activity was—and should remain—firmly embedded in the workings of the social community, and hence embedded in ethics. The analyst of *oikonomia* (household management) reckoned the just price based on reciprocity, not on arithmetic equivalence, and condemned the evils of commercial profit.[1] By the time of Polanyi's essay, economic historians in China had established that the "Qingzhong" 輕重 (lit. "light and heavy"; meaning "price ratio" or "relative value") section of the *Guanzi* 管子 was China's earliest corpus of systematic economic theory.[2] Largely

---

1. Aristotle posited household management (*oikonomia*) and commercial trade (*kapēlikē*) as the two morally oppositional branches of "the art of wealth-getting" (*khrēmatistikē*) (*Politics* 1258a–b). Cf. Aristotle, *Nicomachean Ethics*, 1133a–b.

2. Hereafter, the *Guanzi* refers to the "Qingzhong" chapters that were composed during the Han dynasty, rather than the large older corpus of the philosophical-political

composed between the third and first centuries BCE, the *Guanzi* was championed by Han Emperor Wu's state planners during China's earliest large-scale expansion of imperial frontiers and monetized markets.[3] Unlike Aristotle, who sought to determine a just price that would guarantee exchange (*allagē*) and community (*koinōnia*), the *Guanzi*'s ideal ruler sought to rule the world (*tianxia* 天下) by mastering the mathematical laws of market price that transcended social or political context. As the above-cited rhyming adage suggests, the "Qingzhong" chapters placed economics before ethics, by prioritizing granary-filling strategies over classical ritual propriety (*li jie* 禮節).[4] For its Sunzian world of perennial warfare, the "Qingzhong" offered competitive strategies (*ce* 策), calculations (*shu* 數), and methods (*fa* 法, *shu* 術), for maximizing profit. In contrast to Polanyi's nostalgia for Aristotle, modern scholars of the *Guanzi* have emphasized its strange familiarity. They generally identify its novel proposal that the quantitative relation between commodities and money in circulation determines price as the world's earliest articulation of a (recognizably "modern") quantity theory of money. The political economy described by the *Guanzi* did assume the traditional Chinese model in which the agriculture-based state took responsibility for market regulation and social welfare. However, the "Qingzhong" chapters proposed that the state had to participate in the market to survive, and

---

Guanzi that Liu Xiang compiled into the transmitted book, the *Guanzi*, around 26 BCE. For good English-language introductions to the "Qingzhong" chapters and to their economic and monetary theory, see Rickett, *Guanzi*, 2:337–60 and Von Glahn, *Fountain of Fortune*, 28–32.

3. Modern scholars generally agree that the economic chapters of the composite text *Guanzi* (i.e., "Master Guan")—the "Qingzhong" chapters—were composed by a set of authors distinct from those of the rest of the *Guanzi*. For a useful bibliography on this question, and for arguments that these chapters were largely composed in the Former Han, especially the second century BCE, see Rickett, *Guanzi*, 2:346–57. This departs from Ma Feibai's dating of the text to Wang Mang's interregnum period. Our received version of the composite text *Guanzi* comes from Liu Xiang's edition of the text around 26 BCE. See Rickett, *Guanzi*, 1:25–39.

4. Ma Feibai, *Guanzi Qing zhong pian*, 181, 545: 倉廩實 (*ẓit*) 。則知禮節 (*tset*) 。 More literally: "When granaries and storehouses are full, then there can be understanding of ritual propriety and moderation." This rhyming adage is attributed to Guanzi at *Shiji* 62.2132 and recurs at *Shiji* 129.3255. Emperor Wu's economic adviser, as represented in the *Yantielun* (Debate on salt and iron), discussed below, also cites this line. See Wang, *Yantielun*, 430.

qingzhong economics primarily tutors the reader in the market's cold, calculating logic of accumulation. The *Guanzi* thereby replaced the moral philosopher of traditional "Masters" dialogues (e.g., Confucius, Han Feizi) with the master of the "rules for light and heavy" (*qing zhong zhi fa* 輕重之法): i.e., "the economic expert."

Two types of pedagogy are at play in the *Guanzi*'s Han dynasty "Qingzhong" chapters: the explicit theoretical teachings of the eponymous Guanzi (Guan Zhong 管仲) that unfold through his dialogue with Duke Huan (桓公, 685–643 BCE) of Qi 齊; and the rhetorical aspects of the *Guanzi* as a self-consciously literary text. The fifteen or sixteen extant "Qingzhong" chapters appropriated the historical personae and literary medium of a much older philosophical-political dialogue that the bibliographer Liu Xiang edited into the single, transmitted *Guanzi* around 26 BCE. Although debate remains about dates of composition, most scholars date most of the passages discussed below to the mid-second to early first century BCE.[5] Historians of economic thought have generally approached the difficult language of the *Guanzi* (e.g., *qingzhong*, lit. "light and heavy"; *heng* 衡, lit. "balance") as the technical idiom of a new theory. Aided by the lexicon of modern economics (e.g., "the quantitative theory of money"), such historians continue to "translate" the *Guanzi* within a global history of economic thought, effectively disentangling *qingzhong* theory from its bewildering metaphors. This project of technical translation has been both necessary and helpful but remains insufficient. It helps to de-parochialize Eurocentric histories of economic thought, but also tends to cast ancient concepts as immature "proto" theories divorced from their literary-historical contexts of development. The abstractions that make the *Guanzi*'s "Qingzhong" section recognizable as an "economic" text are, as will be argued below, inextricable from its innovations in genre as well as language. Its choice of dramatic staging, fiction, personification, and metaphorical "jargon" are as important as its explicit account of credit currency.

Qingzhong economics appropriates the dialogue form that is common in "Masters" (*Zi* 子) philosophy, but recasts its moral idiom.[6] The *Debate on Salt and Iron* (*Yantielun*), the only other major economic text to

---

5. For exceptions see Rickett, 2:346–60.
6. On the Masters tradition, see the introduction and Denecke, *The Dynamics of Masters Literature*.

borrow the dialogue form, effectively restores both the preeminence of ritual propriety (*li jie*) and its textual basis in Zhou texts. Although this work does not directly discuss the extant "Qingzhong" chapters, it stages a retrospective court debate over the *qingzhong* policies that were adopted under Emperor Wu. Composed during the classicizing backlash against Emperor Wu that took place in the first century BCE, the *Debate on Salt and Iron* puts the traditional Zhou ideals of the earlier politico-philosophical texts in more favorable light. This Zhou ideal of Mencius, Confucius, and others put ritual propriety (*li* 禮), benevolence (*ren* 仁), and righteousness or integrity (*yi* 義) first. In what later became known as the Confucian Classics, a political-kinship matrix bound rulers and subjects, husbands and wives, and fathers and sons in reciprocal but hierarchical bonds, thereby placing all transactions in a stratified community. Tributary (*gong* 貢) and reciprocal (*bao* 報) exchanges reflected and affirmed these political-kinship bonds. The idealization of the "well-field" (*jingtian* 井田) system, and the (ranked) social classifications of "farmers, artisans, and merchants" (*nong gong shang* 農工商) and of "husbands plowing, wives weaving" (*nan geng fu zhi* 男耕婦織) clarified the agricultural basis of this moral community. Such classical prescriptions, to which this book will frequently return, are more familiar to modern sinologists than those of the various pro-market factions that flourished during Emperor Wu's reign, precisely because generations of classically trained officials, from the Later Han through Qing (1644–1911) dynasties, succeeded in reasserting them. At the same time, the Han Classical Scholars in the *Debate on Salt and Iron* had to update or revise this Zhou ideal. By restoring the traditional moral metaphors *ben* 本 ("fundamental"; "agriculture") and *mo* 末 ("secondary"; "commercial") to the center of the political economy, they reinvented the Zhou ideal with more linguistic creativity and in the context of a more ideologically heterodox, historically dynamic symbolic economy than modern scholarship generally suggests.

Qingzhong 輕重: *Economic Abstraction and Literary Fiction*

Like many Masters dialogues, the "Qingzhong" chapters provoke the reader to look afresh at language and meaning. Just as the *Mencius* begins with the sage's redefinition of "profit" (in ethical terms), so the

"Qingzhong" section frequently tutors the reader in its technical idiom.[7] It introduces new meanings for everyday words that are often drawn from the marketplace, mathematics, or mensuration. These include *heng* 衡 (balance beam or scales); *zhun ping* 準平 and *zhun* 準 (water level); *cheng* 乘 (to multiply), and of course *qingzhong* (standard weight; fluctuation in currency value). Take the following passage, which introduces two principles that generally obtain across the divergent positions of this multi-authored (and often textually corrupt) set of chapters: first, a quantitative theory of money that makes the value of money inversely proportional to the quantity of money; and, second, state intervention into market price to outmaneuver merchants.

桓公問於管子曰：「請問幣乘馬。」管子對曰：「始取夫三大夫之家，方六里而一乘，二十七人而奉一乘。幣乘馬者，方六里，田之惡美若干，穀之多寡若干，穀之貴賤若干，凡方六里用幣若干，穀之重用 幣若干。故幣乘馬者，布幣於國，幣爲一國陸地之數也。謂之幣乘馬。」桓公曰：「行幣乘馬之數奈何？」管子對曰：「 ... 國筴出於穀，軌國之筴，貨幣乘馬者也。今刀布藏於官府，巧幣、萬物輕重皆在賈之。彼幣重而萬物輕，幣輕而萬物重。 ... 人君操穀幣金衡而天下可定也。此守天下之數也。」

Duke Huan asked Guanzi: "May I ask how to calculate money supplies (*bi cheng ma*)?"

Guanzi replied: "Start by collecting taxes from individual plots and from households with three plots. Each six square *li* plot will have one chariot, and twenty-seven men will support each chariot. To calculate money supplies, [calculate] for each six-square-*li* plot: how many fine and poor quality fields it contains; how much grain it produces; the price of grain; the monetary expenses for each six-square-*li* plot; and the monetary expenses for purchasing its grain. Therefore the calculation of money supplies addresses money circulating through a state, and that [circulating] money is made to fit the amount of land in a given state. This is what is called 'calculating money supplies.'"

Duke Huan asked: "How does one carry out these computations based on the calculation of money supplies (*bi cheng ma zhi shu*)?"

---

7. Mencius 1A: "Mengzi had an audience with King Hui of Liang. The king said, 'Venerable sir, you have not regarded hundreds of leagues too far to come, so you must have a way of profiting my state.' Mengzi replied, "Why must your Majesty speak of 'profit'? Let there simply be benevolence and righteousness." Following Van Norden, *Mengzi*, 1.

Guanzi replied: "... State policy is based on its grain supply, but policies that benefit from state financial statistics (*gui guo zhi ce*) depend on calculating commodity and money supplies. Nowadays knife and spade [shaped] money is stored by the official bureaus, so the manipulation of money and the relative prices (*qingzhong*) of all goods lies in the hands of merchants. If money is highly valued (*zhong*), all goods will be cheap (*qing*); if money is devalued (*qing*), all goods will become expensive (*zhong*). ... If the leader of the people controls the balance between grain, money, and gold, he will stabilize the empire. These are calculations for protecting empire."[8]

Duke Huan opens this section, like many others, by questioning a technical term for a *qingzhong* strategy. *Bi cheng ma* 幣乘馬 appears as something needing explanation. Here, as elsewhere, the ruler occupies the position of the unenlightened reader, and Guanzi's response enlightens both ruler and reader. Through Guanzi's explanation one infers the technical meaning of otherwise opaque terms. For example, the phrase *cheng ma* 乘馬 appears several times in the *Guanzi* meaning "to calculate" or "to manage government finances," but also in reference to a system of military taxes (pronounced *sheng ma*). In this case one infers that *bi cheng ma* 幣乘馬 refers to the calculation of money supplies for the state. As throughout the "Qingzhong" section, Guanzi's answer is not a fixed quantity or ratio but, rather, a generalized formula. The calculation here is based on a fixed unit of land (the six square *li* plot), but contingent upon the (variable) production, productivity, and prices of grain among other things. To make calculations the state demands "financial statistics," for which Guanzi uses the term *gui* (軌 literally "the end of a cart axle"). In this case, we derive the meaning of *gui* from another chapter, "Shan Guo Gui" (山國軌 "Using statistics to control state finances"). Guanzi also glosses the phrase *qingzhong* through its etymology—*qing* (light; to be cheap) and *zhong* (to value highly)—correlating price with the relative quantities of money and goods circulating at a given time.

MAKING MONEY UP

The "Qingzhong" chapters do not simply introduce a new economic idiom; they also challenge the reader to rethink conventional relations be-

---

8. Ma, *Guanzi Qing zhong pian*, 383–84. Compare Rickett, *Guanzi*, 2:416–17.

tween linguistic, monetary, arithmetic, and cosmological signs.[9] As discussed in greater detail in chapter 5, other early Chinese texts fixed upon the integrity of the written value (*wen* 文) inscribed on a coin. Anxiety over material erosion, counterfeiting, and seigniorage reflected the broader classical approach to writing (*wen*) itself (i.e., the injunction to match names and things). As a bearer of *wen* (culture, pattern, civilization), circulating Chinese coinage also marked out the cultural-political domain of its issuer, the ruler mandated by Heaven. The "Qingzhong" chapters do not, by contrast, address money as a bearer of *wen*. The quantitative rule of money transcends any written sign, geo-cultural frontier, or heavenly intervention.

管子曰:「昔者癸度居人之國,必四面望於天下。天下高亦高。天下高,我獨下,必失其國於天下。」 桓公曰:「此若言曷謂也?」 管子對曰:「昔萊人善染,練苊之於萊純錙,綢綬之於萊亦純錙也。其周,中十 金。萊人知之,間纂苊空。周且斂馬作見於萊人操之,萊有推 [准] 馬。 是自萊失纂苊而反准於馬也。故可因者因之,乘者乘之,此因天下以制天下。此之 謂國准。」

Guanzi said: "In the past, when *Guidu* [the fictional character Calculate-and-Measure] took residence in another's state, he had to look in every direction at the surrounding world, for if the world's prices were high, he had to also raise prices. If the world's prices are high and ours alone are low, we will necessarily lose this state to the rest of the world."

Duke Huan asked: "What does this mean?"

Guanzi replied: "In the past, the Lai people were skilled in cloth dyeing. Amongst the Lai, a *chun* [11.37 English feet] of silk dyed with purple plants cost only one *zi* (a few ounces of gold) and a *chun* of purple silk ribbon also only cost one *zi*. In the Zhou realm however it cost ten catties [of gold]. When the Lai heard this they secretly gathered the purple plants to use up. The Zhou then assembled counters (*ma*) to serve as pledges to the people of Lai and took control of the silk while the Lai used counters [as their stabilizing monetary standard?] (*zhun ma*).[10] This is a case of the Lai of their own accord losing their purple plants and restoring their monetary standard with mere counters. Therefore use what can be used, manipulate what can be manipulated. This is using the world to control

---

9. See chapter 5 for a further discussion of the *Guanzi*'s approach to money, including its relation to cosmological signs.

10. Here, *tui* 准 has been emended to *zhun* 準, following Ma Feibai and Rickett.

the world. This is what is called 'stabilizing the state through [monetary] standards (*guo zhun*).'"[11]

In this extreme case, Guanzi abstracts money into a pure sign, a pure counter. Here the term *ma* 馬 (literally "horse"), likely a variant of *ma* 碼 (as in *chou ma* 籌碼), refers to a numerical counter or token of exchange.[12] With the careful timing of those familiar with *qingzhong* economics, the Zhou people issue this fiat currency to monopolize the foreign market in Lai silks and demonetize it once this is accomplished. The "Qingzhong" chapters use the term *zhun* 准 to mean "stabilization of prices" or "maintaining stability in state finances," and here it seems to mean establishing mere tokens as a monetary standard. In a world without a transcendental general equivalent, mere counters can purchase valuable silks in one season but in another season be made to signify nothing. By having the Zhou trade in abstract counters rather than, say, counterfeit coins (or even real horses or grain), the *Guanzi* highlights the intrinsically fictional property of money, and the need for a ruler to exploit other peoples' belief that there is a basis for a real currency. As discussed in chapter 5, other early Chinese texts do not approach money in this way.

A context of international exchange helps to generalize this lesson in credit; that is, the people of Lai are foreigners (Yi 夷) who do not belong to the Central States—and who repeatedly occupy the position of "the stupid" in Guanzi's anecdotes. When the people of Lai blithely export their purple silks in exchange for mere counters, they fail to grasp the strictly symbolic property of the monetary instrument. It is worth noting, however, that the people of the Central States (e.g., Liang, Chu) themselves occupy the position of "the stupid" in many other "Qingzhong" chapters. In such dialogues, it is ignorance of *qingzhong* economics, rather than cultural inferiority per se, that explains the defeat of the Lai or of Qi's neighboring states. After all, Duke Huan—and ultimately

---

11. Ma Feibai, *Guanzi Qing zhong pian*, 641–47; cf. Rickett, *Guanzi*, 2:485–86.

12. Following Ma Feibai. The *Liji*'s (禮記) "Tou Hu" (投壺) chapter has the following passage: "[The superintendent] sets up a 'horse' for the victor. If he sets up one horse, then a second, and finally a third, he begs to congratulate the thrower on the number of his horses." (爲勝者 立馬，一馬從二馬，三馬既立，請慶多馬). The Han commentator Zheng Xuan comments: "*ma* is a token of victory" (馬，勝籌也。). See *Li ji*, 966.

the Han dynasty reader of the *Guanzi*—also start out in the epistemological position of the unknowing outsider. There is nothing peculiarly
Zhou ("Chinese") about these credit counters. The Lai people are not
the unchangeable beasts of Later Han historiography and political rhetoric (as discussed in chapter 3), or the "allochronic" primitive of Johannes
Fabian's anthropology.[13] Rather, the Lai here are the panchronic pantopic
ignorant, whom "the wise" (*zhi zhe* 智者) must keep in the dark. In contrast to a dominant classical tradition of acculturating or "transforming"
(*hua* 化) the inferior through knowledge of rituals and texts, Guanzi's
ruler maintains his superiority by hoarding knowledge.

Qingzhong economics transcends time, space, and the material world.
Guanzi advises his ruler to "use the world to control the world" (因天下
以制天下), but Guangzi's world extends beyond the scope of any Zhou
dynasty world map. With flagrant anachronism, the interlocutors discuss
Mount Yin (between Xinjiang and Tibet), the Yuzhi (禺氏) of Central
Asia, Manchuria, and Korea (Chaoxian), all of which entered Chinese
geopolitical horizons and ambitions in the Han dynasty era of Emperor
Wu.[14] Moreover, imaginary places such as "The Plain of All under
Zhou" (*Zhouxiayuan* 周下原) and "Mount Balance" (*Heng shan* 衡山)
are placed in the same fact-fiction continuum with Zhou dynasty Qi
and Han dynasty Central Asia.[15] This is neither allegory, categorical

---

13. Fabian, *Time and the Other*, 32. Fabian describes *allochronism* as "the denial of
coevalness" in anthropology.

14. Commentators beginning with Wang Guowei have interpreted "the Yuzhi" as the
Yuezhi people. The Yuezhi only migrated to the Central Asian mountains after the Han-
Xiongnu wars forced them from the Dunhuang region (modern-day Gansu) around
160 BCE.

15. Mary Poovey's literary analysis of the rise of economic genres in eighteenth-
century Britain offers an interesting contrast. She argues that prior to the mid-eighteenth
century British writers explained the opaque workings of the new credit economy using
undifferentiated modes of imaginative, monetary, and economic writing. This "fact/
fiction continuum" enabled Daniel Defoe's novel *Roxana* to serve as a primer for evaluating credit, using a mix of real and fictional characters, and allowed James Steuart's
Principles of Political Economy to incorporate imaginary characters into its discussion.
During the eighteenth century, a new professional group of economic "experts" became the acknowledged source of the kind of fact-based knowledge that could best
explain the secrets of the market. Writings by Adam Smith and others consciously eschewed the use of abstract fictions in establishing economic "facts." With this breakup
of the fact/fiction continuum, literary and economic genres became differentiated, and
"Literature" was established as a mode of non-factual representation that aesthetically

correspondence, nor pure fiction, but rather a logomythic world: a deliberate mingling of real and imaginary places and peoples. The characters Guanzi, Duke Huan, and Calculate-and-Measure (or henceforth Mr. Calculate-and-Measure), as well as the Zhou and the Lai people, all become a palimpsest of the actual past, the real present, and hypothetical instances. Does this textual blurring of space, time, and reality undermine the text's credibility? Why use a heterotopic, heterochronic literary world that challenges belief—and transgresses literary decorum—to teach the reader about a credit economy? Why use fiction to teach economic fact, especially when teaching the idea that the value of monetary and credit instruments lies not in their intrinsic properties but in mere belief? The role of the character Mr. Calculate-and-Measure, who features elsewhere in the "Qingzhong" chapters, suggests possible answers.

MATHEMATICS AND THE POLITICS OF PERSONIFICATION

Unlike other political-economic texts, the *Guanzi* grounds its authority in a clearly imaginary person. It prefaces the economic parable of foreign exchange with these words, "In the past, when *Guidu* [Mr. Calculate-and-Measure] took residence in another's state he had to look in every direction at the surrounding world." Commentators generally agree that the imaginary economist's name uses the character *gui* 癸 for *kui* 揆, meaning "to calculate" or "estimate," while *du* 度 means "to measure."[16] Mr. Calculate-and-Measure does not supply, or feature in, the historical anecdote of the Lai. He simply serves as the cited authority for Guanzi's lesson in the strategic use of a fiat currency or credit tokens (*ma*) to gain

---

encoded truths that superseded those of the market. See Poovey, *Genres of the Credit Economy*, 1–152. In contrast, the rise of the market economy in early China offers an almost reverse scenario. The *Guanzi*'s market theories introduce a kind of fact-fiction continuum into a discursive context in which only the real (*shi*) was privileged. Emperor Wu's economic advisers championed a text that took the fictional character Mr. Calculate-y as its source of economic expertise. *Qingzhong* economics and rhetoric did not have the same profound effects as in England, and the classical Chinese tradition that historicized markets and devalued imaginative genres remained dominant for centuries thereafter.

16. The *Shiji*'s "Treatise on Pitch-pipe Standards," includes the following: "*Gui* is equivalent to the word *kui* ['measure'; 'estimate']. This means that the myriad things can be estimated and measured [or regulated]. For this reason one says *gui*." (*Shiji* 24.1244: 癸之爲言揆也，言萬物可揆度，故曰癸。). See Ma, *Guanzi Qing zhong pian*, 462; cf. Rickett, *Guanzi*, 2:468.

political advantage. Here and elsewhere the *Guanzi* anchors authority in an abstraction, rather than in the usual rhetoric of historical legitimation by venerated sages that is found in many Masters philosophical dialogues and Han political rhetoric. The *Guanzi* does, at times, recall ancient sages in the manner of Masters texts; for example, it reinvents the legend of Yu by narrating the ancient sage casting coins to help the people (an action Yu did not take in Zhou texts). However, such figures serve as second-order illustrations rather than teachers or cosmological embodiments of *qingzhong* economics.

The "Qingzhong" chapters use personifications of several economic principles or strategies. These personifications are often made to promote and discuss the very principles they embody. These include both positive *qingzhong* principles (e.g., Calculate-and-Measure; Balance [*Heng* 衡]) and negative ones (Great Extravagance [*Tai she* 泰奢]; Idle Fields [*Yitian* 佚田]; Privilege [*Te* 特]). They do not appear elsewhere in Chinese literature. They are clearly fictitious and yet, within the dialogues, belong to the same plane of reality as the historically-based characters (e.g., Guanzi, Duke Huan). Given the traditional classical embrace of the historically real or philosophically true (*shi* 實 "full") over the non-historical or fictional (*xu* 虛 "empty"), the author's use of personification was potentially as scandalous (in literary terms) as the belittling of ethics in *qingzhong* economics. The following passage demonstrates the way in which the text repeatedly draws attention to its own strange mix of historical and imaginary people and places:

桓公問於管子曰：「今欲調高下，分幷財，散積聚。不然，則世且幷兼而無止，蓄餘藏羨而不息，貧賤鰥寡獨老不與得焉。散之有道，分之有數乎？」管子對曰：「惟輕重之家 爲能散之耳。請以令 輕重之家 。」桓公曰：「諾。」 東[柬]車五乘，迎癸乙於周下原。桓公問四因與癸乙、管子、甯戚相與四坐。 桓公曰：「請問輕重之數。」 癸乙曰：「重籍其民者失其下，數欺諸侯者無權與。」

Duke Huan questioned Guanzi: "Now I wish to adjust the relation between those on high and their subjects; to divide up amassed riches; and to disperse accumulated stores. Unless this happens, the accumulation and consolidation (of wealth) in this age will not stop; the hoarding and coveting of stored surplus will never cease; and the poor, the lowly, the widower, the widow, the single, and the elderly will not have access to it [the wealth]. Is there a way to disperse [stored wealth]? Is there a method of distributing it?"

Guanzi replied: "Only a '*qingzhong* expert' (*qingzhong zhi jia*) is able to disperse it. I request that you summon a *qingzhong* expert." Duke Huan said: "I approve." He assembled five chariots to convey Guiyi [Calculate-*y*] from Zhouxiayuan [The Plain of All under Zhou]. Duke Huan met with Guiyi, Guanzi, and [agricultural minister] Ning Qi, and the four of them sat together.

Duke Huan asked: "May I inquire about *qingzhong* methods?"

Guiyi said: "Those who heavily tax their people will lose their subjects. Those [rulers] who frequently deceive their vassal lords will not hold sway over them."[17]

In this extract, the historical adviser Guanzi summons to Duke Huan's court the imaginary Guiyi (Calculate-y), who is the only named "*qingzhong* expert" (*qingzhong zhi jia* 輕重之家) in the "Qingzhong" chapters. As in the passages featuring Mr. Calculate-and-Measure, the *Guanzi* represents economic expertise as a practical body of knowledge that is dispensed by traveling (and competing) "*qingzhong* experts." The methods of calculation (*fa* 法 and *shu* 數) of these experts could be called upon by rulers, in the same way they called upon physicians or "masters of recipes" (*fangshi*). These "*qingzhong* experts" feature three times in the extant *Guanzi* (and nowhere else in early Chinese literature).[18]

Although other Han dynasty texts generally attribute *qingzhong* economic policies to the historical Guanzi, and although the personage Guanzi remains the main exponent of these policies in the *Guanzi*, the text never actually refers to him as an "expert on light and heavy" (i.e.,

---

17. Ma, *Guanzi Qing zhong pian*, 545–46. Cf. Rickett, *Guanzi*, 2:461.

18. In a discussion on the origins of war, Guanzi observes that struggles arise after generations of fathers have distributed their land amongst multiple sons. Amidst the carnage of war, Guanzi says: "*Qingzhong* experts will repeatedly journey amongst [the people], and therefore say: 'Do not give your territory to others. Do not confer wealth on others.'" Ma Feibai, *Guanzi Qing zhong pian*, 381; cf. Rickett, *Guanzi*, 2:416. Elsewhere Guanzi explains: "The stabilization of prices through fiscal management has to be standardized throughout the empire. If your commodities are too cheap then they will be drawn abroad; if they are too expensive, they will be thrown back, and these goods will flow back and forth between rival states, and *qingzhong* experts will compete with each other. When it comes to the ruler of a state, he should take control of this flow and put it to an end." See Ma Feibai, *Guanzi Qing zhong pian*, 160. Rickett, *Guanzi*, 2:366, translates 輕重之家相奪 as "experts who have mastered these fluctuations in price will compete with each other for profit." This suggests a more general rubric of savvy commercialists rather than a group of economic advisers.

as a *qingzhong zhi jia*). Rather, Guanzi explicitly defers in knowledge to Guiyi (Calculate-*y*). In the name, Guiyi, *yi* 乙 names the second heavenly stem, sometimes used as a counter in a hypothetical series (*jia* 甲, *yi* 乙, *bing* 丙, etc.), which renders Guiyi 癸乙 something like "Mr. Calculate-*y*" from "The Plain of All under Zhou" (*Zhouxiayuan* 周下原).[19] Most striking is not the quality of knowledge Mr. Calculate-*y* subsequently imparts—which parallels Guanzi's advice elsewhere—but the text's rhetorical need to introduce this separate personification into the scene. Calculate-*y* is the one who does the talking with Duke Huan, Guanzi, and the agricultural minister Ning Qi. Like Mr. Calculate-and-Measure (Guidu, who is kin in surname), Mr. Calculate-*y* personifies an action or principle fundamental to *qingzhong* policies. Buying and selling at the right times depends on continually estimating or measuring the ever-fluctuating ratio of money and commodities in circulation. Mr. Calculate-*y* personifies the manipulation of specifically non-fixed or hypothetical numbers. Mr. Calculate-*y* is thus a literary abstraction of an economic abstraction.

This unique use of personification might be compared with two traditions. First, within the Masters genre (and within the classical tradition more broadly), the *Zhuangzi* was exceptional in its use of literary personification.[20] What the *Zhuangzi* describes as *yu yan* 寓言 refers to "words lodged" in the mouth of a fictionalized speaker as a literary device.[21] The *Zhuangzi* contains personifications of qualities, natural phenomena, and conventions—for example, Knowledge, Penumbra, Shadow, Aided-by-Ink, Repeated-Recitation. The text uses these to raise skepticism about existence and the efficacy of language, and to parody other philosophical traditions. Unlike the *Zhuangzi*, the *Guanzi*'s (generally overlooked)

---

19. As in the case of Guidu (see note above), in this work *gui* 癸 will be treated as *kui* 揆, following Ma Feibai and Rickett (although the latter transliterates the names as "Guiyi" and "Guidu"). On *Zhouxiayuan*, see Ma Feibai, *Guanzi Qing zhong pian*, 113.

20. The composite text of the *Zhuangzi*, traditionally ascribed to Zhuang Zhou 莊周 (ca. 365–280 BCE), dates from the fourth to second centuries BCE.

21. See chapter 2 for a further discussion of this in relation to Sima Xiangru's *fu*. Modern scholars differ over whether the *Guanzi* belongs to the Daoist lineage (*Dao jia*), as classified in the *Hanshu*'s bibliography, or to the Legalists (*Fa jia*). Although the *Guanzi*'s passion for political hegemony certainly accords better with the latter, its use of personifications and complex metaphorical language bears closer resemblance to that of Daoist texts.

personifications are less pervasive, and belong to a more positive discourse. Mr. Calculate-and-Measure and Mr. Calculate-y both name fundamental *qingzhong* principles to be adopted. Their ahistorical or fictional quality does not provoke an existential crisis (or skepticism about the relation between words and things), but rather emphasizes the "Qingzhong's" transcendence of language, culture, and historical instance. Literary abstractions become useful for teaching how quantitative reasoning and economic abstraction trump anything an ancient sage can say.

Second, *Guanzi's* Mr. Calculate-y evokes traditions of reckoning in mathematics and calendrical systems. Heavenly stems were used to express dates and *qingzhong* economics promoted careful calculation of the timing of purchases and sales. The Han dynasty *Nine Chapters on Mathematical Arts* (*Jiu zhang suan shu* 九章算術) and the excavated *Book of Mathematical Calculations* (*Suan shu shu* 算數書) are the earliest Chinese texts to use the heavenly stems (*jia* 甲, *yi* 乙, *bing* 丙) for mathematical explanations, in the way modern mathematics uses *a, b, c,* or *x, y, z,* and Mr. Calculate-y is suggestive of this. Compare the following mathematical problem from the *Nine Chapters on Mathematical Arts*:

今有甲持錢五百六十，乙持錢三百五十，丙持錢一百八十，凡三人俱出關，關稅百錢。欲以錢數多少衰出之，問各幾何？

Suppose that X has 560 coins, Y has 350 coins, and Z has 180 coins. These three people (*ren*) pass through customs together, and they [collectively] pay a customs duty of 100 coins. If they wish to pay based on their [respective] quantities of coins, how much does each pay?[22]

In this problem, X (*jia*), Y (*yi*), and Z (*bing*) (or A, B, C) stand for hypothetical individuals who own different amounts of money for which they must pay duty as they cross a border.[23] Astronomy and mathematics were

---

22. Bai Shangnu, *Jiu zhang suan shu*, 85. Compare the example in the excavated *Suan shu shu*, strip 132: "行: 甲行五十日" (Traveling: X travels for 50 days). See Peng Hao, *Zhangjiashan Han jian 'Suan shu shu,'* 95. The received text of the *Jiu zhang suan shu* 九章算術 was recompiled by Zhou Cang (d. 152 BCE) and Geng Shoucang (first century BCE); and was later annotated in 263 CE by Liu Hui. See Chemla and Guo, *Les Neuf chapitres*, 82, on the unprecedented use of *jia*, yi, etc., in this way in Chinese mathematical texts.

23. This use of *jia, yi, bing,* for people also recurs in the *Shuihudi* and *Zhangjiashan* legal strips, where these terms are included in discussions of monetary crimes and penalties.

closely related pursuits, and heavenly stems were commonly used for as-
trological instruments: for example, when predicting lucky days to perform certain actions.[24] However, in the above problem the anthropomor-
phized heavenly stems are metonyms rather than personifications; they
embody the mundane hypothesis of the taxpayer, not the correlative relation between cosmic and human action. The *Guanzi*'s Mr. Calculate-*y*
(or perhaps "Calculate-using-*Y*"?) seems to invoke this disenchanted
mathematical idiom.[25] This is important because *qingzhong* experts were
controversial precisely for introducing a radically quantitative approach
to the economy. During the reign of Emperor Wu there was a rise in the
use of statistics, record-keeping, and arithmetic texts, which accompanied the bureaucratization of an expansionist empire and its expanding
markets. Both the *Guanzi*'s "Qingzhong" dialogues and mathematical
texts reflected and enabled this transformation of the political economy.
They provided the technical expertise in economic and financial calculations that the *Guanzi*—and some of Emperor Wu's economic advisers—
insisted was necessary to competitively strengthen the state. The *Guanzi*
re-imagined a cosmocrat, a ruler of *tianxia*, who depended on the mastery not of the environment, or enemies, or ritual propriety, but of the
abstract, ever-fluctuating, quantitative laws of commodity price.

Furthermore, both the *Guanzi* and Han mathematical texts—unlike
the *Zhuangzi*—devote a large proportion of their examples to monetary
or market transactions. The *Book of Mathematical Calculations* and the
(slightly later) *Nine Chapters on Mathematical Arts* include everyday examples that Han dynasty individuals and officials might have encountered: customs payments in bronze coins (as above); interest on money
loans; shared purchases; exchanges of silver and gold by weight; corrections of mistaken tax bills; as well as calculations of the manpower

---

24. See Harper, "Warring States Natural Philosophy and Occult Thought," 820–52;
Tseng, "Representation and Appropriation." Calendrical systems were politicized and Em-
peror Wu reformed the calendar with his "Grand Inception" [*taichu* 太初] in 104 BCE. See
Cullen, "Numbers, numeracy, and the cosmos," and Loewe, *Crisis and Conflict*, 17–36.

25. The *Zhou bi suan jing* 周髀算經 (The Gnomon of the Zhou dynasty), a work on
mathematics and astronomy probably compiled in the Former Han dynasty, includes
the phrase *kui du* ("calculate and measure") in reference to water clock calculations. See
Cullen, *Astronomy and Mathematics*, 191. However, it does not include market transactions as do the two mathematical texts under discussion—and as does the post-Han
Sunzi Suanjing 孫子算經 (The mathematical classic of Sunzi).

required by each county for frontier duty. The *Nine Chapters on Mathematical Arts* also contains a chapter entitled "equalizing transport" (*jun shu* 均輸), an institution first established under Han Emperor Wu to enable the state to more efficiently collect taxes and circulate goods across the empire. Although the "Qingzhong" chapters do not use the term *jun shu*, they propose and explain state control over transportation as a way to help regulate prices and facilitate fair distribution. Both the *Shiji* and *Debate on Salt and Iron* reveal how politically controversial *jun shu* became as one of the key imperial strategies (along with state monopolies and price regulation) that were needed to finance the empire's expansion.[26] The *Nine Chapters on Mathematical Arts*, by contrast, suggests the kinds of mathematical problems raised by the new *jun shu* system—e.g., grain prices, the labor required for distribution, regional taxes, and journey times—and uses a discussion of these problems to tutor the reader in the skills of calculating proportions and ratios.

Like mathematical texts, the "Qingzhong" dialogues use hypothetical scenarios and fictional tales to teach general and abstract procedures. Although Han dynasty mathematical texts did train administrators to perform the calculations required to run a monetized empire, these texts also explored theoretical problems, often embedding these problems in impractical or impossible scenarios.[27] Take for example, the market-driven fantasy of the ever-more productive weaver:

今有女子善織，日自倍，五日織五尺。問日織幾何？

Suppose there is a girl skilful at weaving, who each day doubles her product. In five days she weaves [a cloth of] 5 *chi*. Question: how much does she weave in each successive day?[28]

---

26. E.g., Ma Feibai, *Guanzi*, 445.

27. On this see Cullen, "The *Suan shu shu* 'Writings on Reckoning': Rewriting the History of Early Chinese Mathematics;" Chemla, "Mathematics, Nature and Cosmological Inquiry"; Chemla and Guo, *Les Neuf chapitres*. One might also investigate some shared technical idiom between the "Qingzhong" chapters and mathematical texts: for example, the specialized use of the term *tong* 通 ("communicate").

28. See Bai Shangnu, *Jiu zhang suan shu zhu shi*, 85–86; Chemla, *Les Neuf Chapitres*, 286–89. Cullen, "The Suan shu shu, 'Writings on Reckoning': Rewriting the History of Early Chinese Mathematics," 10–44, emphasizes that this problem was for mathematical not administrative purposes.

Or take the more fantastic case entitled "A fox goes through customs" (*Hu chu guan* 狐出關):

> 狐、貍、犬出關，租百一十一錢。犬謂貍、(貍) 謂狐：而 (爾) 皮倍我，出租當倍(哉)。問出各幾何。得曰：犬出十五錢七分六，貍出卅 (三十) 一錢分五，狐出六十三錢分三。术 (術) 曰：令各相倍也，幷之七爲法，以租各乘之爲實，(實) 如法得一。

A fox, a wildcat, and a dog go through border customs. Their [total] tax is 111 cash. The dog says to the wildcat and the wildcat [also] says to the fox: "Your hide is worth double mine so you should pay double as much tax!"

Question: How much does each pay out?

Result: The dog pays 15 and 6/7 cash; the wildcat pays 31 and 5 parts cash[29]; the fox pays 63 and 3/7 cash.

The method says: Let each one double the next; combine them making 7 the divisor; take the tax and multiply each [of the three numbers] to make the dividend; divide the dividend by the divisor to obtain [each] one's [share].[30]

Here the dog, fox, and wildcat are not personifications, but they populate a clearly fictional world that is somewhat akin to the *Zhuangzi*'s animal parables.[31] The *Guanzi* effectively merges the mathematical question-answer-proof format with the Masters philosophical form of dialogue between ruler and adviser. As throughout the *Book of Mathematical Calculations* and the transmitted *Nine Chapters on Mathematical Arts*, the above case proceeds from a specific imaginary problem to a generalized rule. The conversation between three animals leads to a mathematical question (*wen* 問) and a result (*de* 得); this, in turn, leads on to an algorithmic proof (*shu* 術) that abstracts animals and money into an arithmetic procedure. In a similar, although less rigid fashion, the individual "Qingzhong" dialogues tend to begin with a new problem and to end with a general *qingzhong* "method" or "strategy," often tagged as "This is what is called. . . ." In this light, the "Qingzhong" chapters bring to the political-economic questions of the Masters dialogue both the

---

29. That is, the wildcat pays 31 and 5/7 cash.

30. *Zhangjiashan Han mu zhu jian*, 253, strip 34–35; Peng Hao, *Zhangjiashan Han jian "Suan shu shu" zhu shi*, 52; Cullen, "The Suan shu shu 算數書 'Writings on Reckoning,'" 45, strip 34–35.

31. See Spring, *Animal Allegories in T'ang China* on the later (and distinct) Chinese literary tradition of animal personification.

quantitative, monetized reasoning and the use of hypothetical fictions in mathematical texts. Like Han dynasty mathematical texts, the *Guanzi* prized generality and abstraction. However, the Guanzian use of personification clearly goes further in pushing its readers to consider the *rhetoric* of abstraction.[32]

The Classical Scholars 文學: Returning to Fundamentals (fan ben)

Like the "Qingzhong" chapters, Huan Kuan's *Debate on Salt and Iron* adopted the dialogue form to address the political economy of an expansionist and increasingly monetized empire.[33] There was a broad familiarity with the *Guanzi* during the Former Han, and the *Debate on Salt and Iron* suggests that Emperor Wu turned to those versed in *qingzhong* strategies, such as state monopolies, to finance large-scale territorial expansion.[34] Although the *Debate on Salt and Iron* neither reduced Emperor Wu's politics to the mere implementation of Guanzian theory, nor directly engaged with the "Qingzhong" chapters, it emphasized the need to restore literary and moral decorum to political discourse. That is, the *Debate on*

---

32. Chemla, "Documenting a process of abstraction in the mathematics of ancient China."

33. The first century *Hanshu* bibliography catalogs both subjects under the "Masters" category, but under different sub-categories.

34. The *Shiji*'s joint biography of the historical Guan Zhong and of Yan Ying (another minister) ends with the following authorial comment (*Shiji* 62.2136): "The Grand Scribe comments: 'I have read Mr. Guan's "Mu Min" (On shepherding the people 牧民), "Shan Gao" (On mountains that are high 山高), "Sheng Ma" (On military taxes 乘馬), "Qingzhong" (Light and heavy 輕重), and "Jiu Fu" (On the nine treasuries 九府); as well as Master Yan's *Spring and Autumn Annals*. . . . Since many people possess [copies of] their writings nowadays, I do not discuss [these writings], but instead discuss [Guan Zhong and Yan Ying's] overlooked affairs." It is unclear what the "Qingzhong" here refers to, but it ostensibly refers to an economic text. The term *qingzhong* pervades (what is now known as) the *Guanzi*'s "Qingzhong" section—seven chapters of which are entitled "Qingzhong A," "Qingzhong B," etc., using the celestial stems *jia* 甲, *yi* 乙, etc., as ordinal counters (two of these chapters are now lost). The other four texts listed above belong to the older sections of the *Guanzi* or are lost (e.g., the "Jiu Fu" chapter was lost by Liu Xiang's time). The *Shiji*'s biography emphasizes Guan Zhong's economic savvy, but does not discuss the novel strategies found in the transmitted "Qingzhong" section. On this passage, see Rickett, *Guanzi*, 2:346.

Salt and Iron offered another set of lessons in rhetoric.[35] By juxtaposing these two pedagogic texts today's reader can glimpse the ways in which markets and frontiers became important rhetorical themes for competing approaches to the classical tradition.

In contrast to the *Guanzi*'s semi-fictional world, the *Debate on Salt and Iron* presents a historical scene. It dramatizes a debate that took place in 81 BCE (under Emperor Zhao) over the earlier establishment of salt and iron monopolies, which had taken place under Emperor Wu (in 119 BCE).[36] While ostensibly an economic debate over whether private industrialists or the state should control the highly profitable manufacture of iron and salt, the *Debate on Salt and Iron* unfolds as a postmortem of Emperor Wu's rule and of a much broader ideological debate over the foundations of the political economy. It pits the Imperial Counselor (*da fu* 大夫)—which was an official position that is generally understood to refer to Sang Hongyang 桑弘羊 (152–80 BCE)—as well as the Imperial Counselor's supporters against the "men of learning" or Classical Scholars (*wen xue* 文學) and Worthies (*xianliang* 賢良).[37] Sang Hongyang, a merchant's son famous for his mental calculations (*xin ji* 心計), embodied the state's embrace of *qingzhong* arithmetic reason. Promoted to Superintendent of Agriculture (*Da Sinong* 大司農) under Emperor Wu, Sang Hongyang helped to establish China's earliest state monopolies (*que* 榷), as well as an "equalizing transport system" (*jun shu* 均輸) to ease the transport of goods, institutions for centralized price stabilization (*ping zhun* 平準), and agricultural colonies in Central Asia.[38]

---

35. Esson Gale in Huan, *Discourses on Salt and Iron*, xlii–li, and Nylan, "The Art of Persuasion," 495–498, introduce some aspects of argument and style.

36. Huan Kuan was Governor (*Taishou* 太守) of Lujiang. For helpful accounts and analyses of the debate, see Loewe, "The Former Han Dynasty"; Loewe, *Crisis and Conflict in Han China*; Gale, *Discourses on Salt and Iron*; Lévi, *La dispute sur le sel et le fer*; and Wang Liqi, *Yantielun*.

37. This chapter generally refers to the Classical Scholars and Worthies simply by the former term, since the Classical Scholars are the main representatives of their side, and are the only spokespeople after chapter 41. Similarly, the *Dafu* (Sang Hongyang) dominates his side's defense in the dialogue.

38. Compare Sang with the mathematical expert Geng Shouchang 耿壽昌 (fl. ca. 57–52 BCE), who was well versed in the "distribution of cash" and who instituted the "ever-normal granaries" (*chang ping cang* 常平倉) to regulate grain price. See *Hanshu* 24A.1141.

The *Hanshu's* bibliography listed the *Debate on Salt and Iron* under the Masters rubric. As in other Masters texts there is minimal narrative. The *Debate on Salt and Iron* also renders Sang Hongyang (but never his critics) speechless thirteen times through the dialogue, a common sign of defeat in the philosophical tradition.[39] At the same time, the *Debate on Salt and Iron* gives greater voice to both sides of the argument than do typical Masters dialogues. The *Debate on Salt and Iron* represents political-economic crisis as the product of modern (*jin* 今, *shi* 世) anti-classicist reasoning; and Sang Hongyang confesses he has turned to the scholars for help despite his assiduous attention to all methods of calculation (*ji shu* 計數).[40] In a chapter-length comment at the end of the dialogue Huan Kuan openly criticizes Sang using the same rhetoric used by the Classical Scholars: "[Sang] abandoned himself to profit and to commerce [lit. "the branch"]; he failed to take the beginnings of antiquity as his model" (放於利末，不師 始古).[41] Thus, the *Debate on Salt and Iron*— which was written during the reign of Emperor Xuan (r74–49 BCE), when the state monopolies were still a highly contentious issue—both reflects the political rise of classicists after Emperor Wu and also serves as a kind of manifesto for the return to classical expertise.[42]

Modern scholars have generally explored the relation between the *Debate on Salt and Iron* and *Guanzi* in political and economic terms (e.g., foreign policy, coinage, monopolies). However, the two texts also posited oppositional literary models that have not been sufficiently examined. As shown above, the *Guanzi's* use of new economic terms and of imaginary speakers eschewed classical authority and grounded knowledge in constantly updated quantitative calculations. By contrast, the *Debate on Salt and Iron* conflated the return to the non-expansionist agricultural state (what the *Debate on Salt and Iron* called a "return to the root" *fan ben*) with the return to classical texts ("taking the beginnings of antiquity as model"). The *Debate on Salt and Iron* thereby portrayed the

---

39. This number of instances includes those officials on the *Dafu's* side (御史 the *Yushi* and 丞相 the *Chenxiang*). See Wang Liqi, *Yantielun*, 129, 150, 171, 192, 253, 320, 334, 350, 406, 455, 579, 609, 621, and cf. 291. Typical phrases (usually at the end of a chapter) include: "大夫默然不對" and "大夫不説，作色不應也。"

40. Wang Liqi, *Yantielun*, 128; Ma Feibai, *Yantielun*, 74.

41. Wang Liqi, *Yantielun*, 629–30.

42. On this see the preface to the Hong zhi 宏治 edition of the *Debate on Salt and Iron* by Du Mu 都穆 (1459–1525).

classicist (the expert in classical texts), rather than the expert in quantitative calculations, as the master of the political economy. The following sections explore some of the key terms and models used by the *Debate on Salt and Iron*; through such terms and models the work restored both the moral idiom with which philosophical Masters had traditionally discussed the political economy as well as the ultimate authority of traditional Zhou texts.

BEN 本 (ROOT) AND MO 末 (BRANCH)

The *Debate on Salt and Iron* reasserts the importance of the morally inscribed metaphors *ben* 本 ("root"; "basic"; "primary"; "fundamental") and *mo* 末 ("branch"; "secondary"; "auxiliary") to political-economic debate. At some point in the fourth century BCE—amidst the encroaching urbanization, market-expansion, and deforestation of Warring States China—officials and scholars had begun to figuratively replant trees. They protested the ongoing socioeconomic changes using a new economic metaphor of agriculture as the "root" (*ben*) economy, and commerce as the "branch" (*mo*). Philosophical texts had already established the idiomatic hierarchy of these two terms as moral metaphors, differentiating fundamental (*ben*: root) human values from those that were merely secondary (*mo*: tip, branch). By the Warring States and Qin period some political and philosophical texts, such as the *Book of Lord Shang* (*Shangjun shu* 商君書), *Han Feizi* 韓非子, *Xunzi* 荀子, and the *Spring and Autumn Annals of Master Lü* (*Lüshi chunqiu* 呂氏春秋) also began to extol "the root occupations" (*ben ye* 本業, farmers, weavers). When these works—despite their differences in outlook—praised farming as *ben* and belittled commerce as *mo*, they implicitly grounded their economic metaphors in these moral metaphors.

By the early imperial period (i.e., the Qin and Han dynasties), the widespread introduction of iron implements had revolutionized agriculture, effectively increasing the dependence of agriculture (*ben*) on commercial and artisanal (*mo*) occupations.[43] During the accelerated

---

43. On the "revolution" in pre-Han agriculture, which was primarily brought about by iron implements, animal power, flood control, and irrigation, see Nishijima, "Economic and Social History," 556–57. On the inclusion of the iron industry in *mo*, see Loewe, "Attempts at Economic Co-ordination." On the perceived effects of the iron industry on real trees (as opposed to metaphorical ones) see Major, *The Huainanzi*, 282:

industrial and urban growth of the Former Han—especially during
Emperor Wu's state-sponsored expansion of monetized markets—
some writers re-imagined the positive functions of profit and wealth,
merchants, and money—by reevaluating the relationship of "root" and
"branch" in then-scandalous praise of the "branch" (i.e., commerce).[44]
For example, the "Qingzhong" chapters used the terms in neutral reference to agriculture and commerce precisely to promote state-
regulated markets. And, as will be explored in chapter 3, Sima Qian's
model of unregulated markets in the *Shiji* grounded novel notions of
"root wealth" (*ben fu* 本富) and "branch wealth" (*mo fu* 末富) in market exchange.[45] Modern scholarship often overlooks these transgressive uses of *ben* and *mo* that surfaced during the Former Han.[46] The
Debate on Salt and Iron, however, demonstrates, better than any extant
text the political and literary stakes in the Han dynasty quarrel over
the economic idiom. Within the *Debate on Salt and Iron*, these highly
influential economic metaphors were used in far more dissonant and

---

"Burning down forests in order to hunt;/Stoking kilns with entire logs,/Blowing through
tuyeres and puffing with bellows/In order to melt bronze and iron/That extravagantly
flow to harden in the mold,/Not considering an entire day sufficient to the task./The
mountains are denuded of towering trees,/The forests stripped of their cudriana and
catalpas,/Tree trunks are burned to make charcoal,/Grass is burned to make ash." The
Han dynasty iron industry—using a large-scale technology of the blast furnace that
depended heavily on forest timber from across the empire for charcoal fuel (as well as
on slave and convict labor)—developed alongside bloomer smelting. For an excellent account of archaeological and literary records of the Han dynasty iron industry, see Wagner, *Iron and Steel in Ancient China*. Elvin, *Retreat of the Elephants*, shows how trees, but
not forests, were "part of the rich world of rhetoric and allusion in late-archaic and early
classical China." Competing uses of *ben* and *mo* somewhat complicate this otherwise
very useful argument.

44. On the acceleration of urban growth during the Former Han, followed by decel-
erated growth during the Later Han, see Pirazzoli-t'Serstevens, "Urbanism."

45. Ma Feibai, *Guanzi qingzhong pian*, 445, uses *ben* and *mo* to refer to agriculture
and commerce, respectively. In this context they are presented as interconnected economic sectors to be controlled by the ruler and not as morally-inscribed activities.

46. For useful accounts of the terms *ben* and *mo*, see Loewe, "Attempts at Economic
Co-ordination"; Kern, *The Stele Inscriptions of Ch'in*, 26–27, note 50; Barbieri-Low,
Artisans, 39–44; Tang, "Xian Qin zhu zi jingji zhexue"; Xing Jianguo, "Ben mo guan de
yan bian"; Wagner, *The State and the Iron Industry in Han China*, 25. On the politics of
the use of these terms, see Ye Shichang, *Gudai Zhongguo jingji*, 155 and Guo Moruo,
Nuli zhi shidai, 157–58. Guo situates the rhetoric of *ben* and *mo* within the unsuccessful
class struggle of merchants.

self-reflexive ways than in the previous tradition, and possibly in the post-Han tradition.

The paired terms *ben* and *mo* pervade the *Debate on Salt and Iron*'s sixty chapters, which cover topics ranging from frontiers, currency change, forced labor, and Qin punishments to Ruists (i.e., "Confucian" classicists). The *Guanzi*'s "Qingzhong" chapters very occasionally use *ben* and *mo* as morally-neutral metonyms for agriculture and commerce. When these terms are so used, it is to explain *qingzhong* strategies.[47] By contrast, the *Debate on Salt and Iron*'s Classical Scholars relentlessly re-associate *ben* and *mo* with their origins in moral philosophy. In the opening speech of the *Debate on Salt and Iron*, the Classical Scholars lay out the fundamental, hierarchical opposition between "root" (*ben*) and "branch" (*mo*), and the importance of these terms to any discussion of the political economy. Their *ben* is not so much a metonym for agriculture (as in the *Guanzi*) as an ethical truism: "agriculture-is-the-fundamental-human-value."[48] This foundation of the political economy is the ritual propriety and righteousness (*li yi* 禮義) of a textual antiquity that existed before the rise of monetized markets.

文學對曰：「竊聞治人之道，防淫佚之原，廣道德之端，抑末利而開仁義，毋示以利，然後教化可興，而風俗可移也。今郡國有鹽、鐵、酒榷，均輸，與民爭利。散敦厚之樸，成貪鄙之化。是以百姓就本者寡，趨末者眾。夫 文繁則質衰，末盛則質虧。末修則民淫，本修則民愨。民愨則財用足，民侈則饑 寒生。願罷鹽、鐵、酒榷、均輸，所以進本退末，廣利農業，便也。」

The Classical Scholars replied: "We have heard that the way to administer people begins in guarding against indulgence and ends in broadening the path of virtue, in curbing profits from the 'branch' (*mo li*) and initiating benevolence and righteousness (*ren yi*). If you do not put profit on display then education and cultural transformation can happen and customs can change. Now commanderies and states have monopolies on salt, iron, and liquor, and the equalizing system of market transport, which compete with the people for profit. This will scatter honest and simple people, and turn them greedy and covetous. As a result, those amongst the population practicing the 'root' (*ben zhe*) will be few, while [the numbers of] those rushing to practice the 'branch' (*mo zhe*) will

47. E.g., Ma Feibai, *Guanzi*, 445.
48. For such uses, see Wang Liqi, *Yantielun*, 3–4, 25, 53, 119–20, 161.

proliferate. When civilizations become complex, then [simple] substance declines; when the 'branch' (*mo*) flourishes, then substance is insufficient. Cultivation of the 'branch' (*mo*) leads to indulgence amongst the people; cultivation of the 'root' (*ben*) leads to honesty amongst the people. When people are honest then resources for expenditure will be sufficient; when people are extravagant then there will be starvation in cold [seasons]. We want the abolition of monopolies on salt, iron, and liquor and [the abolishment] of the equalizing system of market transport, in order to promote the 'root' (*ben*) and retract the 'branch' (*mo*), and to increase the profits of the agricultural occupations. This would be expedient."[49]

The opening desire of the Classical Scholars to "curb profits from the branch (*mo li* 末利) and to initiate benevolence and righteousness (*ren yi* 仁義)" resonates with the canonical classical sentiments of the Masters tradition: "The gentleman understands benevolence (*ren* 仁); the petty man understands profit (*li* 利)" (Confucius); and "Why must your Majesty speak of 'profit' (*li*)? There is benevolence and righteousness (*ren yi*) and that is all" (Mencius).[50] The Classical Scholars set up an elaborate series of oppositional associations of "root" and "branch": "honest" and "simple" versus "greedy" and "extravagant" people; "substantial" versus "(superficially) complex" civilization; economic sufficiency versus starvation.[51] They invoke the "branch" (*mo*) five times here to make the basic points that: a) commerce is morally corrupting; b) the state needs to disengage from market activity since state-planning (e.g., monopolies, the equalizing system of market transport) further encourages such immoral commerce; and c) commerce will lead to material insufficiency. Elsewhere the Classical Scholars co-opt the language of profit: to "enrich the state" (*fu guo* 富國), they propose gathering "profits from the soil" (*tu zhi li* 土之利).

The Classical Scholars repeatedly call for a "return to the root" (*fan ben* 反本). Their "root" is an occupation (agriculture), a time (Zhou antiquity), and a set of texts (classical canon). This economics of archaism proposes that the future of China's political economy lies in an idealized agrarian, moral, and textual state:

草萊不闢，田疇不治，雖擅山海之財，通百末之利，猶不能瞻也。是以古者尚力務本而種樹繁，躬耕趣時而衣食足。

---

49. Wang Liqi, *Yantielun*, 1–2.
50. *Lunyu* 37 (*Analects* 4.16); Mencius' opening line at *Mengzi* 9 (*Mencius* 1A1).
51. On this association of *li* with greed see Wang Liqi, *Yantielun*, 4; 598–99.

[The Classical Scholars said:] "If grasses and weeds are not cleared and if fields and farmland are not tended, then even if [the state] monopolizes the wealth of the mountains and seas [i.e., natural resources] and profits from a hundred 'branches' (*mo*) are gained, this still would not be sufficient. Therefore in antiquity they still focused their efforts on the 'root' (*ben*) and planted and sowed abundantly. They cultivated the land themselves according to the season; clothes and food were sufficient."[52]

In this work, the Classical Scholars philologically return to *ben*'s "authentic" meaning. In showing that the care of the "root" is, literally, "planting and sowing abundantly" (and not simply an apt metaphorical figure of such an action) the Classical Scholars can bring into being the moral economy to which *ben* refers. Thus, the classical expert can solve the problem of insufficiency because he best knows the nonmarket conditions of a Golden Age antiquity.

The *Debate on Salt and Iron* does not elucidate actual *qingzhong* strategies but, rather, makes Sang Hongyang defend or ventriloquize *qingzhong*-style economics (e.g., state monopolies) through this classical moral idiom. The *Guanzi* is explicitly cited only four times in the *Debate on Salt and Iron*. In two cases, Sang Hongyang's quotations resemble passages from the "Qingzhong" chapters; in the other two cases, the Classical Scholars draw from the earlier, non-"Qingzhong" sections of the *Guanzi*.[53] Quantitative arguments are rare in the dialogue.[54] Unlike the

---

52. Wang Liqi, *Yantielun*, 25. Following Gao You's 高誘 gloss on *shu* 樹 as *jia* 稼.

53. Although the Classical Scholars invoke the famous phrase "When granaries and storehouses are full, then there can be an understanding of ritual propriety and moderation" (倉廩實而知禮節) that is found both in the pre-Han "Mu Min" 牧民 (On shepherding the people) chapter and in the "Qingzhong" section, the Classical Scholars spin the phrase to mean that a prosperous people act in accordance with ritual propriety (i.e, more consonant with its earlier usage). See Wang Liqi, *Yantielun*, 430, and Ma Feibai, *Yantielun*, 270: "管子曰：「『倉廩實而知禮節，百姓足而知榮辱。』故富民易與適禮。」" For the other passage in which the Classical Scholars quote from the *Guanzi*, see Wang Liqi, *Yantielun*, 578–79; Ma Feibai, *Yantielun*, 394. Ma Feibai proposes about a dozen cases in which the received "Qingzhong" chapters and the *Debate on Salt and Iron* passages offer similar sentiments or nearly parallel passages. However, the quoted passages attributed to Guanzi in the *Debate on Salt and Iron* (that is, the part following "Guanzi says" 管子曰) do not exactly match the received *Guanzi*.

54. The following passage is one exception. Sang Hongyang argues, "Since one *duan* [about 4.62 m] of Chinese silk can obtain Xiongnu goods worth heaps of gold we can diminish the resources of the enemy state"; but then the Classical Scholars recalculate

Classical Scholars, Sang Hongyang uses *ben* and *mo* in overtly strategic
and contradictory ways. Occasionally, he reinforces the traditional hierarchy of these terms. For example, when justifying market intervention
as a means of financing war with the Xiongnu, Sang argues that the
purpose of state monopolies "is not only to profit [the state] but in the
future to build up the 'root' and curb the 'branch'" (非獨爲利入也，
將以建本抑末).[55] More often, however, Sang is made to rhetorically
subvert the original hierarchy of the terms in order to promote commerce (*mo*) as equally necessary (or more immediately important) than
agriculture (*ben*).[56] "Without *mo* pursuit of profit, the *ben* occupations
do not have an outlet (for sales) . . . Farmers and merchants exchange
goods in order that both *ben* and *mo* may profit";[57] "The founders of our
state established the path[s] (*tu*) of *ben* and *mo* . . . therefore if artisans
do not sell, farmers will lack implements; if merchants do not sell, supplies of precious commodities will be cut off."[58] *Mo* ceases to threaten
ben as the over-heavy tree branch in the conventional metaphor. The
interdependence of *ben* and *mo* enables the universal satisfaction of material needs, and the state management of *mo* is precisely the path that
Sang Hongyang seeks to follow. Sang invokes the legendary economic
adviser and self-made, extremely wealthy merchant Fan Li, whose analysis of "the different pathways of *ben* and *mo*" enables him to promote,
rather than suppress, commerce in the service of state and family.[59] In
Sang Hongang's telling, the rivalry is not that between *ben* and *mo*—
between their different paths—but in the direction of *mo* towards the
benefit of the state rather than of the individual.

Sang's computation, "If your calculation includes the labor of plowing and sericulture
and capital expenditure, a single foreign good costs 100 times its value."

55. Wang Liqi, *Yantielun*, 74.

56. E.g., Wang Liqi, *Yantielun*, 2, 4–5, 161, 170–1, 177, 436, 438, 619.

57. Wang Liqi, *Yantielun*, 39–40; on this use of profit, see 177. Cf. *Shiji* 68.2230.

58. Wang Liqi, *Yantielun*, 7.

59. Wang Liqi, *Yantielun*, 436. "When Tao Zhu (i.e., Fan Li) did business, he distinguished the paths of *ben* and *mo*, and counted the activities within a single household,
before his business method was ready. Nowadays the county officials cast agricultural
implements so that the people engage in *ben*, and not in *mo*, and therefore they are not
worn out by cold and hunger." Although Sang Hongyang rhetorically seems to privilege *ben* here (as the people's proper education), he is actually distinguishing between
state and private activities. For an account of Fan Li that uses similar language, see
Shiji 129.3257.

In this way, the *Debate on Salt and Iron* represents Sang Hongyang as someone who seeks at every turn to defeat his opponents through mere rhetorical wordplay rather than by offering constructive economic plans. For example, after the Classical Scholars argue that state monopolies on coinage are incompatible with a "return to the root" (*fan ben*), Sang Hongyang ironically mimics their refrain:

禁禦之法立，而奸偽息，奸偽息，則民不期於妄得，而各務其職；不反本何爲？故統一，則民不二也。

By establishing laws, counterfeiting and faking ceases; when counterfeiting and faking ceases, the people do not expect false gains, and each strives to fulfill his duties. How is this not a "return to the root" (*fan ben*)? Therefore unify [the currency] and the people will not be divided.[60]

Instead of introducing the quantity theory of money or the virtues of monopolies, Sang Hongyang tries to outdo the Classical Scholars in their own moral rhetoric. State laws banning private minting is a "return to the root" because it prevents counterfeiting and guides people back to the ethical fulfillment of their office (*zhi* 職)—a well-known concern of Mencius and other traditional philosophers.[61] In a debate in which both sides accuse the other of using "empty verbiage" (*xu yan* 虛言), such rhetorical appropriations—when juxtaposed with more extended elaborations of their normative values—present one way in which the *Debate on Salt and Iron* makes Sang Hongyang's rhetoric appear more "empty."[62]

Before turning to two economic paradigms that epitomized the classical "return to the root," one should note that women's work did not fit neatly into the rhetorical opposition of "root" and "branch." In the canonical statements of the *Liji* (Rites), the wife "becomes a match to her husband by performing the work of silk, hemp, and cloth, and textiles," and the *Debate on Salt and Iron*'s Classical Scholars reasserted this claim: "Men plowing and women weaving is the great enterprise of empire" (夫男耕女績，天下之大業也).[63] Despite the symbolic pairing

---

60. Wang Liqi, *Yantielun*, 53. In Sima Qian's (critical) description of Sang Hongyang's proposal to Emperor Wu for the "balanced standard," *fan ben* refers to a desired return to farming by merchants, from whom the government wishes to remove control of commercial traffic. See *Shiji* 30.1442.

61. Compare similar rhetorical uses of *ben* at Wang Liqi, *Yantielun*, 27; 52; 335; 578.

62. See Wang Liqi, *Yantielun*, 250–53.

63. *Liji*, "Hun yi" 昏義 (當於夫，以成絲麻布帛之事); Wang Liqi, *Yantielun*, 170–71.

of agriculture and sericulture as the "root" economy, men's occupations provided the default moral example. Plowing always provided a counterpoint to craft (*gong* 工) and commerce (*shang* 商). Women's (textile) work (*nü gong* 女工; *nü shi* 女事; *nü gong* 女功; *nü gong* 女紅), by contrast, could rhetorically belong to either "root" or "branch."[64] There was no corresponding category of all-embracing "manly work." As explored in chapter 4, the *Debate on Salt and Iron's* debate over the productivity of, the different forms of, and the social conditions of women's labor explicitly patterned a much larger conflict over the new kinds of kinship, marriage, and personal desires that were understood both to produce, and to result from, the market economy (*mo*).

JING TIAN 井田: THE "WELL-FIELD"

The influential classical model of the "well-field" or "grid-field" (*jing tian* 井田) anchored the moral economy in the affective bonds of (male-centered) farming. Although the actual historical existence of this model remains unclear, there were *jing tian* advocates from the Warring States through the late imperial period.[65] The system took its name from the Chinese character for well, *jing* 井, whose graphic shape resembled the tic-tac-toe grid of idealized farm units. The most influential exposition of the archaic "well-field" system comes in the *Mencius*:

> [Mencius:] If (those within a *jing* 井) should befriend each other in their comings and goings, help each other in protecting and keeping watch, [and] support each other through illnesses, the people will live in affectionate friendship. [A plot of land] one *li* square is a *jing*. A *jing* is 900 *mu* and at its center is the common field (*gong tian* 公田). The eight families who each privately hold 100 *mu* plots collectively nurture the common field (at the center). Only after they have finished managing the public field do they dare administer their individual (*si*) affairs. This is how one distinguishes them from uncultivated men.[66]

---

64. For examples of the use of *nü gong* to refer to non-commercial, traditional weaving, see, for example, *Hanshu* 28B.1660; Wang Liqi, *Yantielun*, 4–5.

65. On the possibility that the *jingtian* system was an actual practice as well as an ideal during various periods of Chinese history, see Bray, *Agriculture*, 101–2. See also Hsu, *Han agriculture*, 576.

66. See *Mengzi* 92 (*Mencius* 3A3). The *Book of Lord Shang*, the *Zuo Commentary on the Spring and Autumn Annals*, and the *Hanshi waizhuan* (Master Han's Exoteric Commentary [on the *Odes*]) are among the other early texts that promote this model.

Theoretically, land in the Zhou domain was owned by the king, and Mencius describes a system in which tenants pay their lord through labor service on the common field (*gong tian*), and not, as in the Qin-Han period, through rent payments. What Mencius emphasizes here, however, is not the lord-subject bond created by the system, but rather the ties of sodality that were created among the eight families by working together on the common field. The spatial placement of the "common field" at the center of the community—and the temporal order of community labor on the common field *before* farming individual plots—above all promotes community responsibility and spirit, friendship and mutual care. It is the embedding of the economy in society—that is, the inextricability of agricultural labor both from affective ties between peasant families and from the Zhou political hierarchy—that the proponents of the "well-field" idealized. To them, these factors were more valuable than efficiency in output or profit margins.

In *Debate on Salt and Iron* the Classical Scholars call for a return to this archaic "well-field" system: "Thus the Way (*Dao*) of administering the people lies only in modest expenditure, honoring *ben* (agriculture), and distributing land according to the *jing tian* system."[67] Sang Hongyang's contradictory responses exemplify his rhetoric. He and the officials who support him (i.e., the *Yushi* and the *Chenxiang*) first argue that the *jing tian*'s focus on agriculture is inadequate given the already-commercialized present. Later, these officials valorize the *jing tian* as a principle of "putting public duty before oneself"—a system which is better administered through imperial taxation rather than through an archaic labor service system because people generally shirk their duties.[68] Still later, Sang's supporters condemn the hypocrisy of their scholarly critics who, while promoting the *jing tian* system, devote their lives to abstract discourse instead of to economically productive plowing. The Classical Scholars and Worthies must thus defend themselves against the charge that scholarship is un-economic.

"TRIBUTE OF YU" 禹貢

The contested meanings of the "well-field," and of *ben* and *mo*, patterned other oppositional ideals: between the ethics-centered Zhou versus the

---

67. Wang Liqi, *Yantielun*, 26: 故理民之道，在於節用尚本，分土井田而已。
68. Wang Liqi, *Yantielun*, 190, 250.

powerful Qin empires as a paradigm of rule; between Emperor Wu's activism versus Emperor Wen's non-interference; between a future shaped by the patterns of "antiquity" or the exigencies of "modernity"; and between a form of analysis relying on classical citation versus an analysis using recorded statistics and quantitative calculations. In bringing China's frontiers to this set of oppositions, Han scholars and officials debated the "Tribute of Yu." As discussed in the introduction, the *Book of Documents*' section "Tribute of Yu" described the ancient sage Yu dredging the nine lands of the flooded world and thus creating the five tributary zones (see figure 0.2). Sang Hongyang, however, supports a very different world map, one championed by the first Emperor of the Qin 秦始皇帝 (221–210 BCE).[69]

大夫曰:「鄒子疾晚世之儒墨,不知天地之弘,昭曠之道,將一曲而欲道九折,守一隅而欲知萬方,猶無準平而欲知高下,無規矩而欲知方圓也。於是推大聖終始之運,以喻王公,先列中國名山通谷,以至海外。所謂中國者,天下八十一分之一,名曰赤縣神州,而分爲九州。絕陵陸不通,乃爲一州,有大瀛海圜其外。此所謂八極,而天地際焉。《禹貢》亦著山川高下原隰,而不知大道之徑。故秦欲達九州而方瀛海,牧胡而朝萬國。諸生守畦畝之慮,閭巷之固,未知天下之義也。」

The Imperial Counsellor said: "Master Zou [Zou Yan] detested the Ruists and Mohists of later generations, who in their failure to understand the vastness of heaven and earth, and the brightness and clarity of the Way (*Dao*), took [only] one segment of it despite their desire to apply the Way to all nine parts. They upheld but one corner, despite their desire to comprehend the universe. This was like a desire to ascertain a height without a water level, or to draw a circle and a square [shape] without a compass and a square. Thereupon [Zou Yan] deduced the movements [he described in] "Great Sage" and "Ends and Beginnings,"[70] which he used for explanations to the kings and dukes. He first classified the famous mountains and connecting valleys of the Central States (*Zhongguo* 中國), and using this he reached (an understanding of what was) beyond the seas. The so-called Central States constituted only one of eighty-one parts of the world, and he [re]named [the Central States] the "Sacred Land of the Red District" (*Chixian Shenzhou*), dividing [the world] into

---

69. On the more complex relation between Zou Yan's cosmological theory and the First Qin Emperor's political practices, see Aihe Wang, *Cosmology and Political Culture*, 139–43.

70. Following Wang Liqi, Ma Feibai, and Yang Shuda, in following the *Shiji's* list of Zou Yan's works. See *Shiji* 74.2344, and Yang Shuda, *Yantielun*, 66.

nine lands (*zhou*).[71] The cutoff landmasses that did not directly adjoin [lit. communicate] he took as individual lands (*zhou*), and the Great Ocean circled outside them. These were the so-called Eight Extremities[72] and the boundaries of Heaven and Earth met there. The "Tribute of Yu" also records the heights and depths of mountains and rivers and their sources and marshes, but it does not show understanding of the extent of the Great Way. For this reason the Qin state wanted to reach [all] Nine Lands (*jiu zhou*), to attain the Great Ocean, to shepherd the foreigners [as its own people], and to hold court over every state. The anxiety of all who live maintaining acre-plots of land (*xi mou*), and the ignorance of village lane and alleyway [residents], does not comprehend the principle of this world."[73]

Zou Yan's (ca. 305–ca. 240 BCE) cosmological theories were popular in his day, and later, during the reign of the first Qin emperor. But during the Han dynasty, Zou's theories were attacked by Han classicists—and today, Zou Yan's extant work exists only in fragmentary form.[74] In the passage above, Sang Hongyang explains Zou Yan's correction of the classical "Tribute of Yu." That is, Zou Yan takes the nine lands of the Central States (*Zhongguo*), the civilized *oikoumene* of classical accounts, renames it the "Sacred Land of the Red District" (*Chixian Shenzhou*) and diminishes it to only one eighty-eighth of the world. This new map of nine vast continental landmasses (*jiu zhou*) surrounded by an ocean opens up a vast terra incognita that for the First Emperor Qin (and, implicitly, Emperor Wu) demands exploration and conquest. In condemning those obsessed with their "acre-plots of land" (*xi mou*), Sang Honyang implicates the classical "well-field" ideal. His contrast between the ideas presented by Zou Yan and those found in the "Tribute of Yu" redirects the inward-looking vision of agriculturalists outward—towards the militarized borderlands. Elsewhere, Sang repeatedly uses this governmental

---

71. The attack on Yu's geography is more explicit in the *Shiji*'s variant account of Zou Yan's theory: "The Sacred Land of the Red District itself contained nine lands (*zhou*). These were the nine lands put in order by Yu, but they cannot [each] be counted as a 'Land.' Outside the Central States there were nine [Lands] just like the Sacred Land of the Red District, and these were what he called the Nine Lands." See *Shiji* 74.2344.

72. On this see Wang Liqi, *Yantielun*, 566; Ma Feibai, *Yantielun*, 317, 379. On Xunzi's use of the term, see Knoblock, *Xunzi* 3:330, note 48.

73. Wang Liqi, *Yantielun*, 564.

74. *Shiji* 74.2345 contrasts the unhappy lives of Confucius and Mencius with the lavish welcome that Zou Yan received in courts throughout the Central States.

imperative to defend, expand, or explore the frontiers in order to justify large-scale economic planning.

From a comparative perspective, the classicist critique of imperialism takes a strange form. It is not, for example, tied to cross-cultural sympathies with the foreigner (as explored in chapter 3). The Classical Scholars address the textual basis of the expansionist vision, and the relation between non-classical rhetoric and history.

文學曰：「堯使禹爲司空，平水土，隨山刊，定高下而序九州。鄒衍非聖人，作怪誤，熒惑六國之君，以納其説。... 昔秦始皇已吞天下，欲幷萬國，亡其三十六郡；欲達瀛海，而失其州縣。知大義如斯，不如守小計也。」

The Classical Scholars said: "Emperor Yao sent Yu as Superintendent of Works to regulate the waters and land, to mark out the mountains he passed, and to establish the relative [taxes?] for the Nine Lands.[75] Zou Yan opposed[76] the sage men, and composed strange and abstruse (theories), dazzling and confusing the rulers of the Six States in presenting his persuasions. . . . In the past, when the First Emperor Qin had already swallowed up all under Heaven [i.e., established the Qin empire in 221 BCE], in its desire to annex every [other] state it lost its thirty-six commanderies. In its desire to reach the Great Ocean it [the Qin state] lost its [own] provinces and districts. Interpreting the "great principle" in just such as way is not as good as preserving small-scale planning."[77]

The Classical Scholars restore the authority of classical texts by reaffirming the "Tribute of Yu" (and in this longer speech citing the *Spring and Autumn Annals* and the teachings of Confucius). The Classical Scholars dismiss Zou Yan's (to them) outlandish theories and persuasive rhetoric and tie the collapse of the Qin dynasty to its Zou Yan-inspired expansionism (e.g., "in its desire to reach the Great Ocean . . ."). Within the *Debate on Salt and Iron*, a return to the "small-scale planning" of Zhou agriculture is thus not simply a "return to the root occupation" (*fan ben*) in the face of a system of market planning, but is also a call for an end to

---

75. This follows Wang Liqi's suggestion that Yu felled trees as a way of making records, and Ma Feibai's suggestion that *xu* 序 here refers to Yu's taxes (although it might simply refer to his "ordering the land" as Lévi, *La Dispute sur le Sel et le Fer*, 269, takes it). See Wang Liqi, *Yantielun*, 564, and Ma Feibai, *Yantielun*, 380.

76. Following Ma Feibai, *Yantielun*, 380, although this could also be read to mean that Zou Yan was not a sage man.

77. Wang Liqi, *Yantielun*, 564.

imperialist expansion. In other *Debate on Salt and Iron* chapters (on the ongoing Han war with the Xiongnu and the financing of this war), the Classical Scholars condemn the state's overdependence on "military" (*wu* 武) principles, instead of "civil" or "cultural" (*wen* 文) principles.[78] Here the etiology of the world map clarifies the textual basis of this clash. One might note that Huan Kuan does not implicate the *Guanzi* here. The "Qingzhong" chapters of this work tutored the ruler in aggressive hegemonic strategies through the use of a semi-fictional world map (e.g., "The Plain of All Under Zhou") spanning different historical and hypothetical time zones. Both Zou Yan's map and the "Tribute of Yu," by contrast, belong to the same temporal order (even if the Classical Scholars dismiss the former).

Classicism versus Qingzhong *Rhetoric*

The *Debate on Salt and Iron* thus does not give voice to *qingzhong* economics. It does not incorporate the *Guanzi*'s technical terms or alternative literary style. Sang Hongyang speaks in the idiom of his opponents, albeit more reluctantly, more critically, and sometimes more ironically. Like the Classical Scholars, and unlike in the "Qingzhong" chapters, Sang quotes from the Classics or invokes traditional Masters to give rhetorical authority to an argument. For example, although in the *Debate on Salt and Iron* Sang Hongyang condemns appropriations of the *Spring and Autumn Annals* by his political opponents, he himself invokes the work to assert the untrustworthiness of the Xiongnu enemy (and hence to justify an expansionist empire).[79] And although Sang again and again denounces the Classical Scholars' self-promoting "return to antiquity," "lack of concern for present circumstances," and "cherishing of the methods of the Six Arts" (i.e., the Classics), Sang Hongyang actually relies on alternative texts and readings, more heavily than on calculations or statistics, to make his argument. At the same time the *Debate on Salt and Iron* ensures that the political victors of the discussion (the Classical Scholars) demonstrate a "better" literary style than their opponents. For example, the Classical Scholars and Worthies are allotted around four-fifths of the

---

78. For this opposition by the Classicists and for discussions of foreign policy see especially Wang Liqi, *Yantielun*, 160–61, 205–7, 453–55, 510–11, 524–25, 555–57.

79. Wang Liqi, *Yantielun*, 524–25.

dialogue's classical quotations, the majority of which are ascribed to Confucius, Mencius, or one of the Five Classics. The Classical Scholars cite from the *Odes* (*Shi* 詩, which became the *Classic of Odes* [*Shijing* 詩經]) over twenty times to make a point, while Sang Hongyang does so less than half as many times.[80]

In light of the *Debate on Salt and Iron*'s instruction on the moral-political principles and literary style of classicism, it is worth returning to the *Guanzi*'s approach to language and the Classics. The *Debate on Salt and Iron* bids the reader to determine which side is more justified in accusing the other of "empty speech" (the Classical Scholars win out). The *Guanzi*, by contrast, teaches the need to manipulate language. The "Qing-zhong" section's only citation of the poetic *Shi* is part of a lesson in the "use of subtle methods" (繆數). State envoys quote a line to persuade moneylenders to forgive all their debts, redistribute their wealth, and pay tribute at court.[81] Elsewhere, Guanzi offers the following comment:

管子對曰：「動之以言，潰之以辭，可以爲國基。且君幣籍而務，則賈人獨操國趣。君穀籍而務，則農人獨操國固。君動言操辭，左右之流君獨因之。物之始吾已見之矣。物之終吾已見之矣。物之賈吾已見之矣。」

Guanzi replied: "Moving [people] with words and motivating them with speeches may be considered the foundation of the state. Now if you focus on monetary taxation, traders alone will control the ambitions of the state. If you focus on grain taxation, farmers alone will control the stability of the state. But if you use moving words and manipulative speeches, goods will circulate around you and you alone will set matters in motion. We will have gained insight into the production of goods; we will have gained insight into the final [consumption] of goods; [and] we will have gained insight into the price of goods."[82]

Guanzi here solves the economic problem of Qi's dependence on other states for food simply through words and speeches. That is, to prevent others from "controlling the ambitions of the state" one must manipu-

---

80. See Huan Kuan, *Discourses on Salt and Iron*, lii–lvi, for an analysis by Esson Gale of direct quotations in the *Debate on Salt and Iron*.

81. Ma Feibai, *Guanzi*, 659–60.

82. Ma Feibai, *Guanzi*, 674. Partly following Rickett, *Guanzi*, 2:494–95. Compare Ma Feibai, *Guanzi*, 492–93: "Thus the sage is good at making use of what he does not have and in ordering about those who are not his own people. Through moving words and persuasive speeches he is able to gain the allegiance of multitudes of people."

late people through speech. Persuasion, in this context, provides a better strategy than any form of material taxation.

Guanzi clarifies the place of the Classics in *qingzhong* economics in the following section:

桓公問於管子曰:「請問教數。」

管子對曰:「民之能明於農事者,置之黃金一斤,直食八石。民之能蓄育六畜者, 置之黃金一斤,直食八石。...謹聽其言而藏之官...然後置四限,高下令之徐疾,毆屏萬物,守之以筴,有五官技。」

桓公曰:「何謂五官技?」

管子曰:「詩者所以記物也。時者所以記歲也。春秋者所以記成敗也。行者道民之利 害也。易者所以守凶吉成敗也。卜者卜凶吉利害也。民之能此者皆一馬之田, 一金之衣。

Duke Huan asked Guanzi: "May I ask about methods of instruction?"

Guanzi replied: "For those people able to clarify agricultural matters, [you should] establish an award of one catty of gold or an equivalent value in grain of eight *shi*. For those people able to raise the six [kinds of] domestic animals, establish an award of one catty of gold, or an equivalent value in grain of eight *shi*. . . . Listen carefully to their words and store [their information] in public offices. . . . Then establish all the boundaries [for the circulation of goods], adjust the urgency of demands, collect and distribute all goods, [while] maintaining them through fiscal planning and the expertise of the five officials."

Duke Huan asked: "What is the expertise of the five officials?"

Guanzi replied: "Experts in the *Odes* should be used to record [social] matters. Experts in the calendar (*shi* 時) should be used to record harvests. Experts in the *Spring and Autumn Annals* should be used to record victories and defeats. Experts on [sacrifices to] the God of Roads (*Xing* 行) should guide people as to advantageous and disadvantageous routes. Experts on the *Yi* 易 ([Classic of] Changes) should be used to foretell calamity or happiness, while experts in tortoise shell divination may divine bad or good fortune, profit or loss. All those with such abilities should be awarded the amount of land that can be cultivated by a single horse and clothing equal in value to one catty of gold."[83]

Guanzi's "methods of instruction" (*jiao shu* 教數) begin outside the realm of texts. The state is the collector, not the disseminator, of information from

---

83. Ma Feibai, *Guanzi*, 325–26. Largely following the translation of Rickett, *Guanzi*, vol 2, 401–2.

whoever is competent. In this merit-based system, knowledge has a fixed monetary or material exchange value (gold or grain). Like a data bank, the state must buy and store up information: "listen carefully to their words and store [their information] in public offices" (*jin ting qi yan er cang zhi* 謹聽其言而藏之). Knowledge and language have become quantitative as much as qualitative, accumulating like profit reserves in this *qingzhong* world. Experts in classical texts like the *Odes* and *Spring and Autumn Annals* are also brought into this exchange system. However their authority is highly circumscribed and they do not appear elsewhere in "Qingzhong" chapters. Here the classical experts provide useful empirical predictions, statistics, and data, but none of the economic laws and strategies promoted by Guanzi and personified by the fictional character, Mr. Calculate-y.

Conclusion

The *Guanzi*'s "Qingzhong" chapters were an anomaly in the ancient world. Unlike Aristotle, Xenophon, Seneca, Kautilya, or Mencius—to take the most commonly cited cases—the *Guanzi* taught its readers to calculate value (*qingzhong*) in the quantitative terms of the market.[84] It framed its calculations within military ideals of world conquest at a time when the state valorized commercial exchange to finance the largest territorial expansion in China's history. At the same time, the "Qingzhong" chapters propounded at unusual length (about a hundred pages in translation) a disenchanted, non-cosmological theory of value grounded in quantitative relations. As will be explored further in chapter 5, the *Guanzi* disengaged monetary operations from social, cosmological, and ethical concerns to a greater degree than did other extant ancient texts. This generic appropriation of Masters philosophical dialogue transgressed literary as well as ritual decorum. The "Qingzhong" chapters departed from classical conventions in its hybrid mix of real and imaginary characters (e.g., Duke Huan, Mr. Calculate-y), as well as in its heterochronic heterotopias spanning pre-Han, Han, and imaginary worlds (e.g., The-Plain-of-all-under-Zhou, Han Central Asia). Unlike most other classical texts, the *Guanzi* did not assume or assert the superiority of the historical

---

84. As cultural economists have pointed out, all "economic" theory is profoundly ideological, and the *Guanzi* was hardly an exception. See, for example, Sahlins, *Stone Age Economics*.

over the imaginary. Rather it devalued the traditional metaphors and paradigms of the moral economy, drawing in part on the idiom of mathematical abstraction. The work grounded textual authority in personifications of general economic principles (e.g., Mr. Calculate-and-Measure, Mr. Calculate-y), not in the historical words or deeds of ancient sages. The *Guanzi* thereby tutored the reader in the ways that monetary and linguistic values were not necessarily fixed. Although the "Qingzhong" chapters often posit grain as the basis for the value of other goods, these chapters also show how value can be created by manipulating belief. Just as fiat credit currencies could be used to manipulate exchange, so could fictions be used to explain economic laws, and so could rhetorically persuasive speeches manipulate wealthy traders and farmers into compliance with tax requirements.

The *Debate on Salt and Iron* effectively replaced "the Economist" or "economic expert" (*Qingzhong zhi jia*) with "the Classical Scholar" (*Wenxue*) as the expert on political economy. Mastery of classical traditions, not of quantitative calculations, now mattered. The *Debate on Salt and Iron* restored the concrete historical template and moral idiom (*ben* and *mo; jing tian*; "Tribute of Yu") to the Masters dialogue form. The Classical Scholars argued that the archaic Zhou world order, as celebrated in the inherited classical tradition, provided the mimetic template for the future political economy. In this way of thinking, the moral calculations of ritual propriety, not price ratios, lay at the basis for a self-limiting empire that should return its focus to the fundamental (*ben*) agricultural basis of the economy. The *Debate on Salt and Iron* made a return to classical texts the basis for this imagined world order. That is, unlike the *Guanzi*—which grounded its textual authority in overtly fictional demonstrations of the abstract but also on a real quantitative theory of price—the *Debate on Salt and Iron* based its political-economic authority on its own fidelity to a classical tradition. It brought the Masters tradition back to its normative principle of ritual propriety and Zhou history. Discussions of the political economy by Later Han classicists such as Wang Chong 王充 (27–ca. 100), Xu Gan 徐幹 (170–217), and Wang Fu 王符 (ca. 90–ca. 165) would echo the moral sentiments and rhetorical style of the *Debate on Salt and Iron*'s Classical Scholars.[85]

---

85. For example, Wang Chong's chapter, "Destiny and Emoluments" (*Ming lu* 命祿), asserts through quotation that "wealth cannot be obtained through calculations; nobility cannot be achieved through talent and ability" (富不可以籌筴得，貴不可以才能成).

Histories of Chinese literature have overlooked the *Guanzi*'s rhetorical experiments, generally placing the beginnings of fiction in the parables of the *Zhuangzi* or the *Strategems of the Warring States* (*Zhanguo ce* 戰國策).[86] As discussed in the introduction, there was no category of "literature" (*wenxue*) in the Han dynasty, and the belles-lettristic expulsion of texts like the *Guanzi* from the purview of moral-aesthetic style or patterning (*wen*) belonged to the classicizing reaction to Emperor Wu's reign that was found in the *Debate on Salt and Iron* and in works of subsequent centuries. The next chapter explores the possible relations between the *Guanzi*'s quantitative reasoning and the prose-poetic *fu*. It asks whether the *Guanzi*'s "anti-classicist" (or un-classical) values might shed light on a genre otherwise usually appreciated as exemplary of the Chinese belles-lettristic classical tradition.

See *Lun heng jiao shi* 3.21. Wang Fu's chapter on "Concentrating on the Root" (*Wu ben* 務本) in the *Qian fu lun* iterates the moral economic metaphor. See *Qian fu lun jian jiao zheng*, 2.14–23. See also Xu Gan's striking attack on slave ownership and the pursuit of profit in Xu Gan, *Balanced Discourses*, 282–89.

86. See, for example, *The Cambridge History of Chinese Literature*; Luo Yuming, *Zhongguo wenxue shi*; Idema, *A Guide to Chinese Literature*; Lu Xun, *A Brief History of Chinese Fiction*; Nienhauser, *The Indiana Companion to Chinese Literature*; Watson, *Early Chinese Literature*. Compare Zhao, "Historiography and Fiction." For further discussion and bibliography on the Chinese *xiaoshuo* tradition and its origins, see Gu, *Chinese Theories of Fiction*.

CHAPTER 2

Quantification:
Poetic Expenditure in the Epideictic Fu

As they circulate through our lives, we look *through* objects (to see what they disclose about history, society, nature, or culture—above all, what they disclose about us), but we only catch a glimpse of things.

—Bill Brown, *Things*

Someone said, "[The *fu*] has the intricate beauty of misty gossamer." Yang Xiong replied, "It is the scourge of women's work."

—Yang Xiong, *Model Sayings*

Like other forms of Chinese literature, the Han dynasty's most popular literary genre, the epideictic *fu* (*da fu* 大賦 "great *fu*" or 漢賦 "Han dynasty *fu*") includes objects steeped with classical, symbolic determinations. However, this genre's rhythmic catalogs of exotica remain dominated by lists of unfamiliar or apparently non-symbolic things.[1] Unlike the flora and fauna of the *Classic of Odes* and *Elegies of Chu*, China's central poetic traditions, the *fu*'s individual exotica have not raised the critical problem of figurative language. Instead, ancient and modern readers have generally found the meaning of the *things* mentioned in the *fu* in

---

1. For useful approaches to things in literature, see Brown, "The matter of materialism"; Freedgood, *The Ideas in Things*; and Appadurai, "Introduction." Cao Shenggao, *Han fu yu Handai zhidu*, 9–13, divides the *fu*'s things into four categories: 1) things still comprehensible today (e.g., cows, horses) 2) metaphors and classical quotations 3) auspicious and inauspicious objects 4) afterworld people and objects believed as real during Han times.

their collectivity, as an aggregate emblem of accumulation, lavish expenditure, or immoderate empire.

This point of view pervades *fu*-criticism—that is, that the genre reflected the heady materialism of the Han court circles that patronized both the *fu* and the luxury market. Chapter 1 introduced the Former Han debate between the pro-market *qingzhong* economists and the anti-market classicists who sought a return to the traditional agricultural order described in classical texts. As will be further explored in chapter 4, the consumption and production by women of labor-intensive gossamers and embroidery became particularly controversial, and Yang Xiong's 揚雄 (53 BCE–18 CE) abovementioned analogy insinuates the *fu* within this Han dynasty politics of consumption.[2] This commonly used approach has helped to disengage the *fu*, as a literary genre, from a rich tradition of cross-cultural poetics centered on the problem of imagery in Chinese and European traditions.[3] The canonical *Classic of Odes* and its Later Han commentaries have provoked comparative debates over whether Chinese poetry and poetics differs from the Western mimetic tradition in its reliance on correlative cosmology (the belief that all phenomena belong to correlative categories, for example, assuming the first *Ode*'s image of ospreys corresponds to the virtue of the people in the poem).[4] By contrast, the epideictic *fu* has inspired a more material poetics. Philologists, environmental historians, archaeologists, and art historians have sought to match many of the *fu*'s exotica—for example, grapes, chigetai, tarpan, sumac, and Malabar nightshade—not to classically encoded meanings, but to the traffic of words and things in a cross-

---

2. Wang Rongbao, *Fayan yi shu*, 45: 或曰：「霧縠之組麗。」曰：「女工之蠹矣。」 *Du* 蠹, here "scourge," refers to a wood-boring moth or noxious insect. Compare the phrase *guo zhi du* 國之蠹 "vermin of the state" in *Chunqiu Zuozhuan*, 1065 (Xiang 22.1); and the "Wu du" 五蠹 chapter of *Hanfeizi*. See Wang Xianshen, *Han feizi jijie*, 442–55. The meaning of this could also be that the *fu* is like the moth that destroys the silk product, i.e., it destroys something beautiful (perhaps the poetic tradition). The above translation is preferred, given Yang Xiong's other comments on the *fu*, given the ways in which women's craft or women's work (*nü gong*) were discussed during the Han (on which see chapter 4) and given the rare use of the specific phrase "misty gossamer" (*wu hu*), which is discussed further, below.

3. See, for example, Pauline Yu, *The Reading of Imagery*; Saussy, *The Problem of a Chinese Aesthetic*; Cai, *Configurations of Comparative Poetics*.

4. For a further discussion of correlative cosmology and the *Guanzi*'s exploitation of cosmological signs for fiat monetary and credit instruments, see chapter 5.

cultural history of trade and imperial expansion.[5] This differs from the literary debate about whether the *fu*'s lengthy form and ornamental style ultimately preclude it from fulfilling writing's traditional function of promoting classical virtues such as moderation or thrift. Yang Xiong—the conflicted connoisseur, composer, and eventual renunciant, of the *fu*—criticized the *fu* because instead of delivering indirect remonstrance, "it fails to stop" (不已).[6]

This chapter reexamines the *fu*'s aesthetics in the context of the Han politics of literary and visual style. It builds on and complicates the opposition delineated in chapter 1 between the rhetoric of expansionist economics (e.g., use of fiction and personification) and that of its classicizing opponents. It looks at the first epideictic *fu* to be presented to Emperor Wu's imperial court, Sima Xiangru's 司馬相如 (179–117 BCE) "*Fu* on the Excursion Hunt of the Son of Heaven" (*Tianzi youlie fu* 天子游獵賦), and its significance within the development of the genre.[7] This particular *fu* was explicitly structured around an economic metaphor of linguistic expenditure. To better understand Sima Xiangru's literary innovations and the pervasive association of the epideictic *fu* as a genre with extravagance, this chapter explores Han debates about expenditure. It looks at the *fu*'s exploitation of the classical approach to expenditure in terms of the moral ideal of thrift or moderation, as well literary and visual texts that reflected or promoted other values. In particular it looks at the *Guanzi*'s theories of lavish expenditure that were well-known and influential during Sima Xiangru's time, but that are generally overlooked today. In broadening the range of potential resources for Sima Xiangru's aesthetic, this chapter does not align him with a specific ideological faction, but rather suggests his exploitation of ideologically conflicting classical and non-classical styles.

Aesthetic Contradiction in Fu-*studies*

The career of the epideictic *fu* presents us with a conundrum. When Sima Xiangru presented his "*Fu* on the Excursion Hunt" to Emperor Wu (ca. 135 BCE), he thrust an emergent literary genre into the political limelight.

---

5. See the coda for a further discussion of this shift in comparative approach.
6. Wang Rongbao, *Fayan yi shu*, 45.
7. Hereafter abbreviated to "*Fu* on the Excursion Hunt."

With imperial patronage, the *fu* became the Han dynasty's most popular literary form, especially among court circles. However, subsequent *fu* composers and critics attacked precisely those characteristics of the genre that were best exemplified by Sima Xiangru's *fu*. Its ripe ornamentality (extending over 1,500 characters) and structural disingenuity ("deploying a hundred persuasions for a single remonstrance") were discussed in terms of their lack of thrift, not their additive benefits.[8] Dogged by accusations of its failures to morally improve its audiences, the epideictic *fu* seems to have flourished despite, not because of, its signature experiments in length and euphonic language (for example, assonance, rhyme, and rhythm). As one critic has recently summarized:

> During most of the twentieth century, the strongly pejorative view of the *fu* that can be traced back to Yang Xiong has not merely dominated but largely paralyzed the field of *fu* studies. Disparaged as a genre of empty formalism and meaningless verbosity, condemned for its intimate relation to elitist court culture and imperial representation, and charged with neglecting the sincere expression of genuine sentiment, the *fu* was anathema to modern literary criticism.[9]

The paralysis of the *fu* within a century of its inception was partly self-induced. The *Hanshu* biography of Yang Xiong, probably the second most famous *fu*-composer after Sima Xiangru, records that he renounced the genre on the grounds that its readers or listeners never got beyond its signature "gorgeous and lavish words":

---

8. On the preeminence of Sima Xiangru (and his "*Fu* on the Excursion Hunt" in particular) within the *fu* tradition and on the retroactive designation of *da fu* or "epideictic *fu*," see Guo Jianxun, *Cifu wen ti yanjiu*, 105–23; Jian Zongwu, *Sima Xiangru*, 55. The two phrases Guo takes to describe subgenre of the *da fu*, "to display ornament and exhibit refinement" and to "deploy a hundred persuasions for a single remonstrance," draw from traditional *fu*-criticism—taken from *Wenxin diaolong*, 134, and *Shiji* 117.3073, respectively. On the *sao fu*, or "*fu* of frustration," see Wilhelm, "The Scholar's Frustration," 310–19, 398–403. The term "epideictic *fu*" (or epideictic rhapsody) draws from Knechtges's various works, cited below. On dating Sima Xiangru's court presentation, see Jian Zongwu, *Han fu shi lun*, 123–25.

9. Kern, "Western Han Aesthetics," 383–437. For a guide to traditional scholarship on the *fu*, see Zong Fan, *Hanfu yanjiu shilun*; for introductions to traditional and modern scholarship on the Han dynasty *fu*, see Kern, "Western Han Aesthetics"; Gong Kechang, *Studies on the Han Fu*, 1–92.

I believe the *fu* should function as political persuasion. [But] it is forced to speak through categorized examples, the most ornate and lavish phrases, engorged extravagance and overflowing largesse, competing with others so they cannot expand it. Then when it returns to the proper message, the reader has already passed the point (of return) . . . Therefore I stopped and never composed [a *fu*] again.[10]

The *fu* was an unstable genre during this period; it was caught between the paranomastic etymology of *fu* as "display" (*pu* 鋪 or *puchen* 鋪陳), and its reference to the traditional recitation of an *Ode* to make a point in political discourse (*fu shi* 賦詩).[11]

The attack on the *fu*'s failure to make a political point recurred during subsequent dynasties, as some poets continued to imitate the Han *fu* or developed shorter or more regulated subgenres of the *fu*. Many May Fourth modernists and Marxist revolutionaries went on to contrast the "sycophantic," "aristocratic" Han *fu* with the *Classic of Odes* and *Elegies of Chu* as poetic traditions that better reflected social realities or conveyed political criticism.[12] Throughout this critical tradition, the "*Fu* on

---

10. *Hanshu* 87B.3575. 雄以爲賦者，將以風也，必推類而言，極麗靡之辭，閎侈鉅衍，競於使人不能加也，既乃歸之於正，然覽者已過矣。 . . . 於是輟不復爲。 See Zong Fan, *Hanfu yanjiu lun*, 80–83.

11. *Fu* was also one of the three rhetorical devices (*fu, bi, xing*) in Han commentaries on the *Odes*; there *fu* designated a poetic mode of exposition or straightforward description. For a useful account of the semantic evolution and extension of the term *fu* (especially in relation to *bi* and *xing*), see Jia Jinhua, "An Interpretation of the Term *fu* 賦 in Early Chinese Texts." Jia traces the character *fu* 賦 to *wu* 武 "military," through which it came to designate the levying of military service (and possibly levies to meet military expenses); as such, Jia argues that the *fu* referred to "Dawu" 大武, the most important song-and-dance suite in Zhou ceremonies, designating six songs that were merged into the *Zhou song* 周頌 section of the *Classic of Odes*. Pre-Qin texts also used *fu* as a phonetic loan for *bu* 布 "to promulgate," *fu* 敷 "to state" and *pu* 鋪 "to spread," and through this the *fu* acquired further meanings of "to recite poems to promulgate the intention of the king, lord, or state," and "to recite poems to express the author's own intention." See also Levy, "Constructing Sequences."

12. See, for example, Chen Duxiu's "On Literary Revolution": "The 'Airs of the States' in the *Book of Songs* were full of the lowly speech of the streets, and the *Elegies of Chu* employed rustic expressions in abundance, but both were unfailingly elegant and remarkable. In their wake, however, writers of *fu* poetry in the Former and Later Han dynasties raised their eulogistic voices and produced ornate and sycophantic writings, dense with words but sparse in meaning. This was the beginning of the trend in classical aristocratic literature of making artifacts for the dead," in Denton, *Modern*

the Excursion Hunt" has featured as the foundation and emblematic case of the genre's worst tendencies.

Scholarship in Japan, Taiwan, the West, and in the PRC since the 1980s has redressed the political failures of the *fu* in two general ways. The first approach reaffirms the Han *fu*'s political or ethical efficacy; the second embraces the *fu*'s essential disinterest in politics and ethics. In the first approach, the perceived political message of Sima Xiangru's "*Fu on the Excursion Hunt*" usually comprises at least one of the following: a) the promotion of moderation and frugality (*jie jian*); b) a criticism of the extravagance and power of China's regional vassal lords and kings (*zhuhouwang*), many of whom had threatened Emperor Wu's predecessor in the 154 BCE Revolt of the Seven Kingdoms, and whose wealth the *fu*'s imaginary envoys describe; or c) the praise of Emperor Wu and of unified empire. For some scholars, Sima Xiangru conveys his political advice by engaging with the teachings of classical studies (Feng Liangfeng), and especially (an outright or modified) Confucian morality (Yves Hervouet, Jian Zongwu); with the sociopolitics of hunting (Cao Shenggao); or with a broader early imperial theme of universal empire, for which the "*Fu on the Excursion Hunt*" is a literary microcosm, enumerating its possessions (Mark Edward Lewis).[13] Others have tied this *fu*'s political function to the genre's origins, tracing its form through and beyond the poetic traditions of the *Classic of Odes* and *Elegies of Chu* to political memorials (Nakashima Chiaki); or to a range of direct, indirect, and epideictic modes of political rhetoric (David Knechtges); or to the literary principle of enumeration (Dore Levy).[14] Yet other scholars emphasize the *fu*'s departures from traditional aesthetics while articulating its traditional political message (Liu Nanping, Li Tiandao); or positing the Han *fu* as the foundations of China's self-conscious awareness of literature (Gong Kechang).[15] Others emphasize a place for wayward experience in ethical

---

Chinese Literary Thought, 141. On the condemnation of the *fu* during the Cultural Revolution, see Gong, *Studies on the Han Fu*, 5–9.

13. Feng Liangfang, *Han fu yu jing xue*, 252; Hervouet, *Un Poète de Cour*, 243–86; Jian Zongwu, *Sima Xiangru Yang Xiong*, 37; Cao Shenggao, *Han fu yu Handai zhidu*, 154; Lewis, *Writing and Authority*, 317–25.

14. Nakashima, *Fu no Seiritsu to Tenkai*, 339–68; Knechtges, *The Han Rhapsody*, 35; Levy, "Constructing Sequences."

15. Liu Nanping, *Sima Xiangru kao shi*, 81–82; Li Tiandao, *Sima Xiangru fu de meixue sixiang*, 268. Li argues that the *fu* "boldly exposes" the extravagant lifestyle of

traditions: the language and structure of the "*Fu* on the Excursion Hunt" embodies a stock formula of *Classic of Odes* hermeneutics, "using sensual experience (*se* 色) to illustrate ritual," by which the experience of aesthetic pleasure ultimately guides one back to ritual propriety (Martin Kern); or the experience of extravagant waste is necessary for the emperor's political rejection of despotism (Jack Chen).[16]

Arguments for the *fu*'s basic disinterest in political or moral persuasion have emphasized its aim to entertain and intoxicate. Originally an orally performed genre of unsung recitation employing both rhymed and unrhymed lines of wide-ranging lengths, the *fu*'s essential material unit was neither prose nor poetry, but simply *verbal sound*. The *fu*'s signature obsession with rare euphonic words (descriptive binomes) played at the borders between the semantic unit and the asemantic sound. Studies of this new acoustic style point to the formal debt of the "*Fu* on the Excursion Hunt" to traditions of court entertainment, riddles, and incantation in the *Elegies of Chu* (Arthur Waley, Burton Watson); and to exorcism, spells, and hunting chants (Donald Harper). In so doing, these scholars have clarified the mode in which the *fu* both describes its own function, and achieves that function through recitation.[17] Art historians have further embedded the *fu* in history, correlating the *fu*'s descriptive excesses with a Han dynasty visual style and taste for exotica.[18]

To examine the puzzling aesthetics of the *fu*, this chapter builds on and revises these diverse arguments in two ways. First, it approaches the classical ideal of thrift or moderation not as the necessary, authentic way of reading the Han *fu*, but as part of the *fu*'s self-designated politics. If we accept that the *fu* often self-consciously specified its own function, then the "*Fu* on the Excursion Hunt" does indeed concern moral-political persuasion. For the *fu*'s three imaginary interlocutors explicitly attack extravagance, and economic expenditure becomes the central metaphor

---

the upper classes in ways that other genres do not; Gong's *Studies in the Han fu* pushes back Lu Xun's dating (the Jian'an period 196–219 CE) of this self-conscious literary awareness.

16. Kern, "Western Han Aesthetics"; Chen, *The Poetics of Sovereignty*, 268–73.

17. See, for example, Harper, "Wang Yen-shou's Nightmare Poem." As Harper argues, the incantatory language of Wang Yanshou's "Nightmare *Fu*" (*Meng fu*) both describes a nightmare and specifies the *fu*'s exorcising function. Cf. Harper, "Poets and Primates"; Harper, "A Chinese Demonography."

18. See below for further discussion and bibliography.

for speech decorum in their discussion. They condemn excess in words as well as things. By voicing this traditional politics of thrift during the prosaic interludes between their lengthy encomia on hunting parks, they themselves present an aesthetic contradiction. They voice the classical condemnation of extravagance as excess, but the excessive length and euphonic ornament of their boasts that are crucial to the aesthetic playfulness of the genre pattern the quantitative logic of lavish expenditure (the more, the better). Their ornate speeches thus turn their condemnation of ostentation into potential hypocrisy or satire.

Second, and in light of the *fu*'s explicit concern with lavish expenditure, this chapter explores a set of visual and literary sources that ostensibly were not shaped by classical values of moderation. It brings overlooked economic texts to bear on ongoing studies of Sima Xiangru's self-conscious experiments with poetic, non-poetic, classical, occult, material, visual, and institutional genres. The *Guanzi*'s chapter on "lavish expenditure" (*chi mi* 侈靡), which predates the Han "Qingzhong" section, made the argument that market consumption of luxuries stimulates production, thereby increasing employment and revitalizing the general economy. The "Qingzhong" chapters revised this claim but iterated its unusually quantitative approach to spending. This economics of expenditure was well known during the Han but is generally overlooked today. The *Guanzi*'s promotion of "lavish expenditure" largely on economic grounds (consumption creates wealth) was well known, politically influential, and controversial under Emperor Wu. The *Guanzi*'s arguments for and against lavish expenditure provide potentially both formal and political-economic bases for the *fu*'s aesthetic extravagance. Modern assessments of the *fu*'s political nature have, following the classical tradition, taken moderation and frugality as the *fu*'s only viable moral-political message, thus relegating extravagance to the domain of the immoral or apolitical. However, this obscures the political-economic approach to lavish expenditure in the *Guanzi*, in Emperor Wu's historical policies, and among the wealthy patrons of Han art. Former Han proponents of thrift had to struggle to delegitimate lavish expenditure as a positive political alternative. In this light, one might better understand Sima Xiangru's verbal extravagance not as a mere transgression of thrift, but as a self-conscious exploitation of the aesthetic styles and Guanzian dramatizations of lavish expenditure. The next section considers the place of classical economics within Sima Xiangru's "*Fu* on the Excursion Hunt" and its reception in the Han dynasty, before turning to alternate Han dynasty approaches to spending.

THE CLASSICAL ETHIC OF THRIFT

Lavish spending became a particularly fraught issue under Emperor Wu.[19] The contentious debate over state monopolies (the topic of the *Debate on Salt and Iron*) was, according to the *Hanshu*, a reaction against excessive expenditures that characterized his reign.

> The state had inherited the excessive extravagance and military expeditions (奢侈師旅 *she chi shi lü*) of Emperor Wu, so [Du Yannian 杜延年] repeatedly said to General Huo Guang 霍光: "The harvest has failed, and displaced persons have not yet all returned. It would be appropriate to practice the government of the time of Emperor Wen [漢文帝 r. 179–157 BCE], giving an example of frugality and modesty (儉約寬和 *jian yue kuan he*), following the will of Heaven and satisfying the people's sentiments. The harvests will then reciprocate." Huo Guang accepted this: he promoted the Worthies and held discussions on the abolition of the [state] monopolies on liquors, salt, and iron.[20]

This contrast between Emperor Wu's "excessive extravagance" and the "frugality and modesty" of an earlier reign echoed a traditional moral opposition to extravagance in pre-Han and Han classical texts. The *Guanzi* aside, pre-Han and Han classical texts generally promoted a moral ideal of moderation (*jie* 節) that could be cultivated or enacted through everyday social and ritual practices and desires.[21] Moderation was either equated with thrift (*jian* 儉), as in Mohist economics, or, as in the *Analects*, was

---

19. Emperor Wu and his officials clearly ignored the advice presented in the *Masters of Huainan* (*Huainanzi* 淮南子), a guide to political theory and practice presented to the imperial court in 139 BCE (i.e., a few years before Sima Xiangru's recitation). The *Huainanzi* cautioned that the reign of Second Emperor of Qin came to a quick end because he "exhausted every kind of lavish spending (*chi mi* 侈靡)," ignoring poverty and hunger, building a ten-thousand-chariot force and an opulent palace, conscripting villagers and raising taxes. See *Huainanzi ji shi*, 1062; translation largely following Major, *The Huainanzi*, 591. The *Huainanzi* uses the phrase *chi mi* on one other occasion as the conventional antonym of moderation among classicists (*Ruzhe*) who struggle against their appetites. See *Huainanzi ji shi*, 550. The text may include additions up to 122 BCE.

20. *Hanshu* 60.2664. Largely following Wagner, *The State and the Iron Industry*, 20.

21. For passages relevant to relation between extravagance, moderation, and thrift, see Chen, *The Economic Principles of Confucius*, 242–59.

found to be more congenial with thrift than with extravagance: "[Confucius] said, 'Extravagance (*she* 奢) leads to presumption, while frugality (*jian* 儉) leads to shabbiness. Compared to presumption, though, shabbiness is to be preferred.'"[22]

Confucius did not embrace thrift outright, but in cultivating moderation he found it preferable to its recognized opposite, extravagance (*she*). For Han historiographers, this problem of extravagant spending extended far beyond Emperor Wu's state budget. Thus the *Shiji* notes: "While the high ministers and imperial family were competitively escalating their lavish expenditures (*chi mi*), only Gongsun Hong 公孫弘 used moderation (*jie* 節) in dress and food, becoming preeminent amongst all the officials."[23] Here the thrift-tending "moderation" of the hemp-clothed official, Gongsun Hong, is the exception amidst a much broader Han vogue for luxury.

This moral contrast of lavish expenditure with moderation (or thrift) features prominently in Sima Xiangru's "*Fu* on the Excursion Hunt of the Son of Heaven," which takes the form of a dialogue in the regional state of Qi between three imaginary envoys. Sir Vacuous of Chu, Master Improbable of Qi, and the imperial representative Lord No-Such extol the wealth of their respective rulers' hunting preserves, while evaluating each other's speeches within the moral economy of thrift. Their descriptive catalogues of the exotic possessions of these parks occupy the bulk of the *fu*. Although their eulogies are competitive, they criticize each other for boasting.

The interlocutors repeatedly draw attention to the fact that the competition is about the incorrect *representation* of their ruler's things, and not simply about acts of accumulation. As the economic metaphor of linguistic expenditure increasingly dominates their rhetoric, the speakers increasingly focus their complaints on words instead of things, on speech decorum rather than material consumption. For example, take the following excerpts from the prose prefaces to their individual speeches:

> Sir Vacuous: "I enjoyed the King of Qi's desire to boast (*yu kua* 欲夸) about his chariots and horsemen."[24]

---

22. *Lunyu* 7.36; *Mozi* 6.28–35. Mozi argued that when the ruler set an example of frugality the people benefited and the country was well governed.

23. *Shiji* 130.3317. For criticism see *Shiji* 112.2949–52.

24. *Shiji* 117.3003.

Master Improbable: "Your words go wide of the mark (*yan zhi guo* 言之過)! . . . The King of Qi wished to devote his efforts to a hunting catch that would amuse his company—how can you call that boasting (*kua*)? When he asked you what the state of Chu possessed, he wanted to hear about its customs, achievements, and anything further you might add. But now instead of praising the several virtues of the King of Chu, you effusively promote his Yunmeng [i.e., "Cloud-dream"] Park as supreme. You speak extravagantly (*she yan* 奢言) about excessive pleasures (*yin yue* 淫樂) and you glorify lavish expenditure (*xian chi mi* 顯侈靡). If I were you I would not have taken this approach. If things are as you say, you certainly do not enhance the beauty of the state of Chu. If what you speak of exists, you expose your ruler's faults. If what you speak of does not exist, you undermine your own credibility."[25]

Lord No-Such: "You [two] only care about your rivalry (*zheng* 爭) over the pleasures of hunting excursions and the size of parks and preserves, each desiring to employ more wasteful extravagance (*yi she chi* 以奢侈) to beat the other; each surpassing the other with wilder excess (*huang yin* 荒淫)."[26]

The three interlocutors reveal their shared set of values through their (damning) commentaries on each other's displays.[27] Here and elsewhere, two sets of shared criteria emerge. First, in terms of form, content, and intent, one should not show off (*kua*) or compete (*zheng* 爭, *xiang yue* 相越), or take pleasure (*yue* 樂) in showing off; one should not speak in an extravagant manner (*she yan* 奢言, *yi she chi* 以奢侈), nor promote lavish expenditure (*chi mi*). Various cognate terms for immoderation (*she* 奢, *chi mi* 侈靡, *she chi* 奢侈, *mi li* 靡麗, *yin* 淫) are applied interchangeably to behavior and speech. Although the interlocutors dispute who has and has not been boastful or extravagant, they do not dispute the evaluative terms themselves. No one defends lavish expenditure, vacuous language, or the representation of excess. The second shared criterion that they express (and transgress) is that one should not speak above one's own or one's ruler's political station. Sir Vacuous prefaces his description of Chu with the disclaimer that he "does not dare to

---

25. *Shiji* 117.3014–15.

26. *Shiji* 117.3016.

27. Sir Vacuous criticizes the King of Qi; Master Improbable criticizes Sir Vacuous; Lord No-such criticizes Sir Vacuous, Master Improbable, the King of Chu, and the King of Qi; the Son of Heaven criticizes himself.

speak" (*bu gan yan* 不敢言) of his king's preserve, and is inadequate to the task (惡足以言); Lord No-Such will accuse his interlocutors of defaming their rulers and themselves, and of being ignorant of taboos (不知忌諱).[28] The conclusive recognition of shared competitive criteria comes with the open acknowledgement of Sir Vacuous and Master Improbable of their own defeat at the end of the *fu*: "They paled, changed expressions, and disconsolately became lost in themselves. Edging back from the mat they said, 'We . . . have been taught, and hearken to your command.'"[29]

All three interlocutors thus profess the conventional dictates of proper representation: to represent exemplary behavior, to speak according to one's political status, and above all to reject emptiness and extravagance.[30] The economic metaphor they use of "extravagant speech" (*she yan*) is grounded in the classical ideal of moderation (*jie*). When the interlocutors condemn extravagant speech, they affirm the classical preference for thrift (*jian*) over extravagance (*she*) expounded in the *Analects* (above). Although the name of Sir Vacuous (*Zi Xu* 子虛) clearly invokes the phrase "vacuous speech" (*xu yan* 虛言)—that is, the commonplace locution for the kind of unnecessary verbiage that his speech first introduces into the *fu*—the interlocutors do not actually use this phrase. Instead they use the uncommon economic metaphor of "extravagant speech." How, then, in this model of moral calculation, might one measure verbal moderation or extravagance?

THE CLASSICAL ETHICS OF SIZE AND ORNAMENT

From a formal perspective, *size* and *ornament* are two of the signature generic innovations of the epideictic *fu*. The sheer length of the epideictic "big *fu*" (*da fu*) sets it apart from the (shorter and less ornate) earlier *sao*

---

28. These terms and phrases are scattered through the prose sections of this *fu* at *Shiji* 117.3002, 3003, 3014, 3015, 3016, 3043. Compare Sima Qian's use of the phrase 忌諱之辭 ("his words [observed political] taboos") in analyzing Confucius's subtle language when writing about his own times. See *Shiji* 110.2919.

29. *Shiji* 117.3043.

30. See Hervouet, *Le chapitre 117 du Che-ki*, 143, note 2. Hervouet reads the conduct of Wudi and the three protagonists as in conformity with Confucian doctrines. On the distinction between "Confucian" and "classicist" (儒家), see Nylan, *The Five "Confucian" Classics*, 364–65.

fu 騷賦 and later "small *fu*" (*xiao fu* 小賦).[31] Within Sima Xiangru's "*Fu* on the Excursion Hunt*," the narrative outcome of the *fu* appears to correlate speech length with value. The three envoys represent their own conversation as a kind of competition, and the final speech of the imperial representative Lord No-Such wins. If one calculates the relative lengths of speeches, Lord No-Such prevails with a description of the imperial Shanglin Park that is over double the length (about 1,670 characters) of the combined speeches of Sir Vacuous (about 690 characters) and Master Improbable (about 130 characters). Figure 2.1 is an imaginary map that illustrates the relative lengths of these poetic boasts, using the area sizes of the three speech bubbles to (approximately) indicate the speech length.[32] Thus, the longest speech wins in the competition of boasts.[33]

This pattern of expenditure is repeated when we turn to relative use of ornament. The *fu* exploits many of the rhymes and rhythms of China's two traditions of poetry (*shi* 詩 and *sao* 騷), but an important form of acoustic ornament lay in its descriptive vocabulary. Modern scholars have singled out Sima Xiangru's novel patterning of what are now called descriptive binomes as central to the epideictic *fu*'s aesthetics. Descriptive binomes are freely formed bisyllabic compounds that primarily function as evocative euphonic sound words or "vocal gestures."[34] Based in spoken language, their sometimes onomatopoeic, sometimes indeterminate, meanings have posed one of the greatest challenges for ancient and modern translators alike.[35] Each bisyllabic word comprises

---

31. Guo Jianxun divides the *xiao fu* into the *yongwu fu* 咏物賦 and *shuqing fu* 抒情賦. Gong Kechang emphasizes the development from the *sao fu* to Sima Xiangru *da fu*. See also Kroll, "Literary Criticism."

32. In figure 2.1 the speech bubbles contain words (rather than actual excerpts) taken from the respective speeches. The flora and fauna listed in this figure largely come from Knechtges's translations.

33. For each speech, the count only includes the descriptive boast. Thus, this excludes the final prosaic account of the emperor's return to virtuous government.

34. Vocal gesture is Knechtges's translation of Hervouet's term. See Knechtges, *Wen Xuan*, 2:1–13. Harper, "Poets and Primates," 3–4, note 11. On the linguistic background of the rise of bisyllabic words from around 500 BCE through the Han dynasty, see Boltz, *Origin*, 168–77.

35. As Knechtges puts it: "Although descriptive binomes are common in earlier poetry, especially the *Classic of Songs* and the *Chuci*, composers of the *fu* delighted in using as many of these expression as they could, and the rarer the word, the better. Unlike

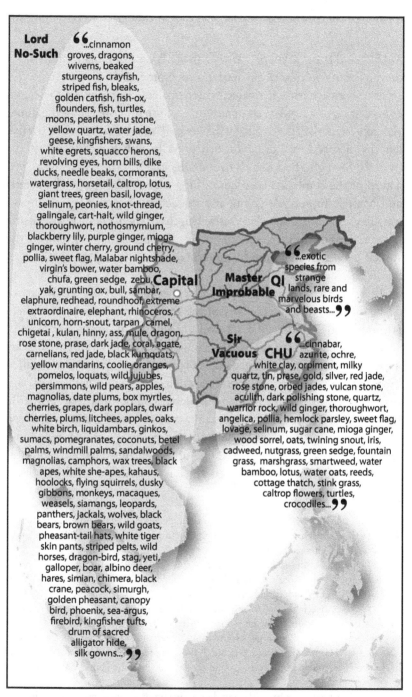

FIGURE 2.1. Map illustrating the relative lengths of the three interlocutors' speeches in Sima Xiangru's "*Fu* on the Excursion Hunt of the Son of Heaven." Lord No-Such's poetic boast of the emperor's exotic possessions is over twice the combined lengths of the boasts of Master Improbable of Qi and Sir Vacuous of Chu.

two characters or graphs, for example 扶與 *fuyu* (probably pronounced *buaja*[36]). Sometimes the meaning or general sense of a descriptive can, as with other common compounds, be derived from one or both of its component graphs.[37] In other cases, however, both graphs seem only to have a phonetic value. Thus the individual graphs 扶 *bua*, "to support," and 與 *ja*, "to give," do not seem to contribute to the understood sense of 扶與 *buaja* to describe the fluttering of a garment. These descriptive words appear in earlier prose and poetic works, and Mei Sheng [or Mei Cheng] 枚乘 (d. 141 BCE), had begun to string them together in his earlier (considerably shorter and less epideictic) *fu*. David Knechtges has, however, argued that Sima Xiangru's *fu* are the earliest extant ones to elaborate descriptive scenes by clustering large numbers of descriptives together.[38] According to Yves Hervouet, Sima Xiangru's surviving *fu* and prose works yield around 220 different descriptive binomes, over half of which are not previously attested (about 115). Since only a small fraction of Han *fu*, and of early Chinese literature in general, has survived, this simply highlights Sima Xiangru's exploitation of socially recognized forms of literary ornament: repetition, synonyms, alliteration, parallelism, rare words, as well as binomial description.

The "*Fu* on the Excursion Hunt" begins its play with euphonic bisyllables (underlined below) in Sir Vacuous's description of the swirling silks of dancers:

於是鄭女曼姬，	Thereupon the women of Zheng, beauteous consorts,
被阿錫，	Wearing silken finery,

---

earlier poets, they did not hesitate to string eight, ten, even a dozen descriptive binomes together in a series." See Knechtges, *Wen Xuan*, 2:3.

36. My reconstructions and transcriptions follow Axel Schussler's phonological reconstructions for the Later Han, and therefore necessarily remain approximate. See Schuessler, *Minimal Old Chinese*. Cf. Knechtges's "*bjah-zah.*"

37. Usually one of the characters is chosen as contributing to the meaning of the binome. Although some Han dynasty readers and writers often did view the graphs selected to write a binome as meaningful, the word itself cannot be analyzed as a combination of the semantic values of the two graphs. See Harper, "Wang Yen-shou's Nightmare Poem," 257–59. For discussions of the role of character-choice in binomes, see also Hervouet, *Un Poète de Cour*, 351–58, and Knechtges, *Wen Xuan*, 2:2–13.

38. On Mei Sheng's "Seven Stimuli" (*Qi fa* 七發) and its relation to traditions of traveling persuasion, "doubled persuasion," and "word magic," see Knechtges and Swanson, "Seven Stimuli for the Prince"; Frankel, *The Flowering Plum*, 186–202; Gong Kechang, *Studies on the Han Fu*, 114–31.

揄紵縞，	Lifting choice taffetas,
尅纖羅，	Bearing exquisite gauze,
垂霧縠；	Unfurling misty gossamer.
襲積褰縐，	<u>Furbelow</u> crisp gathered,
紆徐委曲，	Crinkled down, twisted as
鬱橈谿谷；	Plunging gorges, folded valleys.
袕袕裶裶，	<u>Frou-frou flap-flap</u>,
揚袘卹削，	Hems stretch <u>tailor-trim</u>,
蜚纖垂髾；	Flying sashes, trailing bands,
扶與猗靡，	<u>o'er-soar, sway-sashay,</u>
鏟呷萃蔡，	<u>Plappering susurring,</u>
下摩蘭蕙，	Strokes wort and basil beneath,
上拂羽蓋，	Brushes feathery canopies above,
錯翡翠之威蕤，	Like the <u>lush-brush</u> of halcyon plumes,
繆繞玉綏；	<u>Tangle-dangled</u> pendant jades
眇眇[39]忽忽，	<u>Dim-bedimmed, hazy-hazed,</u>
若神仙之仿佛。	Like immortals, <u>phantaphasms</u>.[40]

To conjure up the popular Han dynasty performance of "long-sleeved dancing" (see figure 2.2) Sima Xiangru creates a soundscape of alliterative bisyllables (*suitsiau* 卹削 "tailor-trim," *hiphap* *dzuits*[b] 鏟呷萃蔡 "plapper susurr," *p*[h]*uaŋbut* 仿佛 "phantaphasms"), at least four rhyming bisyllables (*piektsiek* "furbelow," *buaja* *ɨai*[41]*miai* 扶與猗靡 "o'er-soar, sway-sashay," *ʔuiṅuiu* 威蕤 "lush-brush"), and two pairs of reduplicatives (*miaumiau* *huəthuət* 眇眇忽忽 "Dim-bedimmed, hazy-hazed") one of which alliterates across the line (*punpun* *puipui* 袕袕裶裶 "frou-frou flap-flap").[42] Again, this clustering together of bisyllables was unprecedented among extant *fu* up to that time. Although this patterning of bisyllables is only one indication of sound-ornamentation, it is an important one given its influence on subsequent *fu* composition.

---

39. I follow Hervouet, *Le chapitre 117 du Che-ki*, here in using the *Hanshu* and *Wenxuan* variant of 眇眇 in place of the *Shiji*'s 縹乎.

40. Translation mine, although I have taken the phrase "misty gossamer" from Knechtges's translation, and benefited from both his and Hervouet's translations of, and commentaries on, this *fu*.

41. *ɨai* is preceded by a glottal stop.

42. Hervouet, *Le chapitre 117 du Che-ki*, lists 繆繞 (*kiuṅau*) as a rhyming binome. I was unable to translate 卹削 "trim-tailored," 猗靡 "sway-sashay," 仿佛 "phantaphasms," or 眇眇忽忽 "Dim-bedimmed, hazy-hazed" with attested English words.

In light of Yang Xiong's analogy of the *fu* to "the intricate beauty of misty gossamer" (in this chapter's epitaph), one might note that the rare phrase "misty gossamer" (霧縠 *wu hu*, **muo *gok*) here marks the departure point for the first extended sequence of rhyming and alliterative descriptive binomes in this *fu*. The sweeping sounds of sleeve dancers recur later in this *fu* and in later Han *fu* (including those of Yang Xiong) as a topic for such euphonic, onomatopoeic description. Given that Yang was one of the greatest students of the *fu*—indeed he was invited to court for his ability to imitate Sima Xiangru's style, and he patterned his own *"Fu* on the Barricade Hunt" (*Jiaolie fu* 校獵賦) on Sima Xiangru's *"Fu* on the Excursion Hunt"—the choice of the phrase "beauty of misty gossamer" does not seem insignificant.[43] If we use the clustering of bisyllabic compounds as a partial index of ornament, Lord No-Such's winning description of the imperial park again wins.[44] His speech contains the highest concentration of descriptive binomes (relative to length of speech), as well as the highest number of binomes (150). Master Improbable's account of Qi is much shorter and contains the fewest descriptive binomes. Yves Hervouet's analysis of the use of binomes in different texts, including the poetic traditions of the *Classic of Odes* and *Elegies of Chu* suggest ways in which Sima Xiangru experimented with the texture of sound. Hervouet distinguishes reduplicative, alliterative, and rhyming binomes as three non-exclusive types. In earlier poetic genres reduplicatives comprising two identical syllables comprised the most commonly occurring binome (e.g., 袡袡 **punpun*, "frou-frou," probably an onomatopoeia for

---

43. The phrase, "cloudlike gauze" or "misty gossamer" otherwise only appears once in extant texts, at *Hanshu* 22.1504. For an annotated translation of this rhapsody see Knechtges, *Wen Xuan*, 2:115–36, where it appears as the "Plume Hunt Rhapsody." On its naming as the "Barricade Hunt Rhapsody" (*Jiaolie fu*), for the alternative interpretation of *jiaolie* as "hunting contest," and for a comparison with Sima Xiangru's "Shanglin Park Rhapsody," see Knechtges, *The Han Rhapsody*, 63–80, and Knechtges, *The Han Shu Biography of Yang Xiong*, 106–7 note 249. Knechtges argues that although Yang Xiong demonstrates a greater concern for critique and lesser interest in descriptive catalogs and supernatural fantasy than Sima Xiangru, and although Yang Xiong describes a historical hunt, this is the rhapsody that shows the greatest influence of Sima Xiangru on Yang Xiong.

44. Hervouet, *Un Poète de Cour*, 350, and 337–59, provides the most comprehensive statistical analysis of Sima Xiangru's use of binomes. These statistics are approximate. They largely rely on Hervouet's research except where challenged in subsequent scholarship.

the "rustle of fabric"[45]). The *Classic of Odes* and *Elegies of Chu* commonly use reduplicatives and the limited number of reduplicatives that Sima Xiangru uses in his extant *fu* and prose work generally derive from the *Classic of Odes*. However, the majority of the bisyllables in the "*Fu* on the Excursion Hunt" are alliterative or rhyming.[46]

What is the relation of "extravagance" to length and ornament? If thrift is better (as the interlocutors claim), Lord No-Such's winning speech must be the most frugal. From this perspective, length and ornament have an inverse relation to extravagance (the longer and more ornamental the less extravagant). A closer look at Lord No-Such's speech provides the opposite (and more intuitive) conclusion. Towards the very end of his speech, his imaginary emperor renounces the pleasures of the hunting excursion with a cry, "Alas, this great extravagance is excessive (*tai she chi* 泰奢侈)!" This epiphany follows the passage with the highest concentration of binomes in the *fu*—and the highest concentration of alliterative binomes in the *fu* recorded in the *Shiji* and *Hanshu* biographies of Sima Xiangru. The following six lines, taken from this twenty-line climactic description of the silk-clad women who join the emperor's festivities demonstrate the density of acoustic ornament. Its ten binomes are underlined and in the phonological reconstructions their internal alliteration and rhymes are in boldface.

便嬛綽約	**bianwan *tśʰak?jak*[47]	Bienseance, beaux yeux,
柔橈嬛嬛	**ńuńao *wanwan*	Opiparous tstatske
斌媚姌嫋	**muami *ńamńeu*	Willowily, liefly,
抴獨繭之褕袘	**jas *dok *ken *tśi *jo *jai*	Sweeping hems of sleeves and skirts,
眇閻易以戌削	**miau *jamjek *jə *suitsiak*	Daint swellsome bebroyded
媥姺徶徶	**biansen *piatsit*	Whirl-twirl, sourse deorse.[48]

---

45. Hervouet, *Le chapitre 117*, 39 n7.

46. According to Hervouet, the majority of Sima Xiangru's alliterative binomes are previously unattested (around 65%), a third of which are hapax. Rhyming binomes, such as 扶與 **buaja*, above, have syllables with similar end-sounds and, again, in Sima Xiangru over half (around 55%) are previously unattested. As Hervouet points out, his binome statistics are approximate. Again, it is important to note that rarity is based on the extant archive.

47. Following Schussler 2009: ? indicates a glottal stop.

48. Chinese text and glosses from Hervouet, *Le chapitre 117*; Knechtges, *Wen xuan*, 109, lines 410–15. Author's translation.

Sima Xiangru's descriptive binomes generally have attested but obscure meanings that are, as in the English translation above, possibly inflected by dialect, archaism, and word-play.[49] His euphonies thus only flirt with the kind of regulated nonsense poetry of Lewis Carroll's "Jabberwocky" ("'Twas brillig, and the slithy toves . . ."). Given the oral basis of descriptive binomes, and the variant transcriptions in the (already compromised) *Shiji* and *Hanshu*, it is hard to reconstruct ancient pronunciations. However, even if the soundscape of the original performance is lost, sound-play certainly proliferates in the received written versions. Both the *Shiji*'s *muami* 妩媚 ("liefly"), above, and its *Hanshu* variant (嫵媚), alliterate. The *Shiji*'s alliterative *muami* and *jamjek* 閻易 ("swellsome") are likely rare terms since both are previously unattested, the latter still hapax among extant texts.[50] Sima Xiangru strings together four rhyming binomes ("bienseance," "beaux yeux," "whirl-twirl," "sourse deorse"), three alliterative binomes ("opiparous," "willowily," "liefly") and one reduplicative ("tsatske"). The four four-syllable lines are thus each comprised of two "vocal gestures," many of whose meanings were perhaps as hazy to listeners then as they are to translators now. The alliteration that spills across the more coherent six-syllable lines (*jas, *jo, *jai, *jamjek, *jə, translated there by words beginning with *s-*) onomatopoeically enhances the rustle of silken robes of the sashaying women whose "whirl-twirling" sleeve dances were a staple in Han dynasty art, entertainment, as well as in subsequent *fu*.

This passage thus marks the formal climax in the *fu*, after which the emperor returns to good government (supplying people's needs and opening granaries) and the *fu*'s language becomes more prosaic and less playful with sound patterns. But if length and ornament correspond with extravagance, does Lord No-Such win because of his aesthetic extravagance or despite it? Criticism of Sima Xiangru's work on the grounds of excessively lavish expenditure implicitly correlated his innovations in length and ornament with extravagance. Despite the offi-

---

49. On the rhymes and the dialect of Shu, Sima Xiangru and Yang Xiong's home province, see W. South Coblin, "The Finals of Yang Xiong's Language"; "The Rimes of Chang-an in Middle Han Times, Part I."

50. For this reason, I translate *jamjek* as "swellsome," the only word in the translation passage that is not attested in the Oxford English Dictionary, besides "whirl-twirl" (for which I could not find an internally rhyming equivalent).

cial acceptance of the genre, subsequent epideictic *fu* (at least those that have survived), largely did not surpass this first submission in length and ornamentation.

THE *FU*'S STRUCTURE OF RETURN TO CLASSICAL THRIFT

For classical proponents of thrift (or moderation), Sima Xiangru's ability to harness his long and ornate language to a moral message hinged on the *fu*'s representation of the imaginary emperor's "return" to good government. For some ancient readers, the return to linguistic and moral decorum at the end of the *fu* came just in time; for others it was too late. This concern recurs in Han dynasty comments on Sima Xiangru's "*Fu* on the Excursion Hunt." Readers (or listeners) iterated the same model of thrift espoused by the *fu*'s poetic personae. According to the parallel *Shiji* and *Hanshu* "Biography of Sima Xiangru":

賦奏，天子以爲郎。無是公言天子上林廣大，山谷水泉萬物，乃子虛言楚雲夢所有甚　眾，侈靡過其實，且非義理所尚，故刪取其要，歸正道而論之。

When the ["*Fu* on the Excursion Hunt of the Son of Heaven"] was submitted, the Son of Heaven made Sima Xiangru a Palace Attendant.[51] But where Lord No-such speaks of the increased size of the Son of Heaven's Shanglin Park, and of its mountains and valleys, and rivers and springs, with their myriad things, and where Sir Vacuous (*Zi Xu*) speaks of the rich abundance contained in the Yunmeng Park of Chu, [the *fu*'s] lavish expenditure (*chi mi*) exceeded their reality (*shi*). Furthermore, it did not have the proper respect for righteousness and propriety. Therefore it was abridged and its essential parts selected to be discussed in terms of the return to the proper way (*gui zheng dao*).[52]

Commentators differ over whether the final sentence of this passage actually reports an abridgement of the *fu* and, if so, whether a court censor or Sima Xiangru performs the cuts.[53] The above translation takes *shan* 刪

---

51. A *lang* (Palace Attendant or Gentleman at Arms) was responsible for guarding the palace gates and providing the emperor with mounted and armed escort. See Loewe, *The Men Who Governed China*, 131–38.

52. *Shiji* 117.3043.

53. For rival interpretations of *shan*, see *Shiji* 117.3043; *Hanshu* 57A.2575; *HSBZ*, 32.51a–b. One might compare the prominent uses of *shan* in relation to Sima Qian's work. At *Shiji* 14.511, the Grand Astrologer explains his own construction of a genea-

in the sense of to "cut" or "omit." Those sections that "transgressed the reality [of the parks]" (*guo qi shi* 過其實) and showed insufficient propriety were, in this reading, edited out. In alternate, but also viable, readings of *shan* as to "distill" or "establish," Sima Xiangru "distilled and selected the essential principles, and (the conclusion of the *fu*) discusses them as the return to the proper way." In the former translation, the question looms as to whether our preserved *fu* is the original or abridged version; the latter translation suggests that Sima Xiangru had built critique into the very structure of the *fu*. The concluding section's shift in content, tone, and form, rather than any excisions, brought the *fu* back to the "proper way."

Whichever way we interpret the final sentence, the passage highlights two things that matter here. First, the offending sections of the *fu* (the speeches of Sir Vacuous and Lord No-Such) correspond to the *fu*'s longest and most ornamental sections. Master Improbable's speech, which is by far the shortest and least ornamental, escapes blame (indeed Master Improbable is the one who actually utters the accusation of "extravagant speech"). Second, the "return to the proper way," (i.e., the literal return of the *fu*'s emperor from the hunt to good government) marks a shift in aesthetic as well as moral content. This concluding section is relatively short, occupying only about a quarter of Lord No-Such's speech (less

---

logical table as "the extraction of essential elements (*yao shan*) for those who study and master the ancient writings" (爲成學治古文者要刪焉). The *Hou Hanshu* 40A.1325 records the description by the *Hanshu* historian Ban Biao of Sima Qian's method: "He selected from the [*Zuozhuan*] and *Guoyu* and extracted from (*shan*) the *Shiben* and *Zhanguo ce*" (採左氏、國語、刪世本、戰國策). Cf. *Hanshu* 30.176, which uses the phrase 刪取要用. *Hou Hanshu* 48.1599 records that the first-century CE's Yang Zhong 楊終 "received an imperial edict to edit down (*shan*) the [*Shiji*] into 100,000 or so words" (受詔刪太史公書爲十餘萬言) from the 526,500 characters that the *Shiji* postface records of its own content (*Shiji* 130.3319). Chen Zhi, "Han Jin ren dui Shiji," 221, points out that abridged documents circulated alongside earlier versions. Watson, *Records: Han Dynasty II*, 284, interprets the Sima Xiangru passage above as a scene of censorship, and the recorded *fu* as the uncensored version. By contrast, Hervouet, *Le chapitre 117 du Che-ki*, 143, takes it as a description of Sima Xiangru's own structuring of a Confucian critique of excess in the *fu*. The *Shiji* and *Hanshu* biographies of Sima Xiangru mention, but do not include, a seed-composition entitled "Fu on Sir Vacuous" (*Zi Xu fu* 子虛賦), on the basis of which Emperor Wu first invited Sima Xiangru to court. Hervouet follows the *Wen xuan*, and some (but not all) *fu*-critics in splitting the preserved "Tianzi youlie *fu*" into two (the "Zi Xu *fu*" and "Shanglin *fu*," respectively).

than 15 percent of the entire *fu*). It is also largely shorn of ornamental synonyms, descriptive binomes, and euphonic language.

The *Shiji* and *Hanshu* accepted the legitimacy of the epideictic *fu*'s aesthetics, citing the structural return as its saving grace:

> Sima Xiangru uses "Sir Vacuous" (*Zi Xu*), named for his vacuous speeches (*xu yan*), to praise the state of Chu; "Master Improbable" (*Wuyou xiansheng* 烏有先生), named for the improbability of his affairs, to offer critique on behalf of the state of Qi; and "Lord No-Such" (*Wushi Gong* 無是公), thus named because there is no such person, to clarify the intent of the Son of Heaven. Therefore out of thin air (*kong* 空) he deploys the words of these three people, in order to promote the hunting parks of the Son of Heaven and the vassal lords. His final section (*zu zhang* 卒章) brings it back to moderation and thrift (*jie jian* 節儉), and he accordingly uses it as an indirect remonstrance (*feng jian* 風諫).[54]

The ability of the *fu* to indirectly promote "moderation and thrift" (*jian jie*) here depends entirely on its "final section," which depicts the imaginary emperor's return to good government. For them, the *fu*'s interlocutors personify precisely the modes of unreality (viz. vacuous language, improbable action, nonexistence) that would sustain the condemnation of the *fu*'s aesthetics as "empty formalism." And yet, in this calculus of thrift, the final section just manages to compensate for the vacuous language that comprises the bulk of the *fu*. The empty speeches (*xu, kong*) promoting the wealth of hunting parks clearly correspond to the sections that are not seen as morally "essential."[55]

The end-comments to the *Shiji* and *Hanshu* biographies iterate this assessment: "Although Sima Xiangru abounds in "vacuous words" (*xu ci*) and overflowing persuasions, he essentially returns to moderation and thrift (*jian jie*). How is this different from the indirect remonstrances (*feng jian*) of the *Odes*?"[56] The Han dynasty witnessed the rise in the appreciation of indirect over direct remonstrance in court cul-

---

54. *Shiji* 117.3002; *Hanshu* 57.2533. The *Hanshu* version has *xu* 虛 in place of *kong* 空.

55. "Empty words" *xu yan* 虛言 or *xu yu* 虛語, consistently carry negative connotations. Even Huang-Lao texts which valorize *xu* (Void, on which see below) use the phrase "empty bragging" (虛夸 *xu kua*). See the "Dao and the Law" (*Dao fa*), translated in Yates, *Five Lost Classics*, 51. *Xu yan* is commonly found in the locution, "these are not empty words" (非虛言).

56. *Shiji* 117.3073; cf. *Hanshu* 57.2609.

ture, and indirect remonstrance provided the main justification for literary play (e.g., riddles, fictional anecdotes, and figurative language).[57] From this perspective, "vacuous speech" becomes admissible as an innovative form of indirection. On the aesthetic scales of thrift versus extravagance, the sheer heft of the final, brief critique of excess can outweigh any amount of "vacuous language" without the need for editorial pruning.

ON "EMPTY WORDS"

The above comments on Sima Xiangru's *fu* in the *Shiji* and *Hanshu* invoked a conventional opposition in early Chinese thought between *shi* 實 and *xu* 虛. *Shi* (reality) primarily denoted "material reality," "solidity," "fullness," "truth," and the particular, concrete objects embraced by the more generalized term 物 (*wu*, thing). *Xu* (emptiness, vacuity, falsity, fiction) is personified by Sir Vacuous (*Zi Xu* 子虛), who is named for his "empty speech" (*xu yan*). Sir Vacuous and Lord No Such's speeches constituted the lavish expenditure that "exceeded reality (*shi*)." Within this classical binary opposition, *shi* was always the valorized term, and "empty speech" implied moral as well as aesthetic failure.[58] Yang Xiong and generations of literary critics praised the historiographic *Shiji* as *shi lu* 實錄, that is, as a "true record" or "veritable record."[59] By contrast, the *fu*-composer Zuo Si 左思 (ca. 250–ca. 305 CE) prefaced his *fu* by dismissing his predecessors' works as collectively "empty" (*xu*) in meaning.[60] Viewed from the classical perspective of *shi* (truth), Sima Xiangru's hunting

---

57. See Schaberg, "Playing at Critique."

58. Compare Sima Qian's assessment of certain adulators of Confucius's disciples at *Shiji* 67.2226. On the need to assess the (strategically or militarily) "empty" (*xu*) and "full" (*shi*) in military texts, see Li Ling, *Sunzi yizhu*, 38–45; Li Ling, *Bing yi zha li*, 202–25. Although knowledge of *xu* provides the means for reversal into a position of strength, it still indicates weakness.

59. Wang Rongbao, *Fayan yi shu*, 413. For an excellent discussion of the shifting meanings of this term, see Klein, "The History of a Historian," 323–38.

60. *Shiji* 117.3073; *Hanshu* 87B.3575; cf. *Hanshu* 57B.2609. The *Shiji* end-comment includes what is clearly a later interpolation. See note above on the authenticity of this section and the biography. The *Shiji*'s evaluation of the philosopher Zou Yan resembles that of Sima Xiangru. See *Shiji* 74.2344 and Nienhauser, *The Grand Scribe's Records*, 7:181 n.25. See also the preface to Zuo Si's "*Fu* on the Three Capitals" discussed below.

park sequences exemplified for generations of *fu*-critics unhistorical "empty formalism and meaningless verbosity."[61]

The promoters of a classical, frugal model of the epideictic *fu* thus either tolerated or rejected outright its primary aesthetic departures from other poetic and prose traditions. Those that did accept the genre (e.g., the imperial audience, Sima Qian, Ban Gu) did so for what was familiar about it (the final prosaic remonstrance). Those that did not (e.g., Yang Xiong) denounced its novel use of length and ornamental language ("it fails to stop"). This basic conundrum of the *fu*'s reception (*epideixis* tolerated only for its thrift) is, as we have seen, prefigured within the *fu*. There is a blatant gap between the interlocutors' espoused ideology of frugality and the calculable extravagance of the speech that "wins"; between their advocacy of poetic traditionalism and the stark fact of their experiment. The meteoric ascent of the *fu* as the Han dynasty's leading literary genre therefore invites a reconsideration of other ideals of linguistic decorum.

Elsewhere in the *Hanshu*, in its summary chapter, another model with which to evaluate Sima Xiangru's play with language emerges: "Magnificently patterned but short in utility, Sir Vacuous and Master Improbable with their lasciviously elegant 'imputed speech' (寓言 *yu yan*), were entrusted with persuasion from beginning to end. Rich in knowledge of varieties of things, they held visible colors, and in their ornamentality they became the ancestor of the *ci*, and the leader of the *fu* and *song*."[62] Sir Vacuous's words are not simply "empty words" (*xu yan*), here they are also artful, if lasciviously gorgeous, "imputed speech" or "delegated words" (*yu yan*). The *Zhuangzi* famously discussed this term *yu yan*, whose translations range from "lodging words" to "metaphorical language" and "allegory."[63] *Yu* literally means "to lodge," or "to entrust," and *yu yan* are

---

61. Long after the Han dynasty, narrative "fiction" (represented by *xiao shuo* 小說 and its perceived antecedents) would continue to struggle for a positive valence in Chinese literary criticism, precisely because of the prestige of historiography.

62. *Hanshu* 100B.4255.

63. Translations of this term include: "lodging words" (A. C. Graham), "lodged words (i.e., words dwelling temporarily away from home)" (Haun Saussy), "imputed words" (Burton Watson), "allegories" (William H. Nienhauser), "l'allégorie" (Yves Hervouet), "metaphorical language" (James Legge), "words . . . coming from the mouths of other people" (Brook Ziporyn), "words put in the mouths of others" and "a Han term denoting fictive speech put into the mouth of a fictive personality . . . usually trans-

the words of someone who has been commissioned by another person to plead a particular case and to face its consequences.[64] The *Shiji* characterized all of Zhuangzi's works as *yu yan*, and traditional commentators sometimes explained the term as the guest-host dialogue form. As in Sima Xiangru's *fu*, Zhuangzi uses imaginary people and personifications (including *Wu You* 無有, No-Such or Nonexistence) for conveying messages.[65]

The broader Daoist skepticism of language's ability to reflect the world offers a more affirmative representation of "vacuous speech," correlating experiments in length and ornament with a positive notion of vacuity. The classical condemnation of the *fu*'s language for "transgressing the realities" (*guo qi shi*) of the parks presumed the efficacy of language and its one-to-one correspondence to reality. The matching of *shi*

---

lated as allegory" (J. L. Kroll). For a further discussion of this term, see Spring, *Animal Allegories*.

64. "Delegated words" is preferred since it helps to distinguish this technical term from the quotidian use in English of "to lodge" in relation to language to mean "to put forward" (e.g., to lodge a complaint). A. C. Graham's interpretation of *yu yan* emphasizes the lodger's occupation of another's position: "You temporarily 'lodge' at the other man's standpoint, because the meanings he gives to words are for him the only meanings, and he will not debate on any other basis." However, Zhuangzi here takes the position of the host (who "relies on the outsider"), and the father (who relies on the matchmaker to praise his son). See Graham, *Chuang-tze: The Inner Chapters*, 25–26. Zhuangzi identifies *yu yan* as one of the three modes of discourse that he himself employs, distinguishing it from "tipping-vessel words" (*shang yan* 卮言, or everyday discourse in which different positions can be freely adopted) and "weighted words" (*zhong yan* 重言, or authoritative sayings). See *Zhuangzi* 1098–99 and *Zhuangzi* 27. *Zhuangzi* 948: "Delegated words (*yu yan*) make up nine tenths [of my own], and rely on an outsider to discuss something. A father does not serve as matchmaker for his own son. For a father's praise of his own son would not be as reliable as praises from someone who wasn't the father. Any offence of [these delegated words] would not be mine, but another's. People respond to what they themselves agree with, and reject what they do not agree with." The *Suoyin* commentary on the *Shiji*'s biography of Zhuangzi explains *yu yan* by glossing *yu* 寓 as *ji* 寄, "to lodge" or "to entrust." *Shiji* 63.2143. The Tang dynasty commentator Yan Shigu 顏師古 (581–645) repeats this gloss of *yu yan* in his commentary on the *Hanshu* passage on Sima Xiangru. See *Hanshu* 100B.4255. The Han lexicon *Shuowen jiezi* also glosses *yu* as *ji*. The modern *Hanyu da cidian* glosses *yu yan* as "having speech that is entrusted to [someone else]."

65. *Shiji* 63.2143. See the commentaries of Liu Xiang 劉向 (79 BCE–8 CE) and Zhang Shoujie's 張守節 (fl. 725–735 CE) *Suoyin*, also preserved at *Shiji* 63.2144. Liu Xiang also brings the *Liezi* 列子 into this tradition.

(realities) with their proper names (*ming* 名) was usually the sage-ruler's prerogative in Han dynasty debates about language. *Shi* could designate the real substance, "actuality," or the ontological core of a thing ("that by virtue of which an entity is what it is") and, as such, bore a natural relation to its "name" (*ming*).[66] Alternately, *shi* could refer to the particular object or entity whose *ming* was established by human convention.[67] The *fu*'s interlocutors similarly invoke the inadequacy of language—an approach that resonates better with Laozi's claim that "The Way is constantly nameless" (*Dao chang wu ming* 道常无名) and Zhuangzi's that what is borne by ideas or thought (*yi*) could be not transmitted by words.[68] Although such critiques of books and spoken words were, para-

---

66. "Correlativist" interpretations that developed during the Han dynasty urged the sage to apprehend or coin the name that was naturally and divinely bound to each actuality. Graham, *Later Mohist Logic*, 196–98. For the distinction between "nominalist" and "correlativist" theories, see Makeham, *Name and Actuality*, 35–98. See also Graham, *Disputers of the Tao*, 141. On the controversy over Makeham's distinction between Xunzi's nominalism and Dong Zhongshu's correlativism, see Roetz, "Worte als Namen," 203–17. Roetz argues that Dong was also "nominalist," inasmuch as both he and Xunzi understood that words were "names" of things in the world.

67. Nominalist views of language seem to have dominated the pre-Han period, but also continued to circulate through the Han dynasty. The late Mohist writings and Xunzi's *Zheng ming* 正名 (On the correct use of names), seem to forward the clearest articulation of this theory. *Xunzi* 22.516: "Names (*ming* 名) have no intrinsic object (*shi* 實). They are bound to [some reality] by agreement in order to name that object. The [object] becomes fixed by agreement and custom is established, and it is called the name of that object (*shi ming* 實名)." Largely following Knoblock, *Xunzi*, 130–31. Xunzi outlined criteria by which the sage needed to select for such customary usage "correct names" and, at times, "new names" for *shi*. Names did not necessarily fit their objects, not because there was a true name inherent in a *shi* (as others would claim), but because some names were more logically or coherently appropriate, because some names had become archaic, or because of the arrival of new objects. In A. C. Graham's analysis, the principle of "similarity" underlay naming. Thus, the name "horse" was applied to an object and to anything resembling it, and the name itself only revealed what an object was *like*. The late Mohist *Canon* explicitly stated: "To 'refer' is to give an analogue for the object." See Graham, *Disputers of the Tao*, 141.

68. *Laozi* 32 and *Zhuangzi* 488. Compare the opening lines of the *Laozi* 1: "The Way that can be 'Way'-ed/Is not the constant Way./The name that can be named/Is not the constant name./What has no name is the beginning of heaven and earth,/What has a name is the mother of the myriad things," following the interpretation of Graham, *Disputers of the Tao*, 221. Zhang Dainian characterizes three strands of early thought on language in *Key Concepts*, 477: "The Great Commentary held that language cannot fully express ideas but that symbols can, the Daoists held that language can never ex-

doxically, uttered, written down, and circulated during this period, the language of their transmitted works was notoriously subtle and difficult to decipher.[69] Zhuangzi's use of parables, anecdotes, aphorisms, conundrums, and diverse rhetorical forms drew attention to the paradoxical inadequacy of his own utterances.[70]

Thus far, there are two potential models of language shaping Sima Xiangru's *fu* and its reception: a classicizing one that gauges linguistic decorum in economic terms (lavish expenditure vs. thrift); and another that raises skepticism about language's representative function. The former resonates with the *fu*'s primary economic metaphor of language (lavish expenditure vs. thrift). However, its moral promotion of thrift renders the *fu*'s characteristic length and ornament merely transgressive. By contrast, the Zhuangzian paradigm potentially affirms the *fu*'s play with length, ornament, and blatant departures from *shi*/reality (e.g., "Sir Vacuous") but does not figure language in resonant terms of spending

---

press ideas fully, and the Mohists and Xunzi believed that language can express ideas." Graham characterizes Zhuangzi's theory of language thus: "The most crucial point for Chuang-tzu is that words have no fixed meanings except in the artificial conditions of intellectual debate, in which one may as well accept the opponent's definitions, since they are no more or less arbitrary than others." See Graham, *Chuang-Tzu: The Inner Chapters*, 25–26. The *fu*'s interlocutors themselves vaunted their inability to "name" things. For example, Master Improbable boasts of the King of Qi's hunting preserve (*Shiji* 117.3015, largely following Knechtges's translation):

珍怪鳥獸,	Rare and marvelous birds and beasts.
萬端鱗萃,	Ten thousand kinds gather like fish scales.
充仞其中者,	They so abundantly fill the park,
不可勝記,	They cannot be completely recorded.
禹不能名,	Yu would not be able to name (*ming*) them.

Naming the birds and the beasts was a commonplace example in these language debates, but Sima Xiangru has Master Improbable subvert this trope in boasting that even the legendary sage Yu could not name (*ming*) all his ruler's possessions. See *Shiji* 102.2752 and its parallel account in *Hanshu* 50.2307 on the zoo-keeper's naming of animals. *Xunzi* 22.515: "'Bird' and 'animal' are the names of the largest divisions of things (*wu*)."

69. *Shiji* 63.2156.

70. Compare *Zhuangzi* 925: "The raison d'être of the bait is to get the fish. Once the fish is caught one can forget the bait. The raison d'être of the trap is to catch the rabbit. Once the rabbit is caught one can forget the trap. The raison d'être of words (*yan* 言) is to express ideas (*yi* 意). Once the ideas are grasped one can forget the words. Where can I find someone who forgets words and go speak with them?"

or thrift. In this context of multiple possible (but not entirely satisfactory) templates, the syncretism and contestatory nature of Han dynasty political thought should be emphasized. Some modern scholars have argued that the "*Fu* on the Excursion Hunt" ultimately reflects Confucian values (e.g., Yves Hervouet) or the Huang-Lao *wuwei* (effortless-action) politics popular at the outset of Emperor Wu's reign (e.g., Gong Kechang).[71] However, political factions in Han China did not group neatly under coherent philosophical or political schools. The next two sections explore other potential resources for Sima Xiangru's aesthetics: first, in the visual tastes of wealthy Han nobles who appear not to have espoused classical thrift; and, second, in the *Guanzi*'s theories of lavish expenditure.

These parallels do not align Sima Xiangru with a specific ideological faction, but rather suggest his exploitation of ideologically conflicting classical and non-classical styles.

Lavish Visual and Verbal Style

Modern archaeology has uncovered the packed tombs of those who clearly did embrace lavish expenditure. Han dynasty merchants and nobles believed they would gain access to the afterworld and would protect themselves from an afterlife of want by amassing vast quantities of richly decorated funerary paraphernalia. As will be discussed in chapter 5, many arranged that their remains would be accompanied by real or imitation money, or by goods inscribed with monetary worth, thereby incorporating the logic of the market (that is, the more, the better) into their own plans for the afterworld. Many Han elite lived and died unreformed by classical ideals of funerary moderation. These consumers of lacquerware and bronzes, painting and silk, may not have theorized their materialism as the *Guanzi* did. However, the new Han visual styles that they promoted encoded social values. Art historians such as Martin Powers have reconstructed these historically shifting values through a wide range of analyses (of ornament, size, subject, ritual function, etc.) In so doing, these historians have drawn attention to the shared symbolic repertoire of literary and material texts. Many have usefully matched the *fu*'s exotica—those things not found within the symbolic imagery of classical texts—to visual depictions of the fauna and flora that entered the con-

---

71. Gong, *Studies on the Han Fu*, 137.

sciousness of the expanding Han empire. These scholars have also made analogies between the construction of visual and poetic "scenes" through perspective.[72]

This section builds on such art historical scholarship but broadens the discussion to look at potential parallels in visual and verbal style, and at the politics of the representational medium itself. The imagery of the epideictic *fu*—the long, versified lists of rare flora and fauna; and turbulent scenes with dragons, clouds, and figures with swirling robes, often in cosmic ascent—reflects innovations in the style and content of Han dynasty textiles, bronze and lacquer vessels, mountain censers (*boshanlu* 博山爐), and mat weights accumulated by wealthy Han elites.[73] One might compare this new Han visual style with the *fu*'s acoustic style. As discussed earlier in this chapter, the epideictic *fu* developed as an orally performed genre and the intoxicating *sound* of the *fu* was part of what set it apart from other genres. It exploited rhymes and rhythms and

---

72. Wu Hung, *Monumentality*, 173–76, usefully analogizes visual and literary principles of design, suggesting that Emperor Wu's renovated Shanglin Park mimicked Sima Xiangru's creation of a "microcosm without a focal point." Just as Sima Xiangru presents the park from the ever-shifting perspective of the poet's journey, so the Shanglin Park was restructured around individual "scenes."

73. On reading graphic patterns as paradigms of social order, see Powers, *Pattern and Person*, 111–59, 227–52. Merchants and officials manifested their acquired wealth and rank by accumulating the bronze vessels and material goods that had once been manufactured for aristocratic elites as tokens of fixed, inherited nobility. From the standpoint of graphic design, the repeating geometric patterns found on bronze vessels and silks were joined or replaced by pictorial resemblances. In Powers' explanation, ornament lost its former ideological function—the replacement of modular design with synthetic style marked the political rise of the new bureaucratic and merchant classes over the old familial elites. See also Powers, *Art and Political Expression*. Compare Wu Hung's observation that whereas Warring States pictorial bronze vessels display a "static composition structure . . . by contrast, fluidity characterizes the Han designs in which all objects—mountains, clouds, animals—are incorporated into a constantly shifting circulating system," in Wu Hung, "A Sanpan Shan Chariot Ornament," 52–54. This characteristic depiction of "upward motion" reflected a "deep sense of constant transformation embodied in the Han world view" (ibid., 54). On *boshanlu*, see Erickson, "Images of Mountains," 402–13; for instrument handles (*se rui* 瑟柄) in the shape of *boshanlu* excavated from the Former Han tomb of the King of Nanyue, see Guangzhou shi wenhua ju, *Guangzhou Qin-Han kaogu san da faxian*, 44–45, and Li Linna, *Nanyue cang zhen*, 142–43. My use of art historical scholarship is reductive. On shifts from the Former to Later Han periods, and the sociopolitics of competing tastes in the Later Han, see Martin J. Powers, *Art and Political Expression in Early China*.

introduced a new way of clustering together euphonic words (descriptive binomes). Within Sima Xiangru's collected *fu*, and in later *fu*, this kind of sound-patterning, which was often onomatopoeic, was commonly used to describe scenes of movement, such as the rustle of women's robes, the (imagined) twists of mountain peaks, the crash of waves, and the cloud-borne flight of dragons. Recall Sima Xiangru's use of such verbal orna-ment in his "*Fu* on the Excursion Hunt" to evoke the movement of danc-ers's sleeves: "Frou-frou flap-flap,/Hems stretch trim-tailored,/Flying sashes, trailing bands,/O'er-soar, sway-sashay,/Plappering susurring." The labor of description is lavished less on the women themselves (e.g., their inner qualities or physical beauty) than on their silken garments, whose varieties in texture and name defy English translation. The words evoke through sound the motion of the garments, suggesting in turn a popular Han form of women's dancing involving the twirling of long sleeves. Such "whirltwirling" dancing recur in accounts of post-hunt cel-ebrations that preceded Emperor Wu's return to frugality. Both Yang Xiong and Zuo Si invoke such sleeve dancing in their respective "*Fu* on the Shu Capital."[74]

Art historians have observed that this kind of heightened attention to the intricacy of silk patterns and to the movement of sleeves had become increasingly common across a range of media during the Han dynasty (e.g., jade, ceramic, painted wood, and lacquer).[75] Take, for example, the

---

74. See Yang Xiong, *Shu du fu*, in Gong, *Quan Han fu ping zhu*, 28: 若揮錦布繡 ("Like the dancing brocades and cloths and silks"); and Zuo Si's "Fu on the Three Capitals" (discussed below): 紆長袖而屢舞. Knechtges translates Zuo Si's line as "Twirling their long sleeves, they dance again and again," in the "Shu Capital Rhap-sody," line 305, in Knechtges, *Wen Xuan*, 1:363. The authenticity of Yang Xiong's *fu* re-mains in question. For a tentative argument in favor of its authenticity, see Knechtges, *The Han Rhapsody*, 117–18. On the translation of poetry through the *gestures* of the women of Zheng, as commemorated in Fu Yi's "*Fu* on the Dance" (*Wu fu* 舞賦), see Diény, *Aux origines de la poésie classique*, 75–79. Diény, 67–75, also uses a detailed analy-sis of Han dynasty sculpture and painting to explore the Han dynasty song and enter-tainment practices surrounding the emergence of lyric poetry. He focuses on the icono-graphic content (e.g., whether or not a sculpture represents the rhythmic clapping of hands).

75. For jade dancers, see Erickson, "Twirling Their Long Sleeves"; Guangzhou shi wenhua ju, *Guangzhou Qin-Han kaogu san da faxian*, 276; Wen wu chu ban she, *Zhong-guo kaogu wenwu zhi mei*, 9:130 and 150. For pottery sculptures of dancing women with sleeve movements accentuated, see Xuzhou bowuguan, *Da Han Chu wang*, 154–55. The

ceramic entertainer excavated from the second-century BCE tomb of the King of Chu at Tuolanshan (figure 2.2). The arcs of her layered long sleeves are caught in mid-motion as she bends and arches to imaginary music.[76] Han nobles filled their tombs with jade plaques of sleeve dancers and decorated their caskets with immortals in flowing robes. While early ritual and poetic texts commonly presented a silk garment as an outward sign of status or a synecdoche of female beauty, representations of silk (and of clouds) in motion pervaded Han dynasty visual culture.

What did these ubiquitous sleeve-dancers of Han *fu* and luxurious Han tombs symbolize? Like much of the imagery in the Han *fu*, the dancers have no classical precedent. For the composers of the Han *fu* and their wealthy patrons (and critics), Sima Xiangru's sleeve dancers likely did not recall the demure women of the *Classic of Odes* poetic tradition. Sleeve-dancers do, however, appear in Sima Qian's "Huozhi liezhuan" 貨殖列傳

---

attention to the clothing of the body has parallels in early Chinese tomb sculptures, as well as in the *Classic of Odes*. On the dialogic development of the face and the body in tomb figurines and the importance of silken garments as markers of status or roles (e.g., painted on wood with individual color designs or miniature garments covering the figurines) see Wu Hung, "On Tomb Figurines." For excellent images of these sculptures, see Chen, *Noble Tombs at Mawangdui*, 24, and the plates accompanying Hunan Sheng bowuguan, *Changsha Mawangdui yi hao Han mu*. On the rise of representations of movement in the Han, see Powers, *Pattern and Person*, and Wang, "Crystallizing the 'Bleary Blur.'" Wang situates his own account of the emergence of naturalistic, dynamic, plastic animal forms during the Former Han dynasty within a broader historical shift from the "art of ornament" towards representational art.

76. This analogy between Han acoustic and visual style bears comparison with Aby Warbug's studies of drapery in Italian Renaissance painting and sculpture. Warburg drew on literary tropes of epic winds that writers and critics had already established to argue that an "imaginary breeze" was the external cause of images. The apparent "movement" characteristic of Botticelli's drapery could thus be analyzed by analogies of visual and verbal metaphor. See Warbug, *The Renewal of Pagan Antiquity*, 89–156, and Didi-Huberman, "The Imaginary Breeze." By contrast, sound is the explicit or implicit source (the "external cause") of movement among the sleeve dancers represented in Han dynasty jade, clay, and brick art. In the case of the Tuolanshan dancer, she—and the group of dancers with which she was found—bend in unison to the imaginary sounds of clay musicians included in the set. In the context of the chanted *fu*, words effectively are the music. The verbal medium itself becomes the "external cause" of the moving drapery. The "frou-frou flap-flap" of binomic ornamentation not only provides an acoustic analogy for the visual depiction of twirling dancers in Han art, it also becomes the acoustic impetus.

FIGURE 2.2. Ceramic sleeve dancer from the Former Han tomb of the King of Chu at Tuolan-shan. After Lin, *The Search for Immortality*, plate 30B. Reproduced with the permission of the Xuzhou Museum, Jiangsu Province.

(Account of the commodity producers), within a catalogue of the occu-pations that enabled men and women to flourish or survive in the new money-hungry Han society:

> Wealth, with respect to human emotions and nature, is not taught but is desired by all. . . . Now when the women of Zhao and beauties of Zheng put on their make-up, sound their lutes, flutter their long sleeves, flit about in dancing slippers, with inviting eyes and bidding hearts, and

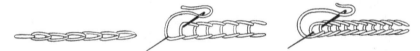

FIGURE 2.3. "Riding the clouds embroidery" (*cheng yun xiu*) from the Former Han tomb of Lady Dai at Mawangdui, Changsha (tomb 1) with illustration (below) of chain stitches. After Chen, *Noble Tombs at Mawangdui*, plate 44. With the permission of the Hunan Provincial Museum.

find a trip of one thousand *li* not too far [to go for a patron], not overly particular about old or young, it is [because they are] in pursuit of immense wealth.[77]

Han dynasty sleeve-dancers were denizens of the market economy who "fluttered their long sleeves" for pay. Those that paid for these dancers (and their clay replicas) were likely not those who espoused classical frugality.

---

77. *Shiji* 129.3271. See chapter 3 for discussions of the *Shiji*'s approach to the market economy.

The theme of "Cloud-riding" (*cheng yun* 乘雲) or "Riding the empty void" (*cheng xu wu* 乘虛無) offers a second case for considering the *fu*'s relation to visual, as well as literary, traditions. Flying about the heavens is a central motif in Sima Xiangru's two most ornamental surviving *fu*. The climactic final stanzas of his "*Fu* on the Mighty One" (*Da ren fu* 大人賦) depict the emperor-like persona: "Riding the empty void, He mounts on high/ Transcending the empyrean, He dwells alone."[78] Sima Xiangru used this same phrase "Riding the empty void" (*cheng xu wu*, *źiŋ *hia *mua 乘虛無) before the turning point in the "*Fu* on the Excursion Hunt*," as the imaginary emperor returns from his hunting extravaganza to his post-hunt banquet epiphany.

然後揚節而上浮，	Then raising His signal flag, He soars aloft,
陵驚風，	Outdistancing the startling wind,
歷駭㵜，	Cleaving the frightful gale,
乘虛無，	*Riding the empty void*,
與神俱，	Joining with the gods,
轔玄鶴，	Trampling the black crane,
亂昆雞·	Upsetting the great fowl,
遒孔鸞，	Harrying the peacock and the simurgh,
促駿鵕，	Tormenting the golden pheasant,
拂翳鳥，	Striking the canopy bird,
捎鳳皇，	Clubbing the phoenix,
捷鴛雛，	Snatching the sea-argus,
掩焦明·	Seizing the blazing firebird.
道盡塗殫，	At journey's end, road's limit,
迴車而還。	Wheeling around His carriage He returns.[79]

The rhythm here hammers out the significance of the return of the imperial chariot. Three-syllable lines are occasionally used in this *fu*, alongside the more common four-syllable lines, as well as a variety of five-, six-, and seven-syllable lines (and longer). The *fu* developed as an orally performed genre, and longer sequences of trisyllables stand out—for example, the twelve-line sequence here leading up to the "journey's end."[80] The syntax

---

78. *Shiji* 117.3062: 乘虛無而上假兮，超無友而獨存。

79. *Shiji* 117.3036. Adapted from Knechtges's translation. Emphasis added.

80. Other sustained three-syllable sequences include: eight and fourteen on hunting in the Yunmneng Park; six describing flora of the landscape; four on the swinging activities of simian creatures (monkey realism); within the Shanglin Park barricade hunt; six describing the material ornamentation of his chariot; eight depicting the capturing

of this entire trisyllabic section conforms to a strict verb-object order (monosyllabic verb followed by a modified noun, two nouns, or a bisyllabic noun), a common pattern in incantatory language. The performance of "*Fu* on the Mighty One" apparently had precisely this incantatory effect. As Han historiographers reported, "When Sima Xiangru presented his ["*Fu* on the Mighty One"], the Emperor was immensely delighted, and felt the vapors of pure clouds floating about, as if he were roaming the expanses of heaven and earth."[81] In gently mocking Emperor Wu's identification with the Mighty One, and in depicting the failure of the *fu* to morally instruct, Han historiographers highlight the *fu*'s key theme and problematic.

From a literary perspective, the phrase "riding the void" (*cheng xu wu*) could have negative or positive connotations. For the classicists who rejected Sima Xiangru's *fu*, the phrase embodied the departure of both the *fu* and its imperial patron from reality (*shi*). When the imaginary emperor left the ground, he clearly entered the realm of fiction (*xu*). Classically trained scholars who found a way to appreciate even the fanciful sections of the *fu* may, however, have drawn on other traditions. For some

---

of various beasts alive and the attire of the hunters; six describing the forms of attack on various creatures (each of the first syllables being a verb of attack). When the Emperor "increases the pace" into the even more remote regions, longer trimeter sequences follow with even greater frequency: ten recounting the Emperor's departure "from the mundane realm," overtaking "scarlet lightning" and shooting ever more supernatural creatures, two on the precision of his arrows, twelve in the void-riding sequence above, six on the topography of his descent, two on the return to various buildings, and two on the singing of mass dancing choruses at the final feast. This rhythm is most common in the more active scenes of hunting. The sequence here invokes an earlier fourteen-line trisyllabic sequence in which "A black crane is hit" (*xuan he jia* 玄鶴加) in the King of Chu's Yunmeng Park hunt. Unlike in this earlier Yunmeng scene, however, the syntax of the entire trisyllabic sequence above conforms to a strict verb-object syntax (monosyllabic verb followed by a modified noun, two nouns, or a bisyllabic noun). Here, the imaginary emperor "tramples the black crane" (*lin xuan he* 轔玄鶴). As in the case of demon curses in *fu*, these trisyllabic sequences may serve as linguistic markers of the Han dynasty *fu*'s function as a form of word magic. For the *fu*'s rhyme schemes, see Suzuki, *Fu shi da yao*. For an analysis of literary accounts of hunting rituals, and of the various forms of visual, verbal, and instrumental imitation used in hunting, see Sterckx, *The Animal and the Daemon*, 123–37. For a detailed reconstruction of archery rituals involving animal hides as targets and hunting incantations, see Riegel, "Early Chinese Target Magic."

81. *Shiji* 117.3063. The *Shiji* has 大人之頌; *Hanshu* 57B.2600 reads 大人賦.

of these scholars, the image invokes a positive politico-philosophical conceptualization of emptiness.[82] In the writings attributed to Laozi, the Way (*Dao* 道) itself was *xu wu* 虛無 ("devoid of form," "emptiness and inaction").[83] Emptiness (*xu*) represented an inner world unshackled by everyday material affairs—a "fasting of the heart" in Zhuangzi's terms.[84] Thus, although the *Shiji* presented Sir Vacuous (*Zi Xu* 子虛) as the negative embodiment of the *fu*'s vacuous speech, "vacuity" (*xu* and *xu wu*) was celebrated within other textual traditions.[85] "The empty void" (*xu wu*) also suggests the politics of *wu wei* 無為 ("non-action" or "effortless action"), grounding "vacuity" in a positive political ideal. This spiritual and political ideal of *wu wei* as an "action that is spontaneous and yet nonetheless accords in every particular with the normative order of the cosmos," was widespread in early Chinese thought, but particularly associated in the *Shiji* with Daoist traditions.[86] In Sir Vacuous's speech,

---

82. *Shiji* 117.3036. This term also appears in his subsequent *"Fu* on the Mighty One." See *Shiji* 117.3062.

83. *Shiji* 63.2156; Knoblock and Riegel, *The Annals of Lü Buwei*, 423–24.

84. *Zhuangzi* 4. See Zhang Dainian, *Key Concepts in Chinese Philosophy*, 77–81. In the cosmogonies of the *Huainanzi* and various Huang-Lao texts, emptiness was a cosmological principle or a vast heavenly void from which the *Dao* emerged. *Huainanzi* 18–19. Within the Huang-Lao tradition, only he who grasps the Dao becomes empty (*xu*) and "The Dao of seeing and knowing is merely vacuity (*xu*) and non-existence." See *The Dao and the Law* (*Dao fa* 道法), *Names and Principles* (*Ming li* 名理), and *Dao the Origin* (*Dao yuan* 道原), in Yates, *Five Lost Classics*, 24, 51, and 101.

85. In the context of the imperial hunt, *cheng xu wu* also recasts the common metaphorical use of "riding a horse" (*cheng ma* 乘馬) for governing the state.

86. See *Shiji* 130.3317: "The affairs of Sir Vacuous, and the persuasions of the *fu* on the Mighty One, were gorgeously extravagant and rich in hyperbole, but gestured towards suasive critique, returning to (the philosophy of) non-action (*wuwei*); *Shiji* 130.3292: "The Daoists [propose] non-action (*wu wei*), also saying that [through it] 'there is nothing left not-done.' Its truths are easy to practice, but its words (*ci*) hard to understand. Its techniques take the empty void (*xu wu*) as their basis, and it takes [natural] causes and compliance as its practice." Scholars of Han dynasty thought generally distinguish Daoism specialists as the main alternatives to the tradition represented by Confucian and Mohist thinkers. Put simply, the former sought to decode the natural rules of cosmos and to harmonize man with them, whereas the latter pursued the sociopolitical reform and regulation of interpersonal relations. These traditions might better be understood as strains, rather than schools, of speculation that permeated mythical, medicinal, military, and divinatory, as well as political and philosophical writings. On the importance of including the Yin-Yang specialists with the Daoists, see Yates, *Five Lost Classics*, 13–14. On the complexity of historicizing and defining Huang-

the King of Chu ascends the Sun-Cloud Terrace at the end of his hunt to demonstrate his politics of *wu wei*. "Riding the empty void" also reworks an attested poetic theme of cloud-riding, exemplified by the shaman-inspired flights of the *Elegies of Chu*. Qu Yuan 屈原 (ca. 340 BCE– 278 BCE), the lyrical persona of its "Encountering Sorrow" (*Li Sao* 離騷), aerially traverses the limits of the world, and the persona of "Far Roaming" (*Yuan you* 遠遊) goes further, "ascending the auroras, ensconced within a floating cloud," explicitly gaining entry to the heavens. Post-dating Sima Xiangru's *fu*, Wang Bao's 王褒 (fl. 60 BCE) "Nine regrets" (*Jiu huai* 九懷) and Liu Xiang's (attrib.) "Nine laments" (*Jiu tan* 九歎) use the phrase "Riding the clouds" (*cheng yun* 乘雲), which the *Huainanzi* and *Han Feizi* had earlier applied to enlightened men and dragons (i.e., paradigms for the ruler).[87] Thus, as modern critics have pointed out, Sima Xiangru's striking phrase simply recasts this *Elegies of Chu* theme for his imperial patron.

From an interdisciplinary perspective, however, Han dynasty artists had already invested the cloud-riding motif with new meanings by the time of the *fu*'s composition. Cloud patterns were one of the most common motifs in Han dynasty art, and the suspension of immortals, exotica, and swirling landscape scenes within and around them pervaded painted, carved, and sculptural design. The excavated inventory slips (*qian ce* 遣策) accompanying the wife of the Marquis of Dai (Mawangdui tomb 1) included in its list of tomb objects "riding the clouds embroidery" (*cheng yun xiu* 乘雲繡).[88] The Marquise of Dai was buried during the second century BCE with a hoard of textile rolls and robes. The "riding the clouds embroidery" record has been matched to two pieces of jacquard silk fabric, one of which is pictured in figure 2.3. "Riding the clouds" likely refers to the repeating geometric pattern of vermilion phoenixes riding cloud

Lao thought and practice, see Guo Zhanbo, "The Huang-Lao School." For an examination of uses of the term *wu wei*, see Slingerland, *Effortless Action*; Csikszentmihalyi, *Readings in Han Chinese Thought*, 48–64.

87. *Huainanzi* chapters 1, 9, 11, and 20; *Han Feizi* chapter 4.

88. Excavated in 1972 from Han Tomb 1 at Mawangdui, Changsha, Hunan. The dimensions of the piece of silk are: length: 39 cm; width: 34 cm. For a technical analysis of the textiles excavated at Mawangdui, see Shanghai Shi fang zhi kexue yanjiu yuan, *Changsha Mawangdui yi hao Han mu chu tu fang zhi pin*. For a discussion of other objects excavated at Mawangdui, including a set of mittens (figure 5.4) see chapter 5.

arabesques. These were auspicious symbols commonly associated with the geographical south in visual and literary texts.

The worked silk medium and elite burial context of the "riding the clouds embroidery" also associate the "riding the clouds" with other values. As also shown in figure 2.3, its manufacture demanded a painstaking chain stitching technique, which raised the layered design above the background. Its value clearly lay in its material worth as a labor-intensive good, as well in its role as an item of auspicious tomb paraphernalia that could prepare the deceased for their journey to the afterworld.[89] Although the origin of the design is not known, textile historians point out that this complex cloud-riding fabric design was one of the most popular patterns in the Han dynasty. Whether the theme originated in the literary or visual arts, it had, by the Former Han, become appropriated by the labor-intensive decorative media prized by lavish spenders. Sima Xiangru may well have been familiar with this kind of design, especially since he came from Chengdu, one the busiest brocade-producing regions of China (in Shu, modern-day Sichuan).[90] By the time Sima Xiangru fashioned the

---

89. Another pair of mitts has the characters for "A thousand taels of gold" (*qian jin* 千金) woven into its ribbons. See Chen, *Noble Tombs at Mawangdui*, 168. On the meanings of these cloud-designs (longevity, auspiciousness), as retrospectively suggested by the characters woven onto later cloud-design fabrics, and for the introduction of the loom by the Later Han dynasty, see Kuhn, "Silk Weaving in Ancient China," 77–114. See also Vainker, *Chinese Silk*, 44–73.

90. Shu workers may well have been familiar with similar designs, and historiographers record that Sima Xiangru and his wife Zhuo Wenjun worked in the Chengdu marketplace before he became a recognized *fu*-composer. The excavation at Mawangdui of wine-vessels and other lacquer-wares that were manufactured in Chengdu suggests the presence of at least some trade relations between Changsha and Chengdu during Sima Xiangru's lifetime. See Chen, *Noble Tombs at Mawangdui*, 131. The origin of manufacture is known from the stamp on the base of the vessels, e.g., "成市草" for "Made in the city of Chengdu," indicating they were made in government workshops there. A painted lacquer *fang*, still holding rice wine-dregs, has the character 米 *mi* (rice) patterned among cloud motifs on the lid. Sima Xiangru would have worked in the marketplace of Chengdu about two and a half decades after the Mawangdui tomb was sealed in 168 BCE. For a discussion of the importance of Han dynasty Shu lacquer production and its export across China, see Wang, *Han Civilization*, 84–99, and Mianyang bo wu guan, *Mianyang Shuangbao Shan Han mu*. For a Later Han dynasty carved depiction of wine-selling and silk-weaving on a single brick-tile from Chengdu, see Gong, *Bashu Handai huaxiang ji*, plates 16–18. Other pieces of fabric or clothing itemized by the burial inventory include the "Abiding faith embroidery" (*xin qi xiu* 信期繡)

emperor's climactic scene of "Riding the Empty Void," cloud-riding was not simply a classical trope, but was also part of the visual vocabulary of the world of lavish expenditure.

Thus, the kinds of visual *comparanda* that ancient and modern critics have brought to bear on the *fu*'s aesthetics—over and above the simple act of comparison—matters. In imitating the rustling sounds or cloud-riding patterns of luxury gossamers, Sima Xiangru helps to introduce into the acoustic medium certain themes whose depiction in visual media was likely shaped by values other than that of the classically-trained elites. In choosing an already decorative medium ("misty gossamer" and other worked silks) as the topic of poetic ornament, he draws on a recognized analogy between verbal and visual patterning. As the fifth-century CE Liu Xie 劉勰 later put it: "Beautiful ideas and clear ideas [in the *fu*]

---

and "Longevity embroidery" (*chang shou xiu* 長壽繡). The *Hanshu* reports that Wen Weng 文翁 (Governor of Shu during Sima Xiangru's time) brought education to those in the region with "uncivilized customs," financing the schooling of local men in the capital by exporting Shu products, specifically Shu cloth (*Shu bu* 蜀布, i.e., brocade) and blades. This follows Yan Shigu's gloss on 布 *bu*. The Shu governor (*shou* 守), Wen Weng, is not mentioned in the *Shiji* but the *Hanshu* includes his biography among those of upright officials. See *Hanshu* 89.3625–27. Emperor Wu's ambassador to Central Asia, Zhang Qian, later reported seeing exports of this Shu cloth (*Shu bu*) as far away as Daxia (Bactria). *Shiji* 123.3166. Compare *Hanshu* 61.2689 and 95.3841. Yang Xiong's and Zuo Si's works both titled "*Fu* on the Shu Capital," would later commemorate the local manufacture of brocade (*jin* 錦) and its worth in gold, and they invoked the patterns of interwoven silk fabric as comparanda for other phenomena. On the importance of Shu brocade (*Shu jin*), see Wang, *Zhongguo si chou ci dian*, 252. Qiao Zhou 譙周 (199–270 CE), a native gazetteer of the Chengdu Plain region, noted: "In Chengdu, when the woven brocade was finished, it was rinsed in the Yangzi's waters and its patterns became much clearer than when it was first finished. Rinsing it in other waters is inferior to the waters of the Yangzi." For this quote and for Zuo Si's use of the Shu dialect word *gui* 䙡 for "cutting silk for clothing," see Knechtges, *Wen Xuan*, 1:360–61. Later histories would echo the local historian Qiao Zhou's 譙周 (199–270 CE) explanation of the superiority of Chengdu's brocade, renaming the river in question "Brocade River." For example, see Li Daoyuan's 酈道元 (d. 527 CE) *Shuijing zhu* 水經注 (Commentary on the classic of waterways), and Chang Qu's 常璩 (ca. 291–ca. 361 CE) *Huayang guozhi* 華陽國志 (Records of the states south of Mt. Hua). See Yang, *Shuijing zhushu*, 33.2754 and Ren, *Huayang guozhi jiao bu tu zhu* 3.153. While Chengdu silk-production was not pre-eminent until the end of the Han dynasty, it was already an established center during the second century BCE. For an introduction to silk production and design during the Qin-Han period, see Zhao, *Zhongguo si chou tong shi*, 83–140. For a map of silk production centers, see ibid., 87.

complement each other as the symbol and the symbolized. They are like red and purple silk in weaving, and black and yellow pigments in painting."[91] In Yang Xiong's comparison of *fu*-composition to the "scourge" of women's craft, however, the visual-verbal analogy concerned the exploitative values of the wealthy consumer. Thus, in taking painted lacquer-ware and embroidery—as opposed, say, to hempen cloth—as potential sources or parallels for the Han *fu*'s imagery and style, one must take into account this contemporary sociopolitics of taste.

The *Debate on Salt and Iron*'s Classical Scholars clarified the ideological values encoded in such desires for decoration: "If men abandon the 'root' for the 'branch,' carving patterns and engravings to imitate birds and beasts, capturing animals by mastering their transformation, there will not be enough grain to eat. If women exquisitely decorate with fine threads to create patterns, maximizing their skill and ingenuity, there will not be enough silk cloth for clothing."[92] The wealthy circles that patronized the *fu* also patronized the new styles of Han wares and purchased luxury items to assert social status. Although the founder of the Han had banned merchants from taking office and riding in carriages, the dynasty saw the political rise of new bureaucratic and merchant classes over the old familial elites. The nouveaux riches became, in Sima Qian's phrase, China's "untitled nobility" (*su feng* 素封).[93] Emperor Wu promoted several officials who belonged to merchant families or who had at some point worked in the marketplace, including his Guanzian economic planner Sang Hongyang (the Classical Scholars's opponent in the *Debate on Salt and Iron*) and Sima Xiangru. As introduced in chapter 1, the *Guanzi* became a well-known and influential text during Emperor Wu's expansion of frontiers and markets. Although modern

---

91. *Wenxin dialong zhu*, 136. See Shih, *The Literary Mind and the Carving of Dragons*. The *Xijing zaji* 西京雜記 (Miscellaneous records of the western capital) has a probably spurious report in which Sima Xiangru had made the comparison himself: "Joining vermilion ribbons to create the pattern, arraying brocade embroidery for the background, one warp, one woof—these are the traces of the *fu*." See Shanghai gu ji, ed., *Han Wei Liu chao bi ji*, 89; following Gong, *Studies on the Han fu*, 19. Although it contains materials concerning the Former Han, the *Xijing Zaji*'s sources and composition probably date to the late Six Dynasties (ca. sixth century CE). Compare the *Hanshu*'s report of Emperor Xuan's defense of the *fu* ("[*Fu*] are like satin").

92. Wang Liqi, *Yantielun*, 40.

93. *Shiji* 129.3271–72.

scholars are right to take classical texts such as the *Classics of Odes* and the *Elegies of Chu* as important resources for the *fu*'s stylistic innovations, renewed attention should be paid to other potential resources: to the Han visual media cultivated by the promoters of the expanding market; and to the literary forms of Han texts that theorized expenditure in quantitative terms, a subject addressed in the next section.

Guanzi's *"Lavish Expenditure"*

The *Guanzi*'s "Lavish Expenditure" (*chi mi* 侈靡) chapter presents what is perhaps the most sustained economic justification for state-sponsored spending to have survived from the premodern world.[94] Just as perceived resemblances between Adam Smith and Sima Qian have renewed interest among modern liberal economists in the latter (beginning with Liang Qichao), so comparisons with Keynesian economics have permeated the new wave of research since the 1950s (beginning with the Marxist historian Guo Moruo). "Lavish Expenditure" was, as Guo put it, "fossilized" for two millennia, neglected for both philological and ideological reasons. Dating to the late Warring States or early Former Han, it is the longest chapter of the *Guanzi* and full of corruptions that only the past half-century of scholarship has helped to clarify. Ideologically, the promotion of lavish spending (on any grounds) jarred with the classical cultivation of moderation, and especially the Mohist economics of absolute frugality. Outside of the *Guanzi*, we find only a few laconic statements supporting lavish spending ("Freely spending is the way to nourish wealth!"; "Thrift (*jie*) causes sheer waste!").[95] Somewhat confusingly, later "Qingzhong" chapters of the *Guanzi* (chapters 68–86) that were probably composed during or shortly after Emperor Wu's reign repudiated this earlier argument for lavish spending. However, unlike the classical attack on lavish expenditure as a form of immoral excess, the *qingzhong* theorists based their critique on an *economic* reevaluation. In their reassessment,

---

94. For good discussions of the *Guanzi*'s *chimi* theory, see Rickett, *Guanzi*, 292–336; Lien-Sheng Yang, "Economic Justification for Spending"; Guo Moruo, "'Chimi' de yanjiu"; Wu Baosan, *Guanzi jingji sixiang*, 143–217; Ye Shichang, *Gudai Zhongguo jingji sixiang shi*, 94–96.

95. *Shiji* 23.1162; *Xunzi* 419. Further justifications for lavish spending seem to disappear from the archive until the Song dynasty (960–1279).

unregulated spending did not promote the flourishing of the market and state. Thus, what remains constant across both the pro-lavish and anti-lavish expenditure positions within the composite Guanzian corpus is a reliance on quantitative reasoning. They calculate or recalculate lavish expenditure policies in more narrowly economic terms, and not moral, cosmological, or purely political ones. Unlike the various sages of the Masters tradition, neither Guanzian position assumes lavish expenditure is a moral transgression.

The introduction of quantitative reasoning into the hitherto ethical question of lavish expenditure is important for considering Sima Xiangru's poetic use of the theme. Given the popularity of parts of the *Guanzi* in the Han, especially among Emperor Wu's economic advisers, Sima Xiangru may have been familiar with some version of the *Guanzi*'s lavish expenditure theory or, depending on its date of composition, with the "Qingzhong" revision.[96] Therefore to better historicize Sima Xiangru's primary metaphor and theme of expenditure it makes sense to explore the *Guanzi* alongside the recognized resources for the *fu*'s aesthetics (e.g., *Classic of Odes*, *Elegies of Chu*, hunting chants). Chapter 1 already tied Guanzian economics to its literary form. To teach its readers how to invent and manipulate fiat and credit currencies, the *Guanzi* introduced a heterochronic, heterotopic world of real and imaginary characters, including the personification of economic abstraction itself ("Mr. Calculate-*y*"). The following section suggests ways in which the *Guanzi*'s oppositional approaches to lavish expenditure provided a resource for Sima Xiangru's experiments with the acoustic medium (length and ornament); the narrative structure of epiphany; and the use of personified interlocutors.

THE GUANZIAN ECONOMICS OF SIZE AND ORNAMENT

The *Guanzi*'s "Lavish Expenditure" chapter (*Chi mi*, chapter 35) offered an economic justification for increased size and ornament. For pro-frugality classicists such as Yang Xiong, the epideictic *fu* involved wasteful work, analogous to that of the exploited weavers of the market economy. The *Guanzi*'s "Lavish Expenditure" chapter, by contrast, correlated work with economic productivity and promoted consumption in the name of

---

96. See the discussion in chapter 1 and *Shiji* 62.2136.

maximizing general employment. In the dialogue between Guanzi (i.e., Guan Zhong) and the Duke of Qi that comprises the chapter, Guanzi promotes state spending as the solution to a depressed economy. Although the dialogue acknowledges the traditional priority of "root" (*ben* 本, agriculture) over "branch" (*mo* 末, craft and commerce), it emphasizes that times have changed (mountains lack trees, marshes lack fish), that people desire profit and material comfort, and that market consumption is the key to economic recovery. High consumption stimulates markets, which in turn boost production, employment, and general economic development. "Without extravagant spending (*chi*), root production cannot be firmly established."[97] Although the chapter also argues that a ruler's lavish spending had political utility, its economic logic of spending is unusually explicit. Unlike the builders of pyramids and medieval cathedrals celebrated by Keynes for their instinctive savvy, the *Guanzi* explicitly theorizes the benefits of spending in economic terms.

Lavish spending by the rich on funerary paraphernalia—a hot topic in Chinese ethics—provides the opportunity to harness work done by women as well as by men, and serves as a means for economic revival:

巨瘞窖，所以使貧民也；美壠墓，所以使文萌也；巨棺槨，所以起木工也；多衣衾，所以起女工也。猶不盡，故有次浮也，有差樊，有瘞藏。作此相食，然后民相利，守戰之備合矣。

Guanzi: "Giant (*ju*) tombs are the means of (*suo yi*) employing poor people; beautiful (*mei*) grave sites for (*suo yi*) employing decorative carvers; giant (*ju*) inner and outer coffins for (*suo yi*) developing the carpentry industry; multiple (*duo*) layers of robes and coverlets to (*suo yi*) develop women's work (*nü gong*). Since these measures will not fully maximize [economic potential] there should be gradations of sacrificial meats, grains, and funerary articles. By enacting such measures we will be able to feed each other, enabling the people to profit from each other. This is a suitable method when preparing for military defense."[98]

The beneficiaries of monumental tombs are not its afterworld-seeking occupants, but rather members of the wider society; and this is highlighted by the fourfold repetition of the construction "[x] 'is the means of' [y] ([x]

---

97. Li Xiangfeng, *Guanzi jiao zhu*, 703. On the location of this passage, see Rickett, *Guanzi*, 306.

98. Li Xiangfeng, *Guanzi jiao zhu*, 688. Text following emendations and glosses of Zhang Dejun, Li Xiangfeng, Guo Moruo, Rickett.

suo yi 所以 [y] *ye* 也)." This rhetoric of instrumentality and strategy demystifies the economic law that binds consumption to production and to universal profit. Lavish expenditure effectively collapses the short-term transactional order of private acquisition into the long-term one. High-spenders convert gains from the market domain to the moral reproduction of society not through taxes, charity, or any political or religious institution, but through the mere economic act of expenditure.[99] Since consumption depends on production, the funeral industry provides employment for poor people, decorative carvers, carpenters, and women workers (i.e., weavers).[100]

The giant size (*ju* 巨) at stake in *Guanzi*'s funerary economy clearly concerns beauty (*mei* 美) as well as number (*duo* 多). Within the aesthetics of lavish expenditure, the value of the big and ornamental lies in the labor required for construction. The bigger and more decorative something is, the more labor is needed, and therefore the more wealth is pumped into the economy. The material expression of beauty not only reduces general unemployment, but also employs precisely those carvers of decorative patterns (*wen* 文) and seamstresses of elaborate robes to whom *fu*-poets would later be compared. The *Guanzi* chapter clarifies the economics of ornament elsewhere: "故嘗至味，而罷至樂。而雕卵然後瀹之，雕橑然後爨之。" ([Guanzi:] Therefore everyone should experience the finest of tastes, indulge in the finest music. Decorate eggs before boiling them! Decorate firewood before burning it!). Some modern economic historians have pointed to the decoration of eggs and firewood as a weak example in *Guanzi*'s lavish expenditure theory—as labor more patently useless than in other examples.[101]

---

99. See Bloch and Parry's "Introduction" to *Money and the Morality of Exchange*, and Carsten, "Cooking Money."

100. "Decorative carvers" follows Liu Shipei's reading of 文明 as 文萌 in Li Xiang-feng, *Guanzi jiao zhu*, 692, which is glossed by Guo, "'Chimi' de yanjiu," 128, as 雕工 and translated by Rickett, *Guanzi*, 319, as "engravers and sculptors."

101. E.g., Ye Shichang, *Gudai Zhongguo jingji*, 95. Hu Jichuang, *Chinese Economic Thought*, 30, likened it to the outcome of burying banknotes in J. M. Keynes's *The General Theory of Employment, Interest, and Money*: "If the Treasury were to fill old bottles with banknotes, bury them at suitable depths in disused coalmines which are then filled up to the surface with town rubbish, and leave it to private enterprise on well-tried principles of *laissez-faire* to dig the notes up again . . . there need be no more unemployment and, with the help of the repercussions, the real income of the commu-

In the *Guanzi's* example, ornament (*diao* 雕, *wen*) becomes a celebrated part of the lavish expenditure economy. The *Guanzi* emphasizes not only the extra labor utilized in egg and firewood decoration, but also the pleasure it brings to the consumer, upon whose taste for luxuries this market-driven model of economic revival depends.[102]

The *Guanzi's* "Lavish Expenditure" chapter thus offers a potential resource for the *fu's* signature play with length and ornament. Just as the *Guanzi* passages above celebrate size (*ju, duo*) and decorative beauty (*diao, mei, wen*), so the *fu's* interlocutors evaluate verbal lavish expenditure (*chi mi*) in terms of length and beauty. Sir Vacuous introduces the *fu's* theme by ridiculing the gap between the real and the boasted size (*duo*) of his host's hunting catch; Master Improbable condemns the lavish expenditure (*chi mi*) of Sir Vacuous, arguing that even if Sir Vacuous's description rings true, such vast possessions fail to constitute the beauty (*mei*) of the state of Chu; and Lord No-Such launches the most lavish description of the imperial preserve with the rhetorical question: "Have you not yet seen immensity and beauty (*ju li* 巨麗)? Have you alone not heard of the Shanglin Park of the Son of Heaven?"[103] To recall, the *fu's* first audience (or Sima Xiangru himself) also criticized those sections where the *fu's* "lavish expenditure (*chi mi*) exceeded their reality (*shi*)." If one considers this *fu* strictly in relation to the classical economics of moderation (*jie*) and frugality (*jian*), then its most striking aesthetic qualities are essentially superfluous. Ornamentation is negatively encoded as transgressively immoderate. The *fu's* interlocutors, however, discuss decorum in terms of lavish expenditure and its synonyms, not moderation or

---

nity, and its capital wealth also, would probably become a good deal greater than it actually is." See Keynes, *The General Theory of Employment, Interest and Money*, 129. Keynes's image of bank note hunting implicitly refashions what he refers to elsewhere as "the form of digging holes in the ground known as gold-mining." He promotes the positive economic utility of employment through apparently wasteful forms of expenditure, including the building of mansions, cathedrals, and pyramids, as well as bank note retrieval.

102. As discussed further below, the aim here is also to produce docile political subjects. Unlike Keynes's intervention into free-market economics, however, the *Guanzi's* quantitative reasoning creates a more separate and enlarged domain of market exchange than in contemporary ethico-political discourse.

103. *Shiji* 117.3016. On the importance of this term *ju*, see Knechtges, "Have You Not See the Beauty of the Large?"

thrift. If, then, one considers the *fu* in terms of quantitative justifications for spending, we find a positive economic model for the bulk of the *fu*. When Master Improbable condemns lavish expenditure, he recognizes enlargement and ornamentation as productive aesthetic work.

Although the complexity of Sir Vacuous's linguistic experiments clearly derive from the earlier *fu*, *sao*, and *shi* poetic traditions, the *Guanzi*'s use of personification, staging, and prosody presented a tradition of writing about economic issues in which form clearly mattered.[104] One might note that the "Lavish Expenditure" chapter includes rhyming verse sequences, for example:

用其臣者		In using your ministers:
予而奪之	(xx **duat *tśɨ*)	Increase and diminish them,
使而輟之	(xx **tyat *tśɨ*)	Employ and finish them,
徒以而富之	(xx **pu *tśɨ*)	Give followers to enrich them,
父繫而伏之	(xxx **bu *tśɨ*)	Use axe and chain to subjugate them,
予虛爵而驕之	(xxxx **kau *tśɨ*)	Give empty ranks to puff them,
收其春秋之時而消之	(xxxxxxx **siau *tśɨ*)	Collect a regular tax to slough them.[105]

The last two characters of the final six lines form three successive pairs of end-rhymes, and all six lines end with the same word ("them" **tśɨ*). The *fu*'s account of Sir Vacuous resonates with the problem here of bestowing empty (**hɨa* 虛) titles, not only in the name of this character (**tsɨ *hɨa* 子虛), but also in the character's boastful (here **kau* 驕 "puffed up") failure to do credit to his ruler (the king of Chu) in the eyes of his interlocutors. The perennial complaint that officials were not worthy of their titles would intensify under Emperor Wu, when ranks were sold to raise funds.[106]

THE GUANZIAN STRUCTURE OF RETURN

The "Lavish Expenditure" chapter also provides a model of spending that resonates with the epiphanic structure of the "*Fu* on the Excursion

---

104. See the discussion of the *Guanzi* and *Debate on Salt and Iron*'s respective uses of dialogue form in chapter 1.

105. *Guanzi*, ch. 35, "Chi mi." Li Xiangfeng, *Guanzi jiao zhu*, 652–53; Rickett, *Guanzi*, 311. My loose translation emphasizes only the end-rhymes.

106. One might compare this to Sima Qian's description of China's wealthiest businessmen as the "untitled nobility," discussed in chapter 3.

Hunt." The Han classicists laid great weight on the final section of "*Fu*
on the Excursion Hunt," which depicts the emperor's return to frugality.
From their perspective, the rest of the epideictic *fu*—the speeches and
hunts, and the lavish expenditure in length and ornament—had minimal moral utility. The *fu* achieved its remonstrative function only after
the emperor's realization.[107] Following this general pattern, the *Guanzi*'s
"Lavish Expenditure" chapter provides an alternate approach that justifies both spending and moderation. It proposed a two-stage political
strategy for the ruler, one of lavish spending followed by a "return" from
spending.

The management of wealth (accumulation, spending) is in the *Guanzi*'s "Lavish Expenditure," as it was in Sima Xiangru's "*Fu* on the Excursion Hunt," part of a political struggle between competing regional powers. At one point Duke Huan asks, "What about exercising control over
the feudal lords?" In his response Guanzi explains the following:

> "If your wealth is equal to that of others, you will face competition; if it
> is twice that of others, the people will be pleased; if it is ten times that of
> others, they will be submissive, if it is a hundred times that of others,
> they will be transformed. You will have achieved [your aim] without
> their realization. People will look forward to the future. Once this has
> come to pass and you have changed the names for things, you may exer-
> cise control over the vassal lords."[108]

---

107. Indeed, the *fu* gestures towards this interpretation by citing a discussion in the
Mencius on the need for a ruler to renounce insatiable pleasures in hunting and wine
and devote himself to opening up granaries and supplying the people's needs. When
Lord No-Such (the imperial representative) cites this passage with "Summoning one's
vassal lords to present tribute is not for their material wealth, but for their 'reports on
their responsibilities'" (*shu zhi* 述職), he negates the use of length and ornament within
a Mencian moral calculus of thrift, *Shiji* 117.3016. On the analogy with *Mencius* 1B.4,
see Knechtges, *Wen xuan*, 2:108; Hervouet, *Le chapitre 117*, 135. Like Mencius, Sima
Xiangru crafts a historical dialogue—also set in the state of Qi—ostensibly to "remon-
strate" against his ruler's profligacy. Like Mencius's Yanzi, Sima Xiangru's Lord No-
Such invokes the necessary linguistic decorum of the vassal lords "reporting on responsibilities" (*shu zhi*). Like Mencius, Sima Xiangru uses hunting as the yardstick for the
moral economy. Indeed, in the final section of his *fu* the imaginary emperor signals his
return to thrift from excessive hunting precisely by opening the granaries to "supply
what is needed" (*bu bu zu*).

108. Li Xiangfeng, *Guanzi jiao zhu*, 705. Largely following the emended text and
translation of Rickett, *Guanzi* 2: 324.

Wealth guarantees political power. As elaborated in greater detail in the later "Qingzhong" chapters, one asserts and maintains hegemony through competitive accumulation ("ten times"; "a hundred times"). The ruler's political rivals are not the merchants, craftsmen, seamstresses, or the general population (whom lavish expenditure seeks to aid), but the hereditary "vassal lords" (*zhuhou*), kings, and nobles.[109] In Sima Xiangru's case, the emperor's representative competes with the representatives of wealthy kings. When the *fu*'s interlocutors condemn each other's rivalry, desire to boast, and "use of more wasteful extravagance to beat each other, each surpassing the other with wilder excess," and when Lord No-Such asserts the tributary obligations of vassal lords, they clarify the political stakes of their verbal jousts.

Unlike traditional texts of frugality (or indeed Keynesian economics), lavish expenditure promoted the ruler's active pursuit of hegemony. Although Guanzi promoted the accumulation of wealth a "hundred times" that of his rivals, the point of lavish expenditure was also to shape the consumptive habits of the wealthy by getting them to spend.

> Duke Huan asked: "How does one bring about reform?"
>
> Guanzi replied: "There is nothing better than lavish expenditure (*chi mi*). If you belittle necessary things (*shi* 實) and respect useless ones (*wu yong* 無用), then you can control[110] other people. Therefore belittle grain and rice, but treat pearls and jade as worthy of honor; show fondness for rites and music but treat (ordinary) production as of little value. This is the beginning of (recovering) the 'root' (*ben*)."[111]

Since the exemplary ruler shapes the tastes and behaviors of his subjects, he can subversively value "useless" (*wu yong*) jades and pearls, and devalue "real" or quotidian necessities (*shi*). As in the *Guanzi*'s "Qingzhong" section on economic theory, the ruler must develop the market to aid the agricultural economy and to deplete the resources of others. Here, however, Guanzi advises manipulating the market by shaping market desires rather than market prices per se. Such imitative desires

---

109. On this term, see Loewe, *The Men Who Governed China*, 283.

110. There are different interpretations of the character *xing* 刑. Zhang Wenhu emends it to *zhi* 制 in the sense of to "control"; He Ruzhang and Guo Moruo to *xing* 型, to "mold" or "shape." Li Xiangfeng, *Guanzi jiao zhu*, 635.

111. Li Xiangfeng, *Guanzi jiao zhu*, 633–34; Wu Baosan, *Guanzi jingji sixiang*, 175–76.

underlie the vogue for the useless (*wu yong*) and the disregard for life's reality (*shi*) that are thematized in the *fu*'s internal poetics and its subsequent reception. The "Lavish Expenditure" chapter goes on to clarify that those with whom the ruler competes politically are—as in Sima Xiangru's *fu*—his rich vassal lords, and not the people "on whose behalf we accumulate wealth."[112]

The second stage of the ruler's lavish expenditure (within this pre-*qingzhong* economics chapter) provides a potential template for the *fu*'s epiphanic return. To stimulate the markets, increase employment, and control his rivals' consumption, the ruler spends lavishly. To maintain political hegemony, however, the ruler then needs to rein in his own personal spending. In the "Lavish Expenditure" chapter, the ruler's use of spending takes the metaphorical figure of a journey from which he must at a certain point "return" (*fan* 返): "Those who wander far, too steeped in their pleasures to return, will be defeated and lost. They are like a wine-vessel with a top too broad for its base, whose contents spill over and destabilize the bottom. Their subordinates are remiss with orders and do not administer well. This failure of superiors and subordinates to provide sufficient mutual support surmounts to ruin."[113] The pleasure-filled journey out is necessary to encourage potential rivals to competitively waste away

---

112. Li Xiangfeng, *Guanzi jiao zhu*, 652–53. "Guanzi said, '. . . If the rich are extravagant (*mi*), the poor can work for them. In this way, the pleasures of the hundred surnames yield all kinds of stimuli and food for those who could not do such things on their own. It is on the behalf (of the people) that we accumulate wealth.'" This largely follows the respective interpretations of Guo Moruo, Wu Baosan, and Rickett. See Guo Moruo, "'Chimi' de yanjiu," 127; Wu Baosan, *Guanzi jingji sixiang*, 180–81; Rickett, *Guanzi*, 310. Three aspects of this passage stand out. First, it naturalizes the desire for market luxuries (*chi*). The ruler here does not shape popular taste, but rather, as in Sima Qian's idealized political economy (addressed in chapter 3) acts in accordance with human desires. The ruler politically benefits from his subjects' pursuit of pleasures that go beyond satisfaction of basic needs (water and clothing) because happy subjects make docile and productive subjects. This is useful especially in times of war. Second, it stresses the need to keep merchants and traders unconstrained, affirming their positive role in the economy. Third, the ruler's hegemony over the feudal lords, rather than over the people per se, is at stake. Here and elsewhere, craftsmen, seamstresses, merchants, and the poor appear as the needy but politically unthreatening economic beneficiaries of lavish expenditure. The vassal lords and the wealthy, however, compete with the ruler as they imitate his expenditure.

113. Li Xiangfeng, *Guanzi jiao zhu*, 680; Rickett, *Guanzi*, 317. This passage is very corrupt and I follow the emendations of Guo Moruo, He Ruzhang, Ding Shihan, and

their politically threatening hoards of capital. "Returning" back is necessary to prevent defeat and political instability.[114] The chapter does not
explain when or how the ruler begins to self-regulate. However, both the
return home and the excess of wine prefigure the turning points for Sima
Xiangru's cavorting emperor in the "*Fu* on the Excursion Hunt."

The *fu*'s turning point comes near the end of Lord No-Such's lengthy
speech, after his florid enumeration of the splendors of the imperial preserve. Lord No-Such describes the imaginary emperor's epiphany during
the post-hunt festivities:

> "Thereupon, in the intoxicated midst of wine and music, the Son of
> Heaven, dizzy and pensive as if lost, says: 'Alas, this great extravagance is
> excessive (*ci tai she chi* 此泰奢侈!)! I idle away time between audiences.
> Without business to attend to I lose track of days, pursuing the Heavenly
> cycle of time by killing and attacking, taking occasional rests here. But I
> fear the exorbitant luxuries (*mi li*) of later generations who in following
> this path will never return (*fan* 反). This is not the way to make and pass
> down your achievements.' Thereupon [the Son of Heaven] ceases his wine-
> drinking, ends the hunt, and commands his officials, saying, 'Let land
> that can be reclaimed and cultivated be made into farmland for the ben-
> efit of the common people.'"[115]

Just as the *Guanzi*'s ruler fears reaching a point of no return (in his journey and in the simile of the unstable and overfilled wine-vessel), so Sima
Xiangru's emperor ends his drinking and hunting lest his heirs "will be
unable to turn back."[116] Both use a language of loss ("as if he had lost
[*wang* 亡] something"). Although the opening up of farmland for the people was a perennial refrain in pro-frugality classical texts, lavish expenditure also legitimizes itself in the discourse of providing for the poor.[117]

Zhang Peilun that Rickett adopts: 逍遙才，臧於荒，返於連，比若是者，必從是儒亡
乎。辟之若尊觶，末勝其本，亡流而下不平。下茍令不治，高下者不足以相待，此謂毀。

114. Cf. Guo, "'Chimi' de yanjiu."

115. Hervouet, *Le chapitre 117*, 134–35; *Shiji* 129.3041. On the *Hanshu* wording of this,
see below.

116. One might compare Guanzi's simile to Zhuangzi's "tipping-vessel speech" (*zhi
yan* 卮言), or everyday discourse in which different positions can be freely adopted. See
Zhuangzi 33.1098–99; *Zhuangzi* 27. See also Fried, "A Never-Stable Word."

117. One might also note, in light of the earlier discussion of "riding the empty void,"
that throughout the *Guanzi*'s "Light and Heavy" chapters—including those that reap-
praise extravagant expenditure—"riding a horse" (*cheng ma*) had the technical meaning
of "to calculate" or "state finances" (and "to multiply" in mathematical texts).

Some modern scholars have understood the *fu*'s late epiphany within a tradition of what might be called the valorized "limit-experience," or thought-experiments in which the empirical testing of the thresholds of pleasures was necessary to attain certain forms of knowledge or self-realization. For example, Mei Sheng's "*Fu* on the Seven Stimuli" details a whole series of pleasure-filled sensory stimulants for a bed-ridden prince, who is finally cured by the proposal that he listen to the words of philosophers and occult masters of techniques.[118] Such *fu* not only described the topic at hand, they also achieved the solution through performance, through the "magic power of words." As the occasion and topic of the *fu* varied, so did its function. If the function of the original "*Fu* on the Excursion Hunt" was to promote lavish expenditure (or at least to show its productive possibilities), then the emperor's limit-experience—and hence the new aesthetics of the epideictic *fu*—prescribes its own utility. Just as ornamental display stimulates production and consumption, so the return to moderation promotes political stability.

PERSONIFYING EXPENDITURE: SIR VACUOUS AND (MR.) GREAT EXTRAVAGANCE

The diverse Guanzian writings on lavish expenditure potentially provided a generic—as well as ideological—resource for Sima Xiangru. The *Guanzi*'s "Lavish Expenditure" chapter offered an economic justification for length, ornament, and the structure of "return"; the *Guanzi*'s later "Qingzhong" ("Light and Heavy") chapters model a literary template for debating lavish spending through staged dialogues that included personified characters. As mentioned above, the *Guanzi* was a multi-authored aggregate of chapters that straddled arguments for and against lavish expenditure. The "Qingzhong" chapters composed in the mid- to late Former Han, probably around the time of Emperor Wu's reign, had the same political ideal of hegemony as the earlier "Lavish Expenditure" chapter, but they disputed the effectiveness of lavish spending

---

118. Kern, "Western Han Aesthetics"; Frankel, "An Early *Fu*." This relation of description to resolution may also be found in the *Wuxingpian* commentary on the *Classic of Odes* that was interred in 168 BCE; this commentary describes a kind of *askesis* by which the reader needs to contemplate the "lesser desires" (*xiao hao* 小好) suggested in the opening Ode in order to recognize his "greater desire" (*da hao* 大好) for proper ritual. See Riegel, "Eros, Introversion, and the Beginnings of *Shijing* Commentary."

for this end. For the "Qingzhong" chapters, the newly discovered law of ceaseless market price fluctuation ("light and heavy," "quantitative theory of money") demanded carefully timed and calculated purchases and sales in order to guarantee supply, and to make competitors economically (and hence politically) dependent. In direct contradiction of the funerary aesthetics of "Lavish Expenditure," Guanzi now argued: "When great officers build high (*gao*) their grave mounds and beautify (*mei*) their tombs, they rob both the farm and marketplace of labor."[119] This critique of lavish expenditure within the later *Guanzi* differed from that of the ethicists of thrift (e.g., Mozi's call for a plain "three-inch thick coffin" standard[120]). For *qingzhong* economists, the flourishing of the market economy was still a primary goal. However, the state planner now needed to observe and manipulate the market, and not merely stimulate it through lavish spending.

Sima Xiangru's "*Fu* of the Excursion Hunt" draws on prose and *fu* traditions of guest-host dialogue, but remains the earliest extant *fu* to use speaking personifications. Within the "Lavish Expenditure" chapter, Duke Huan of Qi plays the traditional role of the benighted ruler in philosophical texts, simply posing leading questions for Guan Zhong (the eponymous Guanzi) to answer at length. The *Guanzi*'s "Qingzhong" chapters transform the basic tenets of this earlier chapter into speaking personifications. Great Extravagance (*Tai she* 泰奢), Privilege (*Te* 特), and Mr. Idle Fields (*Yitian* 佚田) of these Han dynasty "Qingzhong" chapters rehearse the "incorrect" position to be corrected. Great Extravagance makes his entrance as policy informant in the (anti-lavish spending) "Discourse on (Economic) Matters" (*Shi yu*):

桓公問管子曰：「事之至數可聞乎？」管子對曰：「何謂至數？」桓公曰：「泰奢教我曰：『惟蓋不脩，衣服不眾，則女事不泰。俎豆之禮不致牲，諸侯太牢，大夫少牢，不若此，則六畜不育。非高其臺榭，美其宮室，則群材不散。』此言何如？」管子曰：「非數也。」

Duke Huan asked Guanzi: "May I ask about the best method for handling economic affairs?"

Guanzi responded: "What do you mean by best method?"

---

119. Ma Feibai, *Guanzi Qing zhong pian*, 378; Rickett, *Guanzi*, 415.
120. On Mozi's call for 3-cun (about 7 cm) thick coffins, see the surviving "Jie zang" 節葬 ("On moderation in funerals") chapter of the *Mozi*.

Duke Huan said: "[Mr.] Great Extravagance (*Tai she*) taught me, 'If we do not develop carriage-curtain and umbrella production, if clothing does not glut the market, women's industry will not be great (*tai*). Sacrificial rites must use sacrificial animals. If the Greater Lao sacrifice of the feudal lords and the Lesser Lao sacrifice of the great officers do not do so, the six [types of] domestic animals will not multiply. If you do not build high (*gao*) your towers and pavilions, and beautify (*mei*) the palaces and chambers, diverse timbers will not be trafficked.' What do you think of his claim?"

Guanzi: "That is not the (best) method."[121]

As in the case of the fictional characters Mr. Calculate-y and Mr. Calculate-and-Measure in the *Guanzi*'s "Qingzhong" chapters (discussed in chapter 1), there is here an odd hybrid of the historical and the blatantly imaginary in the same representational domain of "reality." The *Guanzi*'s personification of economic principles bears more direct relevance to Sima Xiangru's metaphor of expenditure than to the other early tradition of personification found in the *Zhuangzi*. In Duke Huan's speech, Mr. Great Extravagance is allowed to explain the basic claim of the "Lavish Expenditure" chapter that high consumption of luxury items (like carriage-curtains, or pavilions) stimulates markets and increases employment (women's industry), before Guanzi corrects him.

There is an echo of this passage in the *Debate on Salt and Iron*. The Classical Scholars attack the "extravagance" of Emperor Wu's era throughout the book, and at one point Emperor Wu's economic adviser, Sang Hongyang, argues:

The Imperial Counselor said: ". . . The *junzi* moderates his extravagance but criticizes thrift. . . . Confucius said, 'Excessive thrift puts pressure on inferiors.' . . . Guanzi said: 'If palaces and chambers are not decorated, the timber supply cannot be fully exploited. If kitchens are not stocked, overpopulation by beasts and fowl cannot be checked. Without profits from commerce (*mo*, the "branch"), agricultural occupations (*ben*, the "root") will have no outlet. Without embroidered robes, women cannot be given work.' "[122]

The (classicist) author of the *Debate on Salt and Iron* makes Sang appear rhetorically manipulative. In paraphrasing the *Analects* and quoting

---

121. Ma Feibai, *Guanzi Qing zhong pian*, 175; Rickett, *Guanzi*, 368–69.
122. Wang Liqi, *Yantielun*, 39. See also Ma Feibai, *Guanzi Qingzhong pian*, 33–48.

Confucius (from an unknown source) he omits Confucius's well-known preference for thrift over extravagance. His quotation from the *Guanzi*, also not found in the extant tradition, resonates with Mr. Great Extravagance's claim that "if clothing does not glut the market, women's industry will not be great." Although Sang does not promote extravagance, his quotation and the discussion that follows, both tie the critique of thrift to the need for market expansion and regulation. Such a move to moderate expenditure seems closer to *qingzhong* economic reasoning. It is not the overworked weaver at stake, but the priority of market circulation.

One might also note that both Mr. Great Extravagance and Sir Vacuous are characters in dialogues staged in the state of Qi. *Fu*-scholars have rightly suggested that Sima Xiangru used Qi as a literary reference to Qu Yuan's tradition of *sao*-poetry. Given the *fu*'s primary economic metaphor of lavish expenditure, however, it may also be important that Guan Zhong's economic transformation of Qi was proverbial.

Both the *Guanzi*'s Mr. Great Extravagance and Sima Xiangru's Sir Vacuous personify historically controversial principles that also come under attack within their respective literary dialogues.[123] The *Guanzi*'s use of dialogue to refute an earlier ideological position differs from other recognized literary precedents for the *fu*'s structure, such as Mei Sheng's *fu* or Zhuangzi's "imputed speech." Mr. Great Extravagance expounds the theory of lavish expenditure that (the character) Guanzi criticizes.

---

123. The Marxist historian Guo Moruo made a passing comparison between the *Guanzi*'s and Sima Xiangru's use of personification in discussing why the *Guanzi* contains two contradictory approaches to lavish expenditure: "From this [contradiction] we can see a competitive struggle within theory that constitutes a reflection of sorts of class struggle. These [later chapters] are imaginary stories. Duke Huan and Guanzi need not and did not say such things. The names of the characters 'Great Extravagance' and 'Privilege' one immediately recognizes as mere inventions, akin to [Sima Xiangru's] 'Master Improbable' and 'Lord No-Such.'" See Guo Moruo, "'Chimi' de yanjiu," 157. Guo does not pursue the comparison, but for him the fiction that is "Great Extravagance" reflects the waning historical persistence of lavish expenditure theory through the second century BCE. In this account, the earlier "Lavish Expenditure" chapter reflects the ideology of the merchant or trader, and the contradiction between the *Guanzi* chapters reflects a class struggle between the increasingly powerful (pro-lavish expenditure) merchants and (anti-lavish expenditure) landlords of the Han dynasty. Setting aside his evolutionary framework, Guo's consideration of lavish expenditure in terms of merchant interests (promoting ceaseless market stimulation) usefully sets the stage for Sir Vacuous.

Similarly, "Sir Vacuous (*Zi Xu*) was named for his vacuous speech (*xu yan*)," as the *Shiji* and *Hanshu* observed.[124] Although Master Improbable and Lord No-Such criticize Sir Vacuous's style, he clearly sets a pattern for their own (long and ornamental) speeches, prior to the (brief and unornamented) final section after the emperor's epiphany. Unlike Mr. Great Extravagance, Sir Vacuous and his interlocutors do not promote explicit theories of vacuity, improbability, and nonexistence. Rather, they aesthetically demonstrate such principles. As we have seen, Lord No-Such's emperor registers the limit-point for the *fu*'s lavish expenditure with the cry "Alas, this great extravagance is excessive (*ci tai she chi*)." If the *fu* does indeed exploit the debates over lavish expenditure, then this may be a sly reference to Mr. Great Extravagance. For *tai* (great) and *she* (extravagance) belong to the lexicon of the later *Guanzi* chapters and not to that of "Lavish Expenditure." Mr. Great Extravagance wants women's industry to be great (*tai*); Mr. Privilege elsewhere argues that only "using three hundred burial clothes would be a great stinginess (*tai se* 泰嗇)."[125]

Together, the *Guanzi*'s "Lavish Expenditure" and "Qinghong" chapters open up a complex set of ideological and rhetorical resources for rethinking Sima Xiangru's aesthetics. The "Lavish Expenditure" chapter justifies the length, ornament, and the structure of "return" in Sima Xiangru's *fu*. If some form of *Guanzi*'s "Discourse on (Economic) Matters" chapter was available by the last third of the second century BCE, it offers an alternative template for the *fu*'s "return," staging ideological contradiction through dialogue and speaking personifications. There, Mr. Great Extravagance is allowed to speak at length, before Guanzi takes the opposite position. Although Guanzi rejects lavish expenditure, both interlocutors reason in terms of the political economy, not ritual propriety. If Sima Xiangru did indeed draw on Guanzian and not just classical discourses on lavish expenditure, was the "*Fu* on the Excursion Hunt" for or against lavish expenditure? Or did the *fu*'s aesthetics simply exploit contradiction? Sima Xiangru certainly knew how to play to multiple audiences. Years before he arrived at the imperial court, he found himself hostage to a drinking party of one of the wealthiest industrialists of

---

124. *Shiji* 117.3002; *Hanshu* 57.2533.

125. Ma Feibai, *Guanzi Qing zhong pian*, 378; Rickett, *Guanzi*, 415. Yang Xiong would also later preface his "Barricade Hunt Rhapsody" with a complaint of the "great extravagance" (*tai she*) of Emperor Wu's Shanglin Park.

Han China. Unable to politely decline yet another drunken request from the local magistrate that he entertain them with his lute, Sima Xiangru finally began to play. However, as his biography records, "Sima Xiangru pretended (*miu* 繆) to play out of respect for the magistrate, but actually sounded his desires through his lute to seduce" Zhuo Wenjun, the recently widowed daughter of his host.[126] Sima Xiangru promptly eloped with her, forfeiting her considerable dowry, to work as wine-sellers in the bustling marketplace of Chengdu (Sichuan). Such duplicity in his performance thus did not necessarily violate the classic dictate that "poetry express intent" (*shi yan zhi* 詩言志). He simply negotiated the protocols of different audiences in a single performance as he would, years later, with his "*Fu* on the Excursion Hunt."

Tributary Things

This chapter began with the contrast of the objects and things, between poetic images, whose meanings the classical reader at once decodes (e.g., the *Classic of Odes'* opening image of ospreys as signs of marriage), and the strange fruits listed in the Han *fu*. Many classical readers transformed the *fu*'s semantically opaque *things* into meaningful objects through their quantitative collectivity, as tokens of immoderate economic expenditure. The *fu*'s stylization of things—its lengthy thing-lists in four-syllable rhythms, or its euphonic patterning of the sounds and movements of things—could be decoded as part of a broader Han sociopolitics of taste, in which the aesthetic ornament and length of the poem raised political-economic questions of thrift, excess, lavish expenditure, and so on. Ancient and modern critics of the *fu* have approached the *fu*'s things in terms of the frontiers as well as the market, interpreting them as imperial tributary possessions.[127] In this type of analysis, the *fu* itself is a

---

126. *Shiji* 117.3000.

127. Lewis, *Writing and Authority*, 319–20: "The lists in the verse of Sima Xiangru, and in the other major Han rhapsodies . . . [suggest] that the realm of the emperor contains everything that the world has to offer. This possession of exotic objects was another fundamental feature of Han political power, leading to the notion of 'tribute.'" Knechtges, "The Emperor and Literature," 56–57: "Thus, the hunting park stands *pars pro toto* for the empire at large, and the panoply of rare and exotic objects that [Sima Xiangru] attributes to it are really representations of the profusion of marvelous things that exist within the Chinese cultural sphere . . . . Under [Emperor Wu], the *fu* be-

verbal picture or microcosm of empire. Its rhythmic catalogs of exotic tribute transform the genre into a celebration of unified, expansionist, empire. This tributary model of the *fu* is important for those epideictic *fu* on imperial parks and capitals that thematize empire, and it clarifies the ways in which the genre was historically celebrated or reproached for glorifying empire. At the same time, as in the case of expenditure, the notion of tributary empire was particularly fraught during the period of the *fu*'s development. As discussed in chapter 1, the extent of frontiers and markets and the role of central government in unified empire came under scrutiny, revision, and criticism during the Han. Emperor Wu and his economic advisers sought to establish a massively expanded, commercial-ized empire, in which the state depended heavily on market exchange and not simply on (political) forms of tribute. Han classicists turned to the idealized world of the "Tribute of Yu," seeking a more limited empire centered on the agricultural heartland. The political meaning of "tribute" (*gong* 貢) was, in other words, contested. This final section will briefly address ways in which Sima Xiangru and later *fu*-composers seem to have engaged the metaphor of tribute, and trace the re-alignment of the *fu*'s things with tributary objects after Sima Xiangru's more ambivalent "*Fu* on the Excursion Hunt*."

TRIBUTARY WORDS AND OBJECTS

The notion that the *fu*'s thing-lists should be understood as tribute-lists or tokens of imperial possession has been strengthened by analogy with more overt instruments of imperial regulation of language. Modern scholars have likened the *fu* to the synonymicon (a proto-dictionary and abecedarium) as an imperial treasury of words. Li Si 李斯 (ca. 280–208 BCE), prime minister of the Qin dynasty, introduced the *Cang Jie* 蒼頡 (named after the legendary inventor of writing) to disseminate the proper character forms in Small Seal script. During the Former Han this was combined with other works to produce the *Cang Jie pian* 蒼頡篇, a synonymicon of 3,300 characters entirely in rhyming four-character

---

comes almost exclusively a genre of the imperial court." Hervouet, *Un Poète de Cour*, 306: "L'oeuvre de Sseu-ma Siang-jou se situe plus dans l'espace que dans le temps: elle est avant tout une peinture du monde chinois, de l'univers matériel connu à son époque et, de façon secondaire seulement, une randonnée dans l'histoire chinoise."

lines.[128] It seems no accident that Sima Xiangru and other *fu*-composers such as Yang Xiong also participated in the subsequent revision of these manuals of words aimed at standardizing Chinese writing. Although Sima Xiangru's synonymicon, the *Fan jiang pian* 凡將篇, has not survived, portions of the Han dynasty *Cang Jie pian* have been excavated from sites located across China—including sites at the Han-Xiongnu frontier at Edsin-gol in Mongolia and on ancient routes to Central Asia near Dunhuang in Gansu.

Some portions of Sima Xiangru's *fu* resemble the word-lists of the extant *Cang Jie pian* in their loose classification of things by species and use of four-syllable rhyming lists. Sima Xiangru's *"Fu* on the Excursion Hunt" contains around 350 four-syllable lines, largely consisting of rhyming lists of things, but employs a much broader range of rhythms and rhymes throughout. Compare this line from the *Cang Jie pian*, "Crocodile, dragon, turtle, snake" (蛟龍龜蛇)—with two lines from the *fu*: "Divine turtle, crocodile, alligator, Hawksksbill, soft-shell, trionyx" (神龜蛟鼉，頰瑁涼鼉).[129] The expansion of the *fu*'s reptile list with the addition of the more rare species also typifies its greater tendency toward the atypical. The synonymicon had both technological and ideological functions that are suggested in fragments such as: "Cang Jie created writing/In order to educate later generations" (蒼頡作書，以教後嗣), and "[The Han] united all under Heaven./[It] amalgamated the world within its borders" ([漢]兼天下，海內並廁).[130] Through the transmission of the synonymicon imperial administrators asserted the sovereignty of the regulated script form (over other regional script forms) and insinuated imperial historiography into education. Thus the Han *fu*, like the synonymicon, was a repository of words in an increasingly unified and centralized world of words and things.[131] Of course unlike the administrator's written syn-

---

128. See Greatrix, "An Early Western Han Synonymicon"; Bottéro, "Cang Jie and the Invention of Writing." For the text of the copy of the *Cang Jie pian* to which the above discussion refers, see *Fuyang Hanjian Cang jie pian shiwen*. It was excavated in 1977 from a tomb at Fuyang in Anhui province that was closed in 165 BCE. For the text of other fragments of the *Cang Jie pian*, see Lin Meicun, *Shule he liu yu chu tu Han jian*.

129. *Shiji* 117.3004. This line is identical in the *Hanshu* and *Wenxuan* versions.

130. *Fuyang Hanjian Cang jie pian shiwen* slip C002. The word Han 漢 has been added following transmitted quotations of the *Cang Jie pian*.

131. See Liu Xie, *Wenxin dialong zhu*, 623–24.

onymicon, the Former Han *fu* primarily circulated in oral performance as court entertainment.

Another way of reading the *fu*'s exotica as imperial tribute comes from matching the *fu* to historical tribute. The word *putao* 蒲陶 (grape *vitis vinifera*), for example, appears for the first time in extant literature in Han dynasty historiography, in the *Shiji* and *Hanshu*. It appears in their record of Sima Xiangru's "*Fu* on the Excursion Hunt," supposedly presented to Emperor Wu around 135 BCE. Lord No-Such includes it among his four-syllable lists of imperial possessions:

盧橘夏孰，	Black kumquats that ripen in summer,
黄甘橙榛，	Yellow mandarins, coolie oranges, pomelos,
枇杷橪柿，	Loquats, wild jujubes, persimmons,
楟柰厚朴，	Wild pears, apples, magnolias,
梬棗楊梅，	Date plums, box myrtles,
櫻桃蒲陶，	Cherries, *grapes*,
隱夫鬱棣，	Dark poplars, dwarf cherries,
榙㯓荔枝，	Plums, and lychees
羅乎後宮。	Are spread among the rear palaces. [emphasis added][132]

This un-classical word *putao* also appears in the same historiographies in their respective accounts of Central Asia, in which Emperor Wu's ambassador Zhang Qian opens up new diplomatic and trade routes (later called the Silk Road):

> Hearing of the "heavenly horses" and of the *grape* (*putao*) [Emperor Wu] started communicating with Ferghana and Arsacid Persia [ca. 126 BCE]. From this time on, exotica such as bright pearls, patterned shells, lined rhinoceros-horn, and kingfisher feathers filled the inner palaces . . . hordes of great elephants, lions, fierce dogs, and ostriches were fed in the outer parks. Strange things of diverse regions from the four corners of the world arrived. Upon this, the Shanglin Park was enlarged [emphasis added].[133]

Here, the *Hanshu*'s "Account of the Western Regions" makes Central Asian horses and grapes the reason for Emperor Wu's militarized westward expansion. Grapes were a part of Emperor Wu's infamous "pursuit of exotic things" (*qiu qi wu* 求奇物)—that is, his pursuit of things that

132. *Shiji* 117.3028. Translation following Knechges, *Wen xuan* 2: 91–93. Both the *Hanshu* and *Wen xuan* versions include the *putao* grape.

133. *Hanshu* 96B. 3928. Cf. *Shiji* 3173–74.

he used to awe domestic and foreign subjects. Zhang Qian returned from Central Asia around a decade after Sima Xiangru's presentation of the "*Fu on the Excursion Hunt*." After this the Emperor enlarged his Shanglin Park, the same imperial preserve described in Sima Xiangru's *fu*, precisely to accommodate such exotic tribute exacted "from the four corners of the world." The strange fruit listed in "*Fu on the Excursion Hunt*" thus appear to have anticipated—or even incited—Emperor Wu's subsequent expansion of the park (and the empire).[134]

SIMA XIANGRU'S AMBIVALENT TRIBUTE

Sima Xiangru plays with the idea of the imperial tribute-list in his "*Fu on the Excursion Hunt*."[135] However the cross-cultural relations described in this *fu*, the first to be formally presented to an imperial court, do not resolve into classical patterns of a tributary empire. Unlike later Han *fu* on imperial parks and capitals, the "*Fu on the Excursion Hunt*" highlights *internal* political-economic conflict.[136] The *fu*'s famously florid thing-lists are chanted within a geopolitical context of contestation, not of compliance. As the imaginary map in figure 2.1 illustrates, the dialogue presents three regional sets of exotica. The *fu*'s two regional representatives do submit to the imperial envoy at the end, thereby rendering their own exotic objects simply part of the tributary realm. However, the *fu* remains structured by a critically *dialogic* form of display.[137]

---

134. Some philologists have attempted to account for Sima Xiangru's foreknowledge by interpreting his *putao* as a native Chinese wild grape, but it is also possible that the *Shiji* text is corrupt or that the grape (or news of its existence) entered China earlier than historical sources claim. See Berthold Laufer, "The Grape-Vine," *Sino-Iranica*, 220–45, and Chmielewski, "The Problem of Early Loan Words"; Knechtges, *Wen xuan*, 2:92, note to line 206. Compare Hervouet, *Le Chapitre*, 98, note 6.

135. As Nakashima Chiaki has pointed out, the imperial envoy Lord No-Such quotes two lines from a speech of the Qin adviser Li Si 李斯 (ca. 280–208 BCE) in which Li Si glorifies the exotica of Emperor Qin. See Nakashima, *Fu no Seiritsu to Tenkai*, 345–46, and *Shiji* 117.3038. Li Si was also the author of the *Cang jie* synonymicon, whose similarities to the *fu* were addressed in the discussion above.

136. Cao Shenggao, *Han fu yu Handai zhidu*, 154–55, and Gong Kechang, *Studies on the Han Fu*, 132–62, both argue that this *fu* demonstrates the rivalry between the vassal kings as well as praise for the emperor.

137. Without explicit reference to the "Imperial Hunt Rhapsody," Declercq, *Writing against the State*, 87–92, has explored the rhapsody's formal resemblances to another Han dynasty prose-poetic genre which demanded the dialogue form, namely the *shelun*

The states of Chu and Qi represent rival (imaginary) political-economic centers. Their exotica hint at unofficial land and maritime trade ties that extend across the borders of the Han Empire. This kind of competition between vassal lords and the emperor is addressed in the *Guanzi*'s theories of lavish expenditure (and in Han historiography) but not in the "Tribute of Yu" model.[138] Lord No-Such prefaces his description of the imperial park with the problem of decentralized foreign relations or competing centers of cross-regional exchange. Before his eulogy of the Shanglin Park's exotica he attacks the sovereign pretensions of the state of Qi:

今齊	Now [the state of] Qi
列爲東蕃,	Forms our barrier against aliens to the east
而外私肅慎,	But carries out its own foreign relations secretly with Sushen.
捐國隃限,	It has renounced our state by transgressing its borders,
越海而田,	By crossing the sea to hunt.
其於義固未可也。	Their [neglect] of righteousness certainly should not be allowed.[139]

Before this assertion by Lord No-Such, Master Improbable had extended the imaginary Qi dominion as far as Sushen (Manchuria, Jurchen), a topographic and ethnographic marker of the Han empire's northeastern borderlands. The imperial representative here asserts proper Han imperial

---

設論 "hypothetical questions." Within the traditional poetics of the *fu*, the guest-host dialogue form–like the topic of hunting—is simply a generic variation. On the role of the dialogue in the development of the *fu*, see Liu Chaojian, *Fu wen ben de yishu yanjiu*, 54–71.

138. Xiao Tong's 蕭統 (501–531) influential literary compilation (*Wen Xuan*) has helped to detach and downplay the significance of the *fu*'s dialogue structure, splitting the *fu* into two: the "*Fu* on Sir Vacuous" (presumed to be the *fu* that Emperor Wu heard before inviting Sima Xiangru to court) and the "*Fu* on Shanglin Park." The isolated "*Fu* on Shanglin Park" essentially extracts Lord No-Such's victorious celebration of *imperial* possessions and has since become the most famous of Sima Xiangru's compositions. Having dispensed with the ample boasts of rivals, the *fu* more readily resolves into a monologic display of imperial possessions suspended in a Han imperial present. And yet even this latter, longer section on the imperial park is framed by the competition itself, beginning with Lord No-Such's attack on his interlocutors. (I follow Gong Kechang, *Studies on the Han* Fu, 133–36, in reading the "*Fu* on the Excursion Hunt" as a single rhapsody.)

139. *Hanshu* 57A.2547; cf. *Shiji* 117.3016.

sovereignty over all foreign relations in condemning Qi's "illicit" or "secret" (*si*) relations with the foreign Sushen. One might note that just as Qi illicitly possesses "exotic species from strange lands," so Chu's Yunmeng park contains creatures from the Han-Xiongnu frontier, such as Xiongnu wild asses (*qiongqiong* 蛩蛩 and *juxu* 距虛 are Xiongnu words).[140]

Although the *fu*'s regional envoys submit to the imperial representative, the *fu* itself fails to unfold in the homogeneous space-time of imperial historiography. For this *fu*, compare the *story* (the order of events in chronological time) with the *plot* (the literary organization of events).[141] The fu's story in chronological time is as follows: the King of Chu and the Emperor go hunting in their respective parks (Hunt 1A and 1B, respectively); the King of Chu sends Sir Vacuous to Qi and the King of Qi takes Sir Vacuous and Master Improbable for a hunt (Hunt 2) during which Sir Vacuous boasts of the King of Chu's hunt (Hunt 1A). After hunting (Hunt 2), Sir Vacuous, Master Improbable, and Lord No-Such boast about their respective ruler's parks and hunts.

The *fu*'s plot—the writer's arrangement of events as distinct from the temporal sequence of the story—reverses the order: it begins with Hunt 2 and then has Sir Vacuous recall Hunt 1A, Master Improbable describe Qi's park, and Lord No-Such recall Hunt 1B. This means that neither of the hunting descriptions that comprise the bulk of the *fu* (Sir Vacuous on Hunt 1A and Lord No-Such on Hunt 1B) happen in the real time of the present tense. The *fu* does not follow a spatial logic, or unfold as the live poetic time of description of a single, unified, imperial gaze. Rather, the plot interrupts the conceit of the universal imperial present with the encounter between *plural* regional political centers. This first imperial *fu* (in the sense that it was the first to be formally presented before the Han imperial court) does not yet belong to imperial time, as later *fu* will.

Han historiography helps to contextualize this narrative theme of internal geopolitical rivalries, and of envoys caught between competing centers of exotic accumulation. The *Shiji* and *Hanshu* repeatedly draw

---

140. See Knechtges, *Wen Xuan*, 2:62.

141. In the distinction made by the Russian formalist Boris Tomashevsky, "the story requires not only indications of time, but also indications of cause," and "both story and plot include the same events, but in the plot the events are arranged and connected according to the orderly sequence in which they were presented in the work." See Tomashevsky, "Thematics."

attention to those during the Former Han who equaled, imitated, or challenged the Son of Heaven (*ni yu Tianzi* 擬於天子), added "Emperor" (*di*) to their seals, or took the place of the emperor by "calling their orders [imperial] edicts" (*cheng zhi* 稱制).[142] These were not the enemies without (e.g., the Xiongnu) but rather those within or at the shifting frontiers of the expanding Han empire.[143] Within the *Shiji*, the importance of envoys' words abroad becomes a historiographic factor in the rise and fall of states, and in the Han conquest of the regions around Sima Xiangru's state of Shu (in present day Sichuan) in the southwest. Three of the diplomatic envoys who had accompanied Sima Xiangru on his subsequent diplomatic missions, had to try to convince the King of Dian (in present day Yunnan) and the Marquis of Yelang (in present day Guizhou) to help the Han court find a route to Central Asia via India that would avoid the

---

142. This phrase is not used for legitimate emperors.

143. These included the Empress Dowager Lü, the founding Han emperor's widow, whose biography the *Shiji* and *Hanshu* group among those of early China's male emperors. She is the earliest to "call her orders edicts," and both the *Shiji* and excavated legal statutes from her reign suggest that her orders achieved such status. The other rival "empires" addressed below—including the three regional courts of vassal kings (*zhu hou wang* 諸侯王) who patronized the *fu* prior to Emperor Wu's reign—never received such recognition. These failed imperial pretentions or imaginations nevertheless shed light on the more complex geopolitical context in which exotic tribute—one of the symbolic trappings of the emperor—was trafficked, debated, and celebrated in verse. One should also note that Shu people played an ambivalent role in the imperial expansion into southwestern China as those compelled to help Han armies conquer neighboring regions. As a result of Tang Meng's consumption of Shu betel nut sauce among the Nanyue (Guangzhou) and of Zhang Qian's sighting of Shu cloth in Daxia (Bactria), Shu's location at the southwest frontier of the Han empire took on a new importance. Local leaders, such as Sima Xiangru's father-in-law, had themselves aided and benefited from the Qin colonization of Shu and its native population. Now they were ordered to supply labor and funding to construct the "road through the Southwestern Yi" (西南夷道) into modern day Guizhou and Yunnan in order to find a route to India (and thence to Bactrian allies against the Xiongnu). The *Shiji* records that Sima Xiangru himself initially recommended this costly and unsuccessful project and was sent to his birthplace to annex the regions surrounding Shu. See *Shiji* 116.2994. Later, Sima Xiangru recanted, using a fictional dialogue that, like the "*Fu* on the Excursion Hunt on the Son of Heaven," thematizes the *regional* geopolitics of expansion. Preserved in the same *Shiji* and *Hanshu* biography as his *fu*, this "Letter to the Elders of Shu" resembles the *fu* in its use of the creative envoy as a fictional persona.

Xiongnu and be acceptable to other local groups outside the Han south-western frontiers.[144]

> The King of Dian in dialogue with the Han envoys asked: "Which is larger, the Han [domain] or mine?" And the Marquis of Yelang also asked this. Because the roads between them did not connect, each thought himself ruler of a continent; they did not know about the immensity of the Han [empire]. When the envoys returned, they therefore emphasized in their speech that Dian was a large state, sufficient in its affairs to be attached as an ally. The emperor paid attention to their message.[145]

Local support for the imperial quest to make the unregulated trade route of Shu merchants into the new Han route to the west depended upon the verbal prowess of the envoys. When the two rulers of the neighboring regions remain unconvinced that the Han domain is larger than their own, the Han turns to military action. This episode is part of the conquest narrative of the entire southwest region that includes Dian and Yelang. This dialogue about the competitive size of domains postdates Sima Xiangru's first court presentation of his *fu*. However, it illustrates the commonplace problem confronted by the envoy during the era before Emperor Wu had successfully expanded the frontiers beyond the limited borders indicated in figure 2.1 (compare the expanded borders of China discussed in the introduction and illustrated in figure 0.1). Elsewhere, the *Shiji* juxtaposes the exemplary reports of the Silk Road pioneer Zhang Qian with his careerist followers who "competed in submitting reports that spoke of exotic wonders" and who "exaggerated" (言大 *yan da*) their tales and alienated the foreign states.[146]

Prior to Emperor Wu's reign, *fu* composition flourished in three powerful, regional royal courts, all of which Han historiography associ-

---

144. These three envoys were Wang Ranyu, Bo Shichang, and Lü Yueren.

145. *Shiji* 116.2996.

146. *Shiji* 123.3171. For other critiques of envoys' language or behavior, see *Shiji* 110.2900, 110.2919, 117.3044, 117.3053, 123.3173, and 123.3174. Sima Xiangru's boyhood hero was the legendary third-century BCE official Lin Xiangru, whose verbal prowess on behalf of his state earned him a flattering biography in the *Shiji*. Important here is the traditional license for the envoy's creativity that remained in tension with, but distinct from, the traditional binary of truth/lying (*shi/xu*).

ated with imperial pretensions or ambitions.[147] The *Shiji* and *Hanshu* biographies of Sima Xiangru associated his early *fu*-composition with the specific rivalry between Liu Wu 劉武, King of Liang (r. 168–143 BCE), and Emperor Jing 漢京帝 (r. 157–141 BCE). The latter had no interest in literature, and Sima Xiangru therefore moved from the imperial court to Liang, which had become a center for *fu*-composers. There, he reportedly composed an early version of, or prelude to, the "*Fu* on the Excursion Hunt of the Son of Heaven" (the "*Fu* on Sir Vacuous") during a period when the king of Liang had imperial ambitions. The King of Liang famously established a new hunting park over three hundred square *li* in size and, with his "incalculable" wealth, "manufactured weapons in great quantities, crossbows and spears by the hundreds of thousands; his coffers contained close to one hundred million gold and cash, and more jewels and precious objects than the [imperial] capital itself."[148] The King of Liang, the *Shiji* concludes, "was able to increase his wealth and enlarge his palaces, while his carriages and attire rivaled those of the Son of Heaven. In doing so he also transgressed."[149] Although Emperor Jing named the King of Liang his hunting companion in the Shanglin Park, Emperor Jing did not make him the Heir Apparent.[150] The symbolic trappings of the emperor, including the exotica-filled hunting

---

147. Liu Pi, King of Wu (r. 195–154 BCE), accumulated "wealth that equaled that of the Son of Heaven" and allied with other kings and with the Yue foreigners to instigate the unsuccessful Revolt of the Seven Kingdoms in 154 BCE. Liu An, King of Huainan (r. 164–122 BCE), used his own "Emperor's Seal" (皇帝璽) for a failed coup in 122 BCE, a generation after his father had called his own orders "imperial decrees" and "challenged the Son of Heaven." See *Shiji* 118.3076, and 118.3091.

148. My emphasis. *Shiji* 58.2083, and 58.2087.

149. *Shiji* 58.2089.

150. The 154 BCE Revolt of the Seven Kingdoms coincided with the defensive *heqin*-era against the Xiongnu. Political alliances between those in revolt and the Xiongnu had further threatened the central Han government. The *Shiji* records that the state of Liang was the main ally for the Han throughout the revolt, and the King of Liang would later boast of how his army had effectively saved the Han. See *Shiji* 58.2082 and 108.3077. The young Sima Xiangru was originally an attendant in Emperor Jing's court, and his own move to join the famous rhetoricians of the Liang court resulted from one of the King's several visits to the capital during this time. Although Emperor Jing named the King of Liang his hunting companion in the Shanglin Park, he did not make him the Heir Apparent. As a result, the King of Liang assassinated several imperial advisers and fell dangerously out of favor, before dying prematurely at the end of a private hunt.

park, are important to this anecdote. When Sima Xiangru submitted his "*Fu* on the Excursion Hunt" around 135 BCE, King Liang's ostentatious Eastern Park may well have outshone the still-neglected imperial Shanglin Park.[151] To make Chu and Qi's exotic things signify tributary objects, the *fu* suggests that tribute must adopt a quantitative logic of competitive accumulation.

RESTORING CLASSICAL TRIBUTE

Subsequent Han *fu* on imperial parks and capitals by Yang Xiong, Ban Gu, Zhang Heng 張衡 (78–139 CE), Zuo Si, and others borrowed Sima Xiangru's theme but restored the tributary order of the plot (i.e., the literary organization of events).[152] Collectively, these authors aligned the *fu* with the kind of imperial historiography that prevailed by the Later Han (to be discussed in chapter 3), enabling the more coherent reading of the *fu*'s things as tributary objects.

Yang Xiong, the most acclaimed *fu*-writer after Sima Xiangru, paid poetic homage to Sima Xiangru's "*Fu* on the Excursion Hunt" with two *fu* on imperial hunts in the Shanglin Park. Both were composed around 10 BCE, before Yang renounced the genre for its failure to guide imperial action. In Yang's "*Fu* on the Barricade Hunt" (*Jiaolie fu* 校獵賦), the fictional emperor rejects the extravagance of the Yunmeng Park (once celebrated by Sir Vacuous) and renounces the eponymous "excursion hunts" (*youlie*) of Sima Xiangru's *fu*.[153] Yang's *fu* dispenses, however, with Sima

---

151. The imaginary Sir Vacuous offers a glimpse of the opportunities a low-level official had to glimpse his lord's parks: "I have been fortunate enough to serve as a palace guard (*bi ren* 鄙人) for over ten years. From time to time I have accompanied the King on his excursions as he roamed his posterior park, and I caught a glimpse of what it contains. Even so I have not seen it all." Knechtges, *Wen Xuan*, 2:55.

152. Sima Xiangru himself likely appropriated this theme from a section of Mei Sheng's earlier "Seven Stimuli."

153. See Knechtges, *Wen Xuan*, 2:115–36, where it appears as the "Plume Hunt Rhapsody." On its naming as the "Barricade Hunt Rhapsody" (*Jiaolie fu*), for the alternative interpretation of *jiaolie* as "hunting contest," and for a comparison with Sima Xiangru's "Shanglin Park Rhapsody," see Knechtges, *The Han Rhapsody*, 63–80, and Knechtges, *Han Shu Biography of Yang Xiong*, 106–7, note 249. Knechtges argues that although Yang Xiong demonstrates a greater concern for critique and lesser interest in descriptive catalogs and supernatural fantasy than Sima Xiangru, and although Yang Xiong describes a historical hunt, this is the rhapsody that shows the greatest influence of Sima Xiangru on Yang Xiong.

Xiangru's dialogic frame and replaces the account of an internal rivalry of vassal kings with a triumphant record of imperial expansion.[154] Yang Xiong's autobiographical account in the *Hanshu* also records that this *fu* failed its classical moral-aesthetic aim of moderating imperial behavior. The idealized Emperor Cheng of Yang Xiong's rhapsody curbs his hunting extravagances (as in Sima Xiangru's *fu*). In Yang Xiong's anecdote in the *Hanshu*, however, the real Emperor Cheng (r. 33–7 BCE) ignores the *fu*'s model of moderation and imports exotic beasts to impress his foreign guests (*huren*).

Like his *"Fu on the Barricade Hunt,"* Yang Xiong's *"Fu on the Tall Poplars Palace"* (上長楊賦) describes the glittering imperial Shanglin Park but lacks a description of rival spectacles. Yang Xiong again frames the *fu* as a means of persuading the emperor not to indulge too much in hunting spectacles for foreign guests: "Since I used brush and ink to create my composition, I thus borrow [Mr.] Plume Grove as host and Sir Ink as guest for the purpose of swaying the emperor's opinion." The implicit rivals—representatives of foreign places, rather than of internal regional centers—remain the spectators and recipients of imperial benevolence, rather than the speaking competitors:

今年獵長楊 . . .	This year [the emperor] hunts at Tall Poplars . . .
羅千乘於林莽，	[He] Draws a thousand chariots into forest thickets,
列萬騎於山隅，	Arrays a myriad of cavalry along mountain crags,
帥軍踤阹，	Leads the army, marches them into a compound,
錫戎獲胡。	Allows the Rong and Hu to hunt and capture.

---

154. *Hanshu* 87A.3552; Knechtges, *Wen Xuan*, 2:133: "[The emperor's] beneficent repute soothes the Northern Di; / His martial might shakes the Southern Lin. / Thus, / Kings of the felt and fur tribes, / Chiefs of the Hu and Mo: / Send treasures, come with tribute, / And with raised arms, declare themselves vassals; / The rear of the line forms at Mount Lu." The ability of the emperor's mere reputation of benevolence (*ren sheng* 仁聲), and the righteousness of his martial might (*wu yi* 武義 *wu yi*) in conquering the foreigner recall the archaizing rhetoric of Warring States philosophical texts, and the belligerence of Han dynasty anti-Xiongnu rhetoric. The foreign has, as in many other rhapsodies of the Later Han period, expanded beyond the geopolitical reaches of the Five Classics, extending here as far as Mount Lu, probably the site of the Xiongnu court (near modern day Ulan Bator in Mongolia). Yang Xiong here inserts the Xiongnu within an idealized sinocentric model, as the submissive "kings of the felt and fur tribes." Most importantly, Yang Xiong's treasures are explicitly tribute offerings through which foreigners declare their political subordination.

... 此天下之窮覽極觀也。雖然，亦頗擾于農民。 .... This is the greatest spectacle, the most dazzling sight in the empire. However, it is also rather disruptive for the farmers.[155]

The fictional character Plume Grove responds with an account of China's relations with the outside world that unfolds in dynastic time—from the time of the first Qin emperor, through the reigns of successive Han emperors, from Emperor Gaozu, Emperor Wen, and Emperor Wu, to the present day Emperor Cheng 漢成帝 (r. 33–7 BCE). The space described within the *fu* is that of conquered or submissive territories. Towards the end of the *fu*, the territorial limits of the Han empire has stretched to historical limits:

夫天兵四臨，	[Mr. Plume Grove:] [Our] heavenly armies advance in each of the four directions;
幽都先加，	The Dark Capital [of the north, i.e., the Xiongnu] is the first we gain.
回戈邪指，	[Then] Turning back our spears, we aim them [southward],
南越相夷，	The Southern Yue [tribes] destroy each other.
靡節西征，	Our blazons ubiquitous, we invade the west
羌僰東馳。	The Qiang and Bo flee east.
是以遐方疏俗殊鄰絕黨之域，	Thus in distant regions, [places with] foreign customs, alien districts, and cut-off villages,
自上仁所不化，	Not yet transformed by the Emperor's benevolence,
茂德所不綏，	Not yet pacified by His flourishing virtue,
莫不蹻足抗手，	There are none who fail to move their feet and raise their arms,
請獻厥珍，	To beg to present their treasures [as tribute],
使海內澹然，	Thus making the empire peaceful.
永亡邊城之災，	Never again the calamities of death by the border walls,
金革之患。	[Nor] the sufferings of warfare.[156]

---

155. *Hanshu* 87B.3558. Compare Knechtges, *Wen Xuan*, 2:139.
156. *Hanshu* 87B.3563. Compare Knechtges, *Wen Xuan*, 2:145.

Yang Xiong's *"Fu* on the Tall Poplars Palace" is a historical portrait of the uninterrupted unfolding of tributary empire. Its celebration of expansionist military conquests draws on the classicist tropes of civilizing "transformation" (*hua* 化), "pacification" (*sui* 綏) and the submission of tribute ("begging to present their treasures").

Yang Xiong's approach to frontiers to a large degree reflects a new xenophobic discourse that seems to have emerged in specific relation to the protracted Han dynasty wars with the Xiongnu. Yang Xiong's *fu* follows the narrative shape and tenor of his political memorial to the subsequent ruler, Emperor Ai 漢哀帝 (7–1 BCE), which is preserved in the *Hanshu* "Account of the Xiongnu."[157] This memorial of 3 BCE on Xiongnu affairs also unfolds dynastically, highlighting similar events, and reserving special praise for Emperor Wu's drive against the Xiongnu. Yang Xiong's memorial, which successfully persuaded the emperor to allow the Xiongnu leader to pay court, claimed: "Those of the outer states are by heaven-given nature aggressive as hawks . . . it is difficult to transform them with goodness as they are easily made evil."[158] As will be discussed in chapter 3, the *Hanshu* authors similarly described the Xiongnu as radically untransformable, bestial foreigners in its rewriting of the (more ambivalent) *Shiji*'s "Account of the Xiongnu."

Ban Gu 班固 (32–92) also aligns his own epideictic *"Fu* on Two Capitals" (*Liang du fu* 兩都賦) with the unified perspective of imperial historiography. The two fictional interlocutors of this *fu* boast about the capitals of the Former Han (Chang'an) and Later Han (Luoyang) dynasties that they respectively represent. Each interlocutor narrates the historical achievements of his dynasty and describes its imperial hunting excursions. For both fictional representatives, the Han Empire is a unified entity, and they mark a clear distinction between the exotic imperial possessions within, and the enemy who views these possessions from without. For example, the speech of the representative of the Former Han capital climaxes with a lavish description of Emperor Wu's hunting excursion aimed at overawing the foreign enemy:

---

157. *Hanshu* 94B.3812–16. Yang Xiong's *fu* also ends with Ink Guest conceding defeat.
158. *Hanshu* 94B.2814.

爾乃盛娛游之壯觀，	And then, the grand spectacle of the heady pleasures of the hunting excursion
奮大武乎上囿，	Rouses great martial fervor in the imperial park,
因茲以威戎夸狄，	With this [the emperor] overawes the *Rong* and boasts to the *Di*,
燿威而講事。	Radiating such might, He transacts His affairs.[159]

Ban Gu here evokes and reappropriates its generic template (Lord No-Such's account of the Shanglin Park). Like Sima Xiangru's Lord No-Such, the representative of the Later Han capital goes on to win the argument, in part by condemning the excesses of the Former Han and the superior decorum of the Later Han. However, Ban Gu remaps the rivalry between political centers across historical time (the Former Han capital versus the Later Han capital) instead of across space.

Ban Gu and Yang Xiong thus replace the envoys of the vassal kings (in Sima Xiangru's "*Fu* on the Excursion Hunt") with an explicitly foreign audience (*Rong* and *Di*), strengthening the analogy between the hunt and the *fu* as displays of *imperial* possession. And whereas Sima Xiangru recounts three hunting excursions, Ban Gu, like Yang Xiong, recounts only one. There is no subversive geopolitical space like that opened up by Sir Vacuous's historical recollection. The interlocutors, in their respective dialogues, explore different stages of a single, unified, continuous Han imperial present. As with the *Hanshu* revisions of the *Shiji*'s "Account of the Xiongnu," to be discussed in chapter 3, the universalizing space-time of imperial historiography is founded upon a polar distinction between the speaking Han subject and the mute, alien, enemy without.

Zuo Si's preface to his "Three Capitals Rhapsody" (San du *fu* 三都 賦), composed decades after the fall of the Later Han dynasty, makes explicit the analogy between the *fu* and the classical tribute system.[160] He simultaneously uses the *fu*'s things to resurrect the genre from its dangerous proclivity to fiction:

---

159. *Hou Hanshu* 40A.1347.

160. I do not discuss Ban Zhao's "*Fu* on the Ostrich 大雀" here because of difficulties with its dating, but her composition on the ostrich from the Western Regions fits this tributary model and is cited as such by Ying-shih Yü. Ban Zhao, sister of Ban Gu, was a co-author of the *Hanshu*, and famous author of *Admonitions for Women*. See Swann, *Pan Chao*, 104–7; Idema, *The Red Brush*, 27–28; and chapter 4.

先王采焉，以觀土風。見「綠竹猗猗」則知衛地淇澳之產；見「在其版
屋」，則知秦野西戎之宅。故能居然而辨八方。然相如賦上林而引「盧
橘夏熟」，楊雄賦甘泉而陳「玉樹青蔥」，班固賦西都而歎以出比目，
張衡賦西京而述以遊海若。假稱珍怪，以爲潤色，若斯之類，匪啻于
茲。考之果木，則生非其壤；校之神物，則出非其所。於辭則易爲藻飾，
於義則虛而無徵。

The former kings gathered [the *Odes*] to observe local customs. On reading [the lines from the *Odes*] "Arthraxon and knotgrass, fresh and luxuri-
ant," one learns what the Wei region and the banks of the Qi river produced; on reading "He is in his wooden house" one learns about the
housing [material] of the Western Rong on the wastelands of Qin. Thus
one can use them [the *Odes*] to differentiate every region. However,
[Sima] Xiangru's *fu* on the Shanglin Park [i.e., "*Fu* on the Excursion
Hunt"] refers to "black kumquats ripening in summer"; Yang Xiong's
"*Fu* on the Sweet Springs Palace" depicts "jade trees green and verdant";
Ban Gu's "*Fu* on the Western Capital" [part of his "*Fu* on Two Capitals"]
admires the catching of "paired-eye" [fish]; Zhang Heng's "*Fu* on
the Western Capital" [part of his "*Fu* on Two Metropolises"] describes
the wandering Hairuo [ocean monster]. [In doing so] they fabricated
rare and strange things (*zhen guai*) to make [their *fu*] glisten with color.
These are not the only examples of this kind. If one examines their fruits
and trees, one [finds] they do not grow in the [specified] soils; if one
learns about their supernatural creatures, one [finds] they do not origi-
nate from the [specified] places. In terms of poetic phrasing [their *fu*]
could easily create ornamental embellishments; in terms of meaning
they were empty (*xu* 虛) and without truth.

余既思摹莫蒲二京而賦三都，其山川城邑則稽之地圖，其鳥獸草木則
驗之方志。

When I pondered how to write my "[*Fu* on] Three Capitals" patterned
on [Zhang Heng's] "*Fu* on Two Metropolises," I examined maps for
mountains, streams, towns, and districts, and verified birds, beasts,
plants, [and] trees in regional records.

何則？發言爲詩者，詠其所志也；升高能賦者，頌其所見也。美物者貴
依其本，讚事者宜本其實。匪本匪實，覽者奚信？且夫任土作貢，虞書
所著；辯物居方，周易所慎。聊舉其一隅，攝其體統，歸諸詁訓焉。

Why did I do this? One who expresses his voice in *shi* poetry sings
forth his intent; one who ascends the heights through his ability with
the *fu* commemorates what he sees. One who praises things (*mei wu
zhe* 美物者) values its origins; one who eulogizes actions should
take reality (*shi* 實) as his basis. If they do not [prize] basic origins and

reality, why should the reader trust them? Furthermore, one must determine tribute according to the [quality of] soil, as shown in the "Book of Yu" [of the *Book of Documents*]; and one must differentiate things according to their regional location, as the *Classic of Changes* advises. This [preface] touches upon but one aspect [of the *fu*], addresses their form and generalities, and leads them [to] conform to [philological] glosses and exegesis.[161]

Zuo Si wants *fu*-composition to follow the same (perceived) principles as those of the *Classic of Odes*, and *fu*-criticism to borrow the practices of historicist glossing and exegesis of the *Classic of Odes* that had become canonical by the end of the Later Han. He grounds his own *fu*'s exotica ("rarities and wonders") in historical facts (*shi*), consulting maps and gazetteers to verify the historical location of individual flora and fauna. He frames these exotica as tribute, taking the canonical Tribute of Yu paradigm of the *Book of Documents* as one of the basic templates for the *fu*'s exposition.[162] The later literary analogies of the *fu* to the patterns (*wen*) and to woven or painted designs (e.g., "joining vermilion ribbons to create the pattern"; "black and yellow pigments in painting") reaffirm the notion of the *fu* as an unchanging verbal picture, spectacle, or map of empire and its exotic tributary tokens.

Conclusion

Modern analyses of the development of the *fu* through the Later Han and post-Han period note a general reduction in this poetic form's size and ornamentality—a tendency away from exhaustive enumeration and exotic lists towards the briefer description of fewer, and often simpler and more definite objects. The rise of what came to be known as the "small *fu*" (*xiao fu*) and the *yongwu fu* 詠物賦 (*fu* devoted to single objects or phenomena) accompanied the declining popularity of the "great *fu*" (*da fu*), epitomized by the Han *fu* on imperial hunts and capitals.

---

161. *Wen xuan* 4: 172–74. Compare Knechtges, *Wen Xuan*, 1:337–39.

162. The "Book of Yu" (虞書) chapter discusses Yu's 禹 evaluation of the Nine Lands to establish appropriate tribute. The *Shiji* 29.1405 attributes the above phrase "to determine tribute according to the soil" (任土作貢) to a chapter of the *Book of Documents* (although it is not in the received version).

This chapter has explored the aesthetic development of the lavish earlier *fu* form in relation to the Former Han politics of frontier and market. Sima Xiangru's "*Fu* on the Excursion Hunt," the most influential example of this type, drew on existing classical poetic and *fu* traditions. However the style for which Sima Xiangru was celebrated, and later condemned—his intensification of euphonic ornament and his lengthy catalogs of exotic things—also drew on visual and written traditions that were not shaped by classical values. His literary figuration of lavish expenditure was integral to the innovation of the epideictic *fu*. Sima Xiangru's "*Fu* on the Excursion Hunt" exploited both moral and quantitative metaphors of expenditure. Its imaginary interlocutors articulate a proper classical condemnation of "extravagance" and an advocacy for return to frugal government. However, the signature length and ornament of this *fu* follow the quantitative logic of "lavish expenditure." This paradigmatic epideictic *fu* voiced thrift (the more moderate [or the less], the better), but also passionately espoused expenditure (the more, the better). Its rhythmic catalogs included not only classically recognizable objects, but also unfamiliar things whose sounds and imagery reflected the aesthetic tastes of the market world (for example, the sights and sounds of swirling sleeve-dancers). Within a couple of years of the *fu*'s initial presentation, Emperor Wu launched hugely costly military campaigns into foreign territories. Within decades, the state undertook massive public works projects; introduced state monopolies on iron, salt, liquor, and money; and expanded local and long-distance markets. At a time when the theory and politics of lavish expenditure were being debated, Sima Xiangru's work exploited a range of conflicting positions and generic forms.[163] Pro-thrift classicists such as Yang Xiong sought to re-embed lavish consumption in its exploitative social context, and worried about the relation of the *fu* to classical values. Yang Xiong, Ban Gu, and others contained the subversive potential of the *fu*'s new things by

---

163. His strategy might be compared to Pindar's manipulation of the notion of luxury (*habrosunē*) in Greek choral epinician works. As Leslie Kurke has shown, Pindar made luxury palatable to his civic audience—as well as to the aristocratic elites with whom luxury had long been associated—by redefining it as the outlay required for each athletic victory enjoyed by the public. See Kurke, "The Politics of *habrosune*." In Sima Xiangru's case, the imperial court rather than the broader "community" provides the primary scene of ideological contestation.

specifying their meaning as imperial tribute. By transforming the *fu*'s unfamiliar things into tributary objects, the *fu* could be understood as less about accumulation and competition and more about imperial majesty and unity, less about private wealth and more about the centralized reproduction of the long-term transactional order.[164] The next chapter explores the place of these sociopolitical and geopolitical tensions in the development of Han historiography.

---

164. See the introduction for a discussion of transactional orders.

CHAPTER 3

Competition:
Historiography, Ethnography, and
Narrative Regulation

I stare into the black lenses. He goes on. "A reasonable inference is that the wooden slips contain messages passed between yourself and other parties, we do not know when. It remains for you to explain what the messages say and who the other parties were."
— J. M. Coetzee, *Waiting for the Barbarians*

Like the prose-poetic *fu*, historiography became a medium through which Han writers challenged or reformulated the classical ideal of tributary empire. In the paradigm enshrined in the *Book of Documents* ("Tribute of Yu"), the ruler's foreign and domestic subjects symbolically enacted the hierarchical political order through the annual exchange of material tribute. While the *fu* was embroiled in the Han politics of *things* (e.g., related to lavish spending, tribute, exotica), historiography introduced a new politics of persons. Both ancient and modern scholars have understood Han historiography as a way of introducing new discursive subjects into Chinese literature. Those groups perceived by classicists to pose the greatest threat to the Han dynasty tributary order— commercial profiteers at home and the enemy Xiongnu confederacy abroad—were identified as new types of people through historiography's innovative style of sustained historical, geographical, cultural, and biographical description. This chapter re-examines the representation of these occupants of Han frontiers and markets in the Han dynasty's two historiographies: Sima Qian's *Shiji*, composed before and during Emperor

Wu's activist reign in the Former Han period; and Ban Gu's *Hanshu*, composed during the political establishment of classicism in the Later Han period.[1]

As addressed in chapters 1 and 2, classical scholars traditionally assumed that literary works had a moral or political function. In this context historiography became particularly associated with the task of giving "praise and blame" (*bao bian* 褒貶) to the lives and actions of those it recorded. Thus the historiographic act was ideally another tributary transaction, part of the transmission as well as the historical representation of the ideal world order. The *Hanshu* praised—and self-consciously adopted—the *Shiji*'s new literary format, which comprised Basic Annals, Treatises, Tables, Hereditary Houses, and Accounts. The *Hanshu* also copied long passages from the *Shiji*, leading some scholars, ancient and modern, to treat certain chapters of the *Shiji* and *Hanshu* as more or less interchangeable. Other critics have, however, drawn attention to the *Hanshu*'s explicit criticism of the *Shiji*'s ideology, especially concerning the latter's approach to classicism and commerce. This chapter explores differences in the literary patterning of ideology in these two works. It argues that the *Shiji*'s use of ambiguous metaphors, authorial comments, and competing narrative perspectives disengages the historiographic act from the normative Zhou order. Within the China (or Central States) of the *Shiji* the businessperson (the "commodity producer" *huo zhi* 貨殖) replaces the state as the moral center of the market; at the frontiers, the Han envoys rather than the Xiongnu require regulation. Although the *Shiji*'s "Account of the Xiongnu" (*Xiongnu liezhuan*

---

1. As discussed in the introduction, the *Shiji* and *Hanshu* were composite texts and the *Shiji* has a particularly fraught transmission history. The convention adopted here will be to take Sima Qian as the author of the *Shiji* (with his father, Sima Tan); and to take Ban Gu as the author of the *Hanshu* (with his father Ban Biao 班彪 [3–54 CE], his sister Ban Zhao, and others as co-authors). When examining the *Shiji*'s postface and end comments to individual chapters of the *Shiji* and *Hanshu*—all of which take on an authorial voice—the main aim here will be to reconstruct the text's authorial *persona* (e.g., the "Grand Astrologer" constructed from the authorial comments that follow "the Grand Astrologer says" [*Tai shi gong yue* 太史公曰] at the end of *Shiji* chapters), rather to provide a historical biography of individual authors. One might in this way approach Chu Shaosun's early additions to the *Shiji* from the first century BCE (although generally not discussed in my book) not as inauthentic writings to be dismissed, but rather as distinct first-century BCE texts in themselves.

匈奴列傳, chapter 110) has long been commemorated for initiating the Chinese ethnographic tradition, there are overlooked ways in which the chapter brings its own ethnographic authority into question. The *Hanshu* regulates and clarifies the *Shiji*'s ambivalent moral meanings through editing and reframing. In its cultural ethnographies of frontier and market, the *Hanshu* recasts the Xiongnu as the morally unchangeable foreigner and the biographies of commodity producers into parables of vice. The work thereby corrects the *Shiji*'s un-classical proposals and restores domestic and foreign markets—as well as the historiographer's role—within an updated version of the classical tributary order.

The Shiji *and* Hanshu

Ancient and modern metaphors for the *Shiji* abound: a cloudy mirror, the eyes and ears of a sage, a capital city, a tomb, a microcosm, a universal encyclopedia.[2] To these one might add a marketplace. Despite the parallel content of much of the *Shiji* and *Hanshu*, ancient and modern readers have long emphasized the peculiarities of the former's literary style. Although the *Shiji* represents its task as merely selecting and transmitting reliable and worthy records of the past, it presents events and people from multiple, often irreconcilable, perspectives across different chapters, and across narratives and explicit commentaries.[3] By the Han period, readers had long approached historiography with a hermeneutics of recovery, aiming to reconstruct Confucius's original intentions in the *Spring and Autumn Annals* and the meanings of its commentaries. Modern readers continue to debate the ideological transparency of the *Zuo Commentary on the Spring and Autumn Annals* (*Chunqiu zuozhuan* 春秋左傳); likewise, the *Hanshu* contains recognized passages that constitute

---

2. *Hou Hanshu* 40A.1386; Durrant, *The Cloudy Mirror*; Pan Yinge, *Shiji huozhi zhuan xin quan*; Hardy, *Worlds of Bamboo and Bronze*; Lewis, *Writing and Authority*; Vankeerberghen, "Texts and authors in the *Shiji*." Part of this chapter is based on Chin, "Defamiliarizing the Foreigner."

3. In "The Idea of Authority in the *Shih chi*," Wai-yee Li shows how Sima Qian establishes his moral authority by promoting the task of memorializing human affairs alongside that of elucidating transcendental patterns, and by mediating between a wide spectrum of attitudes in his narrative and commentary, "ranging from ironic detachment to sympathetic identification, from verification to skepticism."

a critique (albeit indirect).[4] However, the problem of the *Shiji*'s implied meanings—that is, the ambivalence or ambiguity of its authorial positions, and its failure to consistently propagate the expected moral message—became far more central to scholarship on the *Shiji* than on the *Hanshu*. Unlike the *Hanshu*, the *Shiji* was periodically celebrated or condemned as a politically "defamatory book" (*bangshu* 謗書).[5] In the specific chapters examined below, Sima Qian allows his variant narratives and metaphorical possibilities to compete with each other for credence in ways that Ban Gu's revised version does not.[6]

The politics of markets and frontiers feature prominently in traditional explanations of the *Shiji*'s "defamatory" nature. Ban Biao, co-author of the *Hanshu*, singled out the "Account of the commodity producers" (*Huozhi liezhuan* 貨殖列傳, chapter 129) as one of the two most dangerous chapters of the *Shiji*.

其論術學，則崇黃老而薄　五經；序貨殖，則輕仁義而羞貧窮；道游俠，則賤守節而貴俗功：此其大敝傷道，所以過極刑之咎也。

In his discussion of techniques and learning [Sima Qian] venerates Huang-Lao and slights the Five Classics. His narration of the "Commodity Producers" devalues benevolence and integrity and shames the poor and needy; that of the way of "Wandering Knights" demeans modesty and moderation and values vulgar achievement. These seriously breached and damaged the proper Way, for which he was punished with the maximum penalty.[7]

In Ban Biao's view, historiography's proper moral function was "praise and blame" and Ban here criticizes the *Shiji*'s ideological underpinning. Sima Qian failed to prioritize the Five Classics and, as Ban Gu elaborated, "In judging right and wrong he [Sima Qian] strays somewhat

---

4. For an introduction to differing views about the transparency of the *Zuo Commentary* and for further bibliography, see Wai-yee Li, *The Readability of the Past*, esp. 29–84. See also Schaberg, *The Patterned Past*; Pines, *Foundations of Confucian Thought*.

5. *Hou Hanshu* 60B, 2006. See Klein, "The History of a Historian." Ban Gu was however imprisoned before his acceptance.

6. This assessment builds on, but departs from, the very useful respective analyses of Nancy Lee Swann's *Food and Money* (in the historiography of money-makers, or "commodity producers"), and Nicola Di Cosmo's *Ancient China and Its Enemies* (in the historiography of the Xiongnu).

7. *Hou Hanshu* 80.1325.

from the Sage" (其是非頗繆於聖人).[8] The *Hanshu*'s method of rectifying the *Shiji* is visible in its approach to the two named chapters. Rather than simply excising the *Shiji*'s biographies of commodity producers (money-makers) and wandering knights (law-breakers who nevertheless heroically protected others) the *Hanshu* selectively copies, expands, and reframes them as those deserving blame, not praise. "What a pity they did not proceed along the proper course of virtue, but succumbed to an inferior way of life. Their deaths and the destruction of their families was not so unfortunate!" interpolated the *Hanshu* into the "Account of the Wandering Knights."[9]

Critics have long differed over the Bans' interpretation of the *Shiji*'s "Account of the Commodity Producers" (which "venerates power and profit and shames the lowly and poor," as Ban Gu rephrased it).[10] The *Shiji*'s view of wandering knights was recognized as more explicitly admiring than its somewhat ambiguous account of commodity producers. The *Shiji* seems to praise commodity producers; but in past centuries some scholars argued that Sima Qian was actually critical of the commodity producers, and that Sima Qian had used the chapter in a classicist vein either to indirectly criticize Emperor Wu's state monopolies and expansionist policies, or to illumine the dangerous impact of the market on society.[11] Since the nineteenth century, other scholars have re-evaluated

---

8. *Hanshu* 62.2737–8. Ban Gu goes on: "In discussing the Great Way he puts Huang-Lao before the Six Classics. His narration of the "[Account of the] Wandering Knights" disparages the inactive scholar and promotes criminal heroes. In transmitting the '[Account of the] Commodity Producers' he venerates power and profit and shames the lowly and poor. This is what clouds [his book]. (論大道則先黃老而後六經，序遊俠則退處士而進姦雄，述貨殖則崇勢利而羞賤貧，此其所蔽也。)

9. *Hanshu* 92.3699. On the *Hanshu*'s treatment of the commodity producers, see below.

10. *Hanshu* 62.2737–8. For a similar sentiment see, for example, Li Mengyang 李夢陽 (1472–1530) in Ling Zhilong, *Shiji pinglin* 6:891.

11. Pan Yinge, *Shiji huozhi zhuan xin quan*; Zhou Rong, *Shi xue tong lun*; Cao Yuanzhong 曹元忠 (1865–1923) and Li Changzhi 李長之 (1910–78) in Zhang Dake, *Shiji yanjiu jicheng*, 6: 612–17. Critics of state monopolies from Ye Shi 葉適 (Song dynasty) to Zhang Jiliang 張際亮 and Wu Yiyin 吳翊寅 (Qing dynasty) iterated the *Shiji*'s criticisms in reference to what they saw as modern day "profiteering" by the state. See Zhang Dake, *Shiji yanjiu jicheng*, vol. 6, 377; 608–609; 613–14. Mao Zan 茅瓚 (1499–?), Min Rulin 閔如霖 (1502–59), Mu Wenxi 穆文熙 (1532–1617) in Ling Zhilong, *Shiji pinglin* 史記評林, 6:900–936. Ye Shichang, *Gudai Zhongguo jingji sixiang shi*, 156, on Sima Qian's novel use of an economic standpoint from which to observe society.

the chapter as a more neutral, but prescient, analysis of the commercial world and of proto-"laissez faire" (*ziyou fangren* 自由放任) or "bourgeois" economics.[12]

This problem of interpretation—of the difficulty of identifying Sima Qian's "true" meaning or object of indirect criticism—has particular resonance with the "Account of the Xiongnu." Ban Biao's above-mentioned claim that Sima Qian was "punished with the maximum penalty"—because of these two chapters (and also because Sima Qian had strayed from classical traditions of thought)—is at odds with the better-known account of Sima Qian's punishment as a result of his involvement in frontier politics. As recounted in the *Shiji*'s final autobiographical chapter, "The Grand Scribe's narrative about himself" (*Taishi gong zi xu* 太史公自序, chapter 130), and the *Hanshu* biography of Sima Qian, Sima Qian faced the death sentence after appearing to defend a Han military general Li Ling 李陵 (d. 74 BCE), who had defected to the Xiongnu.[13] Unable to find the cash to pay for the full commutation of his punishment by Emperor Wu, Sima Qian accepted castration instead of death. He did so to fulfill his promise to his dying father that he complete the *Shiji*. From this dramatic episode came the longstanding conception of the *Shiji* as the work of someone who was artfully encoding his frustrations and a political critique. In this vein, the Ming dynasty commentator Dong Fen 董份 (1510–95) explained the "Account of the Commodity Producers" in terms of Sima Qian's personal experience with Xiongnu politics.[14]

---

12. Guo Songtao 郭嵩燾 (1818–91) and Cao Yuanzhong 曹元忠 (1865–1923) in Zhang Dake, *Shiji yanjiu jicheng*, 6:610–13. Liang Qichao, "Shiji huozhi zhuan xin quan," 35–46; Han Fuzhi, *Liang Han de jingji sixiang*, 64–82; Hu Jichuang, *Concise History of Chinese Economic Thought*, 242–47.

13. *Shiji* 130.3300. Li Ling allegedly confessed: "I have already taken on foreign dress." On the likelihood that Sima Qian completed the chapters involving Han dynasty events (including the "Account of the Xiongnu") after his castration, see William H. Nienhauser, "A Note on a Textual Problem in the 'Shih chi' and Some Speculations Concerning the Compilation of the Hereditary Houses," 39–58. For the longer version of these events, see *Hanshu* 62.2730. This is found in a letter to Sima Qian's friend Ren An 任安, which is preserved in the *Hanshu*'s chapter-length biography of Sima Qian. For Li Ling's statement to Han envoys, not in the *Shiji*, see *Hanshu* 54.2458. See Klein, "History of the Historian" for further discussion and bibliography.

14. Ling Zhilong, *Shiji pinglin*, 6:891–92.

This still-influential approach to the *Shiji* as the lyric expression of the historical Sima Qian stands at the opposite end of a spectrum from studies of the *Shiji* as a textual repository of original imperial archival materials. Both approaches are useful, but the Han dynasty anxiety about the possible political meanings of the *Shiji* matters here for two reasons. First, it helps one to reconstruct the literary expectations and methods of the Han historiographers. Comparison of specific parallel chapters of the *Shiji* and *Hanshu* helps to reveal the ways in which they respectively manipulate metaphor and plot to give (or withhold) praise or blame. Thus the debate over the biography of Sima Qian matters not because its outcome will decode the "true meaning" of individual chapters, but because both the *Shiji* and *Hanshu* problematized or framed specific aspects of their historical narrative using authorial commentary and autobiography. It is precisely because the *Hanshu* discusses Sima Qian's neglect of the Five Classics and praise of moneymaking, and because it recounts Sima Qian's tragic relation to Emperor Wu's frontier politics, that the *Hanshu* revisions of the *Shiji*'s "Account of Commodity Producers" and "Account of the Xiongnu" specifically invite scrutiny.

Second, scholars have often blamed the *Shiji*'s troubled transmission history on its politics. The *Hanshu* composers reported that their copy of the *Shiji* already "lacked ten chapters; they have titles but no text."[15] Early scholars did replace or supplement portions of the damaged text—in some cases with parallel passages from the *Hanshu*—but there is general consensus now that these need to be established on a chapter-by-chapter (or passage-by-passage) basis. Clearly the "Account of Commodity Producers" survived to the Later Han, despite its scandalous content. Three paragraphs that appear towards the end of the "Account of the Xiongnu" and that partly concern Li Ling's infamous defection, have, however, come under suspicion and are excluded here.[16] The broader

---

15. *Hanshu* 62.2724. 十篇缺，有錄無書. See the introduction for a discussion of this broader issue.

16. According to Zhang Yan 張晏 (fl. 3rd c. CE), they were added by first-century BCE scholars Chu Shaosun and Liu Xiang and revised by Ban Biao (i.e., *Shiji* 110.2917–8). The *Suoyin* commentary records Zhang Yan's claim at *Shiji* 110.2919. Giele, "Translator's Note," 305–7, argues that the *Hanshu* version of the "Account of the Xiongnu" is a later work because it improves and "economizes the language," for example by scrapping particles. Honey, "The Han-Shu, Manuscript Evidence," by contrast, concludes that the *Shiji* version post-dates the *Hanshu* version, largely based on lexical variants in

aim is not to use these chapters to generalize about the *Shiji*, but rather, in highlighting literary aspects of chapters that are generally studied by historians, to reconstruct the role of historiography as a generic medium for ideological contestation about Han markets and frontiers.

THE *SHIJI*'S MARKET OF METAPHORS

"Commodity producers" (huo zhi 貨殖).   The *Shiji* begins and ends with an economic geography of China. The very first chapter, "Wu di ben ji" (Basic annals of the five emperors), introduces the tributary order of far antiquity: it recounts Yu's shaping of China's landscape, his organization of tribute, and his pacification of all foreigners within the "four seas." However, the final proper chapter of the *Shiji* before the autobiographical postface describes Han China's economic geography from the perspective of the market. This "Account of the Commodity Producers" introduces a new discursive subject, the "commodity producer" (*huo zhi*), and couples a regional economic geography of China with biographical sketches of prosperous individual commodity producers. This economic portrait of China excludes the six frontier regions whose conquest (or attempted conquest) by Emperor Wu the *Shiji* narrates in its respective chapters on the Xiongnu, Nanyue, Dongyue, Chaoxian, Xinan Yi, and Dayuan. However, the *Shiji* describes both frontier and central regions in terms of their customs (*su* 俗) and products. In the case of the "Account of the Commodity Producers" and the most important of its frontier chapters, the "Account of the Xiongnu," the *Shiji* uses new metaphors and competing narrative perspectives to describe the social transformation wrought by market exchange. In so doing, it defamiliarizes the historiographic act, disengaging its (often unclear) authorial perspective from the moral certainties of the tributary order.

Sima Qian defines the human subject in his final economic chapter on the commodity producers. In his authorial comment, which occupies most of the "Account of the Commodity Producers," the materially ap-

---

the parallel opening paragraph (the "ethnographic logos," on which see below). Since we are still left with the markedly different end comments, the chronology of the received versions of the opening passage does not affect the broader argument here. Chu Shaosun also made signed additions to ten *Shiji* chapters: 13, 20, 48, 49, 58, 60, 104, 126, 127, 128.

petitive body, not political or moral obligations, ultimately makes humans commensurate:

太史公曰：夫神農以前，吾不知已。至若詩書所述虞夏以來，耳目欲極聲色之好，口欲窮芻豢之味，身安逸樂，而心誇矜埶能之榮。使俗之漸民久矣，雖戶說以眇論，終不能化。故善者因之，其次利道之，其次教誨之，其次整齊之，最下者與之爭。

The Grand Scribe comments: I have no knowledge of the time before Shen Nong [the Divine Farmer]. But according to the reports of the *Odes* and *Book of Documents*, from the time of Emperor Shun and the Xia dynasty, ears and eyes have desired (*yu*) the most pleasing sounds and forms; mouths have desired (*yu*) the most savory tastes from pastured animals; bodies have found ease and respite in pleasure; minds have grown grandiose over the glories of power and ability. These habituated (desires) have seeped through the people for such a long time that even if one used detailed arguments to persuade each household, one would not, in the end, be able to transform them. Therefore the competent [ruler] is in accord with [the people/their desires]; the next best [ruler] uses profit (*li*) to guide them; the next best teaches them; the next best disciplines them; the worst competes against them.[17]

Sima Qian universalizes the mind and body's desires for material pleasure and power. He bases his fourfold ranking of rulers on their relation to their appetitive subjects. The most competent ruler is "in accord with" or "follows" them (*yin zhi* 因之); the very worst "competes against them" (*yu zhi zheng* 與之爭). The latter forms the basis for his implicit critique of Emperor Wu's market planning as a form of competition with the people.[18] As when he later rhetorically asks "What need is there of government directives?" Sima Qian implicitly criticizes Emperor Wu's market planning as a form of competition with the people.

---

17. *Shiji* 129.3253. Compare Jia Yi's "five baits," which described the greedy, profit-seeking Xiongnu in terms of their desiring bodily parts (mouths, etc.).

18. *Shiji* 30.1442. Ye Shichang, *Gudai Zhongguo jingji*, 152–57, points out that Dong Zhongshu had previously criticized influential officials for "competing with the people for profit," whereas Sima Qian was criticizing the state-run industrial monopolies that were in place during his time. In the "Treatise on the Balanced Standard," Sima Qian has the exemplary shepherd Bu Shi 卜式 (who voluntarily donates all his sheep to Emperor Wu's treasury) voicing this critique: "District officials should simply administer (property) taxes for food and clothing, but now Sang Hongyang [Wu's economic adviser] has ordered representatives to sit in the markets, arrayed in stalls, peddling goods in the pursuit of profit."

Commentators have debated the *Shiji*'s various uses of the *Laozi* and Daoist texts. The chapter begins with a short repudiation of the *Laozi*'s encouragement of the simple life, one free from material desires, travel, and career ambitions. At the same time, the chapter's low ranking of instruction and disciplining and its claim that without state-regulated activities people "will naturally come without having been summoned" (不召而自來) appears to draw from the *Laozi*.[19] What matters here, however, is the *Shiji*'s introduction of a somehow pre-political *homo economicus*. "Wealth is unlearned and always desired in human nature," Sima Qian states before cataloging the profit-seeking acts of soldiers, murderers, female entertainers, corrupt officials, as well as of any "farmer, artisan, trader and merchant" who simply sets something aside.[20] Sima Qian does not renounce political or moral obligations, but he also articulates a basic bio-economic definition of the human, impervious to differences in occupation, status, or moral behavior.

The *Shiji* introduces the "commodity producer" as the new ethical subject of the market economy. Han writers, as both the *Shiji* and *Hanshu* attest, worried that commerce was breaking down the classical division of Chinese society (that is, of farmers, artisans, and merchants) and upsetting traditional social orders. The pursuit of profit, traditionally restricted to merchants, now crosscut occupations. People were calculating status in terms of someone's monetary "worth," instead of using the official orders of rank (*jue*) or occupation dispensed by the emperor. Pre-Han texts such as the *Xunzi* or the *Book of Lord Shang* had argued that merchants failed to enrich, or had actively impoverished, the state; others like Han Fei and Mencius simply iterated the traditional moral emphasis on agriculture over commerce. The *Shiji*'s "Account of the Commodity Producers" radically displaces the merchant (and his moral baggage) with a new sociological and historical group, the "commodity producer." *Huo zhi*, which is generally translated as "money-makers" or "entrepreneurs," is a rare phrase that literally means "(to make) commodities blossom." At its locus classicus in the *Analects*, Confucius uses

---

19. *Shiji* 129.3254. This appears in both the received and excavated Mawangdui *Laozi*. Pan Yin Ge's *Shiji Huozhi zhuan xin quan* is one of the many commentaries that argue the importance of the *Laozi* quotation.

20. *Shiji* 129.3271.

it, somewhat ambiguously, to compare his wealthy disciple Zigong with his impoverished disciple Yan Hui (who died young):

子曰：「回也其庶乎，屢空。賜不受命，而貨殖焉，億則屢中。」

Confucius said: "[Yan] Hui is almost there but he is perpetually empty. [Zigong] did not accept his lot and he produced commodities (*huo zhi*). If we reckon up his results, then he is often on the mark."[21]

Commentators on the *Analects* have long debated whether Confucius is praising Zigong, Yan Hui, or both here. Since Confucius elsewhere discourages wealth accumulation, does he hold up the impoverished ("empty") Yan Hui as a model for the commercially inclined Zigong? Or does he concede that Zigong succeeds despite his outward turn to commerce?[22]

Sima Qian seems to exploit the moral ambiguity of this passage. On the one hand, Sima Qian presents China's self-made millionaires in a radically positive light. He explains, "They adapted to the changing times, and therefore their [biographies] are worth transmitting."[23] The *Hanshu*'s own "Account of the Commodity Producers" used the opposite interpretation of the commodity producer, presenting a parallel set of biographies as negative moral exemplars. On the other hand, Sima Qian does not praise all profit makers. He conceives the morality of the commodity producers in the traditional terms of classical texts. "When the gentleman (*junzi*) gets rich, he enjoys practicing virtue (*de*); when the mean person (*xiao ren*) gets rich, he uses it to wield force" (君子富，好行其德；小人富，以適其力).[24] "The upright official becomes wealthier over time; the upright merchant [always] ends up wealthy" (廉吏久，久更富，廉賈

---

21. *Lunyu* 11.19.

22. In analyzing Confucius's comparison between Yan Hui and Zigong, He Yan sees Confucius praising Yan Hui as an example to Zigong. Brooks and Brooks, *The Original Analects*, 73 and 77, argue that Yan Hui's acceptance of poverty and achievement through inner meditations are more likely being praised over Zigong's refusal to accept fate and his turning outward to commerce. By contrast, Li Ling, *Sang jia gou*, 215–16, emphasizes the symmetry at stake. One might freely render this alternate interpretation (taking the rhymes 空 and 中): "[Yan] Hui in his ponderings was often in the dark; Zigong refused his fate and prospered; he was often on the mark."

23. *Shiji* 129.3281. 變化有概，故足術也.

24. *Shiji* 129.3255. The wealthy Ren family were loved by their community and ruler because they only used local resources and never ate or drank before completing their duties to their community.

歸富).[25] Commercial profit seekers are, in other words, moral subjects—
junzi and wise men or worthies (*xian ren* 賢人)—who can and must
cultivate their virtue in business. Sima Qian's biographies preserve "the
means by which wise men have become wealthy, to allow later generations to observe and select [what is worthy] from it" (賢人所以富者,令
後世得以觀擇焉).[26] Zigong became Confucius's richest disciple by buying and selling at the right time, and used his wealth to propagate Confucius's teachings around the world. According to the *Shiji*, "[Fan Li
made] one thousand catties of gold three times, and each time distributed it amongst poor friends and distant relatives. This is what is meant
by a rich man who enjoys practicing virtue (*de*)."[27] Sima Qian essentially
shifts the moral agent of wealth redistribution from the state to the individual entrepreneur. The business ethics of such entrepreneurs stands in
stark contrast to Sima Qian's representation of disruptive state planning
in the *Shiji*'s "Treatise on the Balanced Standard." Unlike other advocates of the market (e.g., the "Qingzhong" chapters or Emperor Wu's
economic adviser, Sang Hongyang, in the *Debate on Salt and Iron*), Sima
Qian sanctions market activity with the morality of the profit-seeking
subject and not with that of the ruler of the tributary economy.

"Untitled nobility" (su feng 素封).   The question of whether Sima Qian
was actually celebrating the nouveaux riches and exploring their potential for moral action—or, as others have argued, gently mocking their
pretensions—is further complicated by his use of a particular phrase in
the "Account of the Commodity Producers." In the following passage,
Sima Qian introduces the phrase "untitled nobility" (literally "untitled
fief-holders" [*su feng* 素封])[28]:

> 由是觀之,富無經業,則貨無常主,能者輻湊,不肖者瓦解。千金之家比
> 一都之君,巨萬者乃與王者同樂。豈所謂「素封」者邪?非也?

---

25. *Shiji* 129.3271.
26. *Shiji* 129.3277.
27. *Shiji* 129.3257; compare *Shiji* 120.3280.
28. Both Watson, *Records of the Grand Historian: Han Dynasty*, 2: 454, and Swann,
Food and Money, 464, use the phrase "untitled nobility." The *Zhengyi* 正義 commentary
of eighth-century Zhang Shoujie 張守節 explains *su feng* as a term for those without
office whose profits from their own lands compare with those of an enfeoffed ruler
(*feng jun*).

From this one can see that wealth has no canonical set of occupations. Therefore money has no permanent master. It converges like spokes on a hub upon those with ability; it scatters like shattered tiles away from the worthless. A family with a thousand catties of gold can compare with a lord of a city; the owner of millions (of cash) can enjoy the same pleasures as a king. Surely they are the "untitled nobility" (*su feng*), are they not?[29]

Most ancient and modern readers have understood this passage as a commentary on money's ability to make those of different social status more commensurate with each other.[30] In this interpretation, any savvy commoner of any occupation can, by accumulating a thousand gold pieces "compare" (*bi*) to a lord. Most readers have also argued or assumed that Sima Qian makes this observation sympathetically—that he coins the phrase "untitled nobility" to celebrate the rise of the "commodity producers." Others have, however, suggested that Sima Qian uses the metaphor sarcastically. He mocks the emptiness (*su* 素, literally "uncolored silk") of the pseudo-nobility (*su feng*).[31] Or, in an alternate punctuation and translation of the final sentence, the metaphor names what millionaires, whatever their pretensions, are not ("Are they the so-called title-less lords? No.").[32] Does Sima Qian celebrate, criticize, or

---

29. *Shiji* 129.3282–83.

30. The *Zheng yi* comments, "[It] refers to those who are not officials who privately possess fields or orchards. Through the income from harvesting and [animal-]rearing, their profits make them comparable to an enfeoffed lord." Compare Sima Zhen's 司馬貞 eighth-century CE *Suoyin* 索隱: "It refers to those without social orders [rank, status] or territory who do not receive official salaries and so are called the 'untitled nobility.' *Su* means 'empty.'" Ye Shichang, *Gudai Zhongguo jingji sixiang shi*, 156, sees Sima Qian's introduction of the term *su feng* as a reflection of his novel use of an economic standpoint from which to observe society. Ma Biao, *Qin-Han haozu shehui yanjiu*, 23–28, argues that Sima Qian constructed the *su feng* to show that wealth determined social status and power for those without noble rank, because Sima Qian saw commerce as the best escape from poverty, and because merchants were looked down upon. Ma explains the origins of the *su feng* in the forced resettlement of traders captured by the Qin in the third century BCE (such as the Zhuo family). Bai Yulin, *Shiji jie du*, 2:506–7, defends Sima Qian against the traditional attack (begun by Ban Gu) that Sima Qian despised the poor. Bai argues that Sima Qian used the notion of *su feng* to emphasize the importance of material life and encouraged individuals to use their own abilities to get rich.

31. *Su* 素 refers to uncolored, unpatterned (i.e., pure) white silk.

32. Blue Rhea, "The Argumentation of the *Shih-Huo Chih*," reads this chapter as encouraging the government to curb the rise of profiteers: "[Sima Qian] concludes by

merely document the commodification of social status and the rise of money makers? Sima Qian's lengthy (130-chapter) encyclopedic historiography of the known world begins with an account of those of highest status (emperors) and proceeds through those of lower status (e.g., nobles, foreign neighbors, and professional groups). Excepting the final autobiographical postface ("The Grand Scribe's narrative about himself"), why does his book end with a consideration of the "untitled nobility"?[33] Sima Qian's use of the phrase "untitled nobility" articulated a broader Han anxiety over the challenge that wealth posed to traditional social status. "The merchant may be lowly according today's laws and regulations, but he is [actually] already wealthy and esteemed. We respect the farmer, but he is already impoverished and lowly," argued the Han official Chao Cuo 鼂錯 (d. 154 BCE).[34] Although social orders (*jue* 爵) were dispensed by the emperor and not for sale as such, possessing money appeared able to raise one's status *as if* acquiring an official title. From a historical perspective, the two institutions of social orders and land purchase helped to create the conditions in which the possession of wealth

---

warning that 'pseudo-enfeoffment' obtained through an 'increment of goods' will destroy the basis of the dynasty. The implication is that the government must take measures to control the 'clever' people." Chen, *The Economic Principles of Confucius and His School*, 179, argues: "[Sima Qian] believed in the laissez-faire policy. However he does not go to the extreme. . . . At the end of the whole chapter, he puts this negative answer for the withdrawal of his former statements. In fact, on the one hand, he likes large production, so that he thinks free competition is worthwhile; on the other hand, he hates unequal distribution, so that he employs sarcasm against the rich. To enlarge production and to equalize distribution is his final aim. Therefore, in his conclusion, he comes to the common point of the Confucians."

33. By ending with the suggestion that economic differences might mean as much as political orders of rank, Sima Qian upsets the political ordering of the *Shiji* itself. The *Shiji*'s respective accounts of emperors and of hereditary houses of feudal lords precede those of other groups and individuals, loosely reflecting a proper political order of priority. By placing the "Biographies of the Prosperous" last, Sima Qian relegates such persons to their traditionally low sociopolitical position. However, by then valorizing their abilities and recognizing their true worth (i.e., they are on a par with lords and kings), he undercuts the normative hierarchy. This interplay between what ought to be (as patterned in Heaven) and what actually happened (human choice and action) can be seen elsewhere in his use of "Accounts" (*lie zhuan*) of commoners to reframe or retell events recorded in the "Basic Annals" (*ben ji*) of emperors, e.g., by detailing the illegitimate birth of the First Emperor through the "Account of Lü Buwei."

34. *Hanshu* 24A.1133.

could challenge official rank. Social orders issued by imperial decree came with large gifts of land that were proportional to the given rank, thereby correlating official status with one form of wealth. Since land and orders were widely distributed and inheritable (including by women), a large proportion of the non-slave, non-convicted population held at least the lowest social order and at some point possessed land.[35] The opening up of land for purchase by individuals (*zi tian* 自田) or by households (*hu tian* 户田) during the Qin-Han period exacerbated economic inequality. Small-scale farmers who worked their own plots were highly vulnerable to bankruptcy and debt. The further pressures of taxation (a high poll tax but low land-rate tax) encouraged land sales and the formation of huge estates that either hired wage laborers and slaves or, more generally, rented land back (at a profit) to a rising number of debt-ridden farmers.[36]

Sima Qian was concerned with the one who benefited from this new socioeconomic landscape, not with the dispossessed farmer or the slave. His "Account of the Commodity Producers" introduces the concept of "untitled nobility" between a regional economic geography of China and Forbes-500-style biographical sketches of Han China's mega-rich.

今有無秩祿之奉，爵邑之入，而樂與之比者。命曰「素封」。封者食租稅，歲率戶二百。千戶之君則二十萬，朝覲聘享出其中。庶民農工商賈，率亦歲萬息二千（戶），百萬之家則二十萬，而更徭租賦出其中。衣食之欲，恣所好美矣。故曰陸地牧馬二百蹄，牛蹄角千，千足羊，澤中千足彘，水居千石魚陂，山居千章之材。安邑千樹棗；燕、秦千樹栗；蜀、漢、江陵千樹橘...及名國萬家之城，帶郭千畝畝鍾之田，若千畝巵茜，千畦薑韭：此其人皆與千戶侯等。然是富給之資也，不窺市井，不行異邑，坐而待收，身有處士之義而取給焉。

*Now there are those who do not receive the rewards of official rank or the gifts of honorary titles (*juc*) or [enfeoffed] territory (*yi*), but who enjoy the pleasures comparable (*bi*) to theirs. They should be named "untitled*

<hr>

35. Of the second highest and the lowest of the twenty orders (*jue*) beneath a king, these legal bamboo strips respectively state: "The noble of the interior (*guannei hou* 關內侯) receives 95 *qing* 頃 (about 40,565 English acres) . . . the *Gongshi* 公士 receives 1½ *qing* (about 64 acres)." See Zhangjiashan strips 310 and 312; for gifts of dwelling houses as well, see strips 314–16. See *Zhangjiashan Hanmu zhujian* 172–74. On Han social orders, see Loewe, "Social Distinctions, Groups, and Privileges," 298–307.

36. Hanshu 24A.1132. See Swann, *Food and Money*, 164.

nobility" (su feng).[37] Those who do have fiefs (*feng*) live on taxes from [those renting] their land, with an annual income rate of 200 cash per household. A lord of 1,000 households therefore collects 200,000 cash, from which he pays expenses for gifts for regular audiences at the imperial and local courts. For commoners (*shu min,* i.e., those who do not have titles)—whether farmers, artisans, traders, or businessmen—the annual rate of interest on 10,000 cash is 2,000; and a family with 1,000,000 cash will therefore earn 200,000 [per year],[38] from which they pay the expenses for the commutation of the [military and labor] corvée plus rent and taxes. They [can then] wear and eat whatever they like and indulge in whatever they find beautiful. Therefore it is said that the amount of land (*lu di*) on which one herds 200 hoofs of horses [i.e., 50], or a thousand horns and hoofs of cattle[39] or 1,000 hoofs of sheep; or a marshland (*ze*) in which there are 1,000 trotters of pigs; or a river (*shui*) that houses 1,000 piculs of reservoir fish; or a mountain (*shan*) that houses 1,000 logs of catalpa timber; or 1,000 date trees in Anyi, 1,000 chestnut trees in Yan or Qin, 1,000 citrus trees in Shu, Han or Jiangling . . . and also in the suburbs of a city of 10,000 families in a famous state, 1,000 *mu* of land that yields one *zhong* of grain per *mu,* or 1,000 *mu*

---

37. The parallel *Hanshu* version of this section replaces the first lines (on the *su feng*) with "Under the Qin-Han rule, the vassals and enfeoffed lords [lived off rent and taxes]." *Hanshu* 91.3686. Apart from the italicized sections, the remaining parts are largely similar (with some differences in phrasing).

38. Swann, *Food and Money,* 450, translates the parallel *Hanshu* line: "On the average also [each property of] ten thousand [cash] brings an annual interest rate of two thousand. [Such a] family (*chia,* like those with enfeoffed lands) with a million households *hu* thus derives two hundred thousand [cash]." This interpretation seems to gloss the somewhat ambiguous *Suoyin* comment on the *Shiji* version: 息二千，故百萬之家亦二十萬。("The interest [for 10,000] is 2,000, therefore for a family of 1,000,000 it is also 200,000"). Swann's interpretation works better with the punctuation of Ling Zhilong's *Shiji pinglin* (率亦歲萬息二十。户百萬之家則二十萬) than with the modern *Zhonghua shuju* versions of either the *Hanshu* and *Shiji* chapter (quoted above); the *Hanshu* version omits the bracketed 户 altogether. Since the traditional commentaries do not further clarify this, in this instance the interpretations of Ye Shichang and Watson (of the *Shiji* version), i.e., the "one million" modifies (an elided) "cash," makes more sense than a million households (*hu* 户). Swann's translation and analyses are otherwise very helpful. The term *lü* 率, which I translate twice in this passage as "income rate," is an important term in Han mathematical texts. On this see Chemla, "Documenting a Process of Abstraction."

39. For a parallel use of *lu di,* see Ma Feibai, *Guanzi Qing zhong pian xin quan,* 384. According to the *Ji jie,* which cites the commentary on the parallel *Hanshu* passage, "200 hoofs" means 50 horses, and "1000 horns and hoofs" means 167.

of gardenia or madder plants (for dyes), or 1,000 beds of ginger or leeks—
each person possessing any of these is commensurate (*deng*) with a marquis possessing 1,000 households. *Wealth such as this* (ran shi fu gei) *is [a
form of] capital* (zi).[40] *One does not have to scrutinize marketplaces and
wells, or travel to different cities: one [simply] sits* (zuo) *to receive the bounty;
one's life has the integrity of the scholar without office [even while one] collects income* [emphasis added].[41]

Sima Qian does not simply coin a metaphor; he recasts in economic
terms a philosophically positive notion of the untitled, unblemished, or
"uncrowned" king (*su wang* 素王). In diverse strands of philosophical
thought, the uncrowned king referred to the true sage who failed in his
lifetime to receive the recognition of his true worth (as king).[42] But is
this an earnest or an ironic appropriation? Sima Qian's description of the
essential leisure of the landed rich who "simply sit to receive the bounty"
bears a striking resemblance to Zhuangzi's formulation of the "effortless
action" (*wuwei*) of the uncrowned king.[43] Confucius, often identified as

---

40. *Fu gei* 富給 appears on two other occasions in the *Shiji*, nominalized as 富給者
"the wealthy." At *Shiji* 75.2360, it refers to those wealthy enough to pay the interest on
the loans to the Lord of Mengchang; in Chu Shaosun's addition to *Shiji* 104.2780, it
refers to the materially wealthy (as opposed to the worthy but poor) members of the
suite of Wei Qing 衛青 (d. 106 BCE), Emperor Wu's foremost general.

41. *Shiji* 129.32712.

42. Loewe, *Dong Zhongshu*, 172–77, demonstrates that although Confucius was referred to as *su wang* in Han texts, Confucius himself did not take part "in the formulation and use of the concept of *su wang*, which appears in texts that can in no way be
categorized as 'Confucian.'" According to a later commentator on the *Spring and Autumn Annals* (whose authorship was traditionally attributed to Confucius), supporters
of Zuo Qiuming's 左邱明 Commentary (*Zuozhuan* 左傳) called Confucius the "untitled official" (*su chen* 素臣). See Yang, *Studies in Chinese Institutional History*, 91.

43. The two references to the "uncrowned king" (*su wang*) in the *Shiji* do not, however,
refer to Confucius. See *Shiji* 3.94; 6.277. See *Zhuangzi ji jie*, 457: "Emptiness, stillness,
limpidity, silence, and effortless action (*wuwei*) are the root (*ben*) of the ten thousand
things. To understand them and face south is to become a ruler such as Yao was; to
understand them and face north is to become a minister such as Shun was. To have
them [while] in high office is the virtue of emperors, kings, and the Son of Heaven; to
have them [while] in low office is the way of the dark sage, the uncrowned king (*su
wang*). . . . In stillness you will be a sage, in action a king. Through effortless action
(*wuwei*), you will be honored." Zhuangzi's ideal of *wuwei* comprises, in Edward Slingerland's analysis, "a state in which one's actions are perfectly harmonized with one's
'natural' spontaneous inclinations." Slingerland, *Effortless Action*, 175. Sima Tan associ-
ates *wuwei* particularly with the Daoists (*Shiji* 130.3292), although *wuwei* was used

an "uncrowned king," provides another possible template, since his eminent disciple, Zigong, is included among Sima Qian's commodity producers. The fact that Zigong thus not only plays the role of untitled nobility to an untitled king, but also gives the chapter's eponymous commodity producers (*huozhi*) their name, does not resolve the question of irony. Sima Qian exploits the potential of this ambiguity in naming into existence a societal group that crosscuts occupations, even as the group takes the merchant as its implicit basis.

Sima Qian's notion of untitled nobility calculates status in quantitative market terms. He writes that the pleasures enjoyed by the untitled nobility are the general equivalent of money and social status (for example, "pleasures comparable to [those of fiefholders]"; or "the owner of millions [of cash] can enjoy the same pleasures as a king"), but the market value of accumulated wealth re-tariffs social hierarchies.[44] "Each person possessing" a piece of land with fifty horses or 1,000 chestnut trees in Yan "is commensurate (*deng* 等) with a marquis possessing 1,000 households." The individual entrepreneurial landowner, not the hegemonic Guanzian ruler, itemizes hypothetical produce from non-agricultural marshland or mountains and calculates its monetary value. The parallel *Hanshu* version of this passage omits or replaces those passages underlined above. As discussed below, this helps to block the *Shiji*'s introduction of the moneymaking *junzi* (ethical subject). This includes the above references to the uncrowned nobility and to entrepreneurial landlords who live with the personal safety or "righteousness" (*yi*) of retired scholars. This latter metaphor of the landlord recluse redoubles the scandal of the chapter's earlier assertion that "retired scholars who live concealed in cliffs and caves" desired wealth as much as anyone else.[45]

---

across "schools" or syncretic strains of thought in the pre-imperial and early imperial period.

44. Pan, *Shiji huozhi zhuan xin quan*, 43 and 59, notes the *su feng*'s relation to pleasure although Pan takes the "household of a thousand gold catties" (*qian jin zhi jia*) as the "main thread" running through the account.

45. *Shiji* 129.3271. 隱居巖穴之士. On Ban Gu's condemnation of this, see *Hou Hanshu* 40.1325. The moral inflection of the phrase *chu shi* 處士 is, however, more ambivalent in classical texts. For example, the *Mencius* criticizes the *chu shi*; the *Xunzi* contrasts the good *chu shi* of antiquity with the modern version. *Shiji* 102.2756, 86.2528, uses *chu shi* simply to describe the occupation of particular individuals (wise men, in

Divergent modern economic theories, including those of Marx, Simmel, and Weber, have approached money as an agent of social transformation, making the hitherto incommensurable commensurable. As addressed elsewhere in this book, Karl Polanyi and David Graeber hold money responsible for reorganizing society around quantitative payments instead of qualitative or moral obligations. Although Sima Qian documents the quantitative mode of social transformation perhaps more than any other early observer whose works are extant, his opinion of that change is far less transparent.

通邑大都，酤一歲千 釀，醯醬千瓨 . . . 銅器千鈞， 素木鐵器若巵茜千石，馬蹄躈千，牛千足，羊彘千雙，僮手指千，筋角丹沙千斤， 其帛絮細布千鈞，文采千匹 . . . 子貸金錢千貫，節馹會，貪賈三之，廉賈五之，此亦比 千乘之家， 其大率也。佗雜業不中什二，則非吾財也。

Anyone who, in towns or large cities, sells in a year: 1,000 brewings [of wine], or 1,000 jars of pickles and sauces . . . or 1,000 *jun* of bronze vessels, or 1,000 *shi* of plain wood, or iron vessels, or madder dyes, or [200] horses, 500 cattle, or a couple thousand goats or pigs, or [100] slaves, or 1,000 catties of animal sinews, horns, or cinnabar, or 1,000 *jun* of raw silk, cotton, and fine cloth, or 1,000 bolts of patterned or variegated cloth . . . or interest on a loan of gold and cash worth 1,000 strings [i.e., 1,000,000 cash] from moneylenders, from which greedy merchants can get 30 percent interest and upright merchants can get 50 percent; *such [earnings] make one in general comparable to a family of a thousand chariots. Various other occupations that do not achieve a 20 percent [profit] are not what I see as a source of wealth* [emphasis added].[46]

The thirty-two diverse items on Sima Qian's full list (abridged here) become commensurate in terms of market price and in terms of "achieving a 20 percent" (minimum) annual profit.[47] Sima Qian does not give a

these cases). The *Shiji*'s use of the phrase *shen you chu shi zhi yi* 身有處士之義 here likely recasts the *Book of Lord Shang*'s discussion of occupations (that condemns them), as at *Shiji* 129.3272, discussed below.

46. *Shiji* 129.3274-76.

47. The sentence on money-lending is confusing. Swann, *Food and Money*, 437, translates thus: "[Bringing a net profit] to greedy tradespeople of thirty-three and a third per cent; or to non avaricious *lien* ones of twenty per cent." Watson, *Records of the Grand Historian: Han Dynasty* 2: 450: "A greedy merchant who is anxious for a quick return will only manage to revolve his working capital three times while a less avaricious merchant has revolved his five times." Wu Baosan, *Zhongguo jingji sixiangshi*, 169: "Greedy merchants usually take 30 percent interest; lesser merchants usually take 50

cash figure for these carefully quantified commodities, but his inclusion in the list of the "interest on a loan of gold and cash worth 1,000,000 cash" makes it possible to estimate a cash equivalent, namely 200,000 cash (i.e., 20 percent of 1,000,000 cash). Ding Bangyou's recent study of Han dynasty prices has used this calculated amount to show that Sima Qian's list more or less reflects the commodity prices found in recently excavated documents.[48] Sima Qian, in other words, "compares" (*bi*) various commodities like a merchant. Unlike the critics of the general social mobility of the wealthy (e.g., Chao Cuo), Sima Qian laboriously calculates and records market rates of the convertibility of money, slaves, iron vessels, cinnabar, and political power.

However, the unit of political power, a "family of a thousand chariots" (千乘之家), might trouble the Han dynasty reader. Unlike the "marquis possessing 1,000 households," the phrase "a thousand chariots" is an archaized unit of political domain size found throughout Warring States texts and the rare phrase "family of a thousand chariots" invokes the opening discussion of the *Mencius*, in which Mencius condemns the pursuit of "profit": "When the ruler of a state of ten thousand chariots is assassinated, it will always have been by a family of a thousand chariots. . . . If people put righteousness last and profit first, they will never be satisfied without grasping for more."[49] Despite its representation of the natural desire for profit in the "Account of the Commodity Producers," the *Shiji* praises Mencius's sentiment in its biography of Mencius.[50] The Mencian "family of a thousand chariots" thus puts profit first and hungers to topple the bigger state. Why does Sima Qian use an

---

percent interest." The last seems closest to the traditional commentary on the *Hanshu* version which explains that the greedy merchant actually receives less. Hu, *Concise History of Chinese Economic Thought*, 252, notes the conflation of rate of interest and rate of profit.

48. On Han wine prices, see *Hanshu* 24B.1182, and the discussions at Swann, *Food and Money*, 345, note 712, and Ding Bangyou, *Handai wujia xintan*, 136–39, who makes comparisons with excavated records of price (from Juyan). Ding's discussion of slave prices suggests that Sima Qian's estimate is low compared with evidence from excavated records. According to excavated records slaves went for 15,000–40,000 cash, and prices rose (relative to inflation) during the Han. An adult cost 20,000 and a child 15,000 in the Former Han; by the Later Han they cost 40,000 cash. On the formulation 僮手指千, see traditional commentaries.

49. *Mengzi* 9 (*Mencius* 1A1).

50. *Shiji* 74.2343.

abusive image of the power-hungry—not the more traditional reference to king, lord, or enfeoffed nobility—as the political equivalent for anyone with 200,000 cash capital?[51] Does he iterate the classical distrust of merchants and darkly insinuate that one can endanger the state with a mere 1,000 jars of pickles or 2,000 pigs? Or does he ironically appropriate Mencius precisely to rewrite Mencius's agricultural economic ideal? Since Sima Qian distinguishes (in quantitative terms) between the "greedy" and the "upright" money-lender and frames his chapter with a discussion of the sage businessperson (the *junzi*), it seems likely that, for Sima Qian, those "comparable to a family of a thousand chariots" stand with those "commensurate with the marquis possessing 1,000 households." That is, these persons are the "commodity producers" and the "untitled nobility" who—like so many of the biographical subjects throughout the *Shiji*—are given multiple, morally ambivalent, or often contradictory representations.

"*Root wealth*" (ben fu 本富). The *Shiji*'s use of *ben* 本 ("root," "fundamental"; i.e., agriculture) and *mo* 末 ("branch," "secondary"; i.e., commerce, artisanship, and industry), is also ambivalent. As noted in chapter 1, these were the key terms with which Sang Hongyang and the Classical Scholars debated Emperor Wu's reforms. As with the phrases "untitled nobility" and "commodity producers," Sima Qian uses these terms to enable a new kind of discussion, rather than to coherently express a pro-commerce position. Generally, the *Shiji* faithfully reproduces the traditional meanings of *ben* and *mo* in the words of those he chronicles. Thus the *Shiji* records the normative anti-commercial rhetoric of *mo* as the morally inferior economic sphere to be suppressed (e.g., in its transcriptions of the Qin stele inscriptions and account of Emperor Wen's abolition of land taxes[52]). The work also records the morally neutral idiom of *mo* as commerce used by those who advocated or belonged to the commercial world (e.g., in the record of Jiran's 計然 theory of price: "If you sell grain for 20 [piculs], agriculture will sicken; if you sell it for 90, the 'branch' [*mo*] will sicken").[53] However, the "Account

---

51. The "household of a thousand gold catties" provides a parallel example.

52. *Shiji* 6.245, 10.428. See Kern, *The Stele Inscriptions of Ch'in Shih-huang*, 26 for a discussion of *ben* and *mo* on the Qin stele inscriptions.

53. *Shiji* 129.3256. Jiran advised the King Goujian of Yue 越王句踐 (r. 496–465 BCE).

of Commodity Producers" also recasts "root" and "branch" in a way that aligns both images with positive commercial activity.

今治生不待危身取給，則賢人勉焉．是故本富爲上，末富次之，姦富最下。無巖處奇士之行，而長貧賤，好語仁義，亦足羞也。

Now in running a business one collects income without endangering one's life (*wei shen*), and therefore the wise man directs his efforts towards this. For this reason, "root wealth" (*ben fu*) is best; "branch wealth" (*mo fu*) is next best; "illicit wealth" (*jian fu*) is the very worst. Those who are not reclusive eccentrics but who persist in poverty and lowliness while they keenly discourse on benevolence and righteousness (*ren yi*) have enough to be ashamed about.[54]

This passage introduces the novel phrases "root wealth" (*ben fu* 本富), "branch wealth" (*mo fu* 末富), and "illicit wealth" (*jian fu* 姦富).[55] Some have interpreted these phrases as evidence of Sima Qian's traditional approach to *ben* and *mo* as ranked values in an ordinal series of industries, privileging agriculture over trade, and adding the third category of criminal activity.[56] Others have pointed out that in ranking wealth in terms of the "bodily danger" (*wei shen*), not the traditional morality of occupations, Sima Qian refers back to the wealth of the "untitled nobil-

---

54. *Shiji* 129.3272. The three traditional commentaries do not comment on this passage.

55. *Ben fu* occurs once in the *Guanzi*, *jian fu* once in Jia Yi's *Xinshu*.

56. Sima Qian is thus not saying anything particularly new, and his assertion that *ben* is "best" (*shang*) and *mo* is "next" or "secondary" (*ci*) is basically tautological. Hu Jichuang, *Concise History of Chinese Economic Thought*, 244–45: "By 'fundamental wealth' he [Sima Qian] meant that which came from agriculture, forestry and stockbreeding, while 'peripheral wealth' was that which came from handicrafts and commerce . . . these two categories were fairly universal features of economic thought after the end of the Warring States period." See also Hu Jichuang, *Zhongguo jingji sixiangshi*, 53. Compare Burton Watson's translation: "the best kind of wealth is that which is based upon agriculture, the next best is that which is derived from secondary occupations, and the worst of all is that which is acquired by evil means." Other scholars agree that this statement affirms Sima Qian's traditional respect for agriculture but point out that Sima Qian is actually celebrating wealth (*fu*) acquisition. Han Fuzhi, *Liang Han de jingji sixiang*, 71: "[Sima Qian] had a profound insight into the need and use of wealth, enabling him to guide those doing commerce in getting rich," particularly with the insight that "buying land and engaging in agriculture was the most stable." Compare with Wu Baosan *Zhongguo jingji sixiang shi*, 168, who translates *ben fu* as "agricultural production" (*nongye shengchan* 农业生产) but makes the important point that Sima Qian is stressing ability and "unorthodox" measures of wealth acquisition.

ity" whose "life (*shen*) has the integrity of the scholar without office [even while he] collects income." Root wealth is best not because it is intrinsically more moral or even more profitable than trading but because it is a less risky source of income.[57] Since the opening topic of "running a business" (*zhi sheng*) has specific connotations with trade and commerce in the *Shiji*, all three terms are already tainted with the traditional associations of *mo*.[58] If "branch wealth" refers to the traditional travails of the merchant (who has to "scrutinize marketplaces and wells or travel to different cities," as the untitled nobility does not), and "illicit wealth" (or counterfeit wealth) refers to black market or ill-gotten wealth, then "root wealth" lies in the property (e.g., "1,000 chestnut trees in Yan or Qin") of the untitled noble, the armchair entrepreneur, who simply sits and waits to receive his or her twenty percent annual profit.[59] Poverty implicitly

---

57. Ye, *Gudai Zhongguo jingji*, 152–57. "*Ben fu* refers to getting rich in this way [described at *Shiji* 129.3272]: 'One does not have to scrutinize marketplaces and wells, or travel to different cities: one simply sits to receive the bounty; one's life has the integrity of the scholar without office even while one collects income,' that is, getting rich depends on farming, cattle, forests, fruit, fish, etc., and agricultural income broadly construed. *Mo fu* refers to getting rich by managing artisanal and trading industries, and highly profitable commodities. *Jian fu* refers to getting rich by 'manipulating the laws and committing crimes' [*Shiji* 129.3281]. . . . The hierarchy (between these three) takes 'danger to the body' (*wei shen*) as its measuring stick, and absolutely does not express his high esteem for *ben fu* and low esteem for *mo fu*."

58. *Shiji* 28.1385, 92.2609, 129.3275, 129.3259, 129.3282. Compare *Shiji* 129.3274: "It is said that for a poor person to seek wealth, farming is not as good as the crafts, crafts are not as good as commerce; pricking at one's embroidered patterns is not as good as leaning on the market gate. This means that the branch occupations are the (source of) capital for the poor."

59. The formulation of Sima Qian's claims clearly appropriate and subvert that of the *Shang jun shu*'s 商君書 (Book of Lord Shang) "Calculation in Land" (算地), which sought to banish merchants (and scholars) from his ideal world of farmers and soldiers: "Therefore, if these five kinds of people are also used in the state, then fields will become wasteland and the army will weaken: chattering scholars whose source of capital (*zi*) is their mouth; scholars without office whose source of capital is their righteousness (*yi*); brave men whose source of capital is their energy; skilled craftsmen whose source of capital is their hands; merchants and traders whose capital is their body (*shen*) [since they] must go to every home in the world with their capital [i.e., wares] bundled around their bodies." Lord Shang's metaphorical use of "capital" or "source of capital" (*zi*) mocks the uselessness of the five professions that plague modern times. Sima Qian appropriates his portrait of the righteous (*yi*) scholar without office (*chu shi*). See *Shang jun shu jin zhu*, 63–64.

ranks fourth after the *Shiji*'s ranking of "best," "next," and "worst" wealth. Although the advocates of market expansion in the *Guanzi*'s "Qingzhong" chapters and in the *Debate on Salt and Iron* also argue that external goods are necessary for moral integrity ("Only when granaries are filled up tight can one comprehend what's ritually right"), the *Shiji* at this point seems to go a step further than these other two works.[60] Those who "discourse on benevolence and righteousness" yet choose (to "persist in") poverty become figures of shame. The *junzi* steps into an unregulated market and thrives. Those who remain poor cannot therefore be *junzi*. Does Sima Qian imagine a world in which everyone *should* desire material pleasure and profit; in which ability and honesty somehow guarantee financial success; and in which the market can and should be separated from the political state, as Ban Gu understood him to say? Or, as others have argued, does Sima Qian simply take the emergent world of commerce as a new epistemological subject (for example, "they adapted to the changing times, and therefore their [biographies] are worth transmitting"; or "wise men can learn from them")?[61]

DEREGULATING ETHNOGRAPHY

Sima Qian uses historical change—including the historical emergence of markets—to allow for multiple perspectives to coexist in both the "Account of Commodity Producers" and the "Account of the Xiongnu." Both chapters present a version of the idealized political-economic order of the "Tribute of Yu" but then recount historical changes in customs or practice that undo this ideal. The "Account of Commodity Producers" contains a region-by-region account of China that excludes the frontier colonized during the Han. This regional survey begins with the area called "Within the Passes" (Guanzhong), which was the seat of the Qin capital at Xianyang and the Han capital of Chang'an (modern day Xi'an):

> Guanzhong, from the Qian and Yong rivers east to the Yellow River and Mount Hua has one thousand *li* of rich soil and well-watered wilds. From the time that tribute was given to Shun and the rulers of the Xia dynasty, these have been seen as the best fields [of the Central States, i.e.,

---

60. For this quote, discussed in chapter 1, see Ma Feibai, *Guanzi Qing zhong pian*, 181 and 545; *Shiji* 62.2132 and 129.3255; Wang Liqi, *Yantielun*, 430.

61. *Shiji* 129.3281; compare *Shiji* 130.3319.

China]. . . . Therefore [Guanzhong's] people still follow ways inherited from these former kings. They are fond of sowing grain, and they produce the five grains. They value the land and take acts of excess as serious (crimes). . . . Dukes Wu and Zhao governed Xianyang [during the Zhou dynasty], and for this reason the Han dynasty made their capital [in this region]. People arrived from all four directions converging and gathering like spokes on a wheel to a hub on Chang'an and its surrounding mausoleum towns [i.e., towns established for the construction of imperial mausoleums]. Since the land area was small and the population crowded, [Guanzhong's] people became increasingly good at hustling [lit. "play and manipulation"] in the "branch" occupations [i.e., commerce].[62]

Sima Qian begins with Guanzhong's supreme place in the moral tributary order of the Xia dynasty (i.e., the "Tribute of Yu") but then records the historical transformation of its cities into commercial hubs for those in the "branch" occupations with their business schemes.[63] The regional account maps out market wealth, not tribute to the emperor. Guanzhong's population "is no more than one third that of the empire, but six-tenths of the [empire's] cumulative wealth is there." The ensuing descriptions of the dozens of other regions do not mention tribute but do note the regions' sometimes non-centralized traffic in merchandise with adjacent regions. Take, for example, Sima Qian's account of the northern state of Yan (seat of modern day Beijing):

> Yan, between [the gulf of] Bo and [Mount] Jieshi, also has a capital hub. To the south it communicates with Qi and Yue; to the northeast it borders with the *hu* [i.e., Xiongnu] from Shanggu to Liaodong. Its land is remote and distant, its population sparse and frequently invaded by bandits. Its customs (*su*) can largely be grouped with those of the Zhao and Dai people, but its people are defensive as hawks and are rarely considerate. They are rich in fish, salt, dates, and chestnuts. To the north [Yan's] neighbors are Wuhuan and Fuyu; to the east [Yan] controls the profits from (trade with) Huimo, Chaoxian [i.e., Korea], and Zhenpan.[64]

Here Yan is described as having one of the eight commercial "capital hubs" (*du hui* 都會) dotted across the Central Plains and it has its own

---

62. *Shiji* 129.3261.

63. Compare the similar language and paradigm in the synopsis to *Shiji* 30 found at *Shiji* 129.3306.

64. *Shiji* 129.3265.

"customs" and ethnographic attributes. More importantly, it "controls the profits" from apparently non-tributary trade with areas at or beyond the Chinese frontiers.[65]

While the *Shiji*'s "Account of the Commodity Producers" unsettles the tributary order within the Central States, the *Shiji*'s "Account of the Xiongnu" does so at the borders. The "Account of the Xiongnu" historically maps the Han dynasty's greatest enemy into the tributary order but, as argued below, casts the ethnographic presumptions of this ideal into a negative light. This chapter opens with the longest description of foreign customs found in any *Shiji* chapter, or indeed in all of Chinese literature to that point in history. The *Hanshu* "Xiongnu zhuan" opens with an almost identical passage. These chapters are often read as interchangeable versions of the earliest template for Chinese ethnographic writings (about any peoples).[66] The passage effectively maps Xiongnu ancestry onto the ancient "five-zone" (*wu fu* 五服) schema of the "Tribute of Yu" (*Yu gong* 禹貢).

匈奴，其先祖夏后氏之苗裔也，曰淳維。唐虞以上有山戎、獫狁、葷粥，居于 北蠻，隨畜牧而轉移。...逐水草遷徙，毋城郭常處耕田之業，然亦各有分地。毋文書，以言語爲 約束。...其俗，寬則隨畜，因射獵禽獸爲生業，急則人習戰攻以侵伐，其天性也。其長兵則弓矢，短兵則刀鋋。利則進，不利則退，不羞遁走。苟利所在，不知禮義。自君王以下，咸食畜肉，衣其皮革，被旃裘。壯者食肥美，老者食其餘。貴壯健，賤老弱。父死，妻其後母；兄 弟死，皆取其妻妻之。其俗有名不諱，而無姓字。

The first ancestor of the Xiongnu, called Chunwei, was a descendent of the ruling lineage of the Xia state. From the time of Emperors Yao and Shun, there the Shan Rong, Xianyun, and Hunyu resided among the

---

65. See Swann, *Food and Money*, 442, on this term.

66. Honey, "The Han-Shu, Manuscript Evidence"; and Chen Zhi, *Shiji xin zheng*, 165 and *Hanshu xin zheng*, 421, both note that the archaeologist Huang Wenbi excavated a Han dynasty strip from the ruins of a beacon tower at Tuyin 土堆 near Lake Lop Nor in Xinjiang, in the 1930s. This strip included a phrase with a parallel meaning to that found in the *Shiji* opening passage above: *ren li ze jin bu li* 人利則進不利 [strip broken] (If the people have the advantage, they advance; if they do not have the advantage). It is unclear whether this belongs to a copy of the *Shiji* (or *Hanshu*), if it was a circulating administrative "ethnographic logos" of the kind used by the imperial historiographers, or something else altogether. The archeological location of the strip at the Han-Xiongnu frontier suggests that the Xiongnu could be its subject, but this is not certain.

northern Man, rotating between pastures with their livestock. . . . They [the Xiongnu] move in search of grass and water. They have no walled cities, fixed abodes, or agricultural occupations, but they each have apportioned land. They have no written documents, and they use spoken words to seal pacts. . . . It is their custom when resources are plentiful to make their living by following their livestock and hunting beasts and birds with arrows; but during crises their men practice warfare and invade and plunder. This is their inborn nature. For long-range weapons they use bow and arrow; for short-range weapons they use daggers and lances. If at an advantage, they advance; if at a disadvantage, they depart, not ashamed to beat a retreat. If there is some advantage, they do not understand ritual propriety and righteousness. Everyone from the rulers and kings to their subjects eat the meat of livestock, wear skins and hide, and cover themselves with felts and furs. The strong eat the richest and finest food, while the elderly eat their leftovers. They honor the strong and vigorous and dishonor the elderly and weak. When fathers die, [the sons] marry the stepmothers. When brothers die, they take their [brothers'] wives and marry them. According to their customs, they have personal names but do not observe taboos on them, and they have no surnames or polite names.[67]

The opening genealogy traces Xiongnu ancestry back to the descendents of the rulers of the ancient Xia state. The passage locates and fixes the Xiongnu as political subordinates to the generationally senior Central States.[68] This strategy of creative ethnogenealogy was not uncommon in earlier and subsequent texts. Han dynasty commentators on the *Classic of Odes* glossed the Xianyun of *Ode* 167 ("We have no house, no household/Because of the Xianyun") as the Xiongnu, just as jingoistic Tang dynasty officials would later cast their enemy Uyghurs as the (by then

---

67. *Shiji* 110.2879.

68. Di Cosmo historicizes Sima Qian's ethnogenealogy as a traditional Chinese method of assimilating the Xiongnu into a politically, culturally, and astrologically subordinate position that had previously been occupied by other foreigners. See Di Cosmo, *Ancient China and its Enemies*, 294–304. Cui Mingde, *Liang Han minzu guanxi*, 122–34, esp. 132, similarly uses this passage to show continuities with the *Zuozhuan* tradition; he traces the stance in the *Shiji* of cultural superiority to the Xiongnu back to common attitudes toward foreigners found in earlier historiography. On the processes of constructing a "fictive genealogy" in the formation of the ever-shifting temporal, geographical, ecological, and identificatory borders of the Huaxia (Chinese people), see Wang Ming-ke, *Huaxia bianyuan*.

non-existent) Xiongnu.[69] More importantly, the *Shiji* locates the proto-Xiongnu pastoral rotations among the northern Man 蠻. In the "Tribute of Yu" of the canonical *Book of Documents* (and recorded in the *Shiji*), the Man and the Liu 流 ("nomads") occupy the fifth and outermost "Wilderness Zone" (*huang fu* 荒服) of the concentric Five Zones. Since moral and cultural refinement radiates from the center to which tribute is brought, this region stands at the furthest remove from civilization and political control. The *Shiji*'s chronicle of the northern frontier that follows this introduction explicitly invokes this "Wilderness Zone" and the historical difficulties of getting its occupants to bring tribute (*gong* 貢).

The ethnographic description itself also follows the logic of tribute inasmuch as it describes the politically subordinate as culturally and morally inferior. It unfolds as a litany of lack. The Xiongnu have no written documents, no agriculture, no proper shame, and no proper naming practices. Above all "they do not understand ritual propriety and righteousness" (*bu zhi li yi* 不知禮義), which were key markers of civilization. Xiongnu kinship violations (in marrying stepmothers) and maltreatment of the elderly (in feeding them leftovers) require no explicit condemnation. Such phobic anthropological rhetoric echoes many of the pre-imperial norms of representing foreigners in classical Chinese philosophy, poetry, and historiography.[70] These texts often referred to foreigners with generalizing ethnonyms that were not necessarily their own (such as Yi 夷, Man 蠻, Hu 胡, Fan 蕃) or with collective names such as Four Yi (*si yi* 四夷) or Nine Yi (*jiu yi* 九夷), and generally, but not always, described them as militarily agonistic and morally inferior to the Central States (or the Hua 華, Xia 夏, Zhou 周). Applying an ethical paradigm that divided the world into the civilized and uncivilized, these texts typically stated that the Yi and Di were ignorant of ritual (*li* 禮) and propriety (*yi* 儀), but that they could be enlightened through military force (*zheng* 征 "corrective expedition"; *fa* 伐 "punitive expedition") or

---

69. The Mao commentary says: "The Xianyun are the northern enemy" (玁狁北狄也) and Zheng Xuan comments: "The northern enemy are today's Xiongnu" (北狄今匈奴也). See *Mao shi zhuan jian* 2: 515–16. On the use of the Xiongnu in Tang dynasty archaizing (and jingoistic) rhetoric about the Tujue ("Turkic") people, see, for example, *Jiu Tang shu*, 194A, 5162.

70. On these competing models, see Yuri Pines, "Beasts or Humans."

persuasive example (*yi de lai* 以德來 "to win over through virtue"; *hua* 化 "morally transform"). Chinese geopolitical accounts defined the foreigner as the perennial military adversary invading the historical frontiers or the de facto outsider to the idealized symbolic space of the morally and politically superior Central States. Behind these rhetorics lay the tributary ideal: the expressed desire that all foreigners inhabiting the "four directions" (*sifang* 四方), the "four seas" (*sihai* 四海), the concentric "Five Zones" or (later) the "Nine Zones" (*jiu fu* 九服) outside the Zhou tributary center would join the "inner subjects" (*nei chen* 内臣) of the Central States as its tribute-bearing "outer subjects" (*wai chen* 外臣).[71]

There were important alternatives to this pre-imperial tradition: these same classical texts recorded occasional political alliances binding enemies in the egalitarian language of brotherhood (*xiongdi* 兄弟, *kundi* 昆弟);[72] less hierarchical traditions of guest-host relations (*ke* 客, *bin* 賓)[73]; and a minor tradition of alien wisdom, exemplified by Confucius's claim that foreigners stored ritual knowledge when the Central States fell into moral decay.[74] As discussed in chapter 1, the philosopher Zou Yan (fl. c. 250 BCE), who in his own day enjoyed more popularity than Confucius and Mencius (but whose extant writings are now fragmentary), presented an alternate vision of the world in which the Central States, which he renamed the "Red District's Sacred Region" (*Chixian shenzhou*), constituted only one off-center region of the eighty-one regions of the world's Nine Continents.

ON "THOSE WHO TALK ABOUT THE XIONGNU"

More important than the possible affiliation of the Xiongnu ethnography with one of these rival traditions is, however, the unsettling authorial comment with which the *Shiji*'s chapter closes (each chapter of the *Shiji*

---

71. On *sifang* cosmology as a political discourse, see Aihe Wang, *Cosmology and Political Culture*, 23–74. For the "Tribute of Yu," see Legge, *The Shoo King*, 92–151.; *Shiji* 2.75. On Han dynasty resistance to, and historiographic problems with, the "Tribute of Yu" world order, see *Shiji* 74.2344; Wang Liqi, *Yantielun jiaozhu* 53.564; Gu Jiegang, "Qin Han tongyi de youlai."

72. For the diplomatic metaphor of brotherhood, see Yang Bojun, *Chunqiu Zuozhuan zhu*, 1: 420 and 3: 1176, and Schaberg, *A Patterned Past*, 137, 142–48.

73. Khayutina, "Royal Hospitality and Geopolitical Constitution."

74. *Chunqiu Zuozhuan zhu*, 4: 1389. See Schaberg, "Travel, Geography, and the Imperial Imagination" on this classical figure of the virtuous barbarian ruler.

ends with an authorial comment, and subsequent *Standard Histories* continued to do so):

太史公曰：孔氏著春秋，隱桓之間則章，至定哀之際則微，爲其切當世之文而罔襃，　忌諱之辭也。世俗之言匈奴者，患其徼一時之權，而務諂納其說，以便偏指，不　參彼己；將率席中國廣大，氣奮，人主因以決策，是以建功不深。堯雖賢，興事業不成，得禹而九州寧。且欲興聖統，唯在擇任將相哉！唯在擇任將相哉！

The Grand Scribe remarks: "Confucius, in composing the *Spring and Autumn Annals*, wrote openly about the periods of Dukes Yin and Huan. But when he came to the eras of Dukes Ding and Ai, he [wrote with] subtlety. Because he was writing about his own times he did not give praise [or blame], and his words [observed political] taboos. As for those who talk about the Xiongnu according to contemporary customs, the trouble is that they pursue the expediency of the moment; they are engaged in offering up flattery until they persuade, in order to gain advantage for their partial claims, and they do not compare their strength with ours. The generals consider the Central States to be broad and vast [and so] their spirit is aroused, and the ruler of the people then relies [on these generals' views] to decide his strategy. Consequently, our accomplishments lack depth. Although Yao was worthy, he did not achieve his [governmental] tasks; only when he obtained [the services of] Yu were the Nine Provinces stabilized. Moreover, if one desires to resurrect the sages' pattern of rule, one must select and employ responsible generals and advisers! One must select and employ responsible generals and advisers!"[75]

The *Shiji*'s end comment does not address the Xiongnu at all, but rather turns the critical gaze inwards, addressing the politics of representation, in terms of both the general dangers of writing about one's own era and of the specific distortions in Han discussions of Xiongnu affairs. Sima Qian's reflexive attention to the politics of those who talk about the Xiongnu—in his chapter entitled "Account of the Xiongnu"—reveals that what is at stake are the "contemporary customs" (*shi su* 世俗) not of the ethnographic object but of the ethnographer. Subsequent emulators of Sima Qian's historical ethnography eschewed this rare concern with the politics of representation—it does not appear in any other end comment to chapters on foreigners in any of the *Standard Histories* (from the Han through the Qing Dynasty).

---

75. *Shiji* 110.2919.

The most meaningful allusion to tribute in this passage is in the flattery that "those who talk about the Xiongnu "seek acceptance" (*na* 納) by the emperor. In borrowing the term commonly associated with tribute, Sima Qian mocks the dysfunction of the tribute system at the imperial court as it falsely patterns (through language) relations at the frontiers. This critique of envoys who exaggerate their reports to the emperor in order to gain a higher rank recurs in the "Account of Dayuan," which records, "The accompanying officers and soldiers all competed to submit reports that spoke of exotic wonders, and profits and losses, as part of their own quest to become envoys."[76] In the "Account of the Xiongnu," although Sima Qian invokes the legendary sage Yu, he does so as the model of a well-chosen domestic adviser, not as a symbol of hierarchical frontier relations. Yao wisely selects Yu, just as Han superiors should "select and employ responsible generals and advisers." Sima Qian commemorates Yu for stabilizing the "Nine Provinces" (*jiu zhou* 九州) of China; for after the floods, Yu had delineated the nine provinces and had defined appropriate levels of tribute for each province. Unlike the Five Zones (which the *Hanshu* version would invoke), however, this geographical schema did not delineate the Yi, Di, and Man, or map (or appear to Han scholars to map) tributary zones onto moral-cultural hierarchies. Indeed, Zhang Shoujie 張守節 (fl. 725–35), in his canonical commentary, *Zhengyi* 正義, interprets the anecdote of Yao and Yu as a criticism of Emperor Wu for his inability to choose worthy advisers, the emperor's attention to "the flattery of petty men with empty words," and his aggression against the Xiongnu.

Traditional commentators have long tied this authorial end comment to the *Shiji*'s "Account of the Xiongnu" to the Xiongnu politics that enter Sima Qian's autobiographical postface (chapter 130). Many later commentators echo Zhang's points about the rise of sycophantic verbiage under Emperor Wu and of Sima Qian's allegorical use of language.[77]

---

76. *Shiji* 123.3171.

77. Ye Shi 葉適 (Song dynasty), Mao Kun and Yu Youding 余有丁 (Ming dynasty), and He Zhuo 何焯 and Yang Qiguang 楊琪光 (Qing dynasty) either ponder what Sima Qian was really criticizing (that is, was it Emperor Wu's Xiongnu policy, his choice of ministers, or his neglect of the common people?), or emphasize that Sima Qian used the term "subtle" (*wei* 微) when referring to writing. See Zhang Dake, *Shiji yanjiu*, 6:560–62. Nakai Riken 中井積德 (即中井履軒) (1732–1817) views the need for worthy

Jiao Hong 焦竑 (1541–1620) comments that the Grand Scribe was "deeply dissatisfied with [Emperor Wu], but there were difficulties in speaking openly, and therefore he composed these two lines [about Confucius's writing]. This can be said to be [speaking] 'subtly' [*wei* 微] but 'openly' [*zhang* 章]." The various interpretive traditions of Confucius's *Spring and Autumn Annals* presented it as a text full of subtle moral meanings that readers had to decode or historicize.[78] Sima Qian's autobiographical postface to the *Shiji* modestly distinguishes his mere transmission (*shu* 述) of the *Shiji* from Confucius's creation (*zuo* 作) of the *Spring and Autumn Annals*, but in so doing he echoes Confucius's representation of his own teachings as historical transmission and not creation.[79] Thus when Sima Qian invokes Confucius's composition of the *Spring and Autumn Annals* and the paradigm of the misunderstood sage, he draws attention to the complexity of his own mode and conditions of transmission. The politics of talking about the Xiongnu and of choosing the right generals—the two concerns of the end comment—bind the "Account of the Xiongnu" to the tragic circumstances in which the "Autobiographical Postface" recounts the *Shiji*'s completion.[80]

How does one reconcile the opening and closing perspectives of Sima Qian's "Account of the Xiongnu"? Does Sima Qian's attack on those who talk about the Xiongnu supplement or undermine the opening description of the uncivilized Xiongnu, a people whose ancestors occupied the outermost zone of the "Five Zone" tributary map? An anecdote

---

advisers as central to Sima Qian's lack of clarity in his message. See Takigawa, *Shiki kaichū kōshō*, 9:70.

78. On Dong Zhongshu, whom Sima Qian presents as the leading authority on the *Spring and Autumn Annals*, see *Shiji* 121.3128, 130.3297; Queen, *From Chronicle to Canon*, 124–26. On Sima Qian's departure from Dong Zhongshu's anti-historical method, his relation to competing traditions of *Spring and Autumn Annals* exegesis, and his novel pursuit of meaning in human choices as well as in the moral-political verities patterned in the Heavens, see Wai-yee Li, "The Idea of Authority in the *Shih chi*." See also Li, *The Readability of the Past*, 34–48; Durrant, *The Cloudy Mirror*, 1–27.

79. See Michael Puett, *The Ambivalence of Creation*, 177–212.

80. Ban Gu's end comment excludes this. Ban Gu again dissociates the problem of the politics of representation from his geographical account of the western regions, moving the *Shiji*'s invocation of the problem of envoys' exaggerated speech in the "Dayuan liezhuan" (*Shiji* 123.3171) to the biographies of Zhang Qian and Li Guangli (*Hanshu* 61.2695). As discussed above, the *Hou Hanshu* 80.1325, records Ban Biao's alternate claim that the Sima Qian was punished because of his book.

halfway through the "Account of the Xiongnu" provides a context for this disjunction and illumines the *Shiji*'s subtle regulation of a market of competing narratives. This anecdote concerns a Han defector to the Xiongnu who explicitly turns the gaze of Han ethnographers back toward the Central States. This defector was a tutor to the Han princess who was sent with her to the Xiongnu by Emperor Wen during the renewal of the *heqin* ("peace through kinship") treaty, at a time when the Xiongnu confederacy was still militarily dominant. Upon his arrival at the frontier, Zhonghang Yue left the Han camp to become the personal political adviser to two successive Xiongnu leaders. The *Shiji* records his conversations with both the Xiongnu and the Han envoys at the frontier. Within this long set of discussions, certain passages resonate strikingly with the framing passages of the "Xiongnu zhuan" (the opening and the end comment). Together they serve to defamiliarize Chinese anthropological discourse in an unprecedented way:

漢使或言曰：「匈奴俗賤老。」中行説窮漢使曰：「而漢俗屯戍從軍當發者，其老親豈有不自脱溫厚肥美以齎送飲食行戍乎？」漢使曰：「然。」中行説曰：「匈奴明以戰攻爲事，其老弱不能鬭，故以其肥美飲食壯健者，蓋以自爲守衛，如此父子各得久相保，何以言匈奴輕老也？」漢使曰：「匈奴父子乃同穹廬而臥。父死，妻其後母；兄弟死，盡取其妻妻之。無冠帶之飾，闕庭之禮。」

One of the Han envoys said: "According to Xiongnu customs, [a] they dishonor the elderly."

Zhonghang Yue interrogated the Han envoy: "But according to Han customs, when those joining the military are sent out to be stationed in garrisons, do they not have their elderly kin set aside their own warmest layers and richest and finest [food] in order to send food and drink to those working in the garrisons?"

The Han envoy said: "It is so."

Zhonghang Yue said: "The Xiongnu make it clear that they take warfare and attack as their business. Their elderly and weak are unable to fight, and therefore they give their richest and finest food and drink to the strong and vigorous. And because [the strong] make themselves the protectors and defenders so fathers and sons both protect each other in the long term. How can you say the Xiongnu dishonor the elderly?"

The Han envoy said: "Amongst the Xiongnu, fathers and sons bed together in the same tent. [b] When fathers die, [the sons] marry their stepmothers. [c] When brothers die they take all the [brothers'] wives and marry them. They do not have [our] adornments of caps and girdles, or the proper practices [*li* "ritual propriety"] at watch-gates and courtyards."[81]

Zhonghang Yue treasonably sympathizes with Xiongnu practices ("How can you say the Xiongnu dishonor their elderly?"), and through his reinterpretation of social acts, he undermines the moral authority of the Han envoy. After demonstrating that the wartime sacrifices of the Han elderly to the young manifest a lack of filiality, he revalues the sacrifices of Xiongnu elderly to their young as part of a military system designed to protect their elderly. Zhonghang Yue reverses the ethnographic gaze with the rare phrase, "Han customs" (*Han su* 漢俗). In Han historiography, the term *su* ("customs") generally refers either to foreign practices (in opposition to those of the Central States), or to dynastic norms and popular domestic conventions.[82] However, Zhonghang Yue here contrasts Han customs directly with Xiongnu customs, and not with the customs of another era or dynasty. Since in early Chinese texts the term "Han" (漢) referred to the Han dynastic state (206 BCE–220 CE), to the pre-imperial state of Han, or to the Han River—but never to a culturally or ethnically defined Han people (the post-Han dynasty terms *Hanren* or *Hanzu*)—Zhonghang Yue's phrase reverses the ethnographic gaze.

More strikingly, Zhonghang Yue challenges the claims not only of his immediate interlocutor but also of the opening ethnographic passage of the "Account of the Xiongnu." Compare this excerpt from the opening passage, discussed above.

> [a] The strong eat the richest and finest food, while the elderly eat their leftovers. They honor the strong and vigorous, and dishonor the elderly and weak. [b] When fathers die, [the sons] marry the stepmothers. [c] When brothers die, they take their [brothers'] wives and marry them. According to their customs, they have personal names but do not observe taboos on them, and they have no surnames or polite names.[83]

Zhonghang Yue's dialogue elaborates on the opening passage's theme of Xiongnu cultural failures, echoing its language. It also duplicates the topic order in the opening passage. Both passages proceed from the

---

81. *Shiji* 110.2899–900.
82. See Chin, "Antiquarian as Ethnographer" for a further discussion of this.
83. *Shiji* 110.2879.

Xiongnu's disrespect for the elderly symbolized by the offering of left-over food (a), to Xiongnu sons marrying their stepmothers (b), to brothers marrying their dead brothers' wives (c). The parallels in vocabulary (for example, the phrases "they dishonor the elderly" and "richest and finest food" [a]), and in entire statements in (b) and (c), compel the reader to draw a comparison. The exchange between the Han envoy and the Han traitor becomes more intelligible when read not simply as part of the chronological narrative of the northern frontier that follows the chapter's opening account of Xiongnu customs, but also as a response to, or mimicry of, those opening claims.[84] Through it, the pan-optical eye of the opening passage, whose authority depends upon the invisibility of the ethnographer, becomes embodied in a stock-figure who is worsted in argument with Zhonghang Yue. Originally sent as tutor to the Han princess, Zhonghang Yue redirects his lessons at those sent to educate the Xiongnu in the ways of the Central States.[85] To use the vocabulary of modern anthropology, one might say that Sima Qian

---

84. In Homi Bhabha's model of mimicry in colonial contexts, the native appears to observe colonial discourse but at the same time misrepresents the foundational assumptions of this discourse, differentiating the anti-colonial self by inappropriately appropriating the words of the colonial master. The political conditions of the Han-Xiongnu frontier are different. However, given the status of the "Account of the Xiongnu" as the beginnings of Chinese empirical or imperial ethnography, this play of subversive appropriation within the chapter is in some ways comparable. See Bhabha, *The Location of Culture*, 85–92.

85. In demanding silence, he characterizes the envoy's speech as "twittering and chattering" (*die die er zhan zhan* 喋喋而佔佔), an accusation with a parallel elsewhere in the *Shiji*. In a debate over the proper choice of ministers at *Shiji* 102.2752 (and its parallel account in the *Hanshu* 50.2307), the wise adviser Zhang Shizhi 張釋之 condemns the twittering (*die die* 喋喋) workman at the imperial Shanglin Park who once so impressed the visiting Emperor Wen by naming its exotic animals that the emperor ordered his promotion to the director of the park. If the emperor should choose the workman over the worthy official, Zhang warns, people "will compete in verbal disputation that has nothing to do with reality." Here and in the "Account of the Xiongnu," the kind of empirical truth-claims represented by the workman's and Han envoy's oral reports are dismissed as mere verbosity. Elsewhere, the *Shiji* critically presents Han envoys in distant lands using exaggeration and misrepresentation for profit and power, a worry that recurs in other literary documents. The scholars representing local interests in the *Debate on Salt and Iron*, for example, echo the end comment in the *Shiji*'s "Account of the Xiongnu," in accusing the officers reporting on affairs of the western regions of "seeking after momentary power." See Wang Liqi, *Yantielun* 46.511. *Shiji* 123.3171, also portrays the envoys in the western region as "unbalancing their tales."

illumines the dialogic processes of "participant observation," or ethno-graphic fieldwork, by juxtaposing the claims of the informant with the interventions and cultural assumptions of the ethnographer.[86] In Sima Qian's case, however, there is no Xiongnu informant; it is rather the Han discourse about the Xiongnu, in the chapter's opening and in the figure of the envoy, that comes under scrutiny.[87]

Zhonghang Yue refutes the tributary logic of the chapter's opening ethnography, reverses the ethnographic gaze, and, in his ensuing com-parison of kinship practices (topics b and c), reverses the discourse of cultural superiority:

父子兄弟死，取其妻妻之，惡種姓之失也。故匈奴雖亂，必立宗種。今中國雖詳 不取其父兄之妻，親屬益疏則相殺，至乃易姓，皆從此類。

"When fathers, sons, and brothers die, [the Xiongnu] take [the widowed] wives and marry them, as they hate having the surname group die out. Therefore even when the Xiongnu face political turmoil, the ancestral group is [firmly] established. Now in the Central States although a man clearly would not marry his father's or brother's wife, family members have become so estranged that they kill each other until the dynastic line is changed, and everyone follows this pattern."[88]

Pitting Xiongnu against Han practices, Zhonghang Yue refuses even to use the same terminology. Instead he introduces the new and unfamiliar terms "surname group" (*zhong xing* 種姓) and "ancestral group" (*zong zhong* 宗種) in advocating the Xiongnu system.[89] He directly contrasts the Xiongnu lineage and ancestral groups with the Central States "fam-ily" (*qin shu* 親屬)—a term that the *Shiji* generally uses to refer to the imperial family. His new terms also indirectly counter the vocabulary of descent (*xian zu* 先祖, *miao yi* 苗裔) used in the opening ethnographic statement—vocabulary that would otherwise politically subordinate the

---

86. Clifford, "Introduction: Partial Truths." Sima Qian did not gather information about the Xiongnu through direct observation as he would have in other cases, such as that of the Southwestern Yi (to whom he was sent as an envoy).

87. On the broader use of mock dialogues among Han writers, see Nylan, "Han Classicists Writing in Dialogue."

88. *Shiji* 110.2900.

89. On the translation of "clan," "lineage" and "surname," see Falkenhausen, *Chinese Society in the Age of Confucius*, 23–24, 164–65. On problems in the translation and study of kinship terminology, see Schneider, *A Critique of the Study of Kinship*, 3, 38, and Butler, *Antigone's Claim*.

Xiongnu within the broader Central States family system. Zhonghang Yue's insult of competitive comparison climaxes when he makes the kinship practices of the Central States appear strange and violent. In distinguishing the two systems, he recasts the Central States' "family" (*qin shu*) as the source of its cultural inferiority. Because the Central States have a *qin shu* and not a *zhong xing* or *zong zhong* blessed with the levirate, they, unlike the Xiongnu, are unstable and estranged to the point of dynastic upheaval. The phrase "to change surnames" (*yi xing* 易姓) occurs elsewhere in the *Shiji*, in Confucius's report of the traditional procedure of changing surnames in becoming ruler.[90] But here, in light of the Xiongnu's alternate kinship values (feeding the young well, marrying stepmothers), which enable the young to defend the old and make generational succession smooth, what appears strange and savage are the traditional cycles of dynastic change in the Central States.

This kind of contradiction between sections is not unusual in the *Shiji*. A bald moral statement or character sketch, often at the opening of a chapter, may be undermined or proved inaccurate through ensuing events. So, for example, the "Basic Annals of the First Emperor Qin" juxtaposes the official self-celebrating, epigraphic histories of the Qin dynasty with a narrative of the cruelties and failures of the regime. Likewise, in the chapter on families related to the emperor by marriage, Sima Qian pronounces that "amongst ritual practices only marriage demands complete rigor" before detailing the dramas of ritually incorrect Han consorts.

Zhonghang Yue's rhetoric is more strategic than consistent. In the above example, he reverses the tributary logic, asserting Xiongnu moral superiority. He similarly reduces *heqin* diplomacy to its material transaction: "You should only concern yourselves with the silk, fabrics, rice, and grains that the Han transport to the Xiongnu. Make sure they are of the correct weights and quality—what more is there to talk about?"[91] With tributary rhetoric, he threatens violence should these terms not be met; with tributary logic, he repeatedly cuts off or silences Han attempts at linguistic exchange. In his advice to the Xiongnu, however, he presents an alternate discourse of cultural identity to that of the (inverted)

---

90. *Shiji* 28.1363.
91. *Shiji* 110.2901.

tributary order. He warns the Xiongnu that the market is regulating cultural identity. The *heqin* contract stipulated the opening of markets along the Great Wall and border market activity now threatens the kind of cultural change from Xiongnu to Han customs traditionally associated with tributary subjection (e.g., *zheng* "corrective expedition"; *hua* "morally transform").

> From the outset the Xiongnu were fond of Han silks, fabrics, foods and other goods. Zhonghang Yue said: "The masses of the Xiongnu population will never rival even one [Chinese] commandery. Thus your strength lies in keeping your clothing and food different and in not relying upon the Han for them. *Now if the* chanyu *[i.e. the Xiongnu leader] changes your customs through his fondness for Han goods,* even if Han goods do not exceed twenty percent [of all your goods], Xiongnu loyalties will go over to the Han.[92] So when you come upon Han silks and fabrics, gallop about in them through the grasses and thorns until all the robes and trousers are shred to tatters, to demonstrate their inferiority to the sturdy excellence of wool and furs. Whenever you get a hold of Han foodstuffs, throw them all away to show their inferiority to the tasty nutrition of curds and kumiss." After this Zhonghang Yue taught the *chanyu*'s attendants to keep detailed written records in calculating and assessing their population size, livestock, and goods [emphasis added].[93]

The ultimate strength of the Xiongnu, in Zhonghang Yue's advice to the Xiongnu, does not lie in their inborn cultural or moral superiority or their Sunzian military strategies. The Xiongnu customs that are represented by furs and kumiss may be superior for steppe living—indeed the *chanyu* must persuade his people thus—but it is Xiongnu economic non-reliance on Han imports that will guarantee their political independence. Zhonghang Yue's political calculation follows an economic logic ("even not more than twenty percent"). Somewhat like the Guanzian state economist, he makes the *chanyu* attendants "calculate and assess population size, livestock and goods" (計課其人眾畜物).[94] As addressed in chapter 1, the *Guanzi*'s Han dynasty "Qingzhong" chapters recount

---

92. The traditional *Jijie* explanation here suggests another wording: "Even if [we import] no more than twenty percent of all Han goods." Since 什二 refers to 20% profit at *Shiji* 129.3276, and *Guanzi*, chapter 76, one might also translate this as follows: "If Han goods do not yield more than twenty percent profit [for the Han]."

93. *Shiji* 110.2899.

94. *Hanshu* 94A.3759 has *shi* 識 in place of *ke* 課.

several instances in which one state politically subjects another by manipulating the demand for, and the import of, silk.[95] Unlike the aggressive Guanzian adviser, however, Zhonghang Yue urges defensive avoidance of, not mastery of the border markets.

The *Shiji*'s "Account of the Xiongnu" presents a discordant collection of ethnographies: of Xiongnu as moral inferiors in a tributary paradigm (opening passage); of Xiongnu as superiors and Han as inferiors in a reversed paradigm (Zhonghang Yue to the Han envoys); of commercially available Han-ness (Zhonghang Yue to the Xiongnu); and of the Han as biased ethnographers of the Xiongnu (Zhonghang Yue to the envoys; and Sima Qian's end comment). The dialogic relation between the opening passage and the Zhonghang Yue anecdote aligns Sima Qian's ending comments more closely to those of Zhonghang Yue, and the opening claims with those of the Han envoy.[96] At the same time, these resonances do not resolve into simple praise of the historical figure. The *Shiji* never explicitly recognizes Zhonghang Yue as a model to emulate, and the chapter synopsis in the "Grand Scribe's narrative about himself" refers to the Xiongnu as a source of "worry and harm since the Three Dynasties."[97] How, after all, could Sima Qian present a traitor as an object of praise? Although Sima Qian famously risked his life for defending the reputation of another purported traitor Li Ling, Zhonghang Yue was not a celebrated general defeated and forced to surrender. The figure of Zhonghang Yue serves as a literary device rather than as a paradigm of the good adviser. The Zhonghang Yue episode, more than any place else in the "Account of the Xiongnu," recalls the problems raised by the end comment: problems of writing openly about one's own time, of political bias in Xiongnu reportage, and of choosing the right advisers.

---

95. See Ma Feibai, *Guanzi Qing zhong pian xin quan*, 641–47; Rickett, *Guanzi* 2:485–86 and 501–2. The critique of the collection of state calculations and surveys does, however, occur in the *Hanshi waizhuan* attributed to the classicist Han Ying 韓嬰 (c.200–c. 120 BCE). See *Hanshi waizhuan jin zhu*, 99.

96. Wai-yee Li's phrase in this context is "ironic disjunction." In "The Idea of Authority in the *Shih chi*," Wai-yee Li shows how Sima Qian establishes his moral authority by promoting the task of memorializing human affairs alongside that of elucidating transcendental patterns; and by mediating between a wide spectrum of attitudes in his narrative and commentary that ranged from "ironic detachment to sympathetic identification, from verification to skepticism."

97. *Shiji* 130.3317.

Through the resonances of these three sections (the beginning, the end comment, and the most extended dialogue), it emerges that the overarching problem posed by the Xiongnu was one of representation, not of anthropological difference. Zhonghang Yue's ambivalent status—his ability to be interpreted as traitor, exemplar, or literary signpost—becomes resolved in the context of the parallel *Hanshu* chapter.

The Hanshu's *Tributary Ethnography*

Although the *Hanshu*'s "Memoir of the Xiongnu" (*Xiongnu zhuan* 匈奴 傳) contains an almost identical version of the *Shiji* account, it chronologically extends and reframes its narrative with a radically different authorial end comment. The second half covers Han-Xiongnu relations through the end of the Former Han dynasty (that is, until 25 CE), including the (non-tributary) political submission of the main Xiongnu leader to Emperor Xuan 宣帝 (r. 74–49 BCE) in 51 BCE. Ban Gu's "appraisal" (*zan* 贊) that replaces the *Shiji*'s end comment marks a rhetorical shift within the tributary ideal. It is the longest comment in the entire *Hanshu* and offers an evaluative historical summary of Han-dynasty policies toward the Xiongnu. He distinguishes two main approaches used thus far during the Han dynasty—the *heqin* peace treaty and punitive military expeditions (seeking tributary subjection)—and argues that both are doomed to failure because the Xiongnu *cannot* be morally transformed, as in the traditional model. In the following portions, taken from the appraisal's beginning and end, Ban Gu blames the inevitability of failure on the Xiongnu's inveterate deceptiveness. He supports a third approach, hostile vigilance, which is called the "loose rein" approach (*jimi* 羈縻) and which involves neither military aggression nor political concession:

> The appraisal says: The [*Book of*] *Documents* in warning that "the Man and the Yi disrupt the Central States," the [*Classic of*] *Odes* in speaking of "smiting the Rong 戎 and Di 狄," and the *Spring and Autumn Annals* in saying, "[if the Prince] possesses virtue, it is observed among the four Yi," [demonstrated that] the Yi and Di have long been the cause of disaster. From the rise of the Han dynasty, when were officials with sincere remonstrances and excellent plans ever not planning strategies and presenting and debating many proposals in court? . . . *The ancient rulers measured the earth, establishing the feudal and royal domain at the center, demarcating the nine regions, categorizing the Five Zones* (wu fu) *and the goods of the earth to be brought as tribute* (gong), *and regulating the outer*

and inner. For some they [the ancient rulers] adjusted punishments and laws; for others they made manifest culture and virtue, and their influence over near and distant regions differed. *According to the* Spring and Autumn Annals, *those living inside [the Central States] are the Xia, and those living outside are the Yi and the Di. The Yi and the Di people are greedy and love profit* (貪而好利). They wear their hair down their backs and fasten their garments on the left; they have human faces but the hearts of wild beasts. . . . Therefore the Sage Kings treated them like birds and beasts, neither concluding treaties with them, nor going forth and attacking them. To conclude agreements with them is to waste gifts and suffer deception. To attack them is to exhaust our armies and provoke raids. Their land cannot be cultivated so as to produce food; *their people cannot be made subjects and tamed* (其民不可臣而畜也). For these reasons they are kept outside and not taken as relatives; they are kept distant and not accepted as kin. Official exhortations do not reach these people; the official calendar is not observed in their land. When they come, we must chastise them and oversee their behavior; when they go, we must be prepared and on our guard against them. *If they are moved to admire righteousness and wish to present tribute* (gong), *then we should receive them courteously. We must keep them under loose rein and not cut them off, allowing any wrong course to come from them. This is the constant way of the Sage Kings for regulating the Man and the Yi* [emphasis added].[98]

Ban Gu's appraisal here explicitly validates the tributary model of the "Five Zones" (*wu fu*) implicit in the opening passage (above) of the parallel *Shiji* and *Hanshu* chapters. It assimilates the Xiongnu within its pre-imperial model of a transhistorical ethico-political hierarchy of the Central States over the Yi, Di, and Man. New here, however, is the rhetoric of immutable cultural difference stemming from the political realities of the frontier.[99] Writing by imperial order about the Former Han

---

98. *Hanshu* 94B.3830–34. Largely following Tinios, "Sure Guidance for One's Own Time." Tinios's useful analysis emphasizes the importance of this appraisal within the book as a whole. See also Tinios, " 'Loose Rein' in Han Relations."

99. Elsewhere, the *Hanshu* also includes examples of Xiongnu who do become culturally "transformed," or civilized. Its portrait of Jin Midi 金日磾, the captive son of a Xiongnu king who dramatically rose in favor and office under Emperor Wu, is the most famous example. On the death of Emperor Wu, amidst ongoing Han-Xiongnu hostilities, Jin Midi declines becoming regent [i.e., de facto emperor of China] through his patriotism for China: "I am someone from an outer state (臣外國人). [Becoming regent] would make the Xiongnu disrespect the Han." (*Hanshu* 68.2962) As Ban Gu's authorial statement concludes: "Jin Midi was a foreigner (*yi di*) from a defeated state.

dynasty, just as the Later Han dynasty was resuming hostilities, Ban Gu appraises the past with a view to an ongoing war in which he, unlike Sima Qian, would participate. (Ban Gu was an army commissioner).[100] He conflates the political problem (that "their people cannot be made subjects and tamed") with intractable cultural and geographical differences. Since the Xiongnu cannot be made into full-time tributary subjects (*chen* 臣) or diplomatic relatives (*qi* 戚), they are irremediably "greedy and love profit (*tan er hao li* 貪而好利)" and "have human faces but the hearts of wild beasts." This xenophobic rhetoric of hierarchical statuses exceeds anything within the chapter itself or in the appraisals of other accounts of foreign peoples in the *Shiji* or *Hanshu*.[101]

Although Ban Gu's chapter includes both the opening ethnographic passage and the Zhonghang Yue dialogue, his appraisal transforms their value. Ban Gu's phobic anthropological discourse realigns himself not with Zhonghang Yue but with the Han envoy. Moreover, the *Hanshu* adds another reference to Zhonghang Yue in its biography of the official Jia Yi 賈誼 (201–169 BCE) that is not found in the *Shiji*. In his political attack on *heqin* diplomacy, Jia Yi singles out Zhonghang Yue for blame:

> [Jia Yi:] It is as if the power of empire lies before a single county. The Son of Heaven is the "head" of the empire. Why? Because he is superior. The Man and Yi are the "feet" of empire. Why? Because they are inferior. Now the Xiongnu insolently invade and plunder, failing to give us respect. The sufferings they inflict on the empire have reached the point of destruction. *However the Han annually deliver gold, silks, worked fabrics as offerings to them.* Summons and regulations for the Yi and Di should be in the control of the superior ruler. *Providing tribute for the Son of Heaven is the ritual propriety of the inferior subject* (天子共貢，是臣下之禮 也). *But the "feet" have subversively taken the place of the superior, and the "head" looks back from the place of the inferior. . . . In my humble estimation, the population of the Xiongnu does not exceed that of a large county.* That an empire so great is hampered by the population of a single county

He came to the Han court as an enslaved prisoner . . . but his trustworthy self-conduct was recognized by the ruler, and he became famous through the state and to later generations. . . . What a shining example!" *Hanshu* 68.2967.

100. Ban Gu later took part in the campaigns of 89–91 CE against the Xiongnu. Sima Qian, by contrast, records his own visit to the northern frontier in his critique of the builder of Qin dynasty sections of the Great Wall, Meng Tian 蒙恬 (d. 214 BCE). See *Shiji* 88.2570.

101. See *Hanshu* 95.3837, 96B.3928.

is a disgrace to those of us in office. . . . If you were to put my strategies into practice I would certainly tie the neck of the *chanyu*, take control of his life, and flog the back of a prostate Zhonghang Yue [emphasis added].[102]

Like Zhonghang Yue, Jia Yi compares the relative population sizes of the Central States and Xiongnu.[103] Like Zhonghang Yue, he also interprets the *heqin* payments as symbolic of tribute. However his metaphor of the true imperial "head" sending tribute up to the inferior foreign "feet," casts Zhonghang Yue's ideal as empire upside down. Likewise, Jia Yi's proposal of "five baits" (*wu er* 五餌), recalled in his *Hanshu* biography, identified the border market as the Xiongnu's vulnerability. However, where Zhonghang Yue saw the Xiongnu desire for Han commodities as preventable, and as originally influenced by the *chanyu*'s tastes, Jia Yi assumes that the Xiongnu are the greedy animals who need to be "baited" (*er* 餌) into submission through market exchange and massive material rewards.

It is with the *Hanshu*'s "Memoir of the Xiongnu" that a familiar tradition of ethnographic writing begins—a tradition that assumes the sovereign objectivity of the observer even as it rationalizes the foreign according to a logic of hierarchical difference. The *Hanshu*'s inclusion of Jia Yi's condemnation helps to stabilize Zhonghang Yue as a historical exemplar of the traitor; Ban Gu's end comment simply reaffirms the authority of the envoy and thus of the tributary logic of the opening passage. Lost in the *Hanshu*'s influential reframing of the *Shiji*'s chapter is Sima Qian's implicit affirmation of Zhonghang Yue's criticisms. Sima Qian's end comment echoes Zhonghang Yue's critique of both the Han envoy and the chapter's opening passage but fails to give clear evaluations or solutions. It opens up the chapter to a plurality of ethnographic perspectives, presenting an alternate narrative economy closer in plan to a deregulated market.

REGULATING THE MARKET TALE

The *Hanshu*'s "Memoir of the Commodity Producers" (*Huozhi zhuan* 貨殖傳, chapter 91) similarly restores the tributary ideal. It moves the

---

102. *Hanshu* 48.2241–42, and in a parallel passage in the *Xinshu* 68.
103. In this case the Xiongnu resemble a mere "county" rather than Zhonghang Yue's "commandery."

regional geography of China's markets to its chapter on geography and, in a strategic reversal commonly used in Han dynasty commentaries on the *Classic of Odes*, reframes the biographies of commodity producers as parables of vice instead of virtue.[104] The *Hanshu* excises all passages about the "untitled nobility" and all discussions of the wise "gentleman" (*junzi*) entrepreneur and the honest merchant. In a narrative of moral decline, Ban Gu also restores the normative hierarchy of "root" and "branch." He removes the *Shiji*'s discussion of running a business in terms of "root wealth," "branch wealth," and so forth. The chapter's single invocation of the "root" (*ben*) in this chapter comes at the turning point from an edenic past to the fallen world of the prosperous: "When the house of Zhou became decadent . . . there were none who did not neglect regulations and abandon *ben*. People who sowed and harvested were few; people who traded and peddled were many. There was a deficiency of grain and a surplus of commodities (*huo*)."[105] *Ben*, the work of those who "sow and harvest," appears rhetorically at the moment of its loss. Like the Classical Scholars of the *Debate on Salt and Iron* discussed in chapter 1, the *Hanshu* restores the antagonistic relation between agriculture and commerce, grounding the *ben* economic metaphor back in its moral template.[106]

Ban Gu opens the chapter with a new description of the ways in which people observed social ranks and occupations in the idealized Zhou period, which replaces Sima Qian's comparison of governments and his anatomy of desiring man:

> According to the institutions of the former kings of antiquity, each institution for the orders of honor [*jue* 爵, i.e., social ranks]; for salaries; for presentations; for maintenance; for palaces and chambers; for carriages and clothing; for inner and outer coffins; for worship and sacrifices in life and death—each had differentiated [i.e., graded] categories [for everyone], from the emperor, dukes, feudal lords, and high and lesser officers down to the stableboys, gatekeepers, and nightwatchmen. *With this in order, superior and inferior were in place and people's ambitions stayed settled* [emphasis added].[107]

---

104. On this practice in Han dynasty *Classic of Odes* commentary, see Saussy, *Problem of a Chinese Aesthetic*.

105. *Hanshu* 91.3681.

106. Compare *Hanshu* 91.3679.

107. *Hanshu* 91.3679.

In stark contrast to Sima Qian's closing rhetorical question ("Surely they are the 'untitled nobility,' are they not?"), Ban Gu celebrates, without any ambiguity, the success of the complex system of social orders (*jue*) that naturalizes hierarchical relations. During this golden age, he later adds, "the lowly did not seek to overstep the noble," all discussion of profit (*li*) was limited to the merchants, and the people "esteemed what was right, and looked down upon profit (*li*)." In place of the (potentially) admiring recognition of nouveaux riches, Ban Gu frames the biographies of the prosperous as part of a history of decadence. He closes the chapter with the worst of the money-makers: "Furthermore they became rich through digging up graves, gambling, and ambush. Their transgressions and crimes (*jian*) produced wealth. The followers of (the prosperous) Qu Shu, Qi Fa, and Yong Le still appear as straight as a row of teeth. (However), they harm civilization and destroy customs. They are the road to social chaos."[108] The prosperous are not exemplars of wisdom, but (relatively better or worse) harbingers of social breakdown.

The relative ideological clarity of the *Hanshu* vis-à-vis the *Shiji* in the representation of markets (and frontiers) reflects a broader tendency that ancient and modern commentators have recognized. Although the *Hanshu* offers a history of the Former Han period (unlike the multi-millenia spanning *Shiji*), it introduces a new "Table of Ancient and Modern People" (Gu jin ren biao 古今人表) that morally ranks individuals from the beginning of history to the cusp of the Han dynasty. Its nine columns run from the "most superior sages" (上上聖人), such as Confucius, through variously calibrated "middling" groups to the "most inferior fools" (下下愚人).[109]

Conclusion

Modern scholars have commemorated the *Shiji*'s "Account of the Xiongnu" for introducing empirical ethnography into a continuous, evolutionary history of Chinese writings about its Others ("histories of nationalities" *minzu shi* 民族史) or as the kind of "imperial ethnography"

---

108. *Hanshu* 91.3694.

109. These lowest of fools chronologically end with Yan Yue 閻樂, who ranks even lower than the famously dissolute Second Emperor of Qin whom he overthrew in 207 BCE. See *Hanshu* 20.861–951.

that aids and accompanies imperialist expansion, comparable to European writings about the non-West in the analyses of Edward Said, Mary Louise Pratt, and others. This chapter has shown the difficulties of aligning genre with ideology. The *Hanshu* fits this modern notion of ethnography; the *Shiji*'s assemblage of competing ethnographic narratives and ambivalent metaphors, however, does not. The *Shiji*'s "Account of the Commodity Producers" and "Account of the Xiongnu" present an economic and cultural geography of China whose relation to the classical tributary order remains unclear. The *Hanshu* restored historiography's classical function of praise and blame. Through its clear authorial appraisals, it helped to discursively assimilate those most resistant to becoming Han China's "outer subjects" (*wai chen* 外臣) and "inner subjects" (*nei chen* 內臣). It made the new Han specter of the immutable Xiongnu and created a new literary format of empirical ethnographic description that was continuous with a dominant tradition that assumed Chinese moral and cultural superiority. The *Hanshu* stripped the internal enemy, the "commodity producers," of their moral and social pretensions, omitted the "untitled nobility," and reaffirmed the need for planned markets in the agriculture-centered state. The Xiongnu and the money-maker become opposite sides of the same anti-tributary coin. Although the *Shiji* provided the literary model (and much of the content) for the *Hanshu*, the narrative approaches of the two works differed radically. Ancient and modern scholars have long discussed Sima Qian's so-called laissez faire economics, but they have overlooked his radical critique of ethnographic discourse. As in the case of J. M. Coetzee's fiction (see the epigram at the beginning of this chapter), the *Shiji* illumines the politics of regulating meaning; that is, it explains the conditions that compel the author "to explain what the messages say." Most important in the *Hanshu* rewriting of this narrative, then, is not its removal of the *Shiji*'s un-classical defense of the unregulated market (which later generations would recover), but rather it is the *Hanshu*'s permanent erasure of the *Shiji*'s arresting, unsettling, reflexive and yet internally inconsistent treatment of the very terms and conditions of discourse on frontier and market.

PART II

Practices

CHAPTER 4

Alienation:
Kinship in the World Economy

That the rights and power of women failed to develop can be attributed to the fact that women are well versed in Ban [Zhao] the traitor's book.
> —He-Yin Zhen, "On the Revenge of Women" (1907)

[Kinship] is not a form a being but a form of doing. And [Antigone's] action implicates her in an aberrant repetition of a norm, a custom, a convention, not a formal law but a lawlike regulation of culture that operates with its own contingency.
> —Judith Butler, *Antigone's Claim*

M odern historians have observed that the married couple social unit took on a new political-economic importance during early Chinese empire. Qin-Han laws introduced the marriage-based household as the basic unit of society. Unlike the independent aristocratic polities of the Warring States period, all households were subordinate to the Emperor, and were required to register for the provision of taxes, labor, and military service to the state. During the Former Han, tax penalties on unwed women (but not unwed men) and certain forms of co-residence helped to reduce household size to around four to six persons, thereby increasing the number of households eligible for taxes and services.[1] This nuclear household expanded in size during the Later Han when the

---

1. The annual poll tax of 120 *qian* on all adults over fifteen years of age (*suan fu* 算賦) was doubled for merchants and slaves, and, at least as recorded for the year 181 BCE quintupled for unmarried women between 15 and 30 years of age. See *Hanshu* 2, 91. For very different early twentieth century analyses of the economics of marriage see Chen, *Economic Principles of Confucius*, 269–90, and Liu, *Birth of Chinese Feminism*, 92–104.

classical promotion of filial piety encouraged multiple generations to live together, and when large hereditary lineages regained political power.

Kinship also became politicized at the imperial frontiers. After the defeat of the Han army by the Xiongnu confederacy in 200 BCE, a Han princess was sent to each successive Xiongnu leader along with annual payments to bind the *heqin* 和親 (peace through kinship) treaty that lasted until Emperor Wu resumed war in 133 BCE. During the *heqin* peace the Han official Chao Cuo 鼂錯 (d. 154 BCE) introduced China's enduring strategy of military occupation through colonial settlements (*tun tian* 屯田), recruiting convicts, ex-convicts, slaves, and voluntary migrants with the promise of homes, tax exemptions, and spouses: "County officials should buy (*mai* 買) husbands or wives for migrants, because by nature people cannot settle peacefully for long without a mate."[2]

Recent scholarship has drawn on excavated materials to highlight the tensions between classical prescriptions and lived kinship practices, as well as a historical shift in this dynamic from the Former to Later Han dynasties.[3] To explain this change, especially the increased regulation of women's lives, modern historians have pointed to the political rise of classicism. By the late Former Han and Later Han dynasties, new prescriptive texts specifically for and by women emerged that would remain highly influential for two millennia to come. These most famously included Ban Zhao's *Admonitions for Women* (*Nü Jie* 女誡), condemned by the early twentieth century feminist theorist He-Yin Zhen in the opening epigram. As argued over the preceding three chapters, classicism did not simply evolve in a discursive vacuum. Classicists elaborated and revised traditional claims in and through the new genres that accompanied and enabled Emperor Wu's expansionist economics. This chapter ties the domestic politics of kinship to debates over the political

---

2. Chao Cuo's 169 BCE memorial to Wendi in *Hanshu* 49.2287. Excavated Han administrative documents from the Han-Xiongnu frontier attest to the high proportion of women married at early ages who had been (voluntarily or forcibly) settled at the frontier. Chun-shu Chang's analysis of Juyan documents calculates that approximately 85% of both men and women (who were living in the Han frontier colony of Juyan and who were between the ages of 20 and 57) were married. See Chang, *Frontier, Immigration, and Empire*, 107–28, esp. 126.

3. See for example, Gu Lihua, *Handai funü shenghuo*; Nylan, "Administration of the Family"; Hinsch, *Women in Early Imperial China*; Raphals, *Sharing the Light*; Lewis, *The Early Chinese Empires*; Lewis, *Sanctioned Violence in Early China*.

economy of the frontiers. It argues that the now familiar classical Chinese analogies that produced gendered subjects through work (men plow, women weave) and through kinship relations (husband-wife, lord-subject, father-son) became dominant in opposition to often overlooked Former Han discourses and practices that shaped and were shaped by contact and exchange with the wider world, and that did not always take the marital unit as the ideal form.

Women's Work: The Household and the Silk Road

Silks and textiles were the most important manufactured product of early markets and, as will be discussed in chapter 5, served as a form of money. During the Former Han the expansion of local and long-distance (Silk Road) markets in textiles was enabled both by private enterprise and by large state-run production complexes. The largest of these, which was part of the Three Offices for Garments in the Qi commandery (Shandong), employed several thousand women.[4] As addressed in chapter 1, Warring States and Han texts traditionally discussed the economy using the hierarchical terms *ben* (root, primary, i.e., agriculture) and *mo* (tip, secondary, i.e., commerce). Women's work (*nü gong*) did not, however, fit neatly into this rhetorical opposition. In the canonical statements of the *Record of Rites* (*Liji*), the wife "becomes a match to her husband by performing the work of silk, hemp, and cloth, and textiles," and the Classical Scholars of the *Debate on Salt and Iron* reasserted this claim: "Men plowing and women weaving is the great enterprise of empire."[5] Despite the symbolic pairing of agriculture and sericulture as the "root" economy, men's occupations provided the default moral example. Plowing always played counterpoint to craft (*gong*) and commerce (*shang*). Women's (textile) work (*nü gong; nü shi*), by contrast, could rhetorically belong to either "root" or "branch."[6] There was no

---

4. On these and on the meager archaeological record on women artisans, see Barbieri-Low, *Artisans in Early Imperial China*, 107–14. Lacquer inscriptions provide the best evidence thus far of women's substantial presence in privately-run and government-supervised workshops.

5. *Liji zheng yi* 4001: "Hun yi" (昏義): 當於夫，以成絲麻布帛之事; Wang Liqi, *Yantielun*, 170–71.

6. For examples of the use of *nü gong* to refer to non-commercial, traditional weaving, see for example *Hanshu* 28B.1660; Wang Liqi, *Yantielun*, 4–5.

corresponding category of all-embracing "manly work." Francesca's Bray's observation of late imperial China equally applies to the classical inheritance assumed in the *Debate on Salt and Iron*: "For late imperial officials, agriculture and textile industry were a symbolic pair, insepara- bly bound together as 'correct' male and female work. From this perspec- tive farming and weaving were the activities that constituted at once the moral and material foundation of a proper social order, they were tech- nologies that produced subjects as well as material goods."[7]

During the Han, however, the "correctness" of female work was dis- cussed not simply in traditional terms of fulfillment or negligence, but also with new anxieties about the kind of textile work a woman engaged in and the scale, efficiency, or exploitative conditions of textile produc- tion. Not only were more women leaving their home looms for larger- scale state-run and commercial weaving enterprises, but the vogue for complex weaves and the growth of local and long-distance markets were producing new occupations for women. "If one seeks wealth from poverty," the *Shiji* observed, "pricking at embroidery is not as good as getting one's livelihood from the market (lit. "leaning on the market gates")."[8] The well-studied development of classicizing texts for women (that is, texts that emphasized their exemplary ethical roles as wives and mothers in a stratified society) might be better understood as a reaction, in part, to economic visions of women's primary role as industrious work- ers in the expansionist economy.

QUANTIFYING WOMEN'S WORK

Modern economic historians have highlighted the revolutionary nature of early imperial technological advances in agriculture and the resulting improvements in crop yields. However, it is the figure of the female silk weaver that became exemplary in Han discussions of productivity. Han dynasty mathematical texts, which frequently drew their hypothetical scenarios from the market world, contain problems concerning female but not male productivity. As mentioned in chapter 1, the *Nine Chapters on Mathematical Arts* (*Jiu zhang suan shu*) contains the following prob-

---

7. See Bray, "Toward a critical history," 168; see also Bray, *Technology and Gender*, 184–6, and Kuhn, *Textile Technology*.

8. *Shiji* 129.3274; *Hanshu* 91.3687.

lem: "Suppose there is a girl skilful at weaving, who each day doubles her product. In 5 days she weaves (a cloth of) 5 *chi*. Question: how much does she weave in each successive day?"[9] The earlier *Book of Mathematical Calculations* (*Suan shu shu*) contains a parallel version of this dream of the infinitely more productive weaver, who doubles her production daily. It also poses the following problem: "There are three wives; the eldest one in 1 day weaves 50 *chi*; the middle-aged one in 2 days weaves 50 *chi*; the youngest one in 3 days weaves 50 *chi*. Now their woven product is 50 *chi*. Question: how many *chi* did each manage?"[10]

Although Han mathematical texts explored impractical theoretical scenarios, their examples here, in assessing relative rates of productivity among women (for example, of different age groups) supposedly reflected quotidian problems and made production more efficient.[11] The mathematical problems include examples with activities associated with the traditional occupation of women (for example, performing the measurements required in silk dyeing and silk-boiling). Since a range of received and excavated texts also represent Han dynasty women as buyers and sellers in the marketplace, and as owners and distributers of land, women theoretically could also have peopled the (ungendered) mathematical problems involving monetary price calculations and land-division.[12] Men or husbands are never specified, and the only times women appear in these two mathematical texts are in their roles as weaving workers with variable, quantifiable productivity. There are no extant parallel problems concerning male productivity, whether in agricultural or artisanal occupations.

This seemingly insignificant or incidental detail takes on a greater significance when juxtaposed with *qingzhong* economics. The *Guanzi's*

---

9. For a discussion of this problem in the context of the rhetoric of mathematical texts, see chapter 1. See Bai Shangnu, *Jiu zhang suan shu zhu shi*, 85–86; Chemla, *Les Neuf Chapitres*, 286–89. Compare the *Suan shu shu* version, which omits the discussion of women's age: 女織鄰里有女惡自喜也織日自再五日織五尺問始織日及其次各幾何. See Peng Hao, *Zhangjiashan Han jian "Suan shu shu,"* 56; Cullen, "The Suan shu shu," 22.

10. Peng Hao, *Zhangjiashan Han jian "Suan shu shu,"* 64.

11. See Chemla and Guo, *Les Neuf Chapitres*, 475–81.

12. For a woman's distribution of land in her will in 5 CE, see Hinsch, "Women, Kinship, and Property." For an excellent discussion of women's relation to work, see Hinsch, *Women in Early Imperial China*, 59–78.

"Qingzhong" chapters radically detached women from the classical, marriage-based, household economy. Women's work took on a new significance within the *Guanzi*'s universalizing economic strategies for world hegemony. *Qingzhong* theory quantitatively rationalized women's work in ways that were both parallel to and distinct from men's labor. On the one hand, the state needed to calculate, monitor, and regulate women's work with the same arithmetic precision as men's work because women were equally vital participants in the economy: "If farmers do not plow, someone will consequently go hungry; if a single woman does not weave, someone will consequently freeze."[13] To regulate profits and prices, government statisticians had to calculate: "What is the extent of women's work (*nü shi*) in any given district? How much surplus clothing (do they produce)?"[14] State planners had to "encourage women's fine and delicate [work], and put the returns from their weaving into the state treasury."[15] These textiles appropriated by the state could in turn be used to regulate grain prices or could be stored for times of need. At the same time, women's work became *more* representative, or rhetorically exemplary of, certain specific universal *qingzhong* problems concerning (maximizing) productivity, (manipulating) consumption, and (expanding) world hegemony.

The *Guanzi* tied its broader dream of world domination to the problem of productivity, for which the women's weaving recurs as a solution. In this example, single women in particular assume a new importance:

桓公曰：「何謂來天下之財？」管子對曰：「昔者桀之時，女樂三萬人，端譟晨樂聞於三衢，是無不服文繡衣裳者。伊尹以薄之游女工文繡纂組，一純得粟百鍾於桀之國也。夫桀之國者，天子之國也。桀無天下憂，飾婦女鍾鼓之樂，故伊尹得其粟而奪之流。此之謂來天下之財。」

Duke Huan asked: "What do you mean by attracting the world's wealth?"

Guanzi replied: "In antiquity, during the time of [Xia emperor] Jie, there were 30,000 female musicians. The din of their music [even] at dawn was so loud that it resounded through the three thoroughfares, and there was none amongst them who did not wear patterned and embroidered clothing and robes. Yi Yin put the unattached women (*you nü* 游女, lit. 'roam-

---

13. Ma Feibai, *Guanzi qingzhong pian*, 542.
14. Ma Feibai, *Guanzi qingzhong pian*, 270.
15. Ma Feibai, *Guanzi qingzhong pian*, 129.

ing women') of Bo to work on patterned and embroidered red waist-bands, each *chun* of which obtained 100 *zhong* of grain from Jie's state. Jie's state was the Son of Heaven's state, but since Jie did not grieve for [the welfare of] his state but rather decorated the women who sounded the music of bell and drum, Yi Yin took his grain, and mastered the flow of trade. This is called attracting the world's wealth."[16]

Although the example here is from antiquity, it teaches a general strategy in response to the general question of how to attract the world's wealth (何謂來天下之財？). When the *Debate on Salt and Iron*'s Classical Scholars elsewhere allude to the depravity of Jie, theirs is a parable about the evils of embroidery. Here, however, Guanzi is primarily interested in how to take economic advantage of another state's weakness. At the center of his parable is the usefulness of unattached women as exploitable workers.[17] These women are clearly not part of the marriage-based household economy, thus their greater surplus product of embroidery enables the state to make Jie dependent and hence to "master the flow of trade" (奪之流). Elsewhere, silk and textiles also feature as crucial commodities, mediums of exchange, or tributary items that the ruler uses to gain political hegemony at home and abroad. As discussed in chapters 1 and 5, Guanzi applauds the Zhou people's use of mere fiat "counters" to purchase and monopolize the dyed silks of the naïve Lai foreigners.[18] In other dialogues, he encourages the ruler to manipulate the price or monopolize the supply of certain kinds of textiles to acquire hegemony.

Unlike in the classicizing arguments addressed below, the concepts of marriage and kinship have little use in these economic calculations. The state factory (and hence foreign policy), not the household, benefits from women's productivity. Idle women are potentially useful, not immoral. To maximize silk production, the Guanzian state-planner also needs to regulate sociality and affect. When Duke Huan wanted to lower the

16. Ma Feibai, *Guanzi Qing zhong pian*; 493; cf. Rickett, *Guanzi* 2:447.

17. Ma Feibai and Rickett, *Guanzi* 2: 447, both interpret 游 as "unemployed." The phrase from the *Odes* (Mao 16) suggests unwed young women, as demonstrated in the exemplary citation of this *Ode* in the Former Han dynasty *Hanshi waizhuan*, discussed below. See *Han shi wai zhuan jin zhu*, 3.

18. Ma Feibai, *Guanzi qingzhong pian*, 641–47. For other examples, see Ma Feibai, *Guanzi qingzhong pian*, 307–8 and 695–96.

price of silk, Guanzi ordered trimming the branches of trees by the side
of the road to minimize economically unproductive sociality.

管子對曰：「途旁之樹未沐之時，五衢之民男女相好，往來之市者罷市
相睹樹下，談語終日不歸。男女當壯扶輂推輿，相睹樹下，戲笑超距終
日不歸。父兄相睹樹下，論議玄語，終日不歸。是以田不發，五穀不播，
桑麻不種，璽縷不治。內嚴一家而三不歸則帛布絲纊之賈安得不貴？」

Guanzi said: "Before the branches of trees that lined the pathways had
been trimmed, boys and girls, who were from amongst those people
populating the five main thoroughfares and who were attracted to each
other, met up beneath the trees. They went to and fro whenever the market was closed, chatting together instead of returning home at the end of
the day. Robust adult men and women, manning their carts and pushing
their wagons, would meet up beneath the trees, joking, laughing, and
tussling instead of returning home at the end of the day. Fathers and
elder brothers would meet up beneath the trees to discuss profound
subjects instead of going home at the end of the day. For this reason the
fields were not developed; the five grains were not sown; mulberry and
hemp were not planted; and cocoon and hemp fibers were not spun. If,
on consideration [of all this], in each household these three groups [of
workers] fail to return [home], then how could the price of silk, cloth,
and silk thread and floss not be high?"[19]

In this example, romantic trysts are economically unproductive in
Guanzi's reasoning. The shaded public walkway between market and
home constitutes the main site of profitless "mutual attraction," "joking
and dancing," and "abstruse discussion"—all of which should be elimi-
nated. However, here the reason for regulating sociality is the price of
silk, not ritual propriety. And although male productivity is also af-
fected, it is women's output that is at stake.

The *Debate on Salt and Iron*'s state economists tie Guanzi's use of
women's labor to increase general economic productivity to a longer
historical tradition. These economists do so in justifying the economic
policies that they once used to expand frontiers and markets under
Emperor Wu:

The imperial agent (*yu shi*) advanced, saying: "In the past when Dai
Gong was enfeoffed at Ying Qiu [in the state of Qi], he cleared the fields
and settled there. Since the land was meager and population small, he

---

19. Ma Feibai, *Guanzi qingzhong pian*, 668–69; cf. Rickett, *Guanzi*, 492–93.

developed profits through the path of the 'branch,' maximizing the skills of women's craft (極女工之巧). As a result, neighboring states traded with Qi, and their wealth in livestock and commodities blossomed, and in a generation [Qi] became a mighty state. When Guan Zhong [i.e., Guanzi] was minister to Duke Huan, he carried forward the earlier ruler's task. His use of *qingzhong* [economic policies] caused enough change to make mighty Chu in the south submit, and to make [Duke Huan] the Hegemon over the vassal lords. Now the Imperial Counselor [i.e., Sang Hongyang] has renewed the techniques of Dai Gong, Duke Huan, and Guanzi, unifying control over the salt and iron [industries], developing the profits from mountains and rivers, and producing [literally "letting blossom"] a myriad of commodities. As a result, resources for county officials are plentiful and sufficient; people are not troubled by shortfalls; 'root' and 'branch' profit together; [and] superiors and inferiors have sufficient provisions. This is the result of the directives regarding accounting and calculation, and not from a sole [focus on] plowing, sericulture, and farming."[20]

Sang Hongyang's *qingzhong* methods of "accounting and calculation" (*chou ji* 籌計) trace back to Dai Gong's "development of profits through the path of the 'branch,' maximizing the skills of women's craft." Here "women's craft" exemplifies both the need for the "branch" as compensation for low income derived from poor farmland, and also the universal reasoning of "accounting and calculation" that profits can and should be made by "maximizing" (*ji* 極 "extreme") human labor. The *Shiji* records this same parable of economic success through exploiting women's labor. In its infamous chronicle of the wealthy ("Account of the Commodity Producers"), Dai Gong becomes the earliest money-maker in China's history by "encouraging women's work, and maximizing their use of skill and ingenuity" (勸其女功，極技巧).[21] Such ideals of maximizing the productivity of women have been overlooked within modern accounts of ancient silk markets and the Silk Road.

CLASSICIZING WOMEN'S WORK

Qingzhong economists made women visible as an exploitable engine of expansionist economics. In opposition to this, classicizing scholars

---

20. Wang Liqi, *Yantielun*, 177.
21. *Shiji* 129.3255. Cf. *Hanshu* 28B.1660, which uses 女工.

sought, in different ways, to restore women to the traditional household. Throughout the *Debate on Salt and Iron*'s debate, the Classical Scholars make gender, sexual desire, marriage, and kinship vital to their political-economic claims. They argue that the transformation of women's work by market and state has undermined the marital unit of a moral community. Expansionist wars that tore men away from their villages and wives, and market pressures that forced women out of the home both led to ritually improper mingling between the sexes, and upset or deregulated the proper times (*shi* 時) for marriage meetings. Frontier warfare destroyed the affective bonds and the economic self-sufficiency of the husband-wife pair ("men plough, women weave"); wives wept for the husbands away at the frontier; couples living at the frontier lived in miserable conditions; state levies for war doubled taxes on women and overworked the farmers; women were too busy weaving embroidery to produce sufficient clothes for the family.[22] According to the Classical Scholars, wealth was catalyzing the very destruction of the nuclear couple:

古者，夫婦之好，一男一女，而成家室之道。及後，士一妾，大夫二，諸侯有姪娣九女 而已。今諸侯百數，卿大夫十數，中者侍御，富者盈室。是以女或曠怨失時，男或放死 無匹。

[Classical Scholars:] "In antiquity, the affection between husband and wife, between one man and one woman, was the way to build one's household and chamber. In later times, a knight could have one concubine, a great officer [could have] two concubines, and the vassal lords could have nine women [from the same family]. Nowadays a vassal lord has many hundred [concubines], an auxiliary officer [has] several dozens, those of middling wealth have servants, and the chambers of wealthy men (*fu zhe*) are overflowing [with women]. For this reason there are women who miss their proper time [of marriage] growing jealous alone while there are men who will never have a spouse during their lifetime."[23]

The Classical Scholars protest the market's transformation of marriage practices in terms of the classic economic concerns of equitable distribution and insufficiency. The Han dynasty nouveaux riches, with their overflowing chambers full of concubines, have joined the traditional noble elite in upsetting the ritual propriety of a marriage of "one man and

---

22. Wang Liqi, *Yantielun*, 39, 40, 89–90, 179, 351, 405, 454–55, 464–65, 472–73, 531.
23. Wang Liqi, *Yantielun*, 356; cf. Wang Liqi, *Yantielun* 473; 351.

one woman." This trend results in the unfair and unbalanced distribution of women among powerful men; a growing population of poorer unmarried men; and more women who are demoted to the status of mere concubines. Market growth had tipped the social balance of affect leading to an excess of negative affect (jealousy, loneliness).

The Classical Scholars' opponent, Sang Hongyang, noted the market's transformation of female, rather than male, desire: "The women of Zhao do not discriminate between good and bad; the women of Zheng do not discriminate between locals and those from afar."[24] However, Sang did so to highlight the universal pursuit of self-interest, not to attack the market's corrosion of marital values. As with a man, "If there is a coin on the road, a woman will pick it up."[25] The imperial agent (speaking for Sang's side) even cites an instance in which Confucius violated the ritual propriety governing the separation of sexes.[26] By representing the imperial agent maligning an authority as sacred to the Classical Scholars as Confucius, the *Debate on Salt and Iron*'s classicizing author (Huan Kuan) effectively casts the speaker in ill light. More importantly in this context, the state economists appear unperturbed by the unraveling of gender and kinship norms. What matters for them is women's place in the economic (rather than biological or social) expansion of the state.

The Classical Scholars primarily protested Han dynasty expansionist economics in terms of (implicitly or explicitly) male *ben* and *mo* occupations. When the Classical Scholars specifically discussed women, they highlighted the women's suffering as workers, women's moral duties as frugal consumers, and especially women's kinship role as wives. The Classical Scholars also removed discussions of women's work from economic rationalization. In redefining women's work, they championed the production of the hemp necessary for households over (economically and morally) superfluous silk embroidery (variously 文繡; 飾微治細; 纖微; 黼黻; 綺繡). The plain cloth produced in and for the home (part of the "root") differed from the overly complex weaves produced in large-scale government, manorial, or factory workshops (part of the "branch"). For the Classical Scholars, silk embroidery and complex weaves for local

24. Wang Liqi, *Yantielun*, 228.
25. Wang Liqi, *Yantielun*, 609.
26. Wang Liqi, *Yantielun*, 150.

and long-distance markets placed unconscionable pressures on women workers, and diverted labor from the task of manufacturing sufficient clothing for the general population. A range of earlier classical texts had already presented silk embroidery—and the women who wore such garments—as signs of moral excess. The *Debate on Salt and Iron*'s Classical Scholars condemn "wives and daughters wearing gauzy silks, the servants and concubines trailing linen fabrics."[27] They bemoan the loss of an antiquity in which "commoners could only wear silk once they were elderly, and others all wore hemp"; in which silk was reserved for queens, princesses, and marriage ceremonies; and in which silk was not sold in the marketplace: "Nowadays the rich wear embroidered chiffons and gauzy silks and those of middling wealth wear silks and brocades. The general population commonly wears what only queen consorts once wore . . . . If fine silk is twice the price of raw silk, fine silk should be twice as useful."[28] Although other Han officials did attack the growing disparity of wealth, the Classical Scholars here and elsewhere repeatedly attack the popular adoption of an extravagant lifestyle, epitomized by the sporting of silk. The relative price of raw and worked silk reflects for them precisely the corruption of social values. The Classical Scholars even hold up the Xiongnu as a superior model of economic production saying "[Xiongnu] women do not pay taxes on silks embroidered with excessive skill (*yin qiao* 淫巧); they do not labor over delicate silks and fine gauzes."[29]

The *Debate on Salt and Iron* engaged the Han politics of ornamentality that already considered embroidery as a moral excess. The *Masters of Huainan* (*Huainanzi*)—a political-philosophical text presented to Emperor Wu in 139 BCE—had argued: "Carving, polishing, cutting, and engraving are what harm the tasks of farmers./Embroidering cloth and patterning belts are what impair the labor of women. When the tasks of farmers are abandoned/And women's work is injured/This is the root of hunger and source of cold."[30] Emperor Jing's prior edict of 142 BCE had offered similar sentiments, looking to the imperial couple as the model

---

27. Wang Liqi, *Yantielun*, 119–20. Compare 335–37.

28. Wang Liqi, *Yantielun*, 352.

29. Wang Liqi, *Yantielun*, 555. They also rhetorically praise the fact that Xiongnu men do not have to waste time building houses.

30. Major, *The Huainanzi*, 426–47.

for the household economy: "Ornamental carvings and engraved inlays harm agricultural production. Brocade, embroidery, and vermilion ribbons damage women's work . . . . I [i.e., the Emperor] myself plow and the Empress herself cultivates silkworms in order to provide abundant millet and sacrificial robes to the ancestral temples on behalf of the empire."[31] In a similar vein, the *Debate on Salt and Iron*'s Classical Scholars claim: "If men abandon the 'root' for the 'branch,' carving patterns and engravings to imitate (*xiang* 象) birds and beasts, capturing animals by mastering their movements, there will not be enough grain to eat. If women exquisitely decorate [cloth] with fine threads to create patterns (*wen zhang* 文章), [thus] maximizing their skill and ingenuity, there will not be enough silk cloth for clothing."[32] In this gendered aesthetic model, patterned silks parallel the mimetic designs of artisans as wasteful "branch" labor that leads to economic insufficiency. As discussed in chapter 2, Yang Xiong's analogy between the prose-poetic *fu* and "misty gossamer" was implicitly critical of classical aesthetic ornament. Shortly after Yang Xiong's death, an official proclamation of 7 BCE called for the end of such intricate labor, which was "harmful" to the women laborers themselves.[33]

Han critics understood that the epideictic *fu* celebrated the embroidered sleeves, not the wifely virtues, of its dancing women. By contrast, the *Odes* tradition became a classical vehicle for reasserting the traditional marriage-based household economy. For example, 30 of the 306 moral anecdotes contained in the *Hanshi waizhuan* 韓詩外傳 (Han [Ying's] Exoteric Commentary [on the *Odes*]) addressed the proper actions of women. Attributed to the *boshi* scholar, Han Ying 韓嬰 (ca. 200–ca. 120 BCE), this anthology concluded each of its anecdotes with a verse or section from a selected *Ode*. These anecdotes encoded a set of social values while training the scholar in the important classical practice of apt quotation of the *Odes*. Together the anecdotes make the *Odes* into a resource for political criticism, rather than a text for interpretation. Praise of the frugal life and distaste for the market economy recur throughout the anecdotes: for example, "The gentleman should not speak of exchanging goods or follow the way of a merchant" (士不言通

---

31. *Hanshu* 5.151.
32. Wang Liqi, *Yantielun*, 40.
33. *Hanshu* 11.336.

財貨，不賣於道).[34] In its version of the classical "well-field" (*jing tian*) ideal (discussed in chapter 1), the eight farming families "planned marriages together," in addition to looking after each other in times of need.[35] In another anecdote, Confucius urges his disciple to regard poverty as wealth (夫貧而如富), and praises a washerwoman who rejects bribes.[36] Elsewhere, women's idle play with chestnuts and extravagant use of gauze leads to insufficiency of resources.[37] These moralizing anecdotes also teach the disastrous effects of war and of state intervention in the economy (e.g., increased taxation for public works, increased reliance on state statistics instead of on ritual).[38] In a strikingly political conversation between two women, who are weaving together one night, one woman explains the direct impact of war on her livelihood and family. During the war a horse strayed into the woman's garden, destroying her mallow crop; the ruler sent the woman's sister as a present to an allied ruler; and her brother died while trying to visit her.[39]

The "Mao Prefaces" 毛序 (first century CE) to each individual *Ode* made marriage even more definitive of a woman's life and work.[40] As discussed elsewhere, this commentarial tradition, which later became part of the canonical *Classic of Odes*, contributed to the unprecedented classical focus on women as ethical and political subjects during the Han dynasty.[41] The "Mao Prefaces" to 66 of the 160 songs (of the opening "Airs of States" section) concern female ethics or relations between the sexes:

[*Ode* 1] "The Ospreys" is [about] the virtue of the queen consort.[42]

[*Ode* 2] "The Cloth-Plant Spreads" is [about] the natural disposition of the queen consort. The queen consort is in her parents' household, and

---

34. *Han shi wai zhuan*, 166.

35. *Han shi wai* zhuan, 165.

36. *Han shi wai zhuan*, 429 and 3. Cf. *Han shi wai zhuan*, 11, 73, and 318.

37. *Han shi wai zhuan*, 166.

38. *Han shi wai zhuan*, 37, 91–92, 99, 116, and 224.

39. *Han shi wai zhuan*, 40.

40. For an introduction to the "Great Preface" (*da xu* 大序), the "Small Prefaces" (*xiao xu* 小序), their authorship, and their relation to the *Classic of Odes* commentarial tradition, see Allen, "Postface." The numbering of the poems follows the order of this canonical Mao version.

41. Chin, "Orienting Mimesis."

42. *Mao shi zhu shu*, 12.

therefore her purpose is fixed on the duties of women's work (女功之事); she is economical and frugal; she wears her [carefully] washed clothes; she honors and reveres her teacher. Therefore she is able to return [at the arranged time to visit] her parents, and to transform the empire using a woman's way.[43]

[*Ode* 3] "Cocklebur" is about the intent of the queen consort. It is also about her sense of obligation in assisting her husband in searching for worthies and examining officials. She understands the travails of subordinates. Within [the inner court] she is intent on advancing worthies, but she does not have a mind for using insinuating speech to introduce her own [relatives]. Morning and evening she worries greatly about it, to the point of anxiety and strain.[44]

The "queen consort" is the ethical subject of the "Mao Prefaces" to the opening eight poems of the *Classic of Odes*. In these first three cases it is her kinship position—in relation to her husband (the ruler), her parents-in-law, and her own parents—that gives her an identity, her interiority (her intent, her anxieties), and her work (helping her husband, etc.). Unlike the *Debate on Salt and Iron*, other "Mao Prefaces" elaborate the proper relations between the queen (or wife) and concubines, and pay little attention to the market economy per se. Like the *Debate on Salt and Iron* and *Hanshi waizhuan*, however, the "Mao Prefaces" promote the general importance of marriage for society. They repeatedly propose that individual poems of the *Classic of Odes* offer criticisms or observations of the problem of people who have not wed or will not wed, or the problem of men and women failing to meet at the proper time (especially during times of war).

Scholarship on early Chinese gender has rightly highlighted the significance of Liu Xiang's (79–8 BCE) *Accounts of Exemplary Women* (*Lienü zhuan* 列女傳) and Ban Zhao's *Admonitions for Women* as new kinds of didactic texts for women that emerged in the Han. These texts established highly influential traditions for women over subsequent centuries. That such texts emerged as part of the classicizing tradition seems natural now precisely because the imperial bureaucracy of the Later Han and post-Han period made classicism normative. However, it is important to note that both the kinds of statements that could be made about women

---

43. *Mao shi zhu shu*, 30.
44. *Mao shi zhu shu*, 33.

(e.g., about their productivity) and the literary medium of those proposals (e.g., historicizing, hypothetical, quantitative), was politicized during
the Former Han. The *Debate on Salt and Iron*'s Classical Scholars had
to actively contest the (now often forgotten) *qingzhong* economists who
maximized women's roles in the economic expansion of empire and
minimized their participation in biological and social reproduction. The
Classical Scholars defended classicism (that is, textual expertise, classical
authorities) in part through a new sexual politics—a defense of an agricultural economy and classical reasoning in the name of suffering women
workers and in opposition to the breakdown of traditional marriage roles.

Reconstruction of this historical opposition may help to clarify why
these (later highly influential) didactic texts took on the specific forms
and put forward the claims that they did.[45] Unlike the *Debate on Salt
and Iron*'s Classical Scholars, Liu Xiang and Ban Zhao did not have to
explicitly defend their continual appeal to traditional classical authorities. The political victory of classicism both enabled and constrained
their discursive modes. The representation of the couple as a kinship
unit, not an economic unit, better fit the economics of lineage rule.
Within classicism, Liu and Ban respectively drew on a particular attention to gender, kinship, and desire found in commentaries and in anec-
dotal uses of the *Odes* tradition (as in the *Hanshi waizhuan*). When the
(male) imperial librarian Liu Xiang composed the *Accounts of Exemplary Women*, the earliest (extant) compilation of women's biographies,
he drew generically both on the *Shiji*'s collation of historical biographies
(*zhuan*) and on the *Hanshi waizhuan*'s use of the *Odes*.[46] Each of the
Accounts of Exemplary Women's 104 biographies incorporated a quotation
from the *Odes* tradition and a moral eulogy. Unlike the *Shiji*, which
represented without censure some women's activities in the market and
money economy, the *Accounts of Exemplary Women* exclusively extolled
women's role in the household economy.[47] The *Accounts of Exemplary*

---

45. On Ban Zhao's later influence, see, for example, Ko, *Teachers of the Inner Chambers*; Ebrey, *Women and the Family*; Mann, *Precious Records*; Chen Liping, *Liu Xiang
Lienüzhuan yanjiu*.

46. See Hinsch, "Cross-Genre Influence"; Hinsch, "The Composition of the
Lienüzhuan"; Chen Liping, *Liu Xiang Lienüzhuan yanjiu*, 89–97.

47. As Lisa Raphals has shown, the *Lienü zhuan* showed women using forms of both
rhetorical persuasion (from minister to superior) and instructive argument (from
teacher to student). See Raphals, "Arguments by Women."

Women made exemplars of those women who wove for a living, or who wove despite their own household wealth; and the *Accounts of Exemplary Women* associated such activity with a set of sexual morals that became increasingly embraced as true womanly virtues in the Later Han and subsequent dynasties (e.g., not remarrying, not prostituting oneself). Its assumption—that women's weaving is a virtue—belonged to what Bret Hinsch has called the "moralization of textile manufacture."[48] Unlike the *Guanzi*'s women, whose work is evaluated in terms of quantitative output and profit, these women of the *Accounts of Exemplary Women* become exemplary (for women *and* men) precisely because they produce only enough for a *meager* livelihood. Unlike Guanzi's regulation of sociality and leisure space to maximize productivity (e.g., by cutting foliage around a popular location for socializing), the *Hanshi waizhuan* and *Accounts of Exemplary Women* present the workplace as a social site for the production of the moral economy. They represent mothers and wives making their moral point while at the loom, and women debating while weaving together late at night.

In this context, it makes sense to ask not only what did classicism do to women (i.e., how did classicism shape the representation of women in literature and the bodily activities of these women) but also what did broader discourses about women do to classical practices? On one level, it would appear that the composition, preservation, and prestige of written texts by women during the Later Han, most famously by Ban Zhao, helped to open up classical practices to a broader constituency during the rise of classicism (i.e., to women). However both Liu Xiang's *Accounts of Exemplary Women* and Ban Zhao's *Admonitions for Women* complicate the relation of scholarly activity to gender and to economic work. One of the *Accounts of Exemplary Women*'s most famous anecdotes concerns Mencius's mother:

孟子之少也，既學而歸，孟母方績，問曰：「學何所至矣？」孟子曰：「自若也。」孟母以刀斷其織。孟子懼而問其故，孟母曰：「子之廢學，若吾斷斯織也。夫君子學以立名，問則廣知，是以居則安寧，動則遠害。今而廢之，是不免於廝役，而無以離於禍患也。何以異於織績而食，中道廢而不爲，寧能衣其夫子，而長不乏糧食哉！女則廢其所食，男則墮於脩德，不爲竊盜，則爲虜役矣。」孟子懼，旦夕勤學不息，師事子思，

---

48. Hinsch, *Women in Early Imperial China*, 71.

遂成天下之名儒。君子謂孟母知爲人母之道矣。詩云：「彼姝者子，何以告之？」此之謂也。

[Once] when Mencius was young and he returned from studying, Mencius's mother (*Meng mu*) was spinning and asked: "How far did you get in your studies?" Mencius replied, "As far as before." Mencius's mother took a knife and cut her weaving. Mencius was terrified and asked the reason for this. Mencius's mother said: "Your abandonment of studies is like me cutting this weaving. A gentleman (*junzi*) studies to establish his name, and through inquiry broadens his knowledge, enabling him to reside in peace and tranquility, and in his actions to keep harm at a distance. If you abandon it now, servitude is unavoidable and your disaster and misfortune will not leave you. How would this differ from my weaving and spinning to provide food, and in midcourse abandoning and not completing it, rather than making clothes for my husband, and continuing [to ensure we] never lack in food to eat? A woman who abandons her livelihood [is like] a man who, in neglecting his cultivation of virtue, if he does not become a thief or robber, he becomes a prisoner or corvée laborer." Mencius was terrified, and applied himself to his studies from dawn to dusk without rest. He served his teacher, Zisi, and so became a world famous Ru-scholar. The *junzi* calls Mencius's mother's knowledge of how to become a person the Way of the Mother. The *Ode* says: "That fine gentleman/ How should I respond to him?" This is its meaning.[49]

As Lisa Raphals has pointed out, the anecdote focuses on weaving as a livelihood, not as a skill.[50] Mencius's mother spins and weaves "to provide food," and the analogy of weaving with studying for political office turns her work into an occupation. In another biography, the virtuous wife of Jie Yu of Chu 楚接輿妻 takes on traditionally male and female occupations: "I have served you, my husband, myself taking on the plowing and weaving, to feed and clothe us."[51] There was no conflict between her role as family breadwinner and her virtue. In recognizing women's work as economic, the *Accounts of Exemplary Women* follows many of the earlier Han texts addressed above.

One should also note, however, that that when Mencius's mother treats her own weaving as an economic occupation, her analogy implic-

---

49. *Lienü zhuan*, 20–21. For another Han version of this story, see *Hanshi waizhuan*, 365. See also *Mencius* 1A12.

50. Raphals, *Sharing the Light*, 34. See also Nylan, "The Art of Persuasion," 501–3.

51. *Lienü zhuan*, 44.

itly displaces the traditional pairing of "men plough, women weave." In the *Debate on Salt and Iron*, the Classical Scholars had repeatedly to defend themselves from the charge of being economically useless to society. What is interesting here, then, is the rhetorical use of women's weaving to make the scholar-official occupation an economic activity. The analogy of weaver (mother) to classical scholar-official (son) makes classical scholarship simultaneously a virtuous *economic* occupation and a properly *male* occupation. This pairing thereby de-emphasizes the woman's labor of reading, listening, or instruction—the very practices upon which the *Accounts of Exemplary Women* depends for making women into good mothers. In helping to open classicism up to women, the *Accounts of Exemplary Women* ensured the act of studying would be recognized as kinship when performed by a woman, but as work when performed by a man.

Unlike the above texts, in Ban Zhao's *Admonitions for Women* (which was written in the Later Han and preserved in the *Hou Hanshu* 後漢書 [History of the Later Han]) traditional "wife's work" obscures any broader economic aspect of women's work.[52] In this text, women's work does not correlate with men's in the idealized economy of "men plow, women weave" (or, as in Mencius's mother's case—of women weave, men study). Rather, the product of the "wife's work" (*fu gong* 婦功) becomes the dutiful wife herself. Ban Zhao enjoins her readers to perform wifehood through at least two kinds of work: first, a prescribed set of household tasks and activities; and second, an ethical work on the self that, among other things, reclassifies household work as a demonstration of wifely virtue, identity, and duty, rather than as economically productive or politically significant labor. This latter effort of self-discipline or *askesis* simultaneously draws upon and perpetuates the masculine authority of the Classics and classicism. Ban Zhao discusses the wife's work as part of "wifely conduct" (*fu xing* 婦行):

婦行第四：女有四行，一曰婦德，二曰婦言，三曰婦容，四曰婦功。夫云婦德，不必才明絕異也；婦言，不必辯口利辭也；婦容，不必顏色美麗也；婦功，不必工巧過人也。 ... 擇辭而說，不道惡語，時然後言，不厭於人，是謂婦言。盥浣塵穢，服飾鮮絜，沐浴以時，身不垢辱，是謂婦容。專心紡績，不好戲笑，絜齊酒食，以奉賓客，是謂婦功。此四者，女人之大德。

---

52. The *Hou Hanshu* was composed by Fan Ye 范曄 (398–445 CE). For the text of *Nü Jie*, see *Hou Hanshu*, 2786–91.

[Section] 4. *Wifely conduct.* There are four main types of women's conduct: the first is wifely virtue; the second, wifely speech; the third, wifely appearance; and fourth, wifely work. Wifely virtue doesn't mean you have to be exceptionally talented and bright; for wifely speech you don't need elegance; for wifely appearance you don't have to look beautiful and stunning; wifely work means you don't have to be more skillful than anyone else . . . . To choose one's words when speaking, to refrain from gossip and slander, to speak only when appropriate and not to bore others—this is wifely speech. To wash away dust and dirt, to keep one's clothes fresh and clean, to bathe regularly, and not to soil one's body— this is wifely appearance. To devote oneself to spinning and weaving, not to indulge in banter and laughter, and to neatly prepare the wine and food that is to be served to the guests—that is wifely work. These four areas of conduct constitute a woman's greatest virtue.[53]

Here, the wife's work or "wifely work" (婦功) is non-economic. Although the *Hanshi waizhuan* and *Accounts of Exemplary Women* emphasized the ethical, rather than material, value of women's work, many of their historical anecdotes did represent weaving as a means of livelihood (as in the case of Mencius's mother). The wife in Ban Zhao's treatise, however, labors to be unproductive, or at least to produce an undistinguished product. In contrast to Guanzi's economic success in competitively "maximizing the skills of women's craft" (極女工之巧), Ban Zhao's "wifely work means you don't have to be more skillful than anyone else" (不必工巧過人也). In Ban Zhao's view, to succeed at wifehood one must underperform (i.e., *not* be talented, beautiful, eloquent, or skilful). Work has become transformed into a toilsome daily effort to become unexceptional, and thereby to enact the essence of good wifehood.

Classicism serves as the force of naturalization, that is, by habituating the fundamental principles of social hierarchy encoded within classical texts (through memorization, apt quotation, etc.) one makes a set of attributes and activities appear natural to the core meaning of simply being a wife (and, more obliquely, a husband). As the early twentieth century feminist theorist He-Yin Zhen put it, "Ultimately *the crimes of Ban the traitor were caused by Confucian teachings*."[54] Here, to become a

---

53. *Hou Hanshu*, 2789. Partly following Idema, *The Red Brush*, 39.

54. Emphasis in original translation. He-Yin Zhen also notes: "Once [Ban Zhao's] teachings took root, women began to consider their subjugation to men as their natural lot." See Liu, *The Birth of Chinese Feminism*, 145–46.

wife, to interpret and experience one's own toil and suffering as a kinship duty, and not as productive labor or coerced subjection, one must first know the classical codes. As modern critics have pointed out, Ban Zhao's radical call for the equal education of girls and boys ostensibly comes not on grounds of gender equality—indeed she warns the wife not to see herself as her husband's equal—but as a necessity for a wife to serve the husband.[55] In delimiting wifely work as "wifely conduct," as in the example above, Ban Zhao simply iterates and elaborates the same four topics of bridal education found in the *Rites*' "Hun Yi" 昏義 chapter on marriage (i.e., wifely virtue, wifely speech, wifely appearance, and wifely work). Ban Zhao invokes the *Classic of Odes*, the *Record of Rites*, and *Classic of Changes* throughout, and she introduces her laboring, newlywed self through classical quotation:[56]

鄙人愚暗，受性不敏，蒙先君之餘寵，賴母師之典訓。年十有四，執箕箒於曹　氏，于今四十餘載矣。戰戰兢兢，常懼黜辱，以增父母之羞，以益中外之累。夙夜劬心，勤不告勞。

I am simpleminded and unenlightened and not naturally intelligent. But I enjoyed the doting affection of my late father and relied on the exemplary instruction provided by my mother. When I was fourteen—now more than 40 years ago—I took up dustpan and broom in the Cao family. Trembling with fear, I was always afraid of bringing divorce and dishonor on myself, which would bring shame on my parents and add to the burdens of my relatives. From early morning to late night I put forth my best efforts and toiled without complaining of weariness.[57]

In this opening to the *Admonitions*, the dustpan and broom—not wedding gifts or bells and drums—betoken Ban Zhao's initial entry into the conjugal household. Through her work, her work ethic, and her fear of dishonoring herself and own family she becomes a good wife and daughter-in-law. Ban Zhao autobiographically inscribes, through classical quotation, the experience of the fourteen-year-old sweeper into the textual tradition: she "trembles with fear" (戰戰兢兢, citing the *Classic of Odes*);[58] she toils without "complaining of weariness" (告勞,

---

55. For the discussions of and bibliography on Ban Zhao, see Raphals, *Sharing the Light*, 235–58; Goldin, *After Confucius*, 112–18; Swann, *Pan Chao*.
56. She also cites the (otherwise unknown) *Charter for Women*.
57. *Hou Hanshu* 84.2786. Translation following Idema, *Red Brush*, 36.
58. *Ode* 195. *Mao shi zheng yi*, 420.

citing the *Classic of Odes*).[59] At the same time, this bodily trembling and self-silencing become—as classically tagged or aestheticized experience—precisely what makes her (and her reader) recognize herself as the good wife.

Ban Zhao also represents the conjugal household as a site of sanctioned violence. A metaphor of marriage as warfare permeates Ban Zhao's treatise. As Chen Yu-shih has pointed out, Ban Zhao invokes classical tropes of self-preservation and the avoidance of war.[60] "Treating each other as equals," Ban Zhao argues, will inexorably lead from flirting and teasing to disrespect, discontent, and fights that end with the husband's rage, shouting, beating, and divorce.[61] The specter of sanctioned domestic violence thus necessitates the ascetic and affective labor of the wife in naturalizing inequality. Through her education in moralizing cosmology, she will accept the a priori principle that "yin and yang have their respective nature; men and women have different conduct" (陰陽殊性，男女異行).[62] It is precisely because the daughter has the potential to shout back and "to become a tiger" that she must be classically tamed to recognize herself as the *Odes* subject who "trembles with fear." Ban Zhao's first precept on humility (*bi ruo* 卑弱) begins with a paraphrase of another *Ode*, stating that in antiquity the day after a daughter was born she was "placed under a bed to show her lowliness and weakness" and given a tile (used in the spinning process) "to show she had to get used to hard work" while relatives fasted to signify her task in keeping the ancestral sacrifices.[63] These archaic acts set the symbolic template for Ban Zhao's more codified, more intrusive, "constant way of women" (女人之常道): "living always as if filled with fear"; working from dawn to dusk "taking care of household affairs"; "serving her husband" by

---

59. *Ode* 193. *Mao shi zheng yi*, 409.

60. Chen, "The Historical Template of Ban Zhao's *Nü Jie*."

61. *Hou Hanshu* 84.2788.

62. On yin-yang cosmology and gender, see Raphals, *Sharing the Light*, 139–94; Hinsch, *Women*, 162–66. On the broader context of moralizing cosmology, particularly in the *Hanshu*, see Wang, *Cosmology*, esp. 129–72.

63. *Ode* 189: "Then [the lord] bears a daughter/And puts her upon the ground,/ Clothes her in swaddling-clothes,/Gives her a loom-whorl to play with./ For her no decorations, no emblems;/Her only care, the wine and food,/And how to give no trouble to father and mother." Following the translation by Arthur Waley in Allen, *The Book of Songs*, 162–63. See *Mao shi zheng yi*, 388.

preparing the ancestral sacrifices; never laughing or bantering. Classicism transforms work into the reproduction of the kinship system.

As in the abovementioned case of Mencius's mother, Ban Zhao genders the economics of classical practice, effectively ruling out any potential of writing (or weaving) as a form of livelihood for women. The *Shiji* had listed three standard professions for men: farmers, craftsmen, and merchants (農工商); but the *Hanshu* (which Ban Zhao co-authored) listed four categories of professions in its "Treatise on Food and Commodities": "Scholars, farmers, craftsmen, and merchants, the four [classifications] of people had their occupation" (士農工商，四民有業).[64] Its new order implied a higher ranking of scholars than farmers. Although Ban Zhao's *Admonitions for Women* radically proposes equal education for girls and boys, the girl must interpret her classical training purely as instruction in practices of kinship. She must learn the hermeneutic mode of admiring her own activities (such as sweeping or spinning) as manifestations of proper wifely deportment, not as work per se. Thus Ban Zhao's own work as author of multiple classical works and as tutor for the Empress Dowager paradoxically have no place in her own tract. Weaving, like women's classical training, is defined as a virtuous kinship practice. Kinship practice, not *qingzhong* commodification, alienates the product (silk, writing) from the producer. Despite the Han dynasty growth of silk markets, there is no room for Silk Road history in the classical reproduction of the marital household because the virtuous wife has no surplus product.

*Aberrant Kinship and "Peace through Kinship" (*heqin 和親*)*

The expansionist *qingzhong* fantasy of women's work thus offered an explicit or implicit foil against which classicists elaborated kinship ideals. The Former Han politics of frontiers profoundly shaped classical Chinese discourses of kinship in another way. Following the defeat of the Han imperial army by the Xiongnu in 200 BCE, a new diplomatic practice began that was called *heqin* (peace through kinship). In this new

---

64. *Hanshu* 24A.1117–8. This is not in the *Shiji*. Compare Cui Shi's 崔實 (ca. 103–ca. 170) *Si min yue ling* 四民月令 (Monthly Instructions for the Four Classes of People), an agricultural almanac for the gentleman farmer.

diplomacy, instead of an arrangement in which foreign subjects paid an annual tribute (*gong*) at the imperial court, a *heqin* agreement used the egalitarian language of "brotherly" relations and called for the marriage of a Han princess to a Xiongnu leader. *Heqin* agreements also called for fixed annual payments in silk floss, cloth, and grains from the Han to the Xiongnu; and the opening of Han-Xiongnu border markets. Even though Emperor Wu resumed war against the Xiongnu in 133 BCE, later dynastic rulers would continue to use this foundational form of marriage diplomacy with various states. As modern scholars have pointed out, intermarriage at the frontiers became, by the Later Han period, an enduring Chinese poetic topos that reflected classical anxieties about miscegenation. For example, the *Hanshu* records the lament of Liu Xijun 劉細君 (fl. ca. 110 BCE), the Han princess sent by Emperor Wu to a Wusun leader with whom she has "no verbal communication" (語言不通):

吾家嫁我兮天一方，	My family married me out, to the other side of heaven;
遠託異國兮烏孫王。	They sent me far off to a strange state, to the king of the Wusun.
穹廬爲室兮旃爲牆，	A domed hut became my chamber, its walls made of felt;
以肉爲食兮酪爲漿。	I take meat for my meals, kumiss as my broth.
居常土思兮心內傷，	Living with constant thoughts of my homeland, my heart is wounded inside;
願爲黃鵠兮歸故鄉。	I wish I were a golden swan, returning to its old homestead.[65]

Critics have pointed out that the poem draws on a traditional classical poetic theme of the wife's lament and offers a potential criticism of Emperor Wu's expansionist policies. This figure of the female Han exile, who remained faithful to her homeland while elaborating a phobic ethnography of the northern nomads, would later include the work attributed to the female poet, Cai Yan 蔡琰 (fl. ca. 200 CE) (e.g., "Eighteen Songs of a Nomad Flute") and stories about the Han consort to two successive Xiongnu leaders, Wang Zhaojun 王昭君 (fl. ca. 30 BCE).[66] Cred-

---

65. *Hanshu* 96B.3903.

66. See Kern, "The Poetry of Han Historiography"; Rouzer, *Articulated Ladies*, 157–200, for a useful analysis on anxieties about intermarriage. On Cai Yan, see Levy, *Chi-*

ibly authentic writings attributed to named women in early China are few, and it is worth noting that unlike Ban Zhao's *Admonitions*, the *Hanshu*'s Liu Xijun grounds the classical virtue of the wife precisely on her disloyalty to her husband. In the *Hanshu* account, the succession of women sent abroad prove their enduring political and emotional fidelity to the Han against the odds.[67] To establish the superiority of Chinese *wen* (poetic writing, culture) over the un-sinicized foreigner, the woman can and must challenge the husband-wife bond.

From a classicizing perspective, the *heqin* initiated an enduring tradition of Chinese xenophobic hostility to intermarriage. However, as argued below, Former Han scholars and officials conceived the *heqin* in terms of ritual propriety and tied the politics of kinship at the frontiers to aberrations in kinship at the imperial court. Although now taken as the name for imperial China's earliest form of diplomacy, one which later dynasties continued to use, the *heqin* was discussed with a unique rhetorical playfulness during the Han. Modern scholarship has tended to overlook this attention to the symbolism inherent in the *heqin* ritual. However, during the Han dynasty, officials and scholars disputed the metaphorical meanings of its eponymous kinship (*qin*) ritual. They were concerned as to how or whether the *heqin* could replace the tributary exchange (*gong*) of classical texts as the signifying transaction of the frontiers. The imperial payments to the Xiongnu required by this system could not, after all, be assimilated within the tradition of tributary exchange because the Xiongnu leader did not pay court, give annual gifts, or acknowledge submission. Advocates of the *heqin* practice nevertheless struggled to present this system as a part of a long-term tributary order grounded in ritual propriety (*li*).

nese Narrative Poetry, 80–103; Frankel, "Cai Yan and the Poems Attributed to Her"; Chang, *Women Writers*, 22–30. See also Kwong, *Wang Zhaojun*. The ethnographic vocabulary and tone of distaste found here and elsewhere should also be read as part of the gendered development of a xenophobic discourse, especially after the Former Han. See chapter 3 on differences between ethnographic representation in the *Shiji* and *Hanshu*.

67. When the aging Wusun leader demands that his Han wife marry his grandson, the Han princess begs the Han emperor to refuse, but he does not. Subsequent Han brides to the Wusun prove their skills as spies and strategists. Jia Yi had also argued that in the Xiongnu case, the Han princess and her staff should, serve as spies for the Han government at the frontier and in the border markets.

Prior to the Former Han, *heqin* was an uncommon term, referring to the achievement of harmonious relations—for example, in music and war, among the general population, or within the traditional bonds (e.g., those between father and son, between ruler and subject, or between brothers). On the rare occasions when the term *heqin* was used to describe peace agreements between clans of the same state, or between states, the texts did not specify any ritual or contractual elements. Although some pre-Han texts did record instances where leaders of warring factions gave daughters to opposing leaders as tokens of peace or used an egalitarian diplomatic rhetoric of "brotherhood," they did not use the term *heqin* to describe these actions.[68] The association of these signifying practices with the actual term *heqin* first appears with Han-dynasty literary and epigraphic invocations of the Han-Xiongnu treaty, and only Han texts elaborate the term's various interpretive possibilities.[69] Before and after Emperor Wu ended the *heqin* system in 133 BCE, its apologists struggled to somehow reconcile the defeat of the empire at its own frontier with the ideal political economy of classical texts, substituting the symbolic transaction of the lord-subject hierarchy (tribute) with that of a more egalitarian interpretation of marriage.

---

68. I argue here against Zhang Zhengming's 张正明 otherwise very useful account of the *heqin*, which tries to trace the *heqin* back through pre-imperial texts. The passages Zheng cites from the *Zuozhuan* and *Guoyu* do record diplomatic marriages, but do not use the term *heqin*. When the term *heqin* occurs in a pre-Han text (in reference to a peace agreement between clans from the state of Jin), there is no mention of a marriage ritual. See Yang, *Chunqiu Zuozhuan*, 1074. Likewise, the *Shiji*'s record of a *heqin* between King Qing Xiang of Chu with King Zhao of Qin in 285 BCE does not actually mention a marriage ritual. See *Shiji* 40.1729. Zhang's single example of a *heqin* with foreigners, from the "Qiugong Sikou" 秋官司寇 chapter of the *Zhouli* 周禮—a pre-Han text that first became known in the early Han dynasty—does not clarify this use of the term. See Zhang Zhengming, "Heqin tong lun," 3–24. The "Xiongnu liezhuan" foreshadows the Han dynasty *heqin* with two political "intermarriages," both of which involve the state represented by the wife or female lover subsequently defeating the enemy state of the husband or male lover. The discussion of the political use of marriage (*qin*) to politically pacify (*he*) the Western Rong during the reign of King Xiao of Zhou 周孝王 (r. 872–866 BCE) in the *Shiji*'s "Qin benji" offers a very schematic precedent for the *heqin* debates, although the symbolic meanings of the terms are not questioned. See *Shiji* 5.177.

69. The *Hanshu* uses the term *heqin* in describing later agreements with the Nanyue and the Wusun. See *Hanshu* 64B.2821; 96B.3927.

The *heqin* spanned the first six decades of the Han dynasty and was one attempt to deal with border tensions that overshadowed all four centuries of the Han dynasty. The *Shiji*, *Hanshu*, and *Hou Hanshu* (History of the Later Han), which were the first three books of China's canonical twenty-four Standard Histories (*zheng shi* 正史), each includes a chapter on the Xiongnu. Together, these three accounts chronicle the agonistic relations between the Han dynasty and its single most important enemy.[70] The *Shiji* covers the pre-imperial and early Han history of the northern frontier and the rise of the Xiongnu. It starts with the rise of China's first empire and the joining of the Great Wall during the Qin dynasty (221–206 BCE); continues with the Xiongnu's catastrophic defeat of the first Han emperor, Gaozu (r. 202–195 BCE) in 200 BCE; recounts the establishment, breakdown, and renewal of seven successive *heqin* ("peace through kinship") treaties; and ends in the midst of Emperor Wu's ruthless military campaigns across northern and Central Asia.[71] As discussed in chapter 3, the *Hanshu* includes an almost identical version of this account, but extends the narrative to cover the fragile diplomacy at the end of the Former Han dynasty (that is, until 25 CE). The *Hanshu*'s "Memoir of the Xiongnu" includes the (non-tributary) political submission in 51 BCE of the most important Xiongnu leader, Chieftain Huhanye (*Huhanye chanyu* 呼韓邪單于), to Emperor Xuan 宣帝 (r. 74–49 BCE). The *Hou Hanshu* begins where the *Hanshu* ends, covering the internal divisions of the Xiongnu confederacy and the final defeat and dispersal of the northern and southern Xiongnu states by the final decade of the Later Han dynasty (25–220 CE).

Modern scholars have extensively researched the contractual terms of early *heqin* agreements. Economic analyses of the breakdown of

---

70. For the rich historical scholarship on the relation of the *heqin* to other foreign policy initiatives throughout the Han period, see, for example, Psarras, "Han and Xiongnu"; Di Cosmo, *Ancient China and its Enemies*, chapters 5–6; Lin Gan, *Xiongnu shi*, 44–116; Tinios, "'Loose Rein' in Han Relations." On the Later Han period, see Rafe de Crespigny, *Northern Frontier*, 173–354.

71. One should note that comparative philological analysis of the two accounts has raised the possibility that at least parts of the extant *Shiji* "Account of the Xiongnu" were actually reconstituted from the *Hanshu* version. Honey, "The Case of the 'Hsiung-nu lieh-chuan,'" argues that the opening ethnography of the *Hanshu* predates that of the received *Shiji*. See Nienhauser, Jr., *The Grand Scribe's Records*, Vol. 2, xiii–xxxii, for a cautionary introduction to the relation between the *Hanshu* and *Shiji* texts.

Han-Xiongnu *heqin* have tended to blame the failure of the annual payments and border market exchange to satisfy the material demands of the Xiongnu, resulting in their disruptive cross-border raids.[72] According to this interpretation, the *heqin* marriage ritual is seen as instrumental, as the political trompe l'oeil with which the Han government represented their annual payments not as a reverse tribute to the victorious foreigner, but as a ritual dowry to an equal. Political analyses of Han-Xiongnu relations have emphasized that the *heqin* was a peace (*he*) contract that was repeatedly broken, and ultimately abandoned, due to political misunderstanding and independent military violence by generals on both sides.[73] Such analyses reduce the ritual aspects of *heqin* to being merely symbolic, the continuation of the benign protocols of pre-imperial marriage diplomacy, and these analyses understand the *heqin* contract as the application of traditional marriage diplomacy to the unprecedented situation of imperial defeat. Both of these approaches, then, have, rightly, paid more heed to the quantitative or contractual terms of the *heqin*—such as the value of the gifts or breaches of agreed borders—than to the ritual itself.

Han dynasty officials, however, paid more attention to the actual symbolic practice and moral meaning of the *heqin* form than such historical analyses would suggest.[74] The *Shiji* and *Hanshu* record the centrality of ritual propriety (*li jie* 禮節) to the *heqin*'s original design in their parallel biographies of Emperor Gaozu's most renowned minister, Liu Jing 劉敬.

---

72. E.g., Lin Gan, *Xiongnu shi*, 46.

73. In analyzing the *heqin*'s breakdown, Di Cosmo critiques the strictly economic approach. He argues that the Han failed to grasp fundamental differences in notions of sovereignty. The persistence of independent Xiongnu raids contributed in particular to that political misunderstanding. See Di Cosmo, *Ancient China and its Enemies*, 215–27.

74. For an exceptional literary approach to the *heqin*, see Bulag, *The Mongols at China's Edge*. Bulag critiques Han-centered approaches in frontier historiography, and he provides a genealogy of the *heqin* "marriage-alliance" through Chinese literary history, and its conceptual influence even to the present. Unlike Bulag, who emphasizes enduring symbolic value of the *heqin* as a sign of Chinese self-feminization in the face of "masculine" Inner Asians, I focus on contestation within the Han dynasty archive over the symbolic value of the *heqin*. The observance of ritual propriety in interstate relations features prominently in pre-imperial historiography. One can read the Han-dynasty *heqin* debates about propriety in terms of a conscious Han engagement with the moral economy of pre-imperial historiography.

The observance of ritual propriety in interstate relations features prominently in pre-imperial historiography. In the *Shiji*'s account, after the successful Xiongnu ambush of Emperor Gaozu and his army at Pingcheng 平城 in 200 BCE, Liu Jing devises a "peace through kinship" treaty that will both satisfy the victorious Xiongnu at the present time, but will also somehow turn the *chanyu*'s future "sons and grandsons [into Han] subjects." Liu Jing prefaces his innovative plan with a summary of the problem of Xiongnu kinship impropriety, exemplified by the present *chanyu*'s murder of his father and marriage to his stepmother:

劉敬對曰：「陛下誠能以適長公主妻之，厚奉遺之，彼知漢適女送厚，蠻夷必慕以為閼氏，生子必為太子。代單于。何者？貪漢重幣。陛下以歲時漢所餘彼所鮮數問遺，因使辯士風諭以禮節。冒頓在，固為子婿；死，則外孫為單于。豈嘗聞外孫敢與大父抗禮者哉？兵可無戰以漸臣也。若陛下不能遣長公主，而令宗室及後宮詐稱公主，彼亦知，不肯貴近，無益也。」高帝曰：「善。」欲遣長公主。呂后日夜泣，曰：「妾唯太子、一女，奈何弃之匈奴！」上竟不能遣長公主，而取家人子名為長公主，妻單于。

Liu Jing replied: "If your Honor is sincerely able to have the eldest princess (*di zhang gong zhu* 適長公主) marry [the Xiongnu's *chanyu*], and to send lavish gifts along with her, he [the *chanyu*] will know that the Han [Emperor's] eldest daughter[75] is being sent with material generosity, and, like the Man and the Yi, [the *chanyu*] will inevitably desire her and regard her as his consort. When she has a son, he will inevitably make him his heir, who will in time become the *chanyu*. Why? Because [the *chanyu*] will be greedy for Han material replenishments [of goods]. Your Honor should each year present quantities of the goods that they lack and of which the Han have a surplus, and, by sending rhetoricians, cajole them to use ritual propriety (*li jie*). While [the *chanyu*] Maodun [r. 209–? BCE] is alive he will already be established as your son-in-law. When he dies your grandson will become *chanyu*. And who indeed has heard of a grandson who has dared to defy the propriety (*li* 禮) owed to his grandfather? Without a battle, our army will be able to use this gradual method to subject them. But if Your Honor is unable to dispatch the eldest princess, and orders the imperial household to approach a palace woman and deceptively name her the princess, they will know and will be unwilling to honor or approach her, and we will reap no benefits."

---

75. On the three different terms for the princess used in this passage, see Nienhauser, *The Grand Scribe's Records*, Vol. 8, 285 n. 41.

Emperor Gaozu said, "Good," wishing to send the eldest princess. But Empress Lü wept day and night, saying, "I only have the heir apparent and one daughter. How can you cast her off to the Xiongnu?" The Emperor in the end was unable to send his eldest princess but took the daughter of a commoner, giving her the name of the "eldest princess" and she married the *chanyu*.[76]

According to the *Hanshu*, "Arguments for the *heqin* began with Liu Jing."[77] Here, Liu Jing's anxiety about the appropriateness of *heqin* diplomacy lies not in its contractual terms (giving annual payments, respecting borders), but in the actual marriage ritual that seals the agreement. The traditional political-kinship hierarchies of lord and subject, father and son, and husband and wife provide the ostensible logic of his proposal.

For Liu Jing, the *heqin*'s *qin* (kinship) bears the burden of reproducing the Han moral economy. Ritually correct, procreative marriage will reverse Han-Xiongnu power relations "without a battle." According to the classical ideals of kinship subordination, the Xiongnu leader, in marrying the Han princess, would be compelled to defer to the Han emperor. As a son-in-law, the Xiongnu leader would be placed in a subordinate kinship position to the Han emperor, and would therefore be submissive. The son of the union between the enemy leader and the Han princess in turn would be grandson to the Han emperor. Since rhetoricians will teach ritual propriety (*li jie*) to the Xiongnu, Liu Jing rhetorically asks: "Who has ever heard of a grandson daring to defy the ritual propriety (*li*) owed to his grandfather?" From this perspective, the subsequent inability of the Han to restore proper lord-subject ("tributary") relations reflects their failure to morally transform the foreigner: the Xiongnu continued to dominate the frontiers because the *chanyu*'s son, Laoshang chanyu 老上單于 (r. 174–160 BCE), and grandson, Junchen chanyu 軍臣單于 (r. 160–126 BCE) simply did not observe father-son filial obedience to the Han emperors.

The first violation of ritual propriety to which the Han historiographic accounts draw attention is, however, the relation between husband and wife. After Liu Jing warns the emperor against "deceptively" sending someone other than his eldest daughter, the infamous Empress Lü

---

76. *Shiji* 99.2719.
77. *Hanshu* 94B.3830.

successfully convinces Emperor Gaozu to dispatch a substitute princess. The empress's appeal to the mother-daughter kinship bond is already improper within an androcentric ethical tradition, but even more so when placed above both the empress's own marriage and the diplomatic marriage of her daughter. Through her activist tears ("[weeping] day and night") the empress becomes the agent of exchange in the (normatively male) traffic in women. Empress Lü's protestation that she has "only the heir apparent and one daughter" foreshadows for the reader her future reign (as Empress Dowager) and her improper kinship manipulations of heirs to the throne. As other parts of both the *Shiji* and the *Hanshu* chronicle, it is precisely through the empress's kinship network, anchored in the Lü family, that she orchestrates her own bloody rise to power. Indeed, by the time of this *heqin* debate, Empress Lü's only daughter, Princess Lu Yuan (Lu Yuan gongzhu 魯元公主), was already wedded to the King of Zhao, Zhang Ao 張敖.[78] Their daughter in turn would marry Empress Lü's son, the heir-apparent. After her husband's death, Empress Dowager Lü so dominated political affairs that the *Shiji* includes her biography, but not her son's (Emperor Hui 惠帝 r. 195–188), among its "Basic Annals," a section which is otherwise reserved for emperors.[79]

The impropriety of the *heqin*'s eponymous marriage implicitly resurfaces in an infamous letter that the *chanyu* sends to Empress Lü after the death of Emperor Gaozu.[80] In the *Hanshu* account, the *chanyu* writes,

---

78. Emperor Gaozu stayed at the home of this daughter and her husband, the King of Zhao, on his way back from the very military defeat at Pingcheng that initiated the *heqin* treaty. The King of Zhao demonstrates precisely the "ritual propriety of a son-in-law" that Liu Jing will predict of the *chanyu*. See *Shiji* 89.2582–83. Note that the "Xiongnu liezhuan" reveals the meaning of *yanshi* as mere consort when Maodun kills his "beloved wife" (*ai qi* 愛妻) and gives away "one of his *yanshi*." See *Shiji* 110.2888–89. Han legal texts excavated at Zhangjiashan also attest to the privileges bestowed upon Empress Lü's son-in-law. See *Zhangjiashan Hanmu zhujian*, 210, slips 520–22. On Empress Lü and the Han dynasty use of the term for the renewal of marriage ties between affinal relatives (*chongqin* 重親), see *Shiji* 49.1969; *Hanshu* 96B.3905; Yang Shuda, *Han dai hun sang li*, 20–27.

79. *Shiji* 9.395–422. The *Hanshu* gives Emperor Hui his own chapter. In his comparison of the *Shiji* and *Hanshu*, Hans van Ess, "Praise and Slander," argues that whereas the *Hanshu* emphasizes Empress Lü's cruelty as part of her personal character, the *Shiji* presents it more within the Liu versus Lü political rivalry.

80. The *Shiji* refers to "a letter with insulting language" from the *chanyu* after the death of Emperor Gaozu, and the *Hanshu* includes this letter (and the Empress

"Your Majesty has taken the throne alone, and I reside unsteadily alone. We two rulers do not have pleasure and we lack the means to make ourselves happy. I would like to take what I have and exchange it for what I lack."[81] The irony of his proposition exceeds its indecency. On the one hand, he is pressing the symbolic kinship of the *heqin* to its logical extreme: the marital union of two rulers. On the other, his scandalous proposal redresses the schemes of power reversal, kinship pedagogy, and princess substitution through which the Han court had originally sought to deceive the Xiongnu. He effectively proposes to impose the Xiongnu system of the polygamous levirate, as described by both Han histories, on the Han. As the figurative "brother" to the deceased Emperor Gaozu in the egalitarian rhetoric accompanying the treaty, his marriage to the Empress Dowager would enact the Xiongnu custom of "brothers marrying their [deceased] brothers' wives." As the son-in-law (although not son) of the deceased emperor, the *chanyu* also implicitly recalls the custom of sons marrying their deceased father's wives. This would mark not simply the failure of Liu Jing's plans for proselytizing "ritual propriety," but rather its reversal.

The *chanyu's* use of an economic language of demand and supply— "exchanging what I have for what I lack" (*yi qi suo wu* 易其所無)—also reflects a new Han dynasty discourse of commercial foreign relations. In this context, the *chanyu* both reminds Empress Dowager Lü of her part in taking away what he lacks, namely her only daughter, and he re-objectifies the figure of the *heqin* wife (both the one he already "has" and the Empress Dowager). The idiom of commercial "kinship" (*qin*) recurs elsewhere in Han historiography and in the *Debate on Salt and Iron*. The *Shiji* records, "When the present emperor [Wu] was established, the next *heqin* treaty was sealed, and he treated [the Xiongnu] generously, opened up the border markets, and sent lavish gifts to them. From the *chanyu* down, all the Xiongnu allied (*qin*) with the Han, com-

---

Dowager's response) in full. This is the most significant difference between the parallel sections of the *Hanshu* and *Shiji* accounts. Compare also the two tales of pre-imperial intercultural marriage that preface the Han-Xiongnu *heqin* in both accounts. See Tinios, "Emperors, Barbarians and Historians."

81. *Hanshu* 94.3755. Compare Wang Liqi, *Yantielun*, 524, for the language of market exchange.

ing and going beneath the Great Wall."[82] A political discourse of amity
is here transformed into an economic one as the *heqin*'s act of *qin* comes
to signify the market exchanges between congenial Xiongnu and Han
traders at the border passes.

By contrast, Han officials who opposed the *heqin* strategy rhetorically
exploited the symbolism of the *heqin*'s economic payments. Jia Yi 賈誼
(201–169 BCE) famously excoriates the Han government's annual gifts of
gold, silk, and silk floss as "presenting tribute to the Man and Yi" and
becoming the "vassals of the Rong,"—and in doing so, Jia Yi avoids the
formal term, *heqin*.[83] In the *Debate on Salt and Iron*, Sang Hongyang,
Emperor Wu's chief economist, who helped to finance the resumption
of war with the Xiongnu, goes a step further: "From the rise of the Han
dynasty to the present, we formed friendly relations by binding the *heqin*
agreement, and what we sent to the *chanyu* as betrothal gifts (*pin* 聘)
was extremely lavish. In this way (*ran* 然) they [the Xiongnu] did not
take the rich gifts and lavish bribes as a reason to change and to adopt
moderation, and their violent attacks multiplied."[84] Here, in using the
term "betrothal gifts" (*pin*), a designation for the groom's offering,

---

82. *Shiji* 110.2904. For a similar formulation, see Wang Liqi, *Yantielun*, 524. Compare the complaint of Zhao Tuo, King of Southern Yue (*Shiji* 113.2969): "Now Empress Lu is heeding her slanderous officials, discriminating against me as one of the Man and Yi by severing [trade] in [iron] implements and goods." Jia Yi, in his opposition to the *heqin* in the *Xinshu*, offered a three-pronged approach that involves bribing the Xiongnu with baits. First, he suggested invoking the "Three Principles" (*san biao* 三表) to convince the Xiongnu of Han trustworthiness (*xin* 信), affection (*ai* 愛), and fondness (*hao* 好), as we saw in his metaphor of false maternal affection. Second, he suggested using "Five Baits" (*wu er* 五餌) to corrupt Xiongnu senses and desires. Third, he suggested that the Han government use the high status of the *heqin* princess for strategic purposes. They should increase her staff and through them keep watch on frontier affairs. The *Hanshu* biography of Jia Yi discusses only the first two approaches.

83. *Xinshu*, 153. Cf. *Hanshu* 48.2240. Ying-shih Yü has influentially adopted Jia Yi's argument and rhetoric of reversed tribute. Compare the insistence of the scholars featured in the *Debate on Salt and Iron* on reading the *heqin* and tribute distinct. See Wang Liqi, *Yantielun*, 488.

84. Wang Liqi, *Yantielun*, 488. For the clause 然不紀重質厚賂之故改節, Wang Liqi glosses the character *ji* 紀 as *ji* 記 (to record), whereas Yang Shuda, *Debate on Salt and Iron yao shi*, 57, rejects 紀 as a transcription error for *yi* 以 (to take as, to use). I use Yang's interpretation here, but Wang's would not detract from my argument. On the representation of Sang in the text as *Dafu*, see Chapter 1.

rather than using Liu Jing's term for bridal "gifts" or dowry (*feng* 奉), the speaker highlights a symbolic flaw in the *heqin*'s marriage metaphor and rite.

Liu Jing appeared to use the marriage ritual to transform payments into a symbolic dowry, so that these payments would not be interpreted as tribute. However, Liu Jing's dowry metaphor, which dominates both Han-dynasty and modern analyses of the *heqin*, deserves further scrutiny. For, contrary to his insistence that the *heqin* form propagates ritual propriety, the accompanying gifts go in a direction that does not accord with classical nuptial ideals. Liu Jing's *heqin* transgresses most, if not all, of the six ritual steps of marriage outlined in the canonical *Yi Li* 儀禮 (Book of ceremonies and rites), most significantly in Liu Jing's focus on the gifts that accompany the bride.[85]

Although modern scholars have followed Liu Jing's lead in reading *heqin* gifts as appropriately fulfilling the role of the dowry, the Xiongnu's failure to give gifts in return would have troubled Han observers. For the groom's "presentation of betrothal presents" (*na zheng* 納徵) to the bride's family was the most valued (and most common) step in Han dynasty prescriptive ideals and in practice.[86] Reciprocation by the bride's family, in the form of a dowry, could be practiced, but failure to reciprocate a dowry would have been a notable impropriety.[87] For example, in the *Shiji*'s narrative of Han relations with the Central Asian Wusun people, Emperor Wu's minister respond to the Wusun's request for a Han princess with the following: "There must first be a presentation of betrothal gifts (*na pin* 納聘), and only then should we send a daughter."[88]

---

85. The *Yi Li* did not acquire this name until after the Han dynasty, and addresses the lower-ranked aristocracy rather than the imperial court. See *Shiji* 121.3126; Jack Dull, "Marriage and Divorce in Han China," for a discussion of the six steps.

86. Dull, "Marriage and Divorce in Han China," 48.

87. The phrase used by Liu Jing, *hou feng* 厚奉, appears in one other context in the *Shiji*, in which a rich woman breaks off her first marriage to marry Zhang Er, who receives lavish gifts or dowry (which are apparently unreciprocated); *Shiji* 89.2571. Sima Xiangru offers a parallel case of a transgressive marriage in which the groom receives a large dowry and does not humble himself toward his father-in-law. The importance of the groom's betrothal gifts (*na zheng* or *pin*), is illustrated in the case of the Han minister Chen Ping. According to *Shiji* 56.2052, the bride's wealthy grandmother "lent him money to use for the betrothal gifts (*pin*)." On the dowry, betrothal gifts, and the levirate, see Christian de Pee, *The Writing of Weddings*, 114–16, 218.

88. *Shiji* 123.3170.

The Wusun, after having sent an envoy bearing a gift of horses with the marriage proposal, additionally gave four thousand horses—a gift giving that was not reciprocated—to the Han. In the Han-Wusun alliance (unlike the Han-Xiongnu *heqin* agreements) the gifts flowed in the proper direction, and the presentation of betrothal gifts (*na zheng*) clearly symbolized the giving of tribute (*na gong* 納貢). Thus, while Empress Lü transgressed the *heqin* marriage in having a false princess sent, Liu Jing's original proposal regarding the wedding was already marked as ritually incorrect.

This attention to violation of marriage rituals, whether by Liu Jing, by Empress Lü, or by successive Xiongnu leaders, indexes the much broader Han concern about gender relations in the moral economy, which was already addressed above in the context of women's work. *Qin* 親 and its antonym *shu* 疏 were key terms in traditional political discourse, applicable both to affective relations with the ruler and to filiation within a surname group. Although Emperor Gaozu had declared that only members of the Liu family could inherit the empire, the priority of kinship between blood relations was increasingly challenged during the Han dynasty, as evidenced not only in Han historiography, but also in the location of tombs, diverse statutes on adoption, the emergence of joint tombs, and the rewriting of laws.[89] Liu Jing, the author of kinship diplomacy, began life as a humble sheepskin-clad "Lou Jing" 婁敬, but was rewarded for his uncompromising political advice with the imperial surname Liu 劉.[90] Since women did not take their husbands's surname, Empress Dowager Lü effectively interrupted the reign of her husband's House of Liu. Her ascendancy also marked the beginning of the perennial rise of powerful consort families in Chinese imperial courts (the conflict between the "inner" and "outer" courts). The problem of kinship and imperial succession in the *heqin* debate is thus not simply between Xiongnu and Han, but also between the Liu and the Lü kinship groups at the political center of empire.

---

89. See Wu Hung, *Monumentality*, 162, on the relocation of ministers' tombs beside that of the emperor. On legal support for adoptive relations, and for family relations that are not blood relations but socially constructed, see Queen, *From Chronicle to Canon*, 143–44. For a comprehensive analysis of Han statutes on adoption, see Brown, "Adoption in Han China." See also Nylan, "Notes on a Case of Illicit Sex."

90. *Shiji* 99.2717.

Aberrant transmission of kinship (*qin*) at the center of empire, not simply its frontiers, thus became vital to the establishment of one of imperial China's most important diplomatic protocols.[91] For Liu Jing and *heqin* advocates, intermarriage promised to restore lord-subject relations at China's frontiers despite the improper direction of wedding gifts. It would do so through the Han princess' biological reproduction of the father-son bond between the Han emperor and next Xiongnu leader. The advocates attributed the shortcomings of the *heqin* not simply to sporadic Xiongnu attacks, but also to Empress Lü's transgression of her own husband-wife bond in manipulating the exchange of a *heqin* princess. For *heqin* critics such as Jia Yi and Sang Hongyang, however, the ritually improper direction of marriage gifts betokened, from the outset, a reversal of the proper tribute order. After Emperor Wu terminated *heqin* diplomacy in 133 BCE and instigated a new era of colonial expansion and Silk Road exchange, a more phobic ethnographic discourse emerged. This new attention to the unchangeable or savage customs of foreigners (especially the Xiongnu) appeared not only in subsequent epideictic *fu* (e.g., of Yang Xiong) and Later Han historiography (e.g., the *Hanshu*), as discussed in chapters 2 and 3, but also in a classicizing poetics about patriotic wives sent beyond the frontiers.

Conclusion

Modern scholarship generally approaches the conjugal household as the basic societal unit of the Han dynasty, and treats the expanding Han empire as the replication of this microcosmic unit across macrocosmic space.[92] From the (often conflicting) perspectives of the history of ad-

---

91. Butler, *Antigone's Claim*, 72, defines kinship as follows: "Understood as a socially alterable set of arrangements that has no cross-cultural structural features that might be fully extracted from its social operations, kinship signifies any number of social arrangements that organize the reproduction of material life, that can include the ritualization of birth and death, that provide bonds of intimate alliance both enduring and breakable, and that regulated sexuality through sanction and taboo." Her discussion of the politics and social contingency of kinship in terms of repeated acts and an "aberrant transmission" of norms offers a template for thinking about the Han politics and rhetoric of *qin*.

92. A lucid articulation of this common approach can be found in Mark Lewis's *The Construction of Space* and *The Early Chinese Empires*.

ministrative practice and classical prescription this was largely true. However, by exploring a more complex politics of representation, especially in Former Han discourses of women's work and kinship, this chapter has argued a more interactive, less parallel, relation between frontier and kinship histories. Two of the most important developments in Chinese frontier history—imperial interstate diplomacy (*heqin* peace through kinship) and long-distance tributary trade across Eurasia (that is, the Silk Road)—originated in discourses and practices that departed from classical ideals of kinship. Before Emperor Wu ended the peace with the Xiongnu, Former Han scholars and officials tied the aberrant kinship rituals of the *heqin* to kinship violations in the imperial court. During the expansionist era of Emperor Wu, *qingzhong* economists imagined a kind of interstate Silk Road economy within which the bonds of marriage and sodality had no productive place. In opposition (or contrast) to this, Ban Zhao and other classicists contracted the world of women's work from the economic frontiers to the household. They took the unattached female weaver from the industrious vanguard of the *qingzhong* economic world system and required her to toil at the duties of wifehood and at affirming the prestige of classical texts. The well-known development of classicizing texts for women that emphasized their roles as wives and mothers might thus be better understood as a reaction, in part, to economic visions of women's roles as industrious workers in the expansionist economy. In restoring women to the morality-based household economy, classicists erased local and long-distance markets from the horizon of the female weaver. One might note that when the industrial geographers Baron von Richthofen and Sven Hedin coined and popularized the term Silk Road (*die Seidenstrasse, sichou zhi lu*, etc.) in the late nineteenth and early twentieth centuries they sought to build a transport network linking China and Europe for colonial and commercial advantage.[93] Although these modern geographers cited the Han historiographers, their own concept of a Silk Road possessed a political-economic ambition, a hypothesis, and a strategy—elements that were more characteristic of *qingzhong* economics. The next chapter turns to the most emblematic practice of *qingzhong* economics and the expanded Han market, namely, money.

---

93. On this see Chin, "The Invention of the Silk Road, 1877."

CHAPTER 5

Commensuration:
Counter-Practices of Money

> Money has two sides, symbolised as heads and tails. It is the product of social organisation both from the top down ('states') and from the bottom up ('markets'). It is thus both a token of authority and a commodity with a price. Most economic theories of money focus on one extreme to the exclusion of the other.
>
> —Keith Hart, "Heads or Tails? Two Sides of the Coin"

According to numismatists, Chinese coins had no "heads" side. Unlike their Western counterparts, the coins bore notations of their weight-value but no pictures. Nevertheless, the tension that the anthropologist Keith Hart describes between money as a token of the issuing state's authority ("heads") and its market value as a commodity ("tails") permeates ancient and modern debates about Chinese money.[1] Emura Haruki's recent numismatic study, for example, argues that Chinese coinage began among sixth-century BCE mercantile communities for trade across economic and political borders, and that regional governments subsequently appropriated this medium as an instrument of economic control.[2] In this account, the earliest coinage in Asia circulated in

---

1. Hart, "Heads or Tails?"

2. Emura, *Shunjū Sengoku jidai seidō kahei*. I am indebted to Lothar von Falkenhausen and Richard Von Glahn for their reviews of this book. Studies of ancient Chinese money include Tang Shifu, *Zhongguo gu qianbi*; Peng Xinwei, *Zhongguo huobi shi/A Monetary History of China*; Thierry, *Monnaies chinoises*; Yang, *Money and Credit in China*; Jiang Ruoshi, *Qin-Han qianbi yanjiu*. On important Japanese numismatic scholarship, including Kakinuma Yōhei's recent *Chūgoku kodai kahei keizai shi kenkyū*,

north-central and northern China, along the Eurasian steppe frontiers. This has invited questions about potential trans-regional connections, for Lydia and archaic Greece also saw a rise in the circulation of precious metal coins at around the same time. From this perspective, Chinese money was, in part, the product of a translation and imposition of regimes of value across borders. The primary tension in this analysis is not between (Chinese) "states" and (Chinese) "markets," so much as between "Chinese states/markets" and "cross-border states/markets"—that is, the tension between a China-centered and a trans-regional history of money. The following account of the meanings and pragmatics of Han dynasty money—that is, of the conceptions, workings, and effects of monetary practices—highlights the significance of this more obscured, but already embedded, politics of foreign exchange. To do so, this chapter maps out four sets of competing social and symbolic "counter-practices" of money: burying money (for afterlife exchanges); experimental minting (including coin design); classicizing money (i.e., elaborating money's place in classical ethics and historiography); and quantifying money (according to a market logic). These four approaches either embedded money within cosmological and ethical calculations, or sought to divorce money from such calculations.

Burying Money

The Qin unification of empire (in 221 BCE) helped to eliminate the Warring States problem of "foreign" exchange within China (the Central States) by establishing the round, square-holed bronze *banliang* 半兩 ("half-ounce") as the only imperial coin. The round coin of the original Qin state thereby superseded the forms of the three other major regional currencies of Warring States China: spade-shaped coins of the Central Plain; knife-shaped coins of the east and north (Qi and Yan); and the stamped gold plaques, spade-shaped coins, and bronze imitation cowry coins that had circulated in the south (Chu). As discussed below, subsequent Han debates over private minting, seignorage, coin tampering,

---

see Von Glahn's "Review." On money in China's western regions, see Wang, *Money on the Silk Road*; Wang Yongsheng, *Xinjiang lishi huobi*, Shanghai bowuguan, *Sichou zhilu gudai guojia qianbi*; on Han dynasty casting, see Jiang Baolian, *Han Zhongguan zhu qian yizhi*.

and counterfeiting, led to new monetary forms and practices. These developments culminated in Emperor Wu's successful establishment of a state monopoly on minting, and of the *wuzhu* 五銖 coin as the new imperial coin. This *wuzhu* coin, which like the *banliang* was also round with a square hole, endured from 112 BCE, more or less continuously, until 1912.[3]

However, one important factor is missing from this standard account of the unification of Chinese monetary forms during the rise of empire and the development of China's monetized markets—this is the widespread practice of using afterlife (burial) money. Much of the archaeological evidence for "real-world" money actually relies on an ancient tradition that persisted throughout (and long after) the Han dynasty of burying the dead with money. Burial money helped to mediate between two alien domains, the human and the spiritual. A deceased person was accompanied and aided on the journey to the next world by *sheng qi* (lived objects) and *jiqi* (sacrificial vessels) that were selected from the person's possessions while he or she was still alive, and by *ming qi* (spirit articles) that were made specifically for the tomb.[4] Burial money seems to have fallen into two of these categories, since it included both real-world (lived) money and surrogate money made of a different size or material (e.g., made of clay instead of bronze).

Many Chinese of the time understood the relation between the afterlife and temporal economies to be dynamic and interactive. Household managers prepared inventories (*qian ce*) for their busy underworld counterparts that listed the burial goods accompanying their deceased masters. Han officials prepared contracts for the underworld as they did for the temporal world. Copies of "land contracts" (*diquan* 地券) that specified the buyer, seller, price, the witnesses to the transaction, and the size and location of the tomb's plot were placed both inside tombs and in

---

3. At various stages the *wuzhu* circulated as legal tender across central and southeast Asia, Japan, Vietnam, Korean and Sogdian kingdoms, and Turkic and Uighur khanates. This bronze five-*zhu* (*wuzhu*) coin took its form from the bronze half-ounce (*banliang*) coins established by the First Emperor of Qin. Emperor Han Wudi's *wuzhu* remained the standard, more or less, until the seventh century, when the first Tang emperor re-tariffed similar shaped coins to a decimal system. The same-shaped coins endured in Vietnam until at least 1933.

4. Wu Hung, *The Art of the Yellow Springs*, 87–106.

government administrative offices.[5] "Documents for making a declaration to the earth" (*gaodi shu* 告地書) resembled regular administrative documents. The contract records (*quanci* 券刺) and contract writs (*quanshu* 券書) that were placed in tombs were bipartite documents, with duplicates kept in the world of the living. Such tomb documents reflected the broader integration of religious practices into the same bureaucracy that administered other aspects of early imperial society.[6] More specifically, these documents marked the passing of the deceased from one dominion to another: from the bureaucracy of the Han dynasty's empire to the administrators of the underworld ruler—the Thearch (*di* 帝); Heavenly Thearch (*tiandi* 天帝); Heavenly Sire (*tiangong* 天公). Later Han "celestial ordinances for the dead" or "documents to ward off evil from the tomb" (*zhenmu wen* 鎮墓文) served as a kind of passport, which was supposed to have been issued by the highest deity. These documents addressed the welfare of the surviving family while introducing the deceased to the new administration of the underworld.

Money for this "foreign" underworld economy challenged the normative state/market functions of Han currency (that is, money as a means of exchange, as a method of payment, and as a standard of value). The sheer lack of unity in afterlife currencies—despite the regularization of the money used by the living—is striking. As with other "spirit articles," the material composition of this special type of money held symbolic value. As figure 5.1 shows, some deceased were provided with real money (*banliang, wuzhu*, or gold ingots) (e.g., Liu Kuan 劉寬 [r. 97–87 BCE], the king of Jibei); others were provided with clay coins and ingots (e.g., Lady Dai 軑 [d. before 168 BCE], wife of the Chancellor of

---

5. The earliest authentic land contract dates to 82 CE. Later Han documents reveal a far more complex afterworld bureaucracy than Former Han materials have (so far) yielded. See Seidel, "Traces of Han Religion;" Kleeman, "Land Contracts and Related Documents."

6. As Harper's "Contracts with the Spirit World" puts it: "The point to be emphasized here is that land contracts, *gaodi shu*, and contract documents used in prayer and sacrifice were not likely to be perceived as imitation or forged documents by the people who prepared and used them. Moreover, Han local administration did not constitute a secular authority that was not involved in religious matters." For a similar arguments in earlier contexts, see Sanft's "Paleographic Evidence of Qin Religious Practice from Liye and Zhoujiatai"; Harper, "Resurrection in Warring States Popular Religion."

Tomb	Excavated money	Inventory slip / Basket tag
Mawangdui Tomb 1: Lady Dai, wife of Marquis of Dai (died c. 170 BCE) (Hunan)	One bamboo basket containing around 300 clay ingots with thin gold coating, inscribed with *ying cheng* 郢称.	土金二千斤二笥 "2 baskets of 2,000 catties of clay gold." Basket tag: 金二千一笥 "1 basket of 2,000 catties of gold."
	Around 40 containers, each containing around 2,500–3,000 clay *banliang* 半两 coins (inscribed with *banliang*).	土錢千万篓[簒] 一千 "1,000 containers of 10 million clay coins."
Mawangdui Tomb 2: Brother or son of Marquis of Dai	500 clay ingots. 2,000 clay *banliang* coins.	None
Mawangdui Tomb 3: Marquis of Dai (d. 186 BCE)	One bamboo basket containing 61 pieces of small square and rectangular textiles. One bamboo basket containing over 10 textile pieces; 10 textile pieces were found nearby.	Inventory listings: 聶敝(幣)二笥 "2 baskets of *nie* money." 土錢百萬 "1 million clay coins." 土金千斤 "1,000 catties of clay gold." 聶敝(幣)千匹 Two wooden basket tags, each with "1,000 bolts of *nie* money."
Fenghuangshan Tomb 168 (Hubei)	101 bronze *banliang* coins in a bamboo basket.	錢四貫 "4 strings of coins."
Fenghuangshan Tomb 1	Over 50 bronze *wuzhu* coins.	None
Mancheng, Tomb 1: Prince Liu Sheng (d. 113 BCE) (Hebei)	40 gold ingots; *banliang* coin with auspicious inscription (五穀成).	None

FIGURE 5.1. Table of money and inventory records of money excavated from a selection of Former Han period tombs. See bibliography for sources.

Tomb	Excavated money	Inventory slip / Basket tag
Shuangrushan: Liu Kuan, King of Jibei (r. 97–87 BCE) (Shandong)	20 gold ingots; bronze *wuzhu* coins (unknown quantity).	None
Shuangbaoshan Tomb 1 (Sichuan)	15 bronze *wuzhu* coins; 160 clay ingots.	None
Shuangbaoshan Tomb 2	230 clay ingots; 40 bronze *banliang* coins.	None
Ivolga fortress cemeteries (second to first century BCE) Xiongnu grave 34 (Siberia, Russia)	Bronze *wuzhu* coins; imitation cowries.	None

FIGURE 5.1. (*continued*)

Changsha); and yet others were buried with a mix of metal and clay currencies (e.g., the unknown occupants of tombs 1 and 2 at Shuang-baoshan in Sichuan).[7] Excavated inventories of burial goods appear to acknowledge this distinction between different material forms: for example, the Fenghuangshan inventory refers to its bronze *banliang* as regular *qian* ("4 strings of coins" 錢四貫); and the respective Mawang-dui inventories for tombs 1 and 3 list their clay imitation money as "clay coins" or "earthen coins" (*tu qian* 土錢) and "clay ingots" (*tu jin* 土金). In another example, the inventory for Mawangdui tomb 3—occupied by Li Cang 利倉 (d. 185 BCE), the Marquis of Dai and Chancellor of Changsha—refers to small strips of silk found inside baskets as "*nie* money" (*nie bi* 聶敝[幣]) (figure 5.2). Fixed lengths of silk were used as a form of payment throughout the Han dynasty and the wooden tags that were attached to the tomb baskets enumerate the silk strips in terms of "bolts" (*pi* 匹) of "*nie* money" (*niebi* 聶幣) (figure 5.3).[8] In addition to

---

7. Zheng Shubin suggests that from excavations thus far, it appears that this practice of mixing bronze and non-standard coinage began only in the mid and late Former Han period. See Zheng Shubin, "Qiance de kaogu faxian."

8. Excavated Qin and Han legal documents set the prices for fixed lengths of silk.

FIGURE 5.2. Sample of silk "*nie* money" (*nie bi*) found in a basket in the Former Han tomb of the Marquis of Dai (tomb 3) at Mawangdui, Changsha. After He, *Changsha Mawangdui er, san hao Han mu*, plate 44.1. Reproduced with the permission of the Hunan Provincial Museum.

actual bolts of silk and embroidered pieces (including the "Riding the Clouds" silk design discussed in chapter 2 and shown in figure 2.3), Lady Dai's tomb (Mawangdui tomb 1) held three pairs of silk mitts decorated around the palms with two rings of ribbons bearing the repeating characters *qian jin* 千金 ("1,000 gold [pieces]") (figure 5.4). As shown in figure 5.5, these seal script characters are painstakingly woven into a 0.3-cm-wide band of alternating light and dark shades. The inventory lists these items as *qian jin tao shi* 千金縧飾 ("1,000 gold pieces of/in decorated ribbon" [?]), immediately before it lists the clay ingots and coins.[9] The ribbon's intricately woven phrase transposes a fairly common expression of value from one world to the next, with its material form perhaps evoking the price tag that real-world commodities bore.[10]

---

9. On the rich hoard of silk rolls and textile objects found in tomb 1, see Shanghai shi fang zhi ke xue yan jiu yuan, *Changsha Mawangdui yi hao Han mu chutu fangzhi pin*.

10. See Qin and Han legal documents on this.

FIGURE 5.3. Wooden tag inscribed with "nie bi qian pi" ("1,000 bolts of *nie* money") originally affixed to the basket containing silk strips (see figure 5.2). Excavated from Han tomb 3 at Mawangdui, Changsha. After He, *Changsha Mawangdui er, san hao Han mu*, Plate 88.8. Reproduced with the permission of the Hunan Provincial Museum.

To some extent the diversity in the types of money reflects Former Han changes and regional variations in currency (e.g., the Chu ingot, *banliang, wuzhu*) before Emperor Wu successfully prohibited private minting, and established the *wuzhu* as an empire-wide currency in 112 BCE. However, a diversity (or at least a lack of regulation) in the choice, placement, quantity, and material forms of burial money persisted into the Later Han. Spectacular "coin trees" were buried in Sichuan tombs in

FIGURE 5.4. Pair of silk mitts with ribbons bearing the two characters *qian jin* ("1,000 gold [pieces]"). Excavated from Lady Dai's tomb at Mawangdui, Changsha (tomb 1). After Chen, *Noble Tombs at Mawangdui*, Plate 49. Reproduced with permission of the Hunan Provincial Museum.

the Later Han that appear to draw both on traditional Chinese cosmology and on Indian Buddhist imagery.[11] King Liu Kuan's nineteen large gold ingots were placed next to his head on a jade pillow, with one small gold ingot on his waist; by contrast, bamboo baskets of silk money were found outside the coffin of the Marquis of Dai, in the southern chamber of the tomb. Spirit money may have had different functions at different stages in the soul's journey; however, there was ostensibly no standardized monetary price or tax rate for border crossings between the human

---

11. See He Zhiguo, *Han Wei yao qian shu chu bu*, esp. 212–18; Erickson, "Money trees of the Han Dynasty."

FIGURE 5.5. Detail of the woven characters on the silk ribbons. After He, *Changsha Mawangdui yi hao Han mu chu tu fangzhi,* plate 26. Reproduced with permission of the Hunan Provincial Museum.

and spirit world. In the lavish tomb of Prince Liu Sheng 劉勝 (r. 154–113 BCE), king of Zhongshan, for example, the inclusion of a single *banliang* coin—which was cast with the auspicious tag *wu gu cheng* 五穀成 (Bring the five-grains to fruition), and which lay alongside forty gold ingots—underscores a tendency towards personalizing money.[12] The

12. The source of this information, Xu Limin's "Lun zongjiao," is incorrect, a fact I discovered only late in the publication stage of this book. The coin with an auspicious tag was actually found in Liu Sheng's consort's tomb (Mancheng Tomb 2) as part of a set of twenty bronze coins each bearing a line of a rhyming poem, together with twenty

Prince's gold could conceivably circulate in both human and spirit domains—indeed grave robbery and the theft of buried coins (*yi qian* 瘞錢) is attested in Han texts.[13] Prince Liu Sheng's talismanic *banliang*, by contrast, was symbolically withdrawn from market commerce and re-embedded in the long-term, divinely sanctioned transactional order of agricultural production.[14] The two currencies present in the prince's tomb simultaneously monetized and demonetized human-spirit exchange.

Burial money presents a set of historical counter-practices to the social effects of money that were perceived during the Han—for example, money's tendency to make hitherto incommensurate things or people commensurate (in rank, value, etc.) and to cause people to evaluate things in quantitative terms. Unlike in the world of the *Shiji*'s "commodity producers" (discussed in chapter 3), burial money does not seem to have functioned as a universal yardstick with which to evaluate all other things. Inventories of "spirit articles" accompanying the deceased specified the quantity and material composition of the articles, but did not define the monetary value of each item. Afterworld money seems to function less as a unit of account, a standard of value, and a medium of exchange than it did as a method of payment (for one's entry into the afterworld). In this context, afterworld money, like other tomb articles, served as a store of wealth and as a marker of status.

Take, for example, the quantification of afterworld money. On the one hand, afterworld currencies seem to have been valued on a quantitative basis similar to or identical with that of temporal currencies. For example, Fenghuangshan Tomb 168 included money scales, and in Shuangrushan, Liu Kuan's real gold ingots bore markings that the numismatists Ma Shubo and Wang Yongbo have recently argued refer to numerical measures of weight.[15] The Mawangdui inventories quantify

---

numbered coins, and a die with eighteen sides, likely forming a game set. The above discussion of Liu Sheng's coin may, however, apply to the many Han talismanic coins found elsewhere, for example the gold ingots with inscriptions such as "good fortune" (*ji*) in a Dongbaotai tomb dating to 95 BCE. See Xia Lu, *Shanxi sheng bowuguan*, 201. Liu Sheng's tomb contained 2,317 bronze coins and 40 ingots.

13. *Shiji* 122.3142; *Hanshu* 59.2643.

14. For a brief discussion of Bloch and Parry's notion of long- and short-term transactional orders, see the introduction.

15. For a study of these and other inscribed signs and characters, see Ma Shubo, "Shandong Changqing Shuangrushan Han mu linzhi jin ke hua fuhao de pan shi." See

money in routine ways (coins by number, ingots by catty-weight, silk by bolt), and the massive fortunes represented in these inventories implicate the quantitative logic of the market (i.e., "the more, the better"). Although the Han dynasty clay-to-bronze exchange-rate and the exact functions and purchasing power of clay money remain unknown, one might juxtapose the "10 million clay coins: 1,000 containers" of Lady Dai with the *Shiji*'s claim that 200,000 coins could purchase 200 horses, 1,000 bolts of patterned cloth, 100 slaves or, in the new monetized market economy, entry into ranks of the "untitled nobility." Similarly, although the baskets tags for the Marquis of Dai's silk money list "1,000 bolts of *nie* money," significantly fewer were found (see figure 5.1). And unlike the fixed lengths of silk used in Han dynasty payments, these textile strips came in different square and rectangular sizes (see figure 5.2). Prince Liu Sheng's talismanic coin with "Bring the five-grains to fruition" re-sacralizes numbers, invoking money's non-market functions as a means of tributary payments to the agricultural state.

At the same time, the Lady Dai's household manager clearly did not approach the valuation of his mistress's burial goods with the arithmetic precision of the accountant. In fact, archaeologists have excavated forty (not 1,000) containers, each one containing only 2,500–3,000 coins. Setting aside losses due to thefts, deterioration, or damage during the excavation process—and considering the widely ranging numbers of items listed in Former Han inventories (from a more or less full tally of grave goods to lists of only a few items)—such discrepancies between the amount of inventoried money and excavated money in Han tombs suggest that Han dynasty list makers were commonly given to using large rounded numbers (e.g., *qian wan* 千萬) to designate incalculable (or imprecisely tallied) large amounts.[16]

---

also Beningson, "The Spiritual Geography of Han Dynasty Tombs" and Beningson, *Providing for the Afterlife*, 75, for a good photograph and discussion. On the Fenghuangshan money scales, see Huang Shengzhang, "Guanyu cheng qian heng." Gold ingots and ceramic imitations of gold ingots have been found in many other Han tombs. The size and weight of excavated gold ingots varies, and they generally came either in round disc shapes or horse-hoof shapes. The standard weight of gold was one *jin* (catty) which was equivalent to 10,000 coins (*qian*).

16. According to Zheng Shubin, "Qiance de kaogu," the Mawangdui tomb 1 inventory has a "majority" match; Mawangdui tomb 3 has a "basic match"; Fenghuangshan tomb 168 has a "majority" match.

This rounding and inflation of numbers might be further considered in relation to the kind of self-promoting market "jingles" that Anthony Barbieri-Low has observed in Later Han inscriptions on commodities (often excavated from tombs).[17] Take the following inscription on a lacquer tray found in the tomb of an official of the Han commandery of Lelang (near present-day Pyeongyang, North Korea): 永平十二年。蜀都西工。夾紵行三丸(捖)。治 (直)千二百。盧氏作。宜子孫。牢 "The twelfth year of the Yongping era [69 CE]. / The Western Workshop of the Shu Commandery. / Ramie cored and coated with several layers of mixed lacquer and ash. / Worth twelve hundred [cash]. / Made by the Lu family. / May it bring you sons and grandsons. / Very sturdy."[18] As Barbieri-Low has shown, the product exaggerates its worth ("twelve hundred" coins) and falsely advertises its construction at the eminent state-run factory in Chengdu in Shu. Like the mitts woven with "1,000 gold [pieces]," this tray thus brings the market idiom of profit-seeking exchange and lavish expenditure into the underworld.[19] The inscriptions do not celebrate classical moderation or frugality.

However, one might also point out that the jingle embeds its exaggerated monetary value in other classical ideals. The rare phrase, "It will facilitate sons and grandsons" (*yi zi sun* 宜子孫), is a classical reference to the *Shanhaijing* 山海經 (Classic of mountains and seas). It likely invokes the chapter describing the Western Mountains (where the Queen Mother of the West resides), since the excavated tray bears painted images of the Queen Mother of the West and animals that were associated with immortality. (This reflects a broader cultural association during and after Emperor Wu's westward expansion into Central Asia, between the West and immortality).[20] The *Shanhaijing* describes a tree "with

---

17. For an illuminating account these jingles thus far only excavated from Later Han contexts, see Barbieri-Low, *Artisans*, 138–52.

18. Largely following Barbieri-Low, *Artisans*, 143.

19. On Han debates about lavish expenditure, see chapter 2.

20. On Emperor Wu's various attempts to seek immortality though explorations to the west and east, see, for example, *Shiji* 6.257, 12.476, 123.3179. For good studies of the emperor's quest, see Loewe, *Ways to Paradise*, chapter 4; Wu Hung, *Monumentality*, 126–30. On the *fangshi* who encouraged Emperor Wu, see Puett, *To Become a God*, chapter 6. On the spiritual geography contained within the *Shanhaijing*, see Poo, *In Search of Personal Welfare*, 92–101 and Dorofeeva-Lichtmann, "Mapping a 'Spiritual' Landscape."

round leaves, a white calyx, a scarlet flower with black veins, and fruit like a thick-skinned orange, which if eaten will facilitate sons and grandsons (*yi zi sun*)." The lacquer tray thus subtly performs a double function: it bears the immaterial fruits of immortality for the deceased; and it helps to purchase or redeem (twelve hundred cash's worth of) spiritual favor in multiplying the descendents of the deceased (in the classical, androcentric idiom of reproduction). The tray thus betokens the material and immaterial consumerism of the mutually embedded monetary and cosmological economies. These symbolic and quantitative uses of measurements and numbers in Han tombs point to the underworld's mixed mode of monetary reckoning.

Worlding Numismatics

In addition to the different, but interrelated, logics of burial money versus temporal money, the intercultural relations between Chinese and neighboring numismatic systems complicate China-centered historiography. Numismatists, who generally make a division between Chinese and Western systems of coinage, place the earliest attempt to combine the two systems in the first-century CE kingdom of Khotan.[21] Located in the southwest corner of the Tarim Basin (modern-day Xinjiang), Khotan became a center of silk production along the Later Han dynasty Silk Road. Khotanese coins drew on an existing tradition of bilingual coinage that developed in the Hellenistic states of Central Asia after the conquests of Alexander the Great (d. 323 BCE). However, instead of placing Greek legends (and symbols) on one side and local (e.g., Kharoshthi) legends on the other, Khotan introduced bilingual "Sino-Kharoshthi" coins (figures 5.6 and 5.7). Numismatists such as Joe Cribb and Helen Wang have shown the ways in which Khotan's carefully designed bronze coinage expressed its value in terms legible to the neighboring Kushan and Chinese empires. In manufacture and design, these bilingual coins resembled Kushan, Indian, Hellenistic, Greek, and Lydian coins: they

---

21. Yutian 于闐 in Chinese. Neither the *Hanshu* nor *Hou Hanshu* (History of the Later Han) accounts of Yutian mention its monetary system. The Khotanese coins were unearthed from the ruins of ancient Khotan and also purchased by Aurel Stein in the markets of Yōtkan. See Forsyth, "On the Buried Cities"; Stein, *Ancient Khotan*; Hill, *Through the Jade Gate*, 188–89.

FIGURE 5.6. Obverse of bronze Sino-Kharoshthi coin of Khotanese King Gurgamoya, ca. first century CE, bearing a Prakrit inscription in Kharoshthi script. Reproduced with the permission of the Trustees of the British Museum.

were struck using dies, not cast with molds, as in premodern China; and they a bore pictorial figure (a horse or Bactrian camel), as the standard square-holed Chinese coins did not. The content of the bilingual inscriptions were conventional expressions of their respective traditions. For example, the Prakrit inscription in Kharoshthi script that encircles the picture of a horse on the obverse of the Khotanese coin shown in figure 5.6 gave the issuing ruler's name, together with the traditional epithet of kings "king of kings" inscribed on Central Asian coinage. Its (transliterated) inscription reads: *maharajasa rajatirajasa yidirajasa gurgamoyasa* ([Coin of] great King Gurgamoya, king of kings, King of Khotan). The Chinese inscription on the coin's reverse (figure 5.7), in contrast, stated the *coin's weight*: 銅錢重廿四銖 (Copper coin of weight 24 *zhu*).[22]

---

22. The Khotanese coin also uses the same *xiao zhuan* character style that is commonly used Chinese *wuzhu* coins.

However, neither the weight nor the way in which the Khotanese coin states its own weight are quite "Chinese." Unlike the symmetrically arranged position on Chinese coins of the two characters expressing the coin's weight-value (i.e., *wu* 五 and *zhu* 銖 on the standard first-century Chinese coin), which read horizontally from right to left, the Khotanese coin arranges its lengthier six-character inscription in a circular clockwise design (i.e., in the opposite direction of the Kharoshthi inscription on the obverse).[23] Khotanese coins came in 6- and 24-*zhu* denominations, neither of which had been used in China. And whereas Chinese coins simply stated their nominal weight (usually "5-zhu" *wuzhu*), the Khotanese coin's self-referential use of the term *qian* 錢—the basic fiduciary unit, usually translated as "coin" or "cash" (interchangeable with

---

23. This orientation also resembles that found on Chinese mirror inscriptions.

quan 泉)—was not included on Chinese coins, and thus marks the cultural distance of these Khotanese coins from the Chinese tradition.[24] *Qian* served as the performative utterance, which transformed a hole-less token, with hieroglyphic designs and non-standard weight, into a respectable monetary partner for Chinese coins. The felicity of what was actually a three-way marriage with the early Kushan coinage (of Bactria and northwest India) was further assured by the convenience of the chosen denominations: that is, the big Khotanese *tetradrachm* and the small *drachm* matched the four-to-one ratio of the coin denominations of the neighboring Kushan empire, and one bronze Khotanese *tetradrachm* (weighing 24 *zhu*, i.e., one Chinese ounce) and one *drachm* could potentially be traded (by weight) for six standard 5-*zhu* coins of Han-dynasty China.[25]

Emblematic of Silk Road exchange, these bilingual, bicultural texts thus contributed to the workings of an early interstate economic system, transposing different traditions of aesthetic design and different units of account. These coins likely helped to establish Khotan's position in this Silk Road *oikoumene*. Their "heads" side, symbolic of the issuing state authority (here, King Gurgamoya) asserted Khotan as an international arbiter of ratios of exchange between the Han and Kushan empires. Khotan's Sino-Kharoshthi's coinage also provides a notional template for China's earliest theories of translation which emerged in the Tang dynasty after Buddhist pilgrims (bearing Sanskrit sutras) followed in the tracks of Silk Road merchants: "To translate something means 'to exchange,' that is 'to exchange what one does have for what one does not'" (Kong Yingda, 574–648 CE).[26]

---

24. *Qian* 錢 would not appear on Chinese coins until the Taiping *baiqian* coinage of 256 CE, according to Wang, *Money on the Silk Road*, 44, note 7. Wang Mang's coinage was a brief-lived exception.

25. "The bilingual inscriptions and comparative weights indicate a marriage of the Kushan and Chinese coin systems, which in turn supports the role of Khotan as a land-equivalent of a port of trade." See Wang, *Money on the Silk Road*, xiii, 37–43; Cribb, "Sino-Kharoshthi Coins, Part 1"; Cribb, "Sino-Kharoshthi Coins, Part 2." A *liang* (Han ounce or tael) was 24 *zhu*, and during the first century CE was almost identical in weight to the Bactrian reduced Attic tetradrachm (15.5g) upon which the Sino-Kharoshthi tetradrachm was based.

26. See Behr, "'To translate' is 'to exchange.'"

Commerce and linguistic translation go hand in hand. Although produced by ancient Khotan, such coins implicate Chinese-Khotanese (and potentially Chinese-Kushan) foreign exchange into Han dynasty monetary history.

The traditionally neat division between Chinese and Western coinages has recently faced further scrutiny in scholarly research on one particular set of picture-bearing objects variously called "lead ingots with barbarous Greek inscription," "ingots with foreign inscription," and Han Emperor Wu's *baijin* 白金 ("white metal") coins. These lead (or sometimes clay), saucer-shaped ingots have been excavated across China, especially in the northwest frontier region of Gansu, but also in Anhui and Shaanxi, largely in burial contexts (see appendix for further details). Each ingot bears on the obverse an inscribed dragon (figure 5.8). The reverse bears what some have interpreted as a blundered Greek or foreign inscription, as well as two small identical stamps of a character that some numismatists have identified as an abbreviation for the "imperial privy" (*shaofu* 少府) (figure 5.9).[27] In 1988 a sample of this dragon ingot with foreign inscription was found along with an oval ingot with what appears to be a carapace design, and a square ingot with horse design (see figures 5.10 and 5.11) in Lu'an, Anhui.[28]

Until this discovery in Lu'an, many had assumed these types of ingots were "non-Chinese," possibly Kushan currencies dating to the first or second century BCE (or possibly lead imitations of them, especially

---

27. See the appendix. The burial context of most material samples complicates their identification. They could belong to Han and/or to Han afterworld economies; they could be Han dynasty counterfeits; or, as numismatists from the field point out, many could be modern day forgeries.

28. Li Yong, "Wai wen qian bing kao"; Li Yong, "Lu'an faxian san mei"; Li Yong, "Anhui Lu'an Hanmu." This is the only case in which the three have been found together, and the only case in which the "barbarous Greek" ingot comes from an independently datable context. Li Yong was part of the Wanxi Museum team who oversaw in person the excavation of the Lu'an tomb and wooden coffin in which a bronze wine vessel, a bronze tripod, and two bronze ladles were found along with the ingots. The Lu'an region has been a fruitful site of Han tombs and Li says that the tomb was late Later Han period (though exact details of the dating methodology are not given). The three ingots are currently in a private collection.

FIGURE 5.8. Obverse side of lead ingot or coin with an inscribed dragon, excavated from Lingtai, Gansu province. Reproduced with the permission of Michael Alram.

FIGURE 5.9. Reverse side of lead ingot or coin with blundered Greek or foreign circular inscription and two small Chinese characters. Reproduced with the permission of Michael Alram.

FIGURES 5.10–5.11. Obverse (above) and reverse (below) sides of lead ingot or coin with inscribed dragon and blundered Greek (right); square coin with horse design (middle); and oval coin with turtle design (left), discovered together in Lu'an, Anhui province. Reproduced with the permission of Li Yong.

given their burial context). However, the combination of shapes and pictures of the Lu'an sample has since invited comparison with the *Shiji* and *Hanshu*'s account of Emperor Wu's experimental "three denominations of white-metal currency" (*baijin sanpin* 百金三品) issued in 119 BCE (i.e., before universalizing the *wuzhu* in 112 BCE). For example, the *Shiji* states:

從建元以來，用少，縣官往往即多銅山而鑄錢，民亦閒盜鑄錢，不可勝數。錢益多而輕，物益少而貴。有司言曰：「古者皮幣，諸侯以聘享。金有三等，黃金爲上，白金爲中，赤金爲下。今半兩錢法重四銖，而姦或盜摩錢裏取鋊，錢益輕薄而物貴，則遠方用幣煩費不省。」乃以白鹿皮方尺，緣以藻繢，爲皮幣，直四十萬。王侯宗室朝覲聘享，必以皮幣薦璧，然后得行。又造銀錫爲白金。以爲天用莫如龍，地用莫如馬，人用莫如龜，故白金三品：其一曰重八兩，圜之，其文龍，名曰「白選」，直三千；二曰以重差小，方之，其文馬，直五百；三曰復小，撱之，其文龜，直三百。

Since [the beginning of Emperor Wu's reign] resources had been low, and county officials often went to copper-rich mountains to cast coins, while illegal coin casting amongst the people was beyond computing. Coins became increasingly numerous and lightweight, and goods became increasingly scarce and expensive. An official said: "In antiquity [animal] hide money was used by the vassal lords as gifts and presentations. Metals came in three grades: gold metal was the highest; white metal (*bai jin* 白金) was the middle grade; red metal the lowest. The "half–ounce" coins now in use are supposed by law to weigh four *shu*, but people have tampered with them to such an extent, illegally filing off bits of copper from the reverse side, that they have become increasingly light and thin and the price of goods has accordingly risen. Such currency is extremely expensive to use, especially in distant regions." Therefore [Emperor Wu's officials] made [animal] hide money (*pi bi* 皮幣) from one *chi* (23.1 cm) square pieces of white deer skin with richly decorated hems. Each was worth 400,000 cash. When kings and vassals of the imperial household paid annual court to submit their gifts, they had to present jade [tribute placed on] hide money before they could proceed. They also forged silver (*yin* 銀) and tin into *baijin* ("white metal") [currency]. Since nothing is more useful for Heaven than the dragon, nothing more useful on earth than the horse, and nothing more useful for man than the turtle, they made the *baijin* in three denominations. The first was said to weigh 8-*liang*, was inscribed (*wen*) with a dragon, was named the "white *xuan*," and was valued at 3,000 [cash]. The second was said to be less in weight, was square, was inscribed (*wen*) with a horse, and was worth 500 [cash]. The third was said to be several times less in weight, was oval in shape, was inscribed (*wen*) with a turtle, and was valued at 300 [cash].[29]

Since there were, until recently, no known archaeological samples of these coins or the deer hide money, many modern scholars suspected the existence of the hide money and silver coins bearing pictures of dragons, horses, and turtles.[30] Peng Xinwei and other modern numismatists dismissed as fanciful both the Han historiographic record

---

29. *Shiji* 30.1425–27. Cf. *Hanshu* 24B.1163–64.

30. E.g., Peng, *A Monetary History of China*, 106; Vissering, *On Chinese Currency*, 48. Others have emphasized their function as non-monetary tokens. See, for example, Yang, *Money and Credit*, 51 (on the deerskin) and Scheidel, "Monetary Systems," 148.

and subsequent visual representations that were likely based on these Han records, for example in the respective eighteenth-century works of Qing Emperor Qianlong 乾隆帝 (r. 1735–96) (figure 5.12) and the French Jesuit historian Jean-Baptiste Du Halde (1674–1743) (figure 5.13).[31]

If the excavated lead ingots (or coins) were, indeed, based on a silver currency, they would also be China's earliest attempt to coin a precious metal.[32] Precious metal coinage was not attempted again until 1197— and then, after another long hiatus, in 1890, when the Chinese silver dollar was minted (as a response to the circulation in southern China of Spanish silver coins that had been minted in South and Central America).[33] Whether or not these ingots do reflect the design of Emperor

---

31. In what appears to be a paraphrase of (some version of) the *Shiji* account, Du Halde adds an analogy of the Chinese dragon to the Roman eagle.

> The Chinese gave a mysterious Sense to these Figures: The Tortoise, say they, signifies those who are attach'd to the Earth; the Horse, such as are less wedded to it, and rise above it from Time to Time; and the flying Dragon represents those who are entirely disengag'd from earthly Things. There are other ancient Coins to be found, stampt with Dragons; doubtless, because the *Dragon* is the Symbol of the *Chinese* Nation, as the *Eagle* was of the *Roman*. It is hard to assign what was the just Value of this ancient Money: tho' in my Opinion it ought to be determn'd by the Nature and Weight of the Metal. It is true that Regard has not always been had to that Rule; The Princes, who fix the Value, having often rais'd or lower'd it, as their own Occasions requir'd, or the particular Species grew scarcer.

Du Halde assumes the logic of Western coinage for this comparison—that the dragon like the eagle ultimately represents the stamp of the state (or "Nation" here). See Du Halde, *A Description of the Empire of China*, 332.

32. The burial contexts of most of the excavated samples could explain the substitution of silver for lead.

33. Cribb, "Historical Survey of the Precious Metal Currencies." The second attempt was by the Jin emperor Zhang Zong, who issued silver coins in five denominations in 1197, alongside paper money. No examples of this issue have survived. Silver ingots, used as money, circulated in greater quantities than gold money during the Tang dynasty and, to a lesser extent, during the Song dynasty. Uncoined silver circulated only minimally in early China, especially in comparison with later periods. A third of American silver found its way to China in the sixteenth century, enabling the rise of unregulated private commerce that world historians have explored in revising Europe-centered narratives of capitalism. Von Glahn, *Foun-*

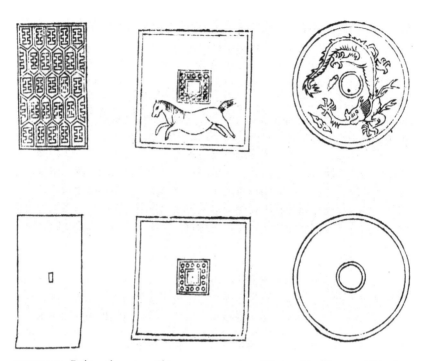

FIGURE 5.12. Eighteenth-century Chinese reconstruction of Former Han Emperor Wu's silver currency (*baijin sanpin*) in Qing Emperor Qianlong's *Qian lu*.

Wu's *baijin*, the numismatic debate alerts us that China's early written record already suggested a breach in the (modern) differentiation between Chinese (non-iconic, bronze) and Western (iconic, silver) coinage traditions. The following section situates the above-mentioned account within a much broader set of classical, "sinifying" practices that have helped to obscure (potentially) intercultural aspects of Chinese monetary history.

_____

tain of Fortune, 83, argues that uncoined and foreign silver circulated in a private market economy that could not be controlled by the state. For further economic analyses, see Frank, *ReOrient*, chapter 3; Flynn, "Money and Growth without Development."

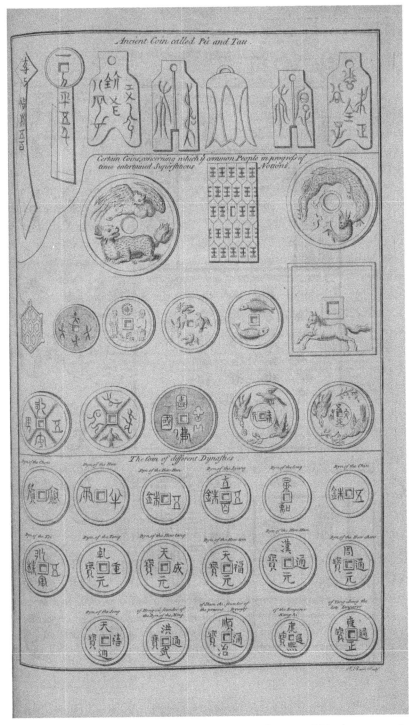

FIGURE 5.13. Eighteenth-century European reconstruction of Emperor Wu's silver currency in Jean-Baptiste Du Halde's *A Description of the Empire of China*.

Classicizing Money

If burial gave money a "foreign" future (inasmuch as the afterlife was a strange and unknown country), discussions of money in classical literature gave money a "Chinese" past. Han dynasty writers embedded the subject of money in competing ethical and cosmopolitical traditions by writing about money in China-centered histories. A coin's inscription was commonly termed *wen* (文, also the term for writing, culture, pattern) and Han historiographers treated money as a transgressive or alien form of *wen*. Despite their different approaches to the monetized market of the Han dynasty (discussed in chapter 3), both the *Shiji* and *Hanshu* highlighted the failure of monetary inscriptions to adequately represent the shared values that governed classical *wen*: as inscriptions of truth/reality (*shi* 實); as cosmological signs; and as patterns of Chinese civilization.[34] As an expression of market logic, the nominal weight-value inscribed on money (e.g., *wuzhu* "5-zhu") presented a counterfeit sort of *wen*. By telling stories of money's origins, as well as fables of debt and interest, classical Han texts debated the broader social and symbolic meanings of money.

WEN: CLASSICAL WRITING VERSUS MONETARY WRITING

Counterfeit values   Han historiographers treated coin inscriptions as a suspicious, transgressive form of writing (*wen*). They recognized that the early imperial state established monetary value through a coin's inscription (*wen* or *wenzhang*). For example, the early second-century BCE *Statute on Coins* 錢律 excavated from tomb no. 247 at Zhangjiashan (Hubei) established that a coin's inscription mattered more than its weight:

錢徑十分寸八以上，雖缺鑠，文章頗可智(知)，而非殊折及鉛錢也，皆為行錢。金不青赤者，為行金。敢擇不取行錢、金者，罰金四兩。

All coins over eight-tenths of a *cun* [approx. 18.5 mm] in diameter, even if they are eroded, [as long as] their inscriptions are somewhat recognizable, and if they are not broken or lead money, may circulate as coins. Gold that has not [turned] green or red is gold that may circulate. Those

---

34. Bottéro, "Cang Jie and the Invention of Writing."

who dare to choose not to take coins and gold that may [legally] circulate will be fined four *liang* of gold.[35]

Limited material erosion of a coin was legally admissible; but imitation in a lower-value metal (e.g., lead) was not. The paramount factor, according to the law, was the legibility of the inscribed weight (*wenzhang* 文章).[36] The *wenzhang* of a coin represented its nominal weight (in this case, likely the "half ounce" *banliang*), rather than its fiduciary value ("one") or its issuing ruler or its issuing mint. Numismatic *wen* was thus a quantitative proposition (that is a proposition of a quantitative value); and the truth of this quantitative proposal would be established by the words written into the state's law, not by the market scales.

However, in contrast to the clear fiats of legal texts, the writings of Han historiographers were troubled by the incommensurability of monetary labels versus the material matter which comprised money, that is, by the incommensurability of money's sign and money's substance. Pre-Han texts did not discuss coin inscriptions and many Han dynasty writers, possibly concerned about the social and economic changes of their time, sought to reclaim or invest this new monetary *wen* (as coin inscription) with non-market, classical values. Although, as discussed in chapter 3, the *Shiji* and the *Hanshu* had very different approaches to the state regulation of the newly monetized marketplace, both works shared the clas-

---

35. *Zhangjiashan Hanmuzhu jian*, 159, strips 197–98. Cf. Strips 199 and 200. On these documents and their dating, see Ōba, "The Ordinances on Fords and Passes" and Li Xueqin, "New Light on the early Han Code." The mid-third-century Qin legal documents excavated from Shuihudi 睡虎地 (Hubei province) specify that good and "bad" (*e* 惡) coins must both circulate as legal tender, but they do not mention the inscription. See Shuihudi Qinmu Zhujian Zhenglixiaozu, *Shuihudi Qin mu zhujian*, 55–56; Hulsewé, *Remnants of Ch'in Law*, 52.

36. The use of *wenzhang* here is striking. Martin Kern's otherwise exhaustive study of uses of the term *wenzhang* in "Ritual, Text, and the Formation of the Canon" argues that up until the late Former Han, *wenzhang* referred to ritual or military insignia, textile patterns, ornaments, ritual forms, the appearance of a ruler or abstract qualities of good rule. At some point in the late Former Han, *wenzhang* starts to refer to writing (especially official writing, classical learning, *wenxue*) and this becomes the dominant meaning in the Later Han. Kern identifies the first-century BCE *Debate on Salt and Iron* as the earliest text in which *wenzhang* refers to writings. Since in that case it refers to legal texts, one might further pursue the relations between monetary and literary genres.

sical assumption that words and writing should represent *shi* ("historical truth," "substance," or "realities"). Both works considered the history of money and drew persistent attention to seigniorage, private casting, metal extraction from coins, and counterfeiting (*jian zhu* 姦鑄 and *dao zhu* 盜鑄).[37] The historiographers used Emperor Wu's silver *baijin* coins—with their anomalous, non-Chinese, and "valueless" inscriptions (*wen*) of dragons, turtles, and horses—as the culminating example of the failure of China's legal tender.[38] Both works noted that counterfeiters of every social status were so numerous that they overwhelmed the penal system: "The *baijin* gradually became so debased (*jian* 賤) that people did not value their use. County officials who used legal statutes to prevent this from happening had no effect. Within a few years the *baijin* was demonetized and ceased to circulate."[39] The *Shiji* and the *Hanshu* added that the authorities had to issue a general amnesty for the "many hundreds of thousands" sentenced to death for illegal casting; and to admit that the number of counterfeiters who were *not* caught was, by this time, "beyond computing."[40]

In addition to their implicit criticisms of Emperor Wu's *baijin* coins, Han historiographers consistently represented *any* form of inscription (*wen*) on coins in a negative light. Three emperors whose coinage reportedly bore inscriptions of each coin's actual weight were the three most reviled in the records (First Emperor Qin; Han Emperor Wu; and Wang Mang the "Usurper"). The *Shiji* and *Hanshu* note that although the weight of the Qin dynasty's standard *banliang* (半兩 "half-ounce") coin "corresponded to its inscription" (*zhong ru qi wen* 重如其文), this prac-

---

37. *Jian* 姦 took on a more limited definition as "sexual offence" in later Ming and Qing legal codes (for which see Sommer, *Sex, Law and Society*, 30–36), but denoted a range of offences in Qin and Han legal codes (including criminal and taboo acts that crosscut political, legal, and ethical realms discussed in early Chinese literature). In the *Shiji*, the referents of *jian* include sexual relations with women in mourning (*Shiji* 106.2825) or with women of the imperial harem (*Shiji* 125.3194); illicit export trade (*Shiji* 123.3166); and grave-robbery (*Shiji* 129.3272).

38. This concern about the *baijin* is iterated in the *Debate on Salt and Iron*. See Wang Liqi, *Yantielun*, 52–53.

39. *Shiji* 30.1434. cf. *Hanshu* 24B.1169.

40. *Shiji* 30.1433; *Hanshu* 24B.1168. Cf. *Shiji* 122.3146; *Hanshu* 24B.1168, 1169; *Hanshu* 90.3654.

tice failed to stabilize prices.[41] Neither book explicitly condemns Han Emperor Wen's 漢文帝 (r. 180–157 BCE) substitution of the Qin's true weight (i.e., twelve-zhu) "half-ounce" coins with underweight four-*zhu* coins on which was inscribed "half-ounce" (四銖錢其文爲「半兩」). However, both tie nonstandard coinage to socio-economic disorder. The *Hanshu* approvingly records Former Han official Jia Yi's wholesale attack on coinage that included the following: "With market stalls using coins of different weights, inscriptions on coins are causing major social havoc" (錢文大亂). Just as, for Jia Yi, commerce was incompatible with the proper agricultural economy (*ben*), so the widespread use of money invited coin tampering. Coin inscriptions both tempted the morally upright into criminal activity and indexed the corruption of traditional values. In these and other ways, historiographers used classical notions of *wen* to embed money within ethical and cosmological contexts. At the same time, in narrating the failure of numismatic *wen* to properly name its object—or to facilitate socially harmonious exchange even when it did—Han dynasty historiographers implicitly asserted their medium (*wen* as writing) as the privileged arbiter of true value.

Counterfeit cosmology   From a numismatic perspective, the development of coinage as a symbolic system was closely tied to that of the tributary and cosmological order. Numismatists trace the signature shape of imperial coins—round with a square center-hole—to the jade discs (*bi*) with circular holes that traditionally circulated in China as gifts and tributary offerings.[42] Excavated Han talismanic coins with auspicious patterns and inscriptions, and coin patterns inscribed on *liubo* 六博 gameboards suggest that some people in the Han dynasty also associated such coins with the popular visualization of Heaven and Earth as a square-within-a-circle.[43] Surprisingly, perhaps, the Han historiographers did not themselves make these cosmological claims. Rather, they showed that whenever the emperor allied monetary inscription and

---

41. *Shiji* 30.1442. *Hanshu* 24B. 1152. The Qin standardization of currency as copper coins and gold (by weight) failed to stabilize prices, thus causing the value of demonetized pearls, jade, and precious items to fluctuate.

42. Thierry, "The Origins and Development of Chinese Coins," 26.

43. Tseng, *Picturing Heaven in Early China*, 37–69 and Tseng, "Representation and Appropriation."

design with cosmological signs as part of his Mandate of Heaven, he did so disingenuously.

Both the *Shiji* and *Hanshu* maintain an attitude of skepticism about Emperor Wu's attempt to make coin inscriptions into Heavenly signs (prior to establishing the standard *wuzhu*):

其後，天子苑有白鹿，以其皮爲幣，以發瑞應，造白金焉。其明年，郊雍，獲一角獸，若麃然。有司曰：「陛下肅祇郊祀，上帝報享，錫一角獸，蓋麟云。」於是以薦五時，時加一牛以燎。錫諸侯白金，風符應合于天也。

After this, white deer appeared in the Son of Heaven's [Shanglin] Park, and their hides were used to make money (*bi*) to display this auspicious sign. *Baijin* [coins] were made along with it. The next year, during the suburban sacrifice at Yong someone captured a beast with one horn similar to a deer. Some official said, "Your Majesty conducted the suburban sacrifices with solemnity and respect, and the Heavenly Emperor above has given lavish recompense, bestowing upon you a one-horned beast. This is probably what is called a unicorn." After this, the emperor visited the Five Altars and added an extra ox to his burnt offerings at each altar. He presented *baijin* to his vassal lords, persuading them that they were tokens corresponding with harmony with the heavens."[44]

In this account, Emperor Wu's deer hide money (*pi bi*, a potential precursor to paper money) is a token, an indexical trace, of an auspicious sign (i.e., the white deer). The *baijin* ("white metal") also acquires cosmological authority by its association with the white color of the auspicious deer. The white deer and unicorn that appear before the casting and circulation of the currency are claimed as signs of Heaven's approval. After all, the capture of a *lin* 麟 (a legendary unicorn) supposedly heralded the advent of the next sage after Confucius. However, the Han historiographers clearly aimed to cast doubt on this claim of divine sanction. They reported the capture of a "beast with one horn similar to a deer" (*biao* 麃); and they record Emperor Wu's advisers as suggesting that "it is probably what is called unicorn" (*gai lin yun* 蓋麟云). In this introduction of an element of uncertainty, the Han historiographers undercut the reader's confidence that the emperor was legitimately presenting the *baijin* as "tokens" (*fu* 符) of heavenly approval.[45]

---

44. *Shiji* 28.1387; cf. *Hanshu* 24B.1169.
45. Compare *Shiji* 28.1387; *Hanshu* 25A.1219.

The *Shiji* and *Hanshu*, in effect, cast subtle aspersions on the emperor's attempt to present coinage as integral to the long-term transactional order. This account of the use of *baijin* falls within an incredulous narrative about the *fangshi* 方士 ("masters of recipes"), which recounts their influence on Emperor Wu as he pursued knowledge about lands of immortality in the distant east and west. By casting suspicion on the sighting of the unicorn, the *Shiji* refuses to validate the representational mode of the Emperor's new money. In the case of the *Shiji*, the authors' sincere belief in cosmological signs lies behind this hermeneutics of suspicion (Sima Tan and Sima Qian successively occupied the position of Grand Astrologer 太史令 *Taishi Ling* at the imperial court). The *Shiji*'s was not a radical skepticism of the possible correlation of cosmological sign and political meaning but, rather, was a critique of precisely the kind of imperial manipulation of signs that the *Guanzi* (as discussed below) promoted.

The scandal of casting coins and claiming them as inscribed tokens of Heaven's Mandate climaxes with the *Hanshu*'s account of the "usurper" Wang Mang (r. 9–23 CE). Wang Mang established his own brief Xin dynasty between the Former and Later Han periods. As the *Hanshu* details in considerable length, Wang Mang legitimated his overthrow of the House of Han with a return to idealized coin designs of the Zhou texts:[46]

> 莽即眞，以爲書「劉」字有金刀，乃罷錯刀、契刀及五銖錢，而更作金、銀、龜、貝、錢、布之品，名曰「寶貨」。

> When Wang Mang was established as the actual [emperor of the Xin dynasty], he took the fact that in writing the character of the [Han dynastic] surname "Liu" [one had to incorporate the characters] "metal" (*jin*) and "knife" (*dao*) [as the pretext for] abolishing the "*cuo*-knife" (*cuo dao*), "*qi*-knife" (*qi dao*), and five-grain (*wuzhu*) coinage. Then, instead, he made gold, silver, tortoise-shell, cowrie, copper, and trouser-shaped

---

46. Wang Mang's radical experiments in numismatic *wen* would include Zhou-styled cowrie and knife-shaped coins and striking social and political nomenclature for his coin denominations (e.g., "emperor," "duke," "marquis," or "adult," "adolescent," etc., coins). Most pertinently here, Wang Mang transformed monetary inscription into an even more explicit form of cosmological-political writing than under Emperor Wu.

["cloth"] denominations, and named them "Precious Currencies" (*bao huo*).[47]

Wang Mang here applies the metonymic tradition of *literary* taboos to the monetary sign system. By the decree of the Han dynasty's founder, every legitimate Han emperor had to possess the surname "Liu" (劉). Wang Mang abolishes three earlier coinages based on three graphic elements of the surname's character: *jin* 金 ("metal"), *dao* 刀 (knife), and *mao* 卯 (one of the twelve "earthly branches" [*di zhi* 地支] used in calendrical notations). The new ruler dismissed the two knife-shaped currencies he had created when acting as regent of the Han dynasty (6–8 CE) (*cuo dao* 錯刀 ["*cuo*-knife"] and *qi dao* 契刀 ["*qi*-knife"]) because "knife" was part of the dethroned Liu surname, along with the universal Han *wuzhu* coinage (presumably because *zhu* 銖 uses the "metal" 金 radical). *Mao* was part of the date (*ding mao* 丁卯) on which Wang Mang seized power from the Lius (Jan. 9, 9 CE). In this way Wang Mang delegitimized earlier currency forms (and inscriptions) as indices of the Liu regime. Coins had become tokens—not as quantitative signs (as in the *Guanzi*)—but as Heaven-mandated *wen*. Writing after the fall of Wang Mang and the restoration of the Han dynasty, the authors of the *Hanshu* exposed the illegitimacy of the interregnum, in part, by presenting Wang Mang's coinage as counterfeit cosmopolitical writing (*wen*).

The civilizational borders of wen   Han dynasty historiographers wrote of foreign money as a foreign sign system, not as a potential medium of exchange. As addressed earlier in this chapter, Chinese and Western coinage traditions diverged in their design and manufacture: that is, Central, Southern, and Western Eurasian coins were struck with dies, used precious metals, and bore pictures; but Chinese coins (apart from Emperor Wu's *baijin*) were cast in molds, bore weight values (not pictures), and used non-precious metals (bronze). Foreign coins enter the Chinese record for the first time in Han historiography as part of an ethnographic, not economic discussion. The topic of foreign money is not included in the long, dynasty-by-dynasty accounts of monetary forms in the *Shiji*'s "Treatise on the Balanced Standard" (*Ping zhun shu* 平準書) or in the *Hanshu*'s "Treatise on Food and Commodities" (*Shi*

---

47. *Hanshu* 24B.1177.

huo zhi). Instead, a possible account of foreign coinage comes in the *Shiji*'s ethnographic "Account of Dayuan [Ferghana]" (*Dayuan liezhuan* 大宛列傳), a notional blueprint for later literary accounts of the "Western Regions" (*xi yu* 西域). In this account, upon returning to Emperor Wu's court (ca. 126 BCE) after his groundbreaking travels in Central Asia, the Han envoy Zhang Qian 張騫 (d. 113 BCE) reported:

以銀爲錢，錢如其王面，王死輒更錢，效王面焉。畫革旁行以爲書記。

[In Parthia (Anxi)] they use silver to make coins. Their coins bear the resemblance of their king's face. When the king dies, they immediately change the coins, putting an imitation of the [new] king's face on them. They draw on leather along horizontal lines to make written records.[48]

In this passage, the *Shiji* (or rather, the envoy Zhang Qian) seems to draw precise attention to the foreignness of Parthia by not using *wen* to describe its coinage and writing. Foreign coins bear iconic resemblances (*ru* 如, *xiao* 效) of the king's face, not *wen*; they also "draw" (*hua* 畫) when making written records (*shu ji* 書記). By contrast, the *Hanshu*'s later "Account of the Western Regions" acknowledges the *wen* on Central Asian coins: "[In the case of Parthian coins] the inscription (*wen*) is only the king's face, and on the reverse is his consort's face" (文獨爲王面，幕爲夫人面).[49] What matters in both examples, however, is that the Han historiographers note the design, but not the potential exchange values, of foreign coins. Coins are cultural objects, not tokens of potentially connected markets. They are, to again borrow Keith Hart's term, all "heads" and no "tails."

This disinterest in "translating" (or inability to discuss) coinage in market terms reflects both a broader ethnographic method and, more specifically, a hostility to the attempted introduction of foreign exchange. The *Shiji*'s ensuing account represents Parthia in part as an inversion of the world of the Central States (China).

其人皆深眼，多鬚髯，善市賈，爭分銖。俗貴女子，女子所言而丈夫乃決正。其地皆無絲漆，不知鑄錢器。及漢使亡卒降，教鑄作他兵器。得漢黃白金，輒以爲器，不用爲幣。

---

48. *Shiji* 123.3162. There is a long-standing debate about the authenticity of this chapter and its relation to the *Hanshu*. The *Hanshu* biography of Zhang Qian does not include this report. See Hulsewé, *China in Central Asia*, 11–39 and Lu Zongli, "Problems."

49. *Hanshu* 96A.3889. Cf. *Hanshu* 96A.3885.

[The people of Parthia] have deep-set eyes and full beards. They are skilled at market commerce, and haggle over a fraction of a penny. By custom they honor their young women (*nü zi*) [or women and children].[50] Men determine what is right based on what young women say. Their land is completely without silk or lacquer, and they did not know how to cast coins[51] and vessels until some soldiers accompanying the Han envoys deserted, defected, and taught them [the Parthians] how to cast [metal] and make other military weapons. When they obtain the yellow or white metal (i.e., gold or silver) from the Han [state], they immediately use it to make utensils and do not use it as money."[52]

Modern historians often use this passage to illumine the biases that pervade classical Chinese texts. The *Shiji* here makes Parthia into a nation of shopkeepers with strange bodies (deep-set eyes and beards), inverted notions of authority (men listening to women, old listening to young), a lack of silk and lacquer, and no knowledge of metal-casting (until educated in this technique by the Chinese). In so doing, the text implicitly reflects what the domain of Chinese *wen* does possess (at least ideally): for example, silk, lacquer, fewer price-hagglers, and more beardless and authoritative men. However, in light of their recorded coin designs and their price haggling, the *Shiji*'s claim that Parthians do not know how to "cast coinage" (鑄錢器) is puzzling.[53] Unless the *Shiji* is registering (without "translating") the distinction between casting and minting, the *Hanshu*'s version, "cast iron vessels" (鑄鐵器), makes better sense. In any case, the passage again suggests the absence of foreign exchange media. Unlike Han dynasty usage of gold or Emperor Wu's *baijin* currency, the Parthians do not use gold or "white metal" (e.g., Emperor Wu's experiment) to make "money" (*bi* 幣).

In narrating the beginnings of (what in modern times became known as) the Silk Road, the *Shiji* presents Chinese attempts at using foreign exchange in a negative light. In the following passage, it suggests the quest for foreign markets had the effect of depreciating standards of speech:

---

50. The text uses *nü zi* 女子.

51. *Hanshu* 96A.3896 has 不知鑄鐵器.

52. *Shiji* 123. 3174.

53. The phrase "haggle over a fraction of a cent" (*zheng fen zhu* 爭分銖) borrows the same locution used elsewhere in Chinese texts for domestic haggling over money. See, for example, *Huainanzi*, 17.218. Compare the use of "higgling-haggling" over price in distinguishing market and non-market trade in Polanyi, "The Economy as Instituted Process."

自博望侯開外國道以尊貴，其後從吏卒皆爭上書言外國奇怪利害，求
使。天子為其絕遠，非人所樂往，聽其言，予節，募吏民毋問所從來，為
具備人眾遣之，以廣其道。來還不能毋侵盜幣物，及使失指，天子為其習
之，輒覆案致重罪，以激怒令贖，復求使。使端無窮，而輕犯法。其吏卒
亦輕復盛推外國所有，言大者予節，言小者為副，故妄言無行之徒皆爭
效之。其使皆貧人子，私縣官齎物，欲賤市以私其利外國。外國亦厭漢
使人人有言輕重，度漢兵遠不能至，而禁其食物以苦漢使。漢使乏絕積
怨至相攻擊。

After the Marquis of Bowang (i.e., Zhang Qian) was honored and en-
nobled for opening the road to foreign states, his accompanying officers
and soldiers all competed to submit reports that spoke of exotic wonders,
and profits and losses, as part of their own quest to become envoys. The
Son of Heaven presumed that the distances involved were so remote that
no person would travel there for pleasure, and so, paying heed to their
speeches, he bestowed on them the official insignia. He recruited officials
and commoners without inquiring into their backgrounds, and sent with
them crowds of people to assist with the necessary provisions, all in order
to expand his path [westward]. On their way back these people were
unable to refrain from embezzling money and goods (*bi wu* 幣物), and
the officials had not carried out their orders. The Son of Heaven was
practiced in this domain. He immediately had them investigated and
accused of such serious crimes that they angrily accepted a new mission
to absolve themselves, reapplying to become envoys. Thus envoys were in
limitless supply, and breaking the law meant little to them. Their accompanying officials and soldiers would also repeatedly come [before
the Emperor] to promote the possessions of foreign states in the most
effusive terms. Those with grandiose claims were awarded the official
insignia; those with lesser claims became their assistants. As a result,
followers of these unscrupulous men who spoke recklessly all competed
to imitate them. These envoys were all the sons of poor people, who
privately took the goods handed to them by county officials. They desired [to buy] cheap goods in markets [to accrue] private profit from
foreign states. These foreign states were fed up with the way each of
these envoys made fluctuating claims (*you yan qing zhong* 有言輕重
lied; spoke of different prices). The locals estimated that the distance for
a Han army to reach them was too great, and so [the locals] prohibited
[sales] of food and goods to [the Han envoys] to make the Han envoys
suffer. Angered that they had been cut off from local stores, the Han
envoys ended up quarreling and fighting each other.[54]

---

54. *Shiji* 123.3171.

As suggested in chapter 3, the text of the *Shiji* reveals prejudices against the poor and those without status. Those beneath the status of envoy who urge Emperor Wu to send delegations to Dayuan clearly belong to the throngs of men who were recruited "without inquiring into their backgrounds," and who embezzled their entrusted goods for private gains in the black market. Although the function of envoys, as recorded in Han and pre-Han historiography, was to deliver messages between their own ruler and another ruler, any unofficial private speech could both debase their identity as envoy and distort their official message. In this text, Emperor Wu "heeds the speeches" (聽其言) of aspiring envoys who "competed to submit reports that spoke (皆爭上書言) of exotic wonders, and profits and losses" and "effusively promoted" (盛推) foreign possessions. In an auction of bidders, the emperor makes "those with boastful speeches" (言大者) his official envoys, rather than "those with more moderate speeches" (言小者), so that other careerists immediately imitated their "reckless speech" (*wang yan* 妄言). These international black market profiteers stand in stark contrast to the *Shiji*'s list of ethical "commodity-producers" (discussed in chapter 3). The speech of these envoys even takes on the property of market exchange: "these foreign states were fed up with the way each of these envoys made fluctuating claims" (*you yan qingzhong*).[55] *Qingzhong* in this novel phrase either describes the envoys

---

55. The exact sense of Sima Qian's phrase remains unclear. The *Shiji* elsewhere uses the phrase *qingzhong* in five basic ways, in which the context inflects it with variously positive, negative, or neutral valences: a) as physical weight, or standard weight; or intentional/unintended fluctuation in weight (*Shiji* 1241; 79.2422; 40.1700; 23.1172, 52.2008); b) as metaphorical weight in the sense of (relative or fluctuating) worth (e.g., of a person, of a currency value) (e.g., *Shiji* 4.168, 30.1442); c) as relative degree (e.g., of rank, seriousness of punishment) or proper standard (e.g., of ritual), (e.g., *Shiji* 23.1161; 68.2230, 102.2755, 118.3093, 119.3102, 107.2846); d) as the name of one of Guan Zhong's well-known works (*Shiji* 62.2136); e) as the economic theory and profitable system established by Guan Zhong for the state of Qi (*Shiji* 30.1442, 32.1487, 62.2133). Given the context and subsequent phrase at *Shiji* 129.3255, this appears to be a technical usage, although the *Suoyin* interprets it as concerning coins and the *Zhengyi* as a reference to shame and dishonor. Ancient and modern commentators have generally interpreted the present context of *you yan qingzhong* as lying, or at least telling "different stories" or varying the relation of their speech to truth. For example, see the *Jijie* commentary at *Shiji* 123.3172: "When the Han envoys spoke abroad, each one said something different than the truth (*qingzhong bu shi* 輕重不實, literally 'lighter and heavier and not true')." The *Hanyu da cidian* cites this *Shiji* line and the *Jijie* comment as the locus classicus for the usage of *qingzhong* as *zhen wei xu shi* 真偽虛實, allowing the context to determine

speech ("false" [in value], i.e., they lied) or refers to the content of their speech (perhaps "value" in the sense of the "price" of goods, i.e., they freely adjusted the prices of their goods for profit). Elsewhere, Han envoys curse or use indecorous speech (*wang yan*) when the residents of Ferghana refuse to accept Emperor Wu's payment in gold for their famous horses.[56] Scandalous, merchant-style speech thus helps to obstruct foreign market transactions.

ETIOLOGIES OF MONEY

Setting aside *qingzhong* economics, foreign money thus did not enter into the new tales of money's origin that emerged during the Han. Modern histories of Chinese economic thought have generally observed a continuity between Zhou and Han legends of money's origins. An inherited pre-Qin myth of sage rulers casting coinage as disaster relief for the needy did indeed remain dominant through the Han period. However, Han writers gave competing meanings to monetary transactions by significantly revising or rejecting this earlier myth. For some, the sages Yu and Tang had cast money to alleviate social suffering, thereby sanctioning a centrally planned market economy. For others, money had arisen naturally in the marketplace to facilitate trade and was therefore best left alone by the state. For yet others, money was a modern invention that deserved no place in state-planned *or* in unregulated markets. Money was, as Former Han official Jia Yi 賈誼 argued, a practice of "plucking

---

the (here negative) valence. Compare Watson, *Records of the Grand Historian, Han Dynasty* II, 242. This uses the figurative sense of *qingzhong* ("b," above) as modifier of an unstated object (i.e., "speech," "claim") of their speaking (*yan*). Within this logic, "light" (*qing*) is a metaphor for "false" (*xu*) and "heavy" (*zhong*) for "true" (*shi*). Although this interpretation is viable, it does not exhaust the possibilities of the *Shiji*'s novel locution. Syntactically, *you yan* is usually followed by what was actually said, either in direct or indirect discourse, rather than being used as a modifier describing *how* what was spoken was spoken. If *qingzhong* is indeed the expressed object, the most likely options would be that the Han envoys "claimed different weights" (as in a, above), "spoke of different values (i.e., prices)" (as in b), or "declaimed Guanzi's economic theories of price" (as in d, or e). The two preceding sentences concern their illegal pursuit of private profit ("These envoys were all the sons of poor people, who privately took the goods handed to them by county officials. They desired to buy cheap goods in markets for private profit on their return from foreign states."). The content of their speeches, in other words, likely concerns marketplace activity (e.g., weights, prices).

56. *Shiji* 123.3174.

bronze" whose popularity had caused the disastrous abandonment of
agriculture. Money encouraged counterfeiting because it was itself a
kind of counterfeit: a fictitious representation of value and an index of social
decline.

What complicates the modern reconstruction of this conflict is not so
much the disagreement over the function of money—as a market commodity or a token of the state—as the rhetorical play with the terminology itself.[57] The term *bi* 幣 was itself more open to redefinition in the
Han than it was in subsequent centuries. Positive attempts now to synthesize documentary and numismatic evidence into a history of Chinese
"money," restrictively conceived as "general purpose money," are complicated by this Han rhetorical playfulness, by historical (and regional)
changes in legal tender, as well as by the ambiguity of pre-Han texts.[58]
Zhou texts generally use *bi* to refer to an offering or gift (often of jade,
silk, or valuables).[59] Only two extended discussions of *bi*, explicitly seen
as coined money, survive from the Zhou. During the far more monetized Qin-Han period, when the universal poll tax on adult men and
women required cash payments, *bi* became the common term for money.
It comprised uncoined gold (*jin* 金) and bronze *qian* (錢) coins that were
round with a square hole.[60] *Qian* (or *quan* 泉 "source" in excavated Han

---

57. See Keith Hart, "Heads or Tails" and Richard von Glahn's use of "cartelist" and
"catallactic" in his very useful introduction to early Chinese monetary theory in *Fountain of Fortune*, 15–47.

58. Just as the *Shuowen jiezi*'s graphic etymology of *bi* ("money") was "silk" (*bo* 帛),
so the term *bu* 布 could refer to actual "textiles" that did serve as a form of payment
through the imperial period (measured by standardized lengths and widths) or to a
pre-imperial coin-type. Similarly, in pre-imperial texts *qian* could refer variously to an
agricultural implement (*yao* 銚 hoe), to a coin that was shaped like that implement, or
to any bronze coin.

59. Anthropologists have used different permutations of Paul Bohannan's distinction between "general purpose" money, which serves as a means of exchange, a measure
of value, and a method of payment (or as a store of value or a unit of account), from
"special purpose" moneys which only performs one or two of these functions. See, for
example, Bohannan, "The impact of money on an African subsistence economy."

60. Gold circulated by actual weight, often as one-catty (*jin* 斤, 245 g) gold cakes,
whereas cast coins circulated by nominal weight, such "half-ounce coins" (*banliang
qian* 半兩錢) or "three-grain coins" (*sanzhu qian* 三銖錢) until Emperor Wu successfully universalized the "five-*zhu* coin" (*wuzhu qian* 五銖錢), which displaced other
coins in 112 BCE. The standardized five-zhu *qian*, which was a round coin with a square

texts) referred to the bronze coin that became the basic fiduciary unit of value with an abstract value of *one* (translated "cash").[61] All currencies and commodities were reckoned in terms of *qian*. Although early imperial *bi* took on the functions modern economists recognize as the hallmarks of general-purpose "money" (e.g., as a means of exchange, a measure of value, or a method of payment), the *Hanshu*, in particular, exploited the historical use of *bi* to refer to the token offerings of the tributary economy, in order to retell *bi*'s history.

The canonical Zhou etiology of the tributary economy found in the *Book of Documents* did not include money. To save humanity after catastrophic floods, Yu explained: "I toiled to transfer between the haves and have-nots, and to change where they lived" (懋遷有無化居).[62] The two surviving Zhou discussions of coined money portray money as the ruler's emergency measure. Both the "Great Rescue" (*Da Kuang* 大匡) chapter of the *Lost Book of Zhou* (*Yi Zhou Shu* 逸周書) and the fifth-century BCE *Legends of the States* (*Guoyu* 國語) tell of kings who cast money

---

hole, took its shape from jade disc offerings, not the pre-imperial agricultural implement *qian*. It was the regional form of coins used in the pre-imperial state of Qin. Similarly, in pre-imperial texts *qian* could refer variously to an agricultural implement (*yao* 銚 hoe), to a coin that was shaped like that implement, or to any bronze coin. According to the *Hanshu*, 28 billion *wuzhu qian* were cast from 112 BCE until the middle of the reign of Later Han Emperor Ping (1–5 CE).

61. On this use in Han wood slips from Eastern Central Asia, see Wang, *Money on the Silk Road*, 13.

62. Karlgren, *Book of Documents*, 9, and Karlgren, *Glosses on the Book of Documents*, 118–19, proposes to translate 懋遷有無化居 as 懋遷有無貨居: "I exchanged and transferred those who had and those who had not hoards of stores." Cf. *Shiji* 85.2506: 此奇貨可居. In light of the ideologically very different uses in the *Shiji* and *Hanshu* at *Shiji* 2.79 and *Hanshu* 24B.1185 (書云「懋遷有無」), this chapter follows the similar interpretations of (pseudo-) Gong Anguo, and of Cai Chen, Couvreur, and Schaberg. The "Tribute of Yu" chapter that describes Yu's labors in bringing order through the nine provinces also makes no mention of money. The *Shiji* version likewise states: "When food was scarce, I moved surplus [food] to where it was lacking, and [helped] people to move residences [i.e., migrate]. The common people were then settled." (食少，調有餘補不足，徙居。眾民乃定). See *Shiji* 2.79. Karlgren translates Sima Qian as follows: "I exchanged—and transferred—the existing and the non-existing—hoarded goods"; Karlgren's *Glosses on the Book of Documents* also notes: "If this was Sima Qian's meaning he violated the Shu text strongly."

to alleviate social suffering in the aftermath of floods and drought.[63] In the former case, King Wen, the founder of the Zhou dynasty, casts money to "rescue" his people; in the latter, a late Zhou adviser recalls this earlier practice of money casting. As the *Legends of the States* narrates:

景王二十一年，將鑄大錢。單穆公曰：「不可。古者，天災降戾，於是乎量資幣，權輕重，以振救民。民患輕，則爲作重幣以行之，於是乎有母權子而行，民皆得焉。若不堪重，則多作輕而行之，亦不廢重，於是乎有子權母而行，小大利之。今王廢輕而作重，民失其資，能無匱乎？... 」王弗聽，卒鑄大錢。

King Jing of Zhou 周景王 (r. 544–520 BCE), in his twenty-first year, proposed the casting of large coins (*zhu da qian* 鑄大錢). Duke Mu of Shan

---

63. The *Lost Book of Zhou* is also known as the *Zhou Shu* 周書 (Book of Zhou). The redaction of the received text of 70 chapters was no earlier than Former Han, but parts of the received text were composed much earlier. Huang Peirong, *Zhoushu yanjiu*, 83–88, includes the "Great Rescue" chapter as chapter 11 of the core 32 *pian* composed in the late fourth to early third centuries BCE. Luo Jiaxian, *Yi Zhou shu yan jiu*, 12–35, uses the parallels between accounts of "mother-child" currency circulation with the *Legends of the States* to re-date the "Great Rescue" chapter to "no later than the Spring and Autumn period" (i.e., 771 to 403 BCE). See also Shaughnessy, "I Chou shu." "The Great Rescue" chapter narrates the response to a huge drought by King Wen 文王 (1099–1050 BCE), the reputed founder of the Zhou dynasty. In this account, money appears among the state-sponsored reforms for the welfare of agricultural communities and traders, respectively. Local authorities distribute public money (賦洒其幣) and the state ensures the circulation of money to facilitate commerce:

於是告四方：游旅旁生忻通，津濟道宿，所至如歸。幣租輕，乃作母以行其子。易資，貴賤以均游旅，使無滯。

Upon this [King Wen] proclaimed everywhere: "Let itinerant traders enjoy extensive travels in circulating [their goods]. Let them have water transport and lodging on their way, and find their destinations [to be] like their places of return. If money (*bi*) is light, make "mother" [money] to circulate [as well as] the "child" [money] (*mu yi xing qi zi*). In the exchange of goods let prices (literally "expensive and cheap") be moderated for itinerant traders so [their trading] never ceases."

See *Yi zhou shu*, 56–63. Light coins become "children" (or sons, *zi*) when heavier "mother" coins are introduced to aid their function as a medium of exchange. The "mother" is a corrective mechanism that here guarantees that the activity of itinerant traders "never ceases." Important to note is the *Lost Book of Zhou*'s framing of the mother-child system as a prescriptive measure. It is part of King Wen's "proclamation." The chapter begins: "In the third year of King Wen of Zhou's residence at Cheng, Heaven sent a huge drought. King Wen composed the 'The Great Rescue' (*Da kuang*) in order to proclaim his administration of his territory, and the vassal lords of his three regions all adhered."

單穆公 (i.e., Shan Qi) said: "This is not right. In antiquity (*gu zhe* 古者), when Heaven sent calamities down, (the ruler) would measure out goods and money (*bi*) and control weights to rescue the people. If the people suffered from light [lightweight money] then he made heavy money for circulation. Thereupon the "mother" would control the "child" in circulation and the people used both to obtain [what they needed]. If the heavy [coins] were inadequate, he [the king] made more light ones for circulation, but did not abolish the heavy ones, whereupon the "child" controlled the "mother" in circulation, and [people] profited from both the big and small. Now if Your Majesty abolishes light [-weight coins] and [only] makes heavy ones, people will lose their property, and how then can they not go bankrupt? . . ." The king did not listen [to Lord Mu], and in the end cast big coins.[64]

In this passage, the ancient ruler "measured out goods and money" (量資幣) for people's welfare after "Heaven sent calamities down." Although king and adviser disagree about the ancient "mother and child" monetary system they do not question the ruler's sanctioned authority over money.[65] This kinship idiom, which configures both king and users of money as the symbolic "father," was unlikely used during the Han, except to describe these archaic practices. The king uses money to harmonize the cosmological exchanges between Heaven and the people (i.e., to prevent bankruptcy), thereby legitimating his authority over the political economy. In Duke Mu's rhetoric, imitation of the ancient past enables the reproduction of the classical, ethics-centered economy, synchronizing the present king's money with the long-term moral transactional order.

The *Shiji* presented the most scandalous revision to the Zhou etiology. It traced money's origins to the marketplace instead of to a state fiat. In the following passage—and more reminiscent of Aristotle and Adam Smith than of other Han dynasty records—Sima Qian uses money to betoken commodity price rather than state authority:

太史公曰：農工商交易之路通，而龜貝金錢刀布之幣興焉。所從來久遠，自高辛氏之前尚矣，靡得而記云。故書道唐虞之際，詩述殷周之世，安寧則長庠序，先本絀末，以禮義防于利；事變多故而亦反是。是以物盛則衰，時極而轉，一質一文，終始之變也。

---

64. *Guoyu*, 118–19. *Hanshu* 24B.1151 records an abbreviated version of this.

65. It may be related to the use of "mother" and "child" to mean a (fractional) denominator and numerator in Han mathematical idiom.

The Grand Scribe [i.e., Sima Qian] comments: When farmers, artisans, and merchants crossed paths to make exchanges, then turtle [shell], cowrie, gold, hoe-shaped, knife-shaped and cloth ("trouser")-shaped money arose (*bi xing* 幣興). This practice comes from remote times, from high antiquity before the Gao Xin Clan [i.e., legendary Emperor Ku], about which [details] are too scanty to record.[66] Thus in the *Book of Documents*' report on the time of [subsequent rulers] Tang and Yu and the *Odes*' transmission of the periods of Shang and Zhou, peace and stability brought the traditional "Gardens" and "Courses" [i.e., the pre-Han educational institutions]—which privileged the "root" (*ben*) and found the "branch" (*mo*) lacking—and used ritual propriety to guard against [pursuit of] profit. Since changes in such circumstance (*shi bian*) are frequent [e.g., war], opposite [sentiments] also therefore arise. From this one can see that what flourishes must decline; when times reach their extreme they turn back; and rude and refined [periods] in turn are endlessly alternating.[67]

Sima Qian here pushes money's origins back into prehistory. Monetary markets existed "from high antiquity before emperor Ku," during the legendary era of the "Five Emperors" (the period with which the *Shiji* begins). Despite the historiographer's explicit and implicit preference elsewhere for reliable written and oral sources, he admits he "has no records" for this period. His account is not therefore constrained by textual occurrences (or absences) of *bi* (as money). *Bi* and *huo*—and the market (*shi* 市) itself—are all synchronic elements of the historically transcendental meeting of paths of "exchange."[68] Unlike all other Han explanations of money, monetary exchange thus belongs to the marketplace not the state. In contrast to the practice of the ancient rulers of the Xia, Shang, and Zhou dynasties in casting coins only after floods and drought to alleviate social suffering in a long-term transactional order, in this *Shiji* account money enables the immediate exchanges between "farmers, artisans, and merchants." Money follows market time that is determined by the perennial "crossing of paths for make exchanges" among farmers, artisans, and merchants. Divorced from natural catas-

---

66. See *Shiji* 1.13 and 1.46 on Emperor Ku, who preceded Emperor Yao, and his questionable historicity.

67. *Shiji* 30.1442; cf. *Shiji* 2489, 2228.

68. On the "barter" hypothesis of money's origins, see Graeber, *Debt*, 21–41.

trophe, money has no naturalized place in the cosmological time of the moral economy.

This passage is part of a highly critical account of Emperor Wu's experiments with planned market activity (which aimed to fund his military exploits abroad and which included attempts to profit from currency changes). Sima Qian portrays Emperor Wu's market regulations as a historic inversion of the proper "cultivated" (*wen*) economy.[69] The "change in circumstances" (*shi bian* 事變) alluded to above points to the wartime era of the profit-seeking state (i.e, the "rude," *zhi*). As seen in chapter 3, the closing chapter of the *Shiji* replaces the redistributive state with the individual Confucian *junzi* entrepreneur as the moral basis of the economy. In disassociating money from the problem of insufficiency (*bu zu*), Sima Qian departs from all other early Chinese stories of money.

One should note that even if the *Shiji*'s etiology considered money as a token of market exchange, this work did not voice approval of private minting. The *Shiji*—along with the *Hanshu*, both sides in the *Debate on Salt and Iron*, and even Tang dynasty officials in post-Han texts—recalled the dangers of Liu Pi 劉濞 (216–154 BCE) and Deng Tong 鄧通 (fl. 170 BCE), China's two most notorious private casters of coins:

---

69. Compare the *Shiji*'s synopsis of the "Treatise of the Balanced Standard" (*Shiji* 130.3306): "Engaging in the practice of money (*bi*) enables exchange (*tong*) between farmers and merchants. In extreme cases it leads to manipulative play, to annexing and consolidating these increases, to competition over opportunistic profits, and to the abandonment of the 'root' [i.e., agriculture] and hastening toward the 'branch' [i.e., commerce]. I made the 'Treatise on the Balanced Standard,' the eighth [treatise], to observe this change in circumstances (*shi bian*)." Although the treatise repeatedly alludes to the opportunism of merchants and landowners, it mainly focuses on what it sees as disastrous state intervention to fund warfare. Thus the "manipulative play," "annexing and consolidating," and "competition over opportunistic profits" (above) that characterize the improper use of money in "rude" times point more directly to Emperor Wu's state planning than to private profiteering. Sima Qian reasserts money's role as a medium of "exchange" (*tong*) between farmers and merchants as the legitimate function of money. The "annexing and consolidation" (*bing jian* 幷兼), the "manipulative play" (*wan qiao* 玩巧), and the "competition" (*zheng* 爭)—invokes the Han rise of powerful landowners and merchants. Rulers in the *Shiji* also "annex and consolidate." Most prominently among them is the First Emperor Qin whose damning portrayal implicitly serves as a template for the *Shiji*'s Emperor Wu (see *Shiji* 6.276, 69.2242. See *Shiji* 30.1425, 112.2961 for reference to powerful individuals who are troublesome for the state).

至孝文時，莢錢益多，輕，乃更鑄四銖錢，其文爲「半兩」，令民縱得自
鑄錢。故吳諸侯也，以即山鑄錢，富埒天子，其後卒以叛逆。鄧通，大夫
也，以鑄錢財過王者。故吳、鄧氏錢布天下，而鑄錢之禁生焉。

By the reign of Emperor Wen "elm-pod" coins had become too numerous and light[-weight], so (in 175 BCE[70]) they [government officials] then
cast four-*zhu* coins inscribed "half-ounce'" (i.e., 12-*zhu*), and they allowed people to freely cast coins for themselves. Consequently [Liu Pi,
King of] Wu, though [only] a vassal lord, exploited his mountains to cast
coins, so that his wealth equaled that of the Son of Heaven, whereupon
he [Liu Pi] used his soldiers to foment revolt. Deng Tong, though [only]
a Grand Counselor, through casting coins amassed resources exceeding
that of a king. Thus the Wu [i.e., Liu Pi] and Deng family coins were
spread throughout the empire, causing the prohibition on casting coins.[71]

In both cases money becomes a problem precisely when used for its
"heads" function, as a mark of the caster's political authority.[72] Liu Pi
used his monetary wealth that "equaled that of the Son of Heaven" to
instigate the unsuccessful 154 BCE Revolt of the Seven Kingdoms, a civil
upheaval that threatened to topple Emperor Jing (Emperor Wu's predecessor). As the *Shiji* elsewhere narrates, the youthful Emperor Jing had

---

70. The *Hanshu* version provides this date; the *Shiji* does not. Swann, *Food and Money*, 232.

71. *Shiji* 30.1419. Commentators gloss *lei* 埒 as *deng* 等. See Ling Zhilong, *Shiji pinglin*, 6: 653.

72. Both figures receive biographical chapters or sketches in the Han historiographies (*Shiji* and *Hanshu*) that complicate their demonization elsewhere. These biographies present private coinage as the means, *not* the original cause, of their political subver-
sion. In narrative terms, subversion begins with the misdeeds of emperors. Warnings from the physiognomy of these individuals—always a mode of truth-telling in the *Shiji*—signal to the reader that the emperor is giving what he should not have given away. The founding Han emperor, Gaozu, gives his nephew Liu Pi the copper-rich King-
dom of Wu, as his "flesh and bones" relative, but the emperor fails to withdraw it when, upon examining Liu Pi's face, he observes "Your face has the appearance of one who will revolt" (*Shiji* 106.2821). Similarly, Emperor Wen bequeaths his favorite Deng Tong the copper-rich mountains of Yandao (in Shu) as a prophylactic against the physiognomist's pronouncement that Deng Tong "will die impoverished and in hunger" (*Shiji* 125.3192). Physiognomists in the *Shiji* reveal in advance the narrative that will subsequently unfold (Liu Pi rebels, Deng Tong dies in poverty); and also, as in these two cases, draw the reader's attention towards the larger moral point of the *Shiji*'s anecdote. In Deng Tong's case, Emperor Wen implicitly acts with hubris when he gives away the mountains of Shu, by imperiously claiming, "The capacity to make Deng Tong rich lies with me." *Shiji* 125.3192.

killed Liu Pi's son during a drunken game of chess, and the unforgiving Liu Pi had later attracted followers by doubling the Han military code's rate of monetary rewards for service.[73]

However, imperial succession is challenged in a very different way in the case of Deng Tong 鄧通, a male favorite of Emperor Wen. The emperor gifts Deng Tong with copper-rich mountains, leading to the "spread of Deng family coins across empire."

文帝嘗病癰,鄧通常爲帝唶吮之。文帝不樂,從容問通曰:「天下誰最愛我者乎?」通曰:「宜莫如太子。」太子入問病,文帝使唶癰,唶癰而色難之。已而聞鄧通常爲帝唶吮 之,心慙,由此怨通矣。

Emperor Wen was once ailing from a boil. Deng Tong regularly blew [on it] and sucked it. Emperor Wen was unhappy and casually asked Deng Tong: "Amongst all under Heaven who loves me most?" Deng Tong replied: "It is proper that no one love you more than the Heir Apparent." When the Heir Apparent entered to inquire about the emperor's illness, Emperor Wen made him blow on his boil, but when he [the Heir Apparent] did so, his discolor [betrayed] his reluctance. Afterwards he heard that Deng Tong regularly blew and sucked [on the boil]. Feeling humiliated, [the Heir Apparent] grew jealous of Deng Tong from this time on.[74]

From a traditional Chinese medical perspective, Emperor Wen's ailment, the *yong* 癰 (boil, clog, or abscess), signals the specific problem of obstructed circulation.[75] This is apt, given the importance of circulation

---

73. See *Shiji* 106.2823 on Liu Pi's fair economic practices and popularity among his subjects prior to this.

74. *Shiji* 125.3193 The *Hanshu* version has 嗽吮 instead of 唶吮. See *Hanshu* 93.3723.

75. On the close relation between *yong* and *ju* abscesses, see Hsu, *Pulse Diagnosis in Early Chinese Medicine*, 123–26. Non-medical literature associated both those afflicted by, and those treating, abscesses (癰 *yong*) with sexual excess. General Wu Qi 吳起 was famous for sucking the abscesses (疽 *jū*) of his soldiers and also for his sexual appetite (好色). See *Shiji* 65.2165–66; *Han Feizi*, 624. In the *Shiji*'s account of physician Chunyu Yi, a fatal abscess (*ju* 疽) was seen to be caused by the ruler indulging in sex after wine. The *Fifty-Two Ailments* of the excavated Mawangdui medical corpus does not propose any causes of abscesses, but its prescription for *yong* (癰), includes: "While spreading the medicine do not eat pork and fish, and do not [have intercourse] with women" (Harper, *Early Chinese Medical Literature*, 293: MSI.E.230). MSI.E.158 also mentions *ju*-abscesses of the testicles. The *Shuo wen jie zi* explains *ju* as "an old *yong*"; and Harper, *Early Chinese Medical Literature*, 290 n. 5, translates *ju* as a "*ju* abscess" (e.g., MSI.E.157–73) and *yong* simply as "abscess" (e.g., MSI.E.225–32), with the etymology of

to the traditional economic idiom (e.g., currency "flow" 流; Yu's postdiluvian tribute system).[76] If the emperor's body here is an implicit metaphor for the economy, Deng Tong (who was a former boatman) occupies the symbolic position of the favored physician-economist. When Em-

---

yong connoting "a 'walled-up' place where pus collects." While *yong* and *ju* are listed as separate ailments, Harper's (276, n. 4) discussion of the two terms suggests *ju* is simply as a type of *yong* (probably rotted and leaky). Furthermore, since the language of sucking (cf. 吮 *chui* and 嗜吮 *jie chui*) is common to the cases of Deng Tong and Wu Qi, and since the diagnostic differences between *yong* and *ju* is not significant, the comparison of Emperor Wen's *yong* abscess with the other cases of *ju* abscesses seems justified. Commentators have also debated whether *Mencius* 9.8 uses the term 癰疽 *yong ju* (abscess-doctor) or the name of the eunuch Yong Qu 雍渠. "[For Confucius to be] hosted by a *yong ju*/Yong Qu and the slave Ji Huan [when staying in Wei] would be without propriety and without Heaven's mandate."

76. Both sides in the *Debate on Salt and Iron* compare the economy to a sick patient and liken their own policies to a physician's acupuncture needles needed to make commodities "flow and circulate" (流通). Deng's outperformance of the Heir-Apparent above resonates with the medical profession's emphasis on non-patrilineal pedagogy, on knowledge of sexual cultivation, on generous gift-compensation for medical services, on the secrecy-shrouded process of inheriting a teacher's position, and on competition between students. Harper, *Early Chinese Medical Literature*, 67, also addresses accounts in the *Huangdi neijing* of professional competition between physicians. On doctors' professional pursuit of wealth, see *Shiji* 129.3271. When, for example, the eminent Han dynasty physician Chunyu Yi was singled out for apprenticeship, his teacher, Yang Qing, warned him: "Take care not to let my sons and grandsons know that you are studying my recipes." *Shiji* 105.2815. Bian Que, the fifth-to-fourth-century BCE pioneer of the diagnosis of the pulse, was a lodging-house manager until mysteriously gifted with the secret recipe books of one of his lodgers. See *Shiji* 105.2785–93. The early conception of medical practice as part of a holistic and occult system (encompassing breath cultivation, sexual cultivation, dietetics, and magic rituals) resonates with other aspects of the *Shiji* and *Hanshu* accounts of Deng Tong: his initial appearance in Emperor Wen's dream; his ability to remain Wen's sexual companion; and his unexplained medical talents. The resonances of the color or discolor (*se* 色) of the reluctant Heir-Apparent's face are both sexual and political. The *se* of one's face was the object of the physician and the physiognomist's gaze; it was an expression of erotic desire; and it was a sign of political legitimacy in five-phase cosmological theory (*wuxing*), which correlated dynastic reigns with one of five colors (*wu se*), five elements, and five directions. When the Heir-Apparent blanched (or blushed), he assumes the symbolic position of the observed patient, not healer. The ailment signaled by the son's *se* becomes a symptom not of eroticized affection (he cannot do what Deng Tong does), but of threatened political succession. See Kuriyama, *The Expressiveness of the Body*, 167–92.

peror Wen dies, and the jealous Heir Apparent becomes Emperor Jing, Deng Tong is charged with smuggling minted coins across the border and "in the end he did not have a single cash to his name."[77]

This tension between the heads function and the tails function of money is taken up in the *Hanshu*'s re-writing of the *Shiji*'s etiology of money. Similar to its subversion of the *Shiji*'s "Account of Commodity Producers" (discussed in chapter 3), the *Hanshu*'s "Shi huo zhi" 食貨志 (variously translated as "Treatise on Food and Commodities" and "Treatise on Food and Money") incorporates the *Shiji*'s monetary history but restores the state origins of money.[78] The first half of this chapter on agricultural history (i.e., on "food") gives the non-monetized tributary legend of Yu its proper place as the basis of the political economy. The second half subsumes money within a generalized history of state-regulated *huo* (commodities). The chapter begins with these sanctioned (and hierarchical) governmental spheres of "Food" and "Commodities/Money":

洪範八政，一曰食，二曰貨。食謂農殖嘉穀可食之物，貨謂布帛可衣，及金刀龜貝，所以分財布利通有無者也。二者，生民之本。二者，生民之本，興自神農之世。斵木爲耜，煣木爲耒，耒耜之利以敎天下，而食足；日中爲市，致天下之民，聚天下之貨，交易而退，各得其所，而貨通。食足貨通，然後國實民富，而敎化成。

The "Great Plan" [the "Hong fan" chapter of the *Book of Documents*] has eight governmental prerogatives (*zheng*): the first was called "Food" (*shi*), the second "Money" (*huo*). "Food" refers to the excellent grains that farmers produce (*zhi* 殖) and things that can be consumed. "Money" refers to textiles and silks that can be worn, as well as gold, knife[-money], turtle shells, and cowries, with which [one can] share out wealth, distribute profits, and supply what is lacking. These two concerns form the basis (*ben*) of sustaining the people, and arose during the era of the Divine Farmer (*Shennong*). [The *Classic of Changes*'s "Appended Statements" says]: "[The Divine Farmer] fashioned wood to make plowshares, bent wood to make plough-handles, and taught all under Heaven the benefits of plowing and weeding," and food (*shi*) was sufficient. "[The Divine Farmer] set up markets at midday, summoned all the people under Heaven, assembled all the *huo* under Heaven, and they traded and exchanged

---

77. *Shiji* 125.3192–93.

78. On the relation of the content of this chapter, *Hanshu* 24, to that of *Shiji* 30 and 129, see Swann, *Food and Money*, especially 399–404.

before returning, each obtaining what [he or she needed]" and so *huo* circulated."[79] With food sufficient and *huo* circulating, the state was replete, people were wealthy, and instruction and cultivation were accomplished.[80]

The *Hanshu* uses the distinction between *shi* 食 (food) and *huo* 貨 (commodities) to explain what *huo* does and does not do. As discussed in chapter 3, the *Hanshu* elsewhere condemns the "commodity producers" (*huo zhi*, literally "[those who make] commodities blossom) that are celebrated by the *Shiji*; and here the *Hanshu* restores food (the "excellent grains") as the proper object of "production." The *Hanshu* does not mention *bi* (money) here—indeed it will not do so until partway through the second half of the chapter (on *huo*), where it makes clear that *bi* is simply one form of *huo*. Given the above definition of *huo*, translators generally translate Ban Gu's *huo* as "media of exchange" or "money." However, the explicit purpose Ban Gu gives for *huo* (and thus *bi*) is not (as it was for Sima Qian in the *Shiji*) to facilitate private "trade and exchange" (*jiao yi*). Rather, it primarily serves as a means for the state "to share out wealth" (*fen she* 分財), "to spread out profits" (*bu li* 布利), and "to supply what is lacking" (*tong wu you* 通有無). Since, the *Book of Documents* specifies that Heaven bestowed the legendary Yu with the "Great Plan" for governing the world after dredging the floodwaters, the *Hanshu*'s citation essentially restores money to the tributary paradigm.

The *Hanshu* authenticates the long-term tributary order of money by exploiting the possible meanings of *huo*. On the one hand, it provides a gloss for the *Book of Documents*' use of *huo* that restricts the meaning of this word to exchange media (cowries, etc.) (As noted above, the *Shiji* does the same for the term *bi*.) Since the *Book of Documents* does not actually suggest this particular reading of *huo*, the *Hanshu*, in effect, smuggles a Han dynasty notion of *bi* (i.e., money) backwards in history (into far antiquity) via the textual occurrence of *huo*.[81] The *Hanshu* does

---

79. The *Hanshu* quotation from the "Appended Statements" of the *Classic of Changes* parallels the received version; however, the recently excavated Mawangdui version of the *Yijing Xici* has an extra character 欲: "each obtained what [he or she] *desired*" (各得其所欲), as opposed to "each obtained [his or her] proper place." See Shaughnessy, *I ching*, 332, n. 118.

80. *Hanshu* 24A.1117.

81. Karlgren translates *huo* as "merchandise" in the *Book of Documents*, 30. Legge, *Shoo King*, 327, translates *huo* as "commodities."

so again in its subsequent quotation from the *Classic of Changes'* "Appended Statements." Commentators on the *Classic of Changes* have traditionally understood that Shennong "assembled commodities" (*ju huo* 聚貨) that the people "traded and exchanged." By reinterpreting the Divine Farmer's (*Shennong*) *huo*, the *Hanshu* potentially upstages the *Shiji's* free-market *bi*. That is, the *Shiji* had placed money's (*bi*) origins in the unregulated markets of high antiquity ("before Emperor Ku") *despite* the lack of records. Since the legendary Divine Farmer (allegedly from the fourth millennium BCE) predates Emperor Ku, the *Hanshu* uses textual "evidence" (its reinterpretation of the "Appended Statements") to reassert the antiquity of state-regulated *huo*. The second half of the *Hanshu's* "Treatise on Food and Commodities" (or "Treatise on Food and Money"), which turns from agricultural history (i.e., "food") to monetary history (i.e., *huo*), admits: "Too scanty are the details to record any money (*huo*), including uses of gold, cash (*qian*), cloth, and silk, before the Xia and Shang dynasties."[82] The chapter's subsequent history of currencies from the Zhou dynasty through the Former Han (and Xin dynasty interregnum) makes no reference to the earlier *huo* of the Divine Farmer described in its opening passage (above). However the "Treatise on Food and Commodities" does restore the Zhou accounts of rulers issuing money (*bi*), (including the *Legends of the States* passage above), which was excluded in the *Shiji's* history of unregulated exchange. On the other hand, the *Hanshu's* "Treatise on Food and Commodities" also uses *huo* in its more traditional sense to refer to market commodities. It alludes to "selling *huo*" (*yu huo* 鬻貨), "exporting *huo*" (*chu huo* 出貨), "the *huo* of the mountains and seas" (*shan hai zhi huo* 山海之貨), and "the myriad *huo*" (*wan huo* 萬貨).

This ambivalent use of *huo* (as commodity and money) enables the *Hanshu* to press its basic point, namely, that market trade, whether or not it involves money, properly belongs to a long-term transactional order determined by a state that places agriculture ("food") and social welfare first. The *Hanshu's* revision of Zhou and *Shiji* historiography treated imperial *bi* as a late appearance in a long-term transactional order that found its purest expression in early classical texts. In place of the *Shiji's* spontaneous "meeting of paths for trading and exchanging," the Divine

---

82. *Hanshu* 24B.1149.

Farmer sets the time of market exchange (midday). The *Hanshu*'s *huo* (as commodities *or* money) belong to the temporality of the (agricultural, tributary) state.[83] For the *Shiji*, Emperor Wu's Balanced Standard represented the fallacy of state intrusion into market activity that characterized this period of decline (of Emperor Wu's reign). For the *Hanshu*, Emperor Wu's Balanced Standard was a passable but less ideal instantiation of the historically transcendent state planned moral economy (agriculture *and* commerce). The *Hanshu*'s classicizing version won out and subsequent dynastic histories adopted the title "Treatise on Food and Commodities" (*Shi huo zhi*) for their economic chapters.[84]

Other genres besides historiography politicized the etiology of money. The *Debate on Salt and Iron*'s clash over money's origins reflects a different quarrel: not over money as token of market versus state ("heads" versus "tails"), but over whether money was necessary at all. To recall from chapter 1, the classicizing *Debate on Salt and Iron* staged a debate between the Guanzian state economist (Sang Hongyang) and the Classical Scholars. The latter pitted their textual expertise against that of the economist. The Classical Scholars sought to reverse Emperor Wu's earlier expansions of market and empire, and to return to the idealized agricultural world of Zhou ethical texts ("return to the root"). Sang Hongyang reappropriated the Zhou myth of emergency state money by inserting money into the (originally moneyless) tributary myth of Yu:

大夫曰：「王者塞天財，禁關市，執準守時，以輕重御民。豐年歲登，則儲積以備乏絕；凶年惡歲，則行幣物；流有餘而調不足也。昔禹水湯旱，百姓匱乏，或相假以接衣食。禹以歷山之金，湯以莊山之銅，鑄幣以贖其民，而天下稱仁。往者財用不足，戰士或不得祿，而山東被災，齊、趙大饑，賴均輸之畜，倉廩之積，戰士以奉，饑民以賑。

---

83. Nostalgia structures both *Hanshu* economic chapters. Ban Gu's end comment to the "Treatise on Food and Money" clarifies that the ideal era of the political economy was that of earliest antiquity with which the chapter began (recorded in the *Book of Documents* and *Book of Changes*). Emperor Wu's state-sponsored economic reforms were in the next class down (其次), and the socially destructive institutional revolutions of the "Usurper" Wang Mang, with which the chapter ends, were next (次) (i.e., the worst). Unlike the *Shiji*, whose cyclical account of history offered the "Treatise of the Balanced Standard" up as a portrait of fallen times, the *Hanshu* presents a chronological narrative of decline.

84. After the popularization of the modern term *jingji* (economics), a 1930s economic journal returned to *Shi huo* for its title.

The Imperial Counselor [i.e., Sang Hongyang] said: "The ruler should seal in Heaven's resources by prohibiting border markets. He should grasp [the strategies of] 'price-stabilization' (*zhun*) and 'taking advantage of the seasons'; [and he should use] *qingzhong* [methods] to govern the people. In bountiful years of piled-up harvests, he should store grain to prepare for times of shortage. In bad years of difficult harvest he should circulate money and goods, letting surplus flow to where there is deficiency. In the past when Yu confronted floods and Tang confronted drought, the people were in dire poverty, and they at times borrowed food and clothing from each other. Yu took the gold of Mount Li and Tang took the bronze of Mount Zhuang, and they [used it to] cast money (*bi*) to buy things for their people, and the world acknowledged their benevolence. Recently our resources were insufficient and some soldiers did not receive their salary, but when Shandong suffered natural disasters and Qi and Zhao had a huge famine we could rely on the livestock [distributed through] the equalizing transport system (*junshu*) and accumulated stores of grain to reward the troops and relieve starving people.[85]

These (serial) origins of money in archaic scenes of rescue conform to the same tributary logic of the Zhou accounts. However, in narrating a pre-Zhou history of the founders of the Shang and Xia dynasties, Sang Hongyang (heretically) prioritizes money. To save the people, the symbolic representative of the Chinese political economy, Yu, does not redistribute grain, dredge canals, and organize agricultural taxes (or tribute)—rather, he "casts money" (*zhu bi* 鑄幣). Sang does not call for a fully monetized economy, but he argues that money has an important place in a centralized mixed economy and that it helps to fund the large-scale military campaigns that were first launched by Emperor Wu. Sang also argues that the *junshu* system's redistributive transport of livestock, first established under Emperor Wu, can also provide disaster relief. A similar version of Sang Hongyang's tale of Yu casting money is preserved in the *Guanzi*'s "Qingzhong" chapters. Unlike in the *Debate on Salt and Iron*, however, the part historical, part-imaginary

---

85. Wang Liqi, *Yantielun*, 25. In the *Guanzi*'s case, people receive humanitarian money to redeem children they have already sold. On this and "taking advantage of the seasons" (守時), see Ma Feibai, *Guanzi Qingzhong pian*, 306–7; cf. Rickett, *Guanzi*, 397. The account in this study complicates Glahn's otherwise very useful analysis of Guanzian monetary theory, which argues: "By Han times this passage had become enshrined as the definitive testament of the origins of money." See Von Glahn, *Fountain of Fortune*, 26.

"Qingzhong" chapters openly promote the exploitation of cosmological tales. As discussed in the next section, *qingzhong* money follows another temporality—a mode of quantitative reasoning, not one of recorded history.[86]

The *Debate on Salt and Iron*'s Classical Scholars protest Sang Hong-yang (and the *Guanzi*'s) monetization of the tributary order by removing money altogether from their idealized antiquity:

文學曰：「古者，市朝而無刀幣，各以其所有易所無，抱布貿絲而已。後世即有龜貝金錢，交施之也。幣數變而民滋偽。夫救偽以質，防失以禮。湯、文繼衰，革法易化，而殷、周道興。漢初乘弊，而不改易，畜利變幣，欲以反本，是猶以煎止燔，以火止沸 也。

The Classical Scholars said: "In antiquity (*gu zhe*) there were markets but no practices of money (*bi*). Each took what he had and exchanged it for what he lacked, 'packing cloth to trade for silk' [from the *Classic of Odes*]. Later generations had tortoise shells, cowries, gold, and cash (*qian*) with which to exchange and give gifts. With frequent changes in currency (*bi shu bian* 幣數變) people have become increasingly deceitful. Use simplicity to rescue us from deceit; use ritual propriety to prevent collapse. Tang and Wen, coming from degenerate times, revised the laws and made transformative changes, and the [principled] way of the Yin [i.e., Shang] and Zhou dynasties arose. The Han dynasty at the outset inherited the evils [of the former period], and [for us] to not make reforms or changes, [but to] pursue profit and change the currency (*bian bi* 變幣), while desiring to return to fundamental values [lit. 'return to the root' *fan ben*] is like using frying fat as a fire extinguisher or using fire to cool boiling water."[87]

In this passage, a golden age of pure barter precedes the degeneration into monetized markets and state-sponsored "changes in currency" (*bian bi*). Notably, the legendary Tang now rescues the people from degeneracy through civilizing laws, not through money. While their opponents used the myth of Yu and Tang as money-casters to justify monopolies on money (alongside those on the salt and iron industries), the Classical

---

86. One might note that the *Shiji*'s etiology, quoted above, outdid this legend (knowingly or not) in pushing the beginnings of money explicitly past Tang and Yu into prehistory.

87. Wang Liqi, *Yantielun*, 53. The latter part of this passage echoes a speech by Dong Zhongshu recorded in the *Hanshu*.

Scholars remove money from antiquity to attack the shift under Emperor Wu from the traditional governmental concern for agriculture to a concern for commerce.

The Former Han official Jia Yi had offered a similar rejection of the very practice of money. The *Hanshu* records his (unsuccessful) memorial to Emperor Wen in 175 BCE that associated money's origins with unnatural material practices:

今農事棄捐而采銅者日蕃，釋其耒耨，冶鎔炊炭，姦錢日多，五穀不為多。善人怵而為姦邪，愿民陷而之刑戮 . . . 令禁鑄錢，則錢必重；重則其利深，盜鑄如雲而起，棄市之罪又不足以禁矣。姦數不勝而法禁數潰，銅使之然也。故銅布於天下，其為禍博矣。

[Jia Yi:] "Agricultural duties have now been abandoned and those who pluck bronze (采銅者) multiply daily. Dropping plow and hoe, they smelt coin molds and blow charcoal. Counterfeit coins (*jian qian* 姦錢) increase daily but the 'five grains' (*wu gu* 五穀) are not increased. Good people have fallen into criminal and evil activity. Honest commoners are trapped and punished by execution. . . . If the prohibition on [privately] casting coins is decreed, coinage will invariably become heavier. Once coins are heavier, [potential] profits from them will increase and illegal casting will spring up like clouds. Even [punishment by] execution in the marketplace will not be able to prevent this. Counterfeiters will be too numerous to be counted and laws prohibiting them will repeatedly fail. Bronze has made the situation this way. Thus the spread of bronze throughout empire will wreak greater disasters."[88]

Jia Yi presents money as the unnatural fruits of "plucking bronze" instead of the traditional "five grains."[89] If his new metaphor plays on the fact that the manufacturing process of Chinese coins originated in that used to make metal plows, then "plucking bronze" makes people abandon both the proper agricultural occupation and the auxiliary production of

---

88. *Hanshu* 24B.1155.

89. In a similar vein, the official Gong Yu 貢禹 (127–44 BCE) later contrasted the value of minerals and comestibles, "Pearls, jade, gold, and silver cannot be eaten when one is hungry, nor worn when one is cold. However those that value them are many because the emperor finds a use for them. . . . Therefore the enlightened ruler values the five grains and belittles gold and jade." See *Hanshu* 24B.1176. Like "harvesting bronze," the metaphor of eating gold denaturalizes the (presumed) object of value.

agricultural implements.[90] Money is an agent of social transformation that causes the catastrophic abandonment of agriculture. For this reason, Jia Yi later calls for all bronze to be returned to the imperial treasury; for the state to monopolize and regulate bronze coins; and for "those who harvest bronze for casting [coinage] to return to plowing fields." Jia Yi also attacks money as a false system of value. Coinage inevitably leads to counterfeiting because it is itself a counterfeit system of value. Thus Jia Yi goes on to advise that the emperor should dispense gifts of bronze "vessels and weapons" to truly "discriminate between the noble and the lowly." As addressed above, Jia Yi's condemnation of the "major catastrophe wrought by coin inscriptions" was part of the classical concern about money as a form of "writing" (*wen*).

PARABLES OF DEBT

As a social as well as symbolic system, money was closely associated with the problem of debt. The Qin-Han opening up of land for purchase made small-scale farmers who worked their own plots highly vulnerable to debt. Harvest failures and a high poll tax (coupled with a low land tax) encouraged land sales and the formation of huge estates. The estate owners then often rented land back (at a profit) to the rising number of debt-ridden farmers. Children could be pawned (*zhu zi* 贅子) in return for food, clothing, or cash.[91] Legal texts address different problems faced by debtors in repayment, including the redemption of punishment (*shu* 贖). (This term was also applied to payments for the liberation of bond servants and slaves.)[92] In Qin legal documents women counted as half of a male in reckoning redemptions, rations, and labor, unless the women "use the needle to make embroidery" (in which case they were

---

90. Thierry, *Origins and Development*, 33: "An impression was made in a clay mould of the desired coin, then rims and characters were added with a pointed tool. The same procedure was used to make the reverse. When the obverse and reverse moulds were joined together, molten metal was poured into the whole. Once the metal was cooled, the mould was broken to retrieve the coin."

91. *Hanshu* 64A.2779.

92. On slavery and bondage, to which this study has not given the attention it deserves, see Wilbur, *Slavery during the Former Han Dynasty*; and Yates, "Slavery in Early China." On debates about "slave society" in China, see Guo Moruo, *Nuli zhi shidai*; Dirlik, *Revolution and History*.

equivalent to a male).[93] As noted in chapter 3, Sima Qian failed to redeem his own penalty of castration due to insufficient funds. To pay off their debts, many were forced into convict labor ("grain-pounding" for women, "wall-building" for men).[94] Corvée service and the penal system might be understood as part of this broader Han politics of debt.

David Graeber's *Debt: The First 5,000 Years* makes a basic distinction between a moral obligation and an economic debt.[95] Debts, unlike obligations, can be precisely quantified with money and, as such, transform human relations into a form of mathematics. Indeed the Han dynasty's *Nine Chapters on Mathematical Arts* helps with just such a calculation:

今有人持錢之蜀，賈利十三。初返歸一萬四千，次返歸一萬三千，次返歸一萬二千，次返歸一萬一千，後返歸一萬。凡五返歸錢，本利俱盡。問本持錢及利各幾何？

Suppose a person brings cash to Shu for commerce at a profit of 10:3 [i.e., an interest rate of 30 percent]. The first return brings 14,000; the next 13,000; the next 12,000; and finally 11,000. The cash from these five returns exhausts the entire capital and profit. Question: How much was the cash capital brought in and how much was the profit?[96]

Here, the ability of cash to regularly "return" yet more cash is strictly a mathematical problem devoid of human relations. Staged in the famously wealthy markets of Shu (modern Sichuan, and Han dynasty birthplace of the *fu*-composers Sima Xiangru and Yang Xiong), this problem puts the reader in the position of the profit-seeking lender or investor. Other Han texts, however, embedded this quantitative dynamic of loans and interest in different ethical and cosmopolitical contexts.

In the face of growing anxiety over debts and loans (*zhai* 責; *dai* 貸), Han texts placed new responsibilities, variously, on the moneylender (*cheng dai jia* 稱貸家; *cheng dai zhi jia* 稱貸之家; *zi qian jia* 子錢家),

---

93. Hulsewé, *Remnants of Ch'in Law*, 61–62. See also Nylan, "Administration of the Family," 272.

94. On *ju* 居 in legal texts, see Hulsewé, *Remnants of Ch'in Law*, 17–18.

95. Graeber, *Debt*, 21–41.

96. *Jiu zhang suan shu*, 181. See Chemla, *Les Neuf Chapitres*, 592–95. In contrast to the common use of *ben* 本 (primary; agriculture) and *mo* 末 (secondary; commerce) in philosophical discussions of the economy (discussed in chapter 1), *ben* here refers to monetary "capital" (in opposition to *li* 利 "interest"). One might note that Shu is the only place name other than the capital Chang'an to appear in extant Han mathematical texts.

the debtor, and the underworld spirits. Some Han texts condemned money-lending outright as had pre-Han texts like the *Book of Lord Shang* 商君書.[97] Liu Xiang's classicizing *Accounts of Exemplary Women* (discussed in chapter 4), for example, contains a didactic moral anecdote about a mother who rejects the money that her son, Tian Jizi 田稷子, gives her because he has gained it by taking interest on a loan. The mother explains that taking profit from interest is an unfilial act (*bu xiao* 不孝). As an official, Tian Jizi has violated the relation between ruler and subject; as a son, he has disgraced his mother's house.[98] The *Hanshi waizhuan* brings loans into the broader affective bonds of the classical "well-field" (*jing tian* 井田) society (discussed in chapter 1). This text (originally used to demonstrate exemplary uses of the *Odes*) recounts that neighbors not only worked on a shared portion of land; but also says, "In sickness they shared the anxiety; in difficulty and distress they aided one another. Those who had, loaned to those who had not (有無相貸); they invited each other to food and drink; they planned marriages together."[99]

Other texts, however, elaborated a more complex ethics of money-lending: for example, when, how, to whom, or why and how much interest should (or should not) be taken were discussed with greater precision. As discussed in chapter 3, the *Shiji* suggested, for the first time, that the businessperson could—and should—become an ethical subject (*junzi*). Debt comprised one such set of financial dealings in which individual morality (over and above any actions of the state) could reap material rewards. The *Shiji*'s biographies of the fourth-century BCE Su Qin 蘇秦 (a moral debtor) and Lord Mengchang 孟嘗君 (a morally-incorrect moneylender who was corrected by his agent) underscore the importance of an ethical approach to debt. Su Qin starts off poor and despised, and is forced to borrow 100 coins; on gaining office, esteem, and fortune he repays his debt with 100 pieces of gold, and redistributes his wealth

---

97. *Shangjun shu*, 122, offers one of the clearest pre-Han condemnations of money lending.

98. *Lienüzhuan*, 25–26. The mother of Tian Jizi clarifies that the loan is monetary; compare the simpler version in *Hanshi waizhuan*, 366. The *Debate on Salt and Iron*'s Classical Scholars deplored the debts burdening the poor. See Wang Liqi, *Yantielun*, 335. Wang Fu (ca. 90–165 CE), *Qian fu lun*, 113, in another classicist vein, condemned the rich for refusing to lend money to the needy.

99. HSWZ Ch. 4.13. Following Hightower, *Han Shih Wai Chuan*, 138.

to friends.[100] Lord Mengchang, by contrast, lends money to poor peasants to finance his household of guests and retainers.[101] He is angered
when the guest he sends to collect his interest forgives the debts of those
who are too poor to pay up. In response, the guest explains that Lord
Mengchang needs to think about "interest" (*xi* 息) in broader terms, since
desperate peasants will otherwise simply flee.

The *Guanzi*'s "Qingzhong" dialogues, to which the next section will
turn, treated debt as a political and economic opportunity. In this text,
Guanzi teaches strategies by which the state can use gifts, token money,
language, and gestures, to make wealthy moneylenders understand their
moral obligations and forgive debt.

桓公曰：「崢丘之戰，民多稱貸，負子息，以給上之急，度上之求。寡人
欲復業產，此何以洽？」管子曰：「惟繆數為可耳。」

Duke Huan said: "During the battle of Zhangqiu, a great many people
[went bankrupt from] borrowing money and bearing the burden of interest in order to supply their sovereign with his pressing needs and meet
his expenses. Now I wish to restore them to their production. How can I
manage this?"

Guanzi said: "This can only be done through the use of subtle
methods."[102]

Here, as so often in the "Qingzhong" chapters, the state military budget
creates an economic crisis. To solve this problem, Guanzi advises the
ruler to use a "subtle method" (繆數). By honoring the moneylenders
with jade discs (*bi* 璧), an invitation to court, and calling them "mother
and father of the people" (民之父母)—a term traditionally reserved for
the Heavenly mandated ruler—the moneylenders are flattered into destroying their loan contracts and distributing their own wealth to the
needy. A second dialogue advises gathering careful statistics on popular
debt, before introducing a special-purpose money from government supplies of brocade. By commanding all those who pay tribute at court to
henceforth present such brocade, Guanzi creates demand *ex nihilo*: "Its
price will rise to ten times its original cost." The state then uses its supply

---

100. *Shiji* 69. 2262.
101. *Shiji* 75. 2351–63.
102. Ma Feibai, *Guanzi Qingzhong pian*, 659. Largely following Rickett, *Guanzi* 2:
490–1.

of brocade to pay the moneylenders. Duke Huan says, "Now I possess ornate brocade-covered drumsticks and drums that have an average value of ten thousand cash. I wish to use them to pay the interest [that] my poor people owe you, thereby relieving them of their contractual obligations" (寡人有鏤枝蘭鼓, 其賈中純萬泉也。願以爲吾貧萌決其子息之數, 使無券契之責。).[103] In both cases related above, the ruler is taught to exploit the fact that he can create and regulate value. As discussed in chapter 1, the *Guanzi* taught that "moving [people] with words and motivating them with speeches may be considered the foundation of the state."[104]

Such divergent Han writings about monetary interest embedded debt within the sphere of moral obligation (or exploited the rhetoric of moral obligation in the case of the *Guanzi*). They heightened awareness of human responsibility in the dynamics of debt. One might note that the excavated human-spirit contracts, by contrast, give spiritual authorities a far greater role in debt-forgiveness. The deceased carried the "burdens of debt" (*fu zhai* 負責) of the living into the afterlife. A set of first-century CE contracts prepared before and after a sick woman's death suggests the authority of the spirit world over debts of the living and the dead. It contains the recurring formula: "May living people not be encumbered with debt; may dead people not be penalized" (生人不負責, 死人毋適).[105] Donald Harper has argued that such bipartite contracts reflect a Han dynasty shift in human-spirit interactions, from an interaction centered on gifts to one concerned with debt. Instead of simply giving prayers and sacrifices to the spirits (in the expectation of return favors), people set up contractual relations that placed themselves in debt to the spirit world for a credit of favor from the spirits.[106]

---

103. Ma Feibai, *Guanzi Qingzhong pian*, 631. Following Rickett, *Guanzi* 2: 482–85.

104. Ma Feibai, *Guanzi Qingzhong pian*, 674.

105. The Xuning 序寧 slips also include: 生者不負責(債), 死者毋適(讁). See Harper, "Contracts with the Spirit World" for the text and an annotated translation and discussion. The provenance of the Xuning slips is unknown. They comprise eight contract writs and six contract records.

106. Harper, "Contracts with the Spirit World," 256. Harper links this Han anxiety about the "burden of debt" to an older concept of the "blame" (*ze* 責) placed on humans by spirits, and to the commodification of prayer and sacrifice. One might also note a congruent notion of cosmic employment. Pre-Han and Han texts used the term *tian lu* 天祿 (Heavenly emoluments) to figure the ruler (or ethical subject) as the sala-

Quantifying Money

The *Guanzi*'s "Qingzhong" chapters have no such respect for the spirit world. They teach their readers to assess money in terms of quantitative relational values (*qingzhong*), not the cosmological values of human-spirit relationships or the classical values of the China-bound moral-literary (*wen*) tradition. Since the relative amount of commodities and money in circulation determines money's true worth, the *Guanzi* is disinterested in monetary inscriptions (*wen*). It approaches money's intrinsic problem of sign and substance as an opportunity to exploit the sign's infinite possibilities, not to assert the superiority of the classical interpretation of sign as writing, culture, decorum, cosmological pattern, or Chinese civilization. As introduced in chapter 1, the *Guanzi*'s hybrid mix of real and imaginary characters transgressed the classical hierarchy that placed historical writing over fictional writing. It grounded textual authority in personifications of general economic principles (e.g., the fictional characters Mr. Calculate-and-Measure and Mr. Calculate-y), not in the historical words of ancient sages. Its suggestion that the general equivalent was related to the linguistic as well as monetary domain invites comparison with Ferdinand de Saussure's account:[107]

> To determine what a five-franc piece is worth one must therefore know:
> (1) that it can be exchanged for a fixed quantity of a different thing, e.g.,
> bread; and (2) that it can be compared with a similar value of the same
> system, e.g., a one-franc piece, or with coins of another system (a dollar,

---

ried officer of Heaven: "If there is hardship and poverty within the four seas, Heavenly emoluments will forever cease" (四海困窮，天祿永終). *Lunyu*, 20.1. For interpretations of this passage, see Slingerland, *Analects*, 231. Compare the version in the spurious (post-Han) "Counsels of Great Yu" chapter of the *Book of Documents*, and Mencius's use of the term in *Mencius* 5B3. The term *lu* 祿 has positive connotations in the *Analects* and *Mencius* (as profit does not). On the Later Han discussion of 命祿 *ming lu* (destiny and emoluments) in Wang Chong's *Lunheng*, in which *ming* concerns lifespan and *lu* refers to one's destined allotment of wealth and status, see Seidel, "Buying One's Way to Heaven: The Celestial Treasury in Chinese Religions." *Ming lu* refigures the quantitative connotations of *lu* 祿 "salary, reward, remuneration." Like a contract, the Heaven-conferred mandate (*ming* 命), or credit of dominion, burdens the ruler with the responsibility for the material well-being of its inhabitants.

107. Saussure himself drew from economics. On this, see Maurer, "The Anthropology of Money." See also Goux, *The Coiners of Language*, 3–22, 135–43, and Spivak, "Scattered Speculations."

etc.). In the same way a word can be exchanged for something dissimilar, an idea; besides, it can be compared with something of the same nature, another word.[108]

Like the five-franc piece, Guanzi's fiat currencies ("horse" [*ma* 馬] counters) showed their worth through their exchange for the precious foreign silks of the naïve Lai people.[109] Guanzi's profit-making strategy depended precisely on the worthlessness of these counters in relation to Zhou currency (or goods). Unlike Saussure's work, of course, the *Guanzi* does not analyze language or the creation of linguistic value. Its use and promotion of fiction and manipulative words simply challenges the classical injunction that names (*ming*) should match realities (*shi*). It implies, rather than explicates, an analogy between coins and words as semiotic systems. The juxtaposition with Saussure does, however, help to illumine the profound gulf between *qingzhong* theory and other approaches to money. The "Qingzhong" chapters do not "flatten" human relations altogether (Duke Huan is still Guanzi's ruler), but they allow for the dangerous imagination of a world without the grounded, transcendent values (and moral community) of traditional ritual and scholarly practice. As elaborated below, the *Guanzi* defends (or "dis-embeds") money from cosmological, sinifying, and classicizing practices.

DISENCHANTING MONEY

Guanzian economics provides a disenchanted theory of signs. It mocks belief and argues the economic *utility* of fabricated cosmic signs. This is significant given the pervasiveness both of cosmological thinking during the Han period and, as recent scholarship has shown, of a modern assumption that *all* traditional Chinese thought and poetics was enthralled to "correlative cosmology."[110] To clarify, correlative cosmology—the belief that all phenomena belong to correlative categories—was once

---

108. Saussure, *Course in General Linguistics*, 115.

109. Ma Feibai, *Guanzi Qingzhong pian*, 641–47. See my chapter 1's discussion.

110. Correlative cosmology originally became a stereotype of universalized Chinese thought in modern European sociology. See, Puett, *To Become a God*; Ekström, "On the Concept of Correlative Cosmology"; Rawson, "Cosmological Systems as Sources of Art, Ornament and Design"; Saussy, "Correlative Cosmology and its Histories"; Aihe Wang, "Correlative Cosmology."

understood to explain China's profound difference from the West. Since words were part of the same interactive dimension of experience as things, and not an independent sign system, the Chinese failed to develop an alphabet; since Chinese poems and paintings were stimulated "responses" to, rather than representations of, phenomena, no Chinese theory of mimesis emerged.[111] The classical ordering of a world according to the "five elements" (*wuxing*) and *yin* and *yang* helped to explain China's failure, among other things, to achieve the rationalism of the European Protestant cradle of capitalism.[112] Over recent years, scholars have criticized this claim on different grounds. First, the term *correlative cosmology* was coined by Western sinologists for what is essentially a historically commonplace phenomenon or universally available way of looking at the world. Second, and more importantly, correlative cosmology was not a universal Chinese cultural belief or a shift from religion to naturalism, but rather a historically situated political rhetoric. Michael Puett has argued that correlative thinking emerged only in the late Warring States "as a language of critique against the dominant notions of the time, and it remained a language of critique and opposition throughout the early imperial period" and Jessica Rawson's study of burial and visual practices in the Han suggests a self-reflexive adoption of correlative cosmology.[113]

As addressed above, Han material and literary practices embedded money in diverse cosmological traditions. The deceased were buried with different currencies for use in human-spirit commerce. Historiographers mocked imperial attempts to use monetary inscriptions as reflections of signs of Heavenly approval, but they did so precisely because they understood that all forms of writing (*wen*) reflected Heavenly signs. In the apocryphal account of the invention of written characters, Cang

---

111. See Chin, "Orienting Mimesis." The issue of correlative cosmology was also raised in chapter 2 in the comparison between interpretive traditions of imagery in the *Classic of Odes* and the epideictic *fu*.

112. On the attack on *yin-yang wuxing* cosmology by early-twentieth-century Chinese intellectuals, see Aihe Wang, "From Structure of Mind to Embodied Practice." On Weber's relation to China, see Puett, *To Become a God*, 1–25. See also Sivin, "State, Cosmos, and Body," and Yates, "Cosmos, Central Authority, and Communities in the Early Chinese Empire."

113. Puett, *To Become a God*, 145–200; Rawson, "Cosmological Systems as Sources of Art, Ornament and Design."

Jie "looked up [to Heaven]" before looking down and around.[114] For Guanzi, in contrast, those who believe in heavenly signs are "the stupid" (愚者) whom the ruler needs to exploit:

龍門於馬謂之陽，牛山之陰。管子入復於桓公曰：「天使使者臨君之郊，請使大夫初飭，左右玄服，天之使者乎！天下聞之曰：『神哉齊桓公，天使使者臨其郊！』不待舉兵，而朝者八諸侯。此乘天威而動天下之道也。故智者役使鬼神而愚者信之。」

Dragons fought to the north of Madu and Mount Niu. Guanzi entered and reported the matter to Duke Huan saying, "Heaven has sent down envoys to your suburbs. I suggest that you, My Lord, have your great of-ficers don black robes and your officials of the right and left wear dark colors when welcoming these envoys from Heaven." When the rest of the world heard about it they exclaimed, "Truly divine! For Duke Huan of Qi, Heaven has sent down envoys to his suburbs! Without any need for the duke to raise arms, eight feudal lords came to pay court. This is the way to utilize the awesomeness of Heaven to exert one's influence on the world. Thus the wise make use of the spirits while only the stupid believe in them."[115]

The *Guanzi* does not record strange signs or events for the purpose of interpretation—as in the cases of Sima Tan and Sima Qian (the court astrologers) who, for example, use celestial observations to introduce the Xiongnu into a correlative map of heaven and earth, in order to explain and predict China's military activities in Inner Asia.[116] Many of the an-ecdotes contained in the *Shiji* also validate the work of wise diviners, physiognomists, and oneiromancers, by recording their predictions (based on signs) and then narrating their historical fulfillment. Guan-zian signs, by contrast, are floating signifiers to be seized. The ruler "uses spirits" and "exploits the awesomeness of Heaven" (乘天威). "The wise" or knowledgeable (智者) know how to use spirits (鬼神) to make others politically submit. The stupidity of the stupid lies in their sheer credulity in correlative cosmology (i.e., in a fixed correspondence between earthly sign and heavenly referent).

---

114. On the *Shuowen jiezi* and Cang Jie legend, see Bottéro, "Cang Jie and the In-vention of Writing."

115. Ma Feibai, *Guanzi Qingzhong pian*, 651–52; largely following Rickett, *Guanzi*, 2: 488.

116. See *Shiji juan*, 27, and Di Cosmo, *Ancient China and Its Enemies*, chapter 8, on this.

The *Guanzi* urges the economic exploitation of other people's correlative assumptions. It explicitly advises "gaining control of a spirit to use as a treasure" (御神用寶), using the example of a turtle dug up by someone in a suburb. In the narrative, Guanzi advises Duke Huan to claim that the turtle is the son of the Eastern Sea; and the turtle is worshipped as a "priceless treasure." During wartime, the ruler uses this turtle treasure as a pledge, or credit token, in return for the grain supplies from a wealthy local family that enable his subsequent military victory. Immediately after this:

桓公立貢數：文行中七年龜中四千金，黑白之子當千金。凡貢制，中二齊之壤筴也。

Duke Huan established a tribute tariff in which a *wenxing* (文行, literally "patterned ways") was seven [thousand gold pieces], a *niangui* (年龜, lit. "year turtle") was four thousand gold pieces, and a *heibai zhi zi* (黑白之子, literally "child of black and white") stood at one thousand gold pieces. This tribute system as a whole yielded twice the usual amount of tribute from the land of Qi.[117]

Commentators have suggested that the "patterned ways," "year turtle," and "child of black and white" either designate three different kinds of turtle carapaces, or refer to inscribed jades, turtle carapaces, and cowrie shells, respectively. Duke Huan takes advantage of the cosmologically sanctioned tributary ritual to increase his gold reserves. The *Guanzi* ties this strategy to wartime needs: "When the state is in crisis, produce such treasures [such as the turtle to serve as pledges]. When the state is at peace, control the flow of goods."[118] This is significant given the military impulses behind Emperor Wu's economic reforms and, as addressed above, the partly tributary circulation of his fiat *baijin* ("white metal") currencies.

The *Guanzi* provides uses, not meanings, for dragons and turtles. It makes the economist the poet of cosmological signs. When the *Shiji* and *Hanshu* mockingly tied Emperor Wu's *baijin* coins (inscribed with dragons, turtles, and horses) and deer-hide money to the sighting of "what is probably called a unicorn," they denounced precisely what Guanzian economics proposed. Guanzi creates or manipulates correspondences out of political-economic necessity, not by transgressing true values (*wen*).

---

117. Ma Feibai, *Guanzi Qingzhong pian*, 338–39; cf. Rickett, *Guanzi*, 2: 403–5. Here as in many passages, there are textual corruptions.

118. Ma Feibai, *Guanzi Qingzhong pian*, 339.

For the historiographers, the *baijin* fell on the wrong side of their Janus-faced historiography of money that distinguished the true and the counterfeit in both legal and cosmopolitical terms. In their narratives of implicit "praise and blame," the imperial proponents of the *baijin* were as guilty as the hundreds of thousands charged with counterfeiting this money. Heaven lurks behind their monetary histories as the general equivalent, or at least as arbiter of the general equivalent. They cast suspicion not on the system of symbolic correspondences itself ("Since nothing is more useful for the heavens than the dragon, nothing more useful on earth than the horse, and nothing more useful for man than the turtle, they made the *baijin* in three denominations"), but rather on the legitimacy of its interpretation.

The *Guanzi* is the only early text besides the *Shiji*, *Hanshu*, and *Debate on Salt and Iron* to explicitly invoke "white metal" (*baijin*) and "[animal] hide" (*pi*) as possible forms of money (*bi*). It names them as two of the seven "strategic" resources that are useful for manipulating prices (*qingzhong*) and hence "the world" (*tianxia*).

桓公問於管子曰：「吾聞海內玉幣有七筴，可得而聞乎？」管子對曰：「陰山之礝磻，一筴也；燕之紫山白金，一筴也；發、朝鮮之文皮，一筴也；汝漢水之右衢黃金，一筴也；江陽之珠，一筴也；秦明山之曾青，一筴也；禺氏邊山之玉，一筴也。此謂以寡為多，以狹為廣。天下之數盡於輕重矣。」

Duke Huan asked Guanzi: "I have heard that within the seas there are seven strategic uses (*ce*) of jade and money (*bi*)—might I hear about them?"

Guanzi replied: "Nephrite from Mount Yin offers one strategy. White metal (*baijin*) from Mount Zi in Yan offers one strategy. Patterned [animal] hide (*wen pi* 文皮) from the Fa and Chaoxian peoples offers one strategy. Gold metal from the right-hand (i.e., southern) reaches of the Ru and Han rivers offers one strategy. Pearls from the Yangzi and Yang rivers offer one strategy. Malachite from Mount Ming in Qin offers one strategy. Jade from the mountains bordering the Yuzhi offers one strategy. This is called using scarce [resources] to make plenty and using the scanty to become vast. The best [economic] calculations for the world (*tianxia*) derive from *qingzhong* methods."[119]

---

119. Ma Feibai, *Guanzi Qingzhong pian*, 460; cf. Rickett, *Guanzi*, 438. This passage from the chapter now entitled "Calculate and Measure" (*Kui du*), probably dates to the same period as the other *qingzhong* texts, i.e., the latter half of the second century BCE.

Crucial to note is that *baijin* and patterned hide, like gold and jade, have no intrinsic value determined by Heaven. The ruler himself does not need to wait for an auspicious sign. Whether or not the excavated ingots or coins (figures 5.8, 5.9, 5.10, and 5.11) are indeed related to the recorded *baijin* currency, it is *Guanzi*'s disenchanted economics that offer the best (and hitherto overlooked) account for understanding the calculations behind Emperor Wu's failed numismatic experiment.[120] One might further speculate on Emperor Wu's unusual decision to coin silver (as well as on the "barbarous Greek" inscription on excavated ingots) in light of the *qingzhong* approach to foreign exchange.

FOREIGN EXCHANGE

The *Guanzi*'s quantitative economics reduces all world currencies to theoretically exchangeable moneys whose designs never demand translation. In contrast to the China-centered histories of money, the *Guanzi* incorporates foreign exchange into the basic tenets of *qingzhong* economics. Unlike the opaque, spirit-dependent workings of the afterlife economy, such exchanges are governed by universalized quantitative laws:

桓公曰：「四夷不服，恐其逆政游於天下而傷寡人。寡人之行，爲此有道乎？」管子對曰：「吳越不朝，珠象而以爲幣乎？發、朝鮮不朝，請文皮毤服而以爲幣乎。禺氏不朝，請以白璧爲幣乎。崑崙之虛不朝，請以璆琳琅玕爲幣乎。故夫握而不見於手，含而不見於口，而辟千金者珠也，然後八千里之吳越可得而朝也。一豹之皮，容金而金也，然後八千里之發、朝鮮可得而朝也。懷而不見於抱，挾而不見於掖，而辟千金者，白璧也，然後八千里之禺氏可得而朝也。簪珥而辟千金者璆琳琅玕也，然後八千里之崑崙之虛可得而朝也。故物無主，事無接，遠近無以相因，則四夷不得而朝矣。」

Duke Huan said: "The four *yi* [i.e., all foreigners] have not [politically] submitted themselves and I worry that their political transgression will spread through the world and harm me. What path of action should I take for this?"

Guanzi replied: "Since the states of Wu and Yue have not come to court, pearls and ivory should be used as money (*bi*). Since the Fa and Chaoxian have not paid court, I request our use of patterned hides and fur clothing as money (*bi*). Since the Yuzhi have not paid court, I request our use of white jade discs as money (*bi*). Since those of the Kunlun deserts

---

120. See the Appendix for bibliography on alternative interpretations.

have not paid court, I request our use of lapis lazuli and *langgan* gems as money (*bi*). Therefore a pearl held unseen in a hand or mouth will be used as a thousand pieces of gold, and we can obtain the Wu and Yue eight thousand *li* away and make them pay court. Since one leopard skin will be like a thousand pieces of gold the Fa and Chaoxian eight-thousand *li* away will be obtained and pay court. Since a white jade held tight unseen against one's chest or under one's armpit will be used as a thousand pieces of gold, we can obtain the Yuzhi eight thousand *li* away and make them pay court. Since a lapis lazuli and *langgan* gem (fashioned in) a hair-clasp and earring will be used as a thousand gold pieces, we can obtain [i.e., defeat] [the inhabitants] of the Kunlun deserts eight thousand *li* away and make them pay court. Therefore if resources are not commandeered,[121] economies will not connect, those distant from each other will have nothing to use for their common interest and the four *yi* will not be obtained and come to court."[122]

Anything, in other words, can be made into money, regardless of historical precedent: pearls, ivory, lapis lazuli, leopard skins. These exotica have exchange equivalents in gold (e.g., "a pearl . . . will be used as a thousand pieces of gold," or as one thousand catties of gold). Once the ruler pronounces them money (*bi*), it is their quantity in relation to that of circulating commodities (and to other currencies) that will matter. Here the "scarcity" of raw materials—as well as the ruler's ability to harness these resources and to intimately control their circulation as money—will empower him. Money, in this context, does not alienate human relations; rather, it brings strangers closer into the relations of subjection. Establishing common currency becomes a means of political conquest.

Qingzhong money transcends Chinese culture. The *Guanzi* never alludes to monetary inscriptions (*wen*) in its dialogues except in this context of foreign "patterned [animal] hide" (*wen pi* 文皮). The scene of foreign exchange discussed in chapter 1 borrowed Zhou dynasty geography ("The Zhou then assembled 'counters' [*ma* 馬] to serve as pledges to the people of Lai and took control of the silk while the Lai used counters as their stabilizing monetary standard"). Here, however, the *Guanzi*

---

121. Lit. "goods have no ruler" 物無主, i.e., the ruler needs to harness unused resources. Alternately: "if no commodity is made preeminent," following Guo Moruo and Ma Feibai.

122. Ma Feibai, *Guanzi Qingzhong pian*, 560; Li Xiangfeng, *Guanzi jiao zhu*, 1440; cf. Rickett, *Guanzi*, 464.

locates many of the material resources for money at the geographical horizons not of Zhou dynasty Qi but of the Han dynasty empire. Mount Yin belongs to the Kunlun range between Xinjiang and Tibet, and the Yuzhi 禺氏 are now identified with the Yuezhi 月氏 of Central Asia. As commentators have pointed out, the Yuezhi only migrated to the Central Asian mountains after Han-Xiongnu wars forced them from the Dunhuang region (modern-day Gansu) around 160 BCE; and the *Shiji* preserves reports about the Yuezhi by Emperor Wu's envoy Zhang Qian. These distant places mark the western and northwestern limits of Han dynasty exploration and expansion. In Guanzi's earlier example, patterned hide comes from Manchuria and from Chaoxian (Korea), both of which lie in the far northeast that was colonized during the Han. The state of Yan (the source for *baijin* in that example) was on the Han empire's northern border with the Xiongnu (and Mount Ming might be a mistake for Nan-shan [南山 southern mountains] located in the southwest). Guanzi, with flagrant anachronism, stages his Zhou dynasty dialogue on foreign exchange within the geopolitical horizons and ambitions of the Han-dynasty era of Emperor Wu. At the same time, the subjunctive, hypothetical mode of the generalized lesson (and its fictional personae) clarifies that the *tianxia* of money is not Han political empire but the transhistorical "world."

Conclusion

The anthropologist Bill Maurer has observed that within recent anthropological and literary scholarship on money there is an "emphasis on modern money's distinctive qualities of commensuration, abstraction, quantification, and reification."[123] That Han texts variously promoted and lamented many such tendencies does not mean that they had precociously entered the world of modern money. At the same time, the Han case shows the difficulties of assuming complete dissonance between the worlds of ancient and modern money.[124] The universalizing quantitative

---

123. Maurer, "The Anthropology of Money."

124. Compare Anne Carson's approach to the fifth-century BCE Simonides (the first Greek poet to charge a price for his poetry) as someone born into "an early, severe form of economic alienation," in a society on the border between two economic systems "where traditions of gift exchange coexisted with commodity trade and a flourishing money economy." Carson, *Economy of the Unlost*, 10–44.

laws of the *Guanzi*'s "Qingzhong" chapters made all world currencies potentially exchangeable. These chapters promoted foreign exchange through the creative invention of credit and fiat currencies for economic profit and political conquest. In contrast to common Han burial practices, the *Guanzi* mocked and exploited the belief in cosmologically sanctioned currencies. Burial money thus belonged to a very different mode of foreign exchange. The diverse currencies and contracts prepared for human-spirit commerce did not follow the same transparent, quantitative, logic. Unlike the aggressive, hegemonic Guanzian ruler, the deceased would meet the "foreign" world of the spirits with payments and appeals for debt-relief. In contrast to both of these, the dominant classical tradition brought money into the domain of Chinese ethics by treating it as an inferior form of writing (*wen*). It highlighted the failure of monetary inscriptions (*wen*) to conform to the shared values governing classical *wen*: as inscriptions of truth or reality (*shi*), as cosmological signs, and as patterns of Chinese civilization and history. To debate the proper relation of money to the state, society, and market, historiographers and classicists invented new etiologies of money and new parables of debt. Money became a new site for explaining and asserting the preeminence of the classical tradition. Unlike the *Guanzi*, within whose part-historical, part-imaginary world neither linguistic nor monetary signs had a universal equivalent, classical discourses grounded money in classical Chinese values. With the political rise of classicism after Emperor Wu's reign, these non-*qingzhong* texts helped to keep real or imaginary commerce with foreign worlds out of Chinese monetary history.

Coda: Counterhistory, Connected Histories, and Comparative Literature

If the student fails to get the author's basic point, then reading his book will be like Zhang Qian arriving in Bactria without any capacity [for engaging with] the Yuezhi.
—Huang Zongxi (1610–95), *Directions to the Reader of Case Studies of Ming Confucians*.

Globalization takes place only in capital and data . . . . Information command has ruined knowing and reading.
—Gayatri Spivak, *An Aesthetic Education in the Era of Globalization*.

Although grounded in Chinese literary and cultural history, this book began and developed as part of a broader interest in seeing what happens when one takes cross-cultural and connected histories, rather than national history, as the framework for literary inquiry. In this coda I will try to clarify my intention for this book: that is, I hope this work will help to open up a space for early interculturality in approaches to comparative literature and, conversely, that it will suggest avenues for approaching contact historiography from a literary perspective.

Let me begin with material archaeology. Recent excavations of literary and material texts have opened up both the canon and the cultural frontiers of ancient China. The painstaking transcription, translation, and interpretation of a motley array of excavated texts (e.g., medical fragments, tax documents, silk paintings) are now at the vanguard of antiquarian studies. Frontier archaeology has created new centers of culture. Han-era burial sites from Syria to Korea, from Chennai to Xinjiang, attest not only to the extent and complexity of the ancient networks of trade and cultural exchange but also to the widespread hybridization of symbolic practices. As someone working in comparative literature as well as sinology, I was struck that art historians and economic historians were using these new texts and sites to link ancient China with the wider world, but that most literary scholars were not. The kind of critical attention to China's contact zones that inspired this book—work on Tang-dynasty Buddhism, research into the nineteenth-century Opium Wars, and so on—was limited to later historical contexts.[1]

Comparative analyses of pre-Tang Chinese literary aesthetics have, by contrast, largely used an approach based on a traditional canon and an Axial Age model of independent civilizations. For Karl Jaspers, the real meaning of the synchronous rise of "imagery, concrete representation, and myth" in the Axial Period (800–200 BCE) lay in the foundation, during this period, of a universal history that led to better understanding of others (especially those of other faiths) and thus of the self.[2] While many comparatists have rejected the significance of synchronicity, they continue to reproduce two of Jaspers's assumptions about ancient civilizations: first, that these civilizations developed independently; and second, that the same civilizations developed into particular modern cultures, thereby enabling transhistorical, civilizational notions of Self and Other.[3] In the last few decades, incisive comparative studies of

---

1. See Mair, *Painting and Performance* and *T'ang Transformation Texts*; Liu, *Tokens of Exchange* and *The Clash of Empires*. Liu models a more critical two-way encounter than Mair's focus on eastward influence. Liu has usefully extended her notion of "translingual practices" beyond linguistic translation to include material circulations across borders. In its original formulation, "the study of translingual practice examines the process by which new words, discourses, and modes of representation arise, circulate, and acquire legitimacy within the host language due to, or in spite of, the latter's contact/collision with the guest language." See Liu, *Translingual Practices*, 26–27. Other useful rubrics for analyzing linguistic and symbolic exchange in modern and early modern contexts of colonialism and globalization include: "transculturalism" (Mary Louise Pratt); "colonial mimicry" (Homi Bhabha); "planetarity" (Gayatri Spivak); "flexible citizenship" (Aihwa Ong); "affective communities" (Leela Gandhi); "minor transnationalism" (Françoise Lionnet and Shu-mei Shih); "signifying" (Henry Louis Gates); "cosmopolitan literature" (Sheldon Pollock); and "connected histories" (Sanjay Subrahmanyam).

2. Jaspers, "Philosophy and History"; Roetz, "The Axial Age Theory."

3. On the invention of Greece and Rome as the isolated civilizational foundations of the European race, see Bernal, *Black Athena*; Burkert, *The Orientalizing Revolution*. On

traditional Chinese literary aesthetics have helped to historicize and deconstruct East-West comparisons, and to demythologize stereotypes of *China* and of the *West* in modern Western and Chinese imaginations. The explicitly comparative literary studies of Alexander Beecroft, Zong-qi Cai, François Jullien, Hyun Jin Kim, Ming Dong Gu, Mu-chou Poo, Haun Saussy, Pauline Yu, and Zhang Longxi have, often in oppositional ways, used China to revise conventional understandings of European and Chinese aesthetic traditions, and to challenge the cultural biases animating European structuralist, poststructuralist, and deconstructionist studies.[4] And yet, the focus of these comparisons on texts such as the *Classic of Odes* and the other Confucian Classics (and their commentaries) has had the unintended effect of re-canonizing the canon and of perpetuating a mirage of an antiquity in which China was not in contact with the outside world, and in which China's aesthetics developed

---

the classical, ethnological, and archaeological discourses through which a transhistorical Han ethnicity reaching into antiquity has been produced, see Chin, "Antiquarian as Ethnographer."

4. Li Zehou, *The Chinese Aesthetic Tradition*; Yu, *The Reading of Imagery*; Owen, *Readings in Chinese Literary Thought*; and Gu, *Chinese Theories of Reading and Writing* are influential comparatively situated accounts of the Chinese tradition that basically comprises the Confucian Classics and their commentaries, as well as *Zhuangzi*, the *Elegies of Chu*, and in the post-Han period Liu Xie's *Wenxin dialong* [Literary Mind and the Carving of Dragons] as well as Chan Buddhist texts. Zong-qi Cai's more explicitly comparative *Configurations of Comparative Poetics* draws on a similar archive. Cai clarifies three modes of comparing Chinese and Western traditions of literary criticism: an intracultural perspective which "distinguish[es] Western and Chinese poetics each as a largely self-contained system rooted in its own intellectual and cultural traditions"; a cross-cultural perspective "overcome[s] the politics of similitude and polemics of difference"; and a transcultural perspective provides the "evaluation of similarities and differences." See Cai, *Configurations of Comparative Poetics*, 239–55. These are useful but exclude the possibility an ancient contact zone. For incisive comparative projects, see Beecroft, *Authorship and Cultural Identity*; Saussy, *The Problem of a Chinese Aesthetic*; and Zhang, *Allegoresis*, all of which focus on the *Odes* tradition. See also Jullien, *In Praise of Blandness*; Zhang, *The Tao and the Logos*; and Gu, *Chinese Theories of Fiction*. My point in reducing these works to their sources is not to belittle their critical claims upon which my own scholarship depends, but to note the unintended effect of their collective textual choices. The comparative studies of Poo, *Enemies of Civilization* and Kim, *Ethnicity and Foreigners* (as well as Di Cosmo, *Ancient China and Its Enemies*) crucially make frontiers central to the problem of representation. Unlike these, however, I do not approach the problem of representation from the perspective of a predetermined object of representation (the foreigner).

in isolation from the wider world.[5] Likewise, comparative studies of China and Greece underemphasize or overlook recent reconsiderations of Greco-Roman literary and aesthetic traditions as part of an interactive ancient Mediterranean *oikoumene*. As the antiquarian's view of literary history increasingly acquires a radical openness in compass and cultural identity, the comparatist's version remains retrospectively ossified along Axial or national lines.

Thus, for me, Michel Foucault's famous invocation of "a certain Chinese encyclopedia" at the beginning of *The Order of Things: An Archaeology of the Human Sciences* poses a very different kind of problem from that raised by other comparatists. To recall Foucault's opening:

> This book first arose out of a passage in Borges, out of the laughter that shattered . . . all the familiar landmarks of my thought—*our* thought, the thought that bears the stamp of our age and our geography. . . . This passage quotes a "certain Chinese encyclopedia" in which it is written that "animals are divided into: (a) belonging to the Emperor, (b) embalmed, (c) tame, (d) suckling pigs, (e) sirens, (f) fabulous, (g) stray dogs, (h) included in the present classification, (i) frenzied, (j) innumerable, (k) drawn with a very fine camelhair brush, (l) et cetera, (m) having just broken the water pitcher, (n) that from a long way off look like flies." In the wonderment of this taxonomy, the thing we apprehended in one great leap, the thing that, by means of a fable, is demonstrated as the exotic charm of another system of thought, is the limitation of our own, the stark impossibility of thinking *that*.[6]

Among China scholars, this passage has become a litmus test for Foucault's relation to Orientalism. Some have argued that Foucault does not

---

5. This literary scholarship joins the hugely important and inspiring comparative studies of Greco-Roman and Chinese science, thought, social practices, gender relations, and empires, which also generally take non-contact as the point of departure. In addition to the above-mentioned works, see Kuriyama, *The Expressiveness of the Body*; Lloyd and Sivin, *The Way and the Word*; Raphals, *Knowing Words*; Mutschler and Mittag, *Conceiving the Empire*; Scheidel, *Rome and China*; and Zhou, *Festivals, Feasts, and Gender Relations*. See also Graeber, *Debt*, and Moretti, *The Novel*. Again my purpose is not to criticize the function of defamliarization that juxtaposition of alien cultures enables, but rather to draw attention to the critical spaces for alternative forms of comparative work on antiquity.

6. Foucault, *The Order of Things*, xv.

exoticize China (Zhang Longxi, Ming Dong Gu).[7] He is, after all, openly using a *fictional* China to symbolize a totally incomprehensible disorder (the heteroclite), which will serve as a foil and provocation to Foucault's historical archaeology of the unspoken, unseen, unconscious orders of experience that produced and constrained the possibilities of knowledge during different periods of European history.[8] For Haun Saussy, by contrast, Foucault's invocation of China exemplifies a broader rhetorical reliance on the notion of China as an *anti-type* in early French poststructuralist and deconstructionist analyses.[9] The idea of the Chinese encyclopedia, over and above its explicitly fictional basis, enables the reader to contemplate stepping out of the history Foucault is about to tell "by making it possible to imagine a tabula rasa on which no categories would be set down in advance."[10] For me, however, the question of China in *The Order of Things* does not concern China's presence as an anti-type or an exotic fantasy, but rather China's absence from the archaeology itself. Foucault's awe-inspiring account traces two epistemic shifts in notions of language, living things, and economic facts, from the Renaissance (pre-1650) to the Classical period (1650–1800), and from the Classical to the Modern (1800–1960s) period.[11] Fundamental to the

---

7. See Zhang Longxi, *Mighty Opposites*, 19–54; Gu, *Sinologism*. Mary Franklin-Brown's study of the medieval European encyclopedia has suggested that the European florilegium-as-encyclopedia had more in common with Borges's fiction than with Foucault's orders. See Brown, *Reading the World*. One might also note that the stereotype of the traditional Chinese approach to language and thought as structured by "correlative cosmology" in European sinology resembles the Renaissance Europe of Foucault's account.

8. For Catherine Gallagher, Foucault's laughter represents the "limit experience of counterhistory," that is, his experiential rather than intellectual apprehension of the possible nonexistence of order. The passage also exemplifies the rhetorical role of the anecdote and idiosyncratic voice in counterhistories. See Gallagher, *Practicing New Historicism*, 49–74. Compare Leslie Kurke's *Coins, Bodies, Games, and Gold*, 3.

9. Saussy, *Great Walls of Discourse*, 146–82.

10. Chinese ontology and (ostensibly) nonphonetic writing serve as the antitype through which Derrida, Sollers, and others think through the differences between structuralism and poststructuralism. For them, "China is what deconstruction will turn the world into." Saussy, *Great Walls of Discourse*, 150.

11. Foucault replaces the conventional five-hundred-year evolutionary history of biology, linguistics, and economics, with his account of the underlying rules that governed theories and concepts across different kinds of texts during different historical periods. (Foucault's account of the Renaissance largely covers the 1500–1650 period.) As he put

shift from the Renaissance world of resemblance—in which words and things, money and stars, were part of the same cosmological sign system of the world—to the Classical world—in which tables of identity and difference structured knowledge and value was formed through exchange and quantitative laws of money—is the rise of the French Physiocrats, the classical economists who, as Foucault points out, saw wealth as coming from the land. Foucault does not, however, mention that the Physiocrats self-consciously acknowledged their debt to Chinese analyses that used land as the basis of wealth. Had *The Order of Things* included (along with Borges's fictional Chinese encyclopedia) the writings of eighteenth-century Jesuits such as Jean-Baptiste Du Halde (see figure 5.13 for his included drawings of Emperor Wu's silver coins), which introduced Chinese analyses of wealth to Europe, Foucault might have released his metaphorical archaeology from its civilizational assumptions.[12]

Can material archaeology help one to rethink "critical" archaeology? Without well-documented forms of literature from China's neighbors (e.g., Xiongnu poetry), can one conduct a study of "contact comparative literature" (that is, is it possible to analyze this period by taking into account historical exchange across, or hybridity within, aesthetic traditions)? *Savage Exchange* proposes "yes" to these questions. It attempts to historicize Chinese literature in ways that do not privilege an anachronistically restrictive notion either of China or of aesthetic practice. It gives an account of inter-cultural China and of Han classicism from the

---

it, he placed "side by side, a definite number of elements: the knowledge of living things, the knowledge of the laws of language, and the knowledge of economic facts," and "relate[d] them to a philosophical discourse that was contemporary with them." Foucault, *The Order of Things*, x–xi.

12. Foucault is not interested in the reasons for epistemic shifts or in the history of individual thinkers. What matters to him is, for example, that the opposing schools of Physiocrats and Utilitarians rely on the same theory of value. Translated texts (from outside Europe) might, however, have fit into Foucault's analytic structure as part of the "intradiscursive dependencies (between the objects, operations and concepts of a single formation)" that Foucault seeks to define. See Foucault, "Politics and the Study of Discourse," 58–59. Foucault's archaeological metaphor thus has the same (unintended) monumentalizing effect with respect to East and West as Li Zehou's cultural-psychological "sedimentation" (*jidian*) of the Chinese aesthetic tradition. Their (spatial) metaphors are grounded in nationalist and civilizational paradigms of archaeology at the expense of the frontiers. Lost in figuration are the connected histories that stretch long into premodernity.

perspective of an enlarged history of symbolic media and practices. It puts the noncanonical, nonliterary, and visual texts (e.g., economic, mathematical, and ethnographic texts, as well as Sino-Kharoshthi and Chinese coins) in the foreground alongside familiar classics. Largely following New Historicist, postcolonial, and feminist studies, I ask how such minor texts and practices can transform the way we look at the canon, and I examine the historical and evaluative processes by which canons (and master narratives) are made and sustained.

Savage Exchange began with two non-canonical Masters dialogues, the *Guanzi*'s "Qingzhong" chapters and the *Debate on Salt and Iron*, and showed how they used different literary styles to model rival ideals of the political economy. The *Guanzi* grounded its radically quantitative economics in literary abstractions (e.g., Mr. Calculate-y) rather than in classical propriety. The Classical Scholars (Wenxue) of the *Debate on Salt and Iron* restored traditional agricultural ideals by reasserting the authority of the classical texts in which those ideals were patterned. Chapters 2 to 5 tracked the rise—and the containment—of quantitative modes of reasoning, as applied to a range of canonical and noncanonical symbolic practices: the prose-poetic *fu*, historiography, mathematical texts, women's weaving, and money. Competing Han perspectives were encoded through formal innovations and adjustments within these same genres and practices.[13] The Han-dynasty rise of the classicist as encoder of an enduring Chinese aesthetic ideology might thus be appreciated not only in terms of correlative thinking and the structures of imperial bureaucracy (e.g., the canonical Mao-Zheng interpretation of the *Classic of Odes*; or the traditional examination system), but also as an outcome of a battle between the economist and the classicist (or the money-counting globalist and the text-citing sinocentrist).

This *imaginary* history of contact was what I found missing in the new empirical studies of the Silk Road, and was what I hoped to begin to supply. The events of *Savage Exchange* take place not in battlefields,

---

13. Unlike Lukacs's theory of genre (the integrated world of epic versus the alienated modern novel), or Chen Duxiu's analysis of traditional poetic forms (the "lowly street speech" of the *Odes* versus the "sycophantic" *fu*), or Leslie Kurke and Ian Morris's differentiation of Greek poetic forms by performance occasion (the aristocratic symposium versus civic chorus), genre does not in the Han instance necessarily align with ideology.

markets, and administrative fiats but in poetic, prose, and visual what-ifs and would-thats. It documents the Han-dynasty emergence—and classical containment—of hypothetical perspectives that interrupted traditional understandings of the world but did not necessarily enlarge capacities for action at this time. One might think of these two types of history in terms of Raymond Williams's distinction between the "indicative" mode of literary narration that describes what happened or was happening, and the "subjunctive" mode that "introduces a perspective that is actually not socially or politically available."[14] The subjunctive perspectives of the Former Han do not add up to a tectonic shift in deep ideological form; to a new stage in Smithian, Marxist, Polanyian, or world-systems meta-narratives; or to a precocious consciousness in the evolution of Chinese economic rationalism (or "Confucian capitalism") that continued from antiquity to the present.[15] Rather, these subjunctive per-

---

14. Williams, "Forms of Fiction in 1848." Williams was describing divergent modes within the emergent nineteenth-century English realist novel. This subjunctive "hypothesis of a perspective, a feeling, a force, which [the protagonist] knows not to be in the existing balances of forces that was there to be observed" differed, Williams argued, from the more explicit ideological forms of contemporary Russian and French novels in which, in Georg Lukacs's influential account, the protagonist's personal experience of the limitations of his life enables his discovery of the objective limits conditioning society. For an elaboration of this subjunctive in relation to postcolonial and "ahimsaic" historiography, see Leela Gandhi's *The Common Cause*.

15. Twentieth-century historians of China have revised Marxist and Smithian historical frameworks by rejecting nineteenth-century Orientalist paradigms of an unchanging China. Within Adam Smith's "stationary" economic state of China and Karl Marx's stagnant, despotic "Asiatic mode of production" (iterated by Max Weber and Karl Wittfogel), the Qin-Han (221 BCE–220 CE) beginnings of a unified empire was little different from its Qing dynasty (1644–1911) ends. On this, see R. B. Wong, *China Transformed*; and Brook, "Capitalism and the Writing of Modern History." For early Chinese Marxist attempts to fill China's "blank page" in Marxist world history by periodizing dynastic history according to Morgan-Engels evolutionary stage-theory, see for example Guo Moruo, *Zhongguo gudai shehui*. Both Japanese and Chinese Marxists remained concerned with the particularity of China's experience of those universal historical stages. Since China had not developed industrial capitalism, commerce in China's long feudal period (beginning variously in the Zhou or Qin-Han period and extending to the Qing) took on a new importance. Fan Wenlan, "Zi Qin Han qi Zhongguo chengwei tongyi guojia," argued that the emergence of commodity markets and "common economic life" (as well as Han nationality [*Hanzu*]) in the feudal Qin-Han period, as described in the *Shiji*, did not herald the beginnings of capitalism as it did in medieval Europe. This contradicted Marx's association of nationality-formation

spectives signify the unrealized, dead-end hypotheses with no immediate progeny that challenge teleological narratives of economic thought. The Han-dynasty quarrel over money's propensity to abstract, to quantify, or

---

with capitalism. Pre-capitalist market development thus marked one of the many differences between China and Europe's respective paths to capitalism. For early critiques of the "sprouts of capitalism" narrative, see Nishijima Sadao's "Economic and Social History of Former Han"; and "Formation of the Early Chinese Cotton Industry." Adam Smith's *Wealth of Nations* (1773) argues that China, despite its highly developed markets and superior wealth, had already by the thirteenth century maximized its natural and human resources. Mark Elvin's *Pattern of the Chinese Past* implicitly affirms Smith's view, but focuses on the role of the economics of technology—the ability to motivate and finance technological innovation—in propelling China to lead the world economy (circa 900–1300) before reaching its "equilibrium point" or "high-equilibrium trap." In Elvin's account, expanded since by Gang Deng and others, the Han empire's unprecedented monetization, its expanded (if not yet popular) markets, and its use of the crossbow, mounted archery, and foreign mercenaries essentially prefigure the popularized markets, paper money, mechanized industry, and gunpowder warfare of the Song dynasty. R. Bin Wong, Giovanni Arrighi, and others have since argued that Smithian market dynamics *did* extend into late imperial China (circa 1500–1900). Rather than explaining the "Great Divergence" (Kenneth Pomeranz) between European and Chinese economies in terms of China's failure to develop industrial capitalism ("stationary state," "high-equilibrium trap"), they show how late imperial China's cash cropping, handicrafts, and market development did follow a Smithian dynamic. Wong's *China Transformed*, 74–77, traces back to the Han dynasty the bureaucratic and ideological logic ("political imagination") of an "economically viable peasantry," whose welfare legitimated governments of successive agrarian empires. Arrighi's *Adam Smith in Beijing* further argues that late imperial China, not modern Europe, followed Smith's path of "natural" market development, contrasting the modern West's capitalist "Industrial Revolution" (capital-intensive, energy-consuming, class-based, large-scale production) and East Asia's Smithian "Industrious Revolution" labor-intensive, energy-saving, household-centered, small-scale production). (Arrighi borrows and develops the term "industrious revolution" from Hayami Akira and Kaoru Sugihara.) For an introduction to the 1950s primitivist-substantivist debate on ancient Mediterranean societies, see Morris, "Forward"; Polanyi, *Trade and Market in the Early Empires*. Karl Polanyi set aside East Asia (see, for example, Polanyi, "The Economy as Instituted Process"); but Rostovsteff, *The Social and Economic History of the Hellenistic World*, 864–65, does incorporate cross-regional trade, including the "silk route" caravan trade to China, into his analysis. Barbieri-Low's *Artisans*, positions Han China as a counter-example to Polanyi's argument that there were no price-setting markets in antiquity. Ying-shih Yü's *Zhongguo jin shi zong jiao lun li* and "Business Culture and Chinese Traditions" offers an account of pro-commerce Confucianism. He uses Weberian categories (such as impersonality) to propose a multi-millennia-spanning evolution of Chinese "merchant culture" or "business culture" that developed in spite of state discrimination against merchants.

to make the hitherto incommensurable commensurate troubles modern assumptions of analytic dissonance between the worlds of pre-modern (or so-called primitive) and modern money. But this does not constitute a narrative bridge.

In re-examining the first-century BCE rise of classicism, *Savage Exchange* offers a counterhistory of literary aesthetics as well as of economic thought.[16] In contrast to studies that make the prestige of writing (*wen*) emblematic of cultural China (ancient and modern), *Savage Exchange* denaturalizes the authority of Chinese writing (and the literary canon) and historicizes the embattled rise of textualism itself. It argues that the ossified literary-cultural-ritual-aesthetic matrix of *wen* (writing, pattern, Chinese civilization, etc.) that is used in modern literary and comparative accounts of China became hegemonic after the Former Han period—not simply through the iterations of generations of classicizing imperial bureaucrats in an inevitable evolution that culminated in the systematic anthologies and poetics of Xiao Tong's *Selections of Literature* (Wen xuan) and Liu Xie's *The Literary Mind and the Carving of Dragons* (Wenxin diaolong)—but also after a historical contestation with Former Han dreams of quantitative value (*qingzhong*) and calculation (*ji*).

Let me summarize by making two basic points. First, comparative literature can and must pay attention to premodern histories of contact. Material archaeology has de-centered the literary classics that once comprised Chinese literature and the study of this enlarged repository of literary and visual symbolic practices shows that many of these practices were embedded in contexts of inter-cultural exchange. *Savage Exchange* shows that Han dynasty literary aesthetics developed in self-reflexive relation to a larger world. This was exemplified through an array of short-lived metaphors and unrealized aesthetic ambitions: the *Shiji*'s critique of ethnography; Sima Xiangru's poetic exotica; the idiom of border-market "kinship" (*qin*); Emperor Wu's foreign-looking silver coinage; and the *Guanzi*'s Central Asian horizons of *qingzhong* economics. This

---

16. In Foucault's "Nietzsche, Genealogy, History" counter-memory opposes the themes of history as recognition, as a continuity, and as knowledge. I draw on Catherine Gallagher and Stephen Greenblatts's New Historicist elaboration of counterhistories that aim in this vein to "make apparent the slippages, cracks, fault lines, and surprising absences in the monumental structures that dominated a more traditional historicism." See Gallagher, *Practicing New Historicism*, 17, 49–74.

mode of "worlding" early Chinese literary aesthetics—of exploring its experiments and exchanges with other traditions—comes not from analyses of difference and identity (e.g., comparisons with ancient Greek or postmodern thought), but rather from historicizing cultural exchange. Although *Savage Exchange* has largely focused on Chinese-language texts (and materials found in China) I hope that future projects can go on to demonstrate the two-way (or multiple-way) aspect of those exchanges.

Second, the materialist historiography of world-systems might benefit from a broader set of interpretive approaches to primary documents and data. Archaeologists, historians of world history, and world systems theorists rely on vast amounts of secondary scholarship on individual states, regions, or literary traditions to interpret the ways in which the (roughly) contemporaneous Roman, Parthian, Persian, Mauryan Indian, Kushan, and Chinese Han empires, and their neighbors, were connected or integrated by trade and cumulative investments in state and industrial infrastructure (as well as by war, diplomacy, and intermarriage).[17] The scholarship that they synthesize and footnote on the Chinese Silk Road tends, in an "indicative" mode, to extract empirical data from Chinese texts.[18] From this perspective, the *Shiji*'s record of Zhang Qian's arrival in Bactria matters but the *Guanzi*'s hypothetical dialogue about linking Central Asian and Chinese monetary economies does not. An *imaginary* history of the Silk Road makes outside contact a question of meaning,

---

17. Andre Gunder Frank and Barry Gills's "5,000-Year World System" takes capital accumulation, not the capitalist mode of production, as the marker of the capitalist world system. The authors redefine capital to include not only classic wage-labor capitalism, but also monetary and non-monetary, state and private, forms of production and accumulation of wealth (e.g., technology, temple luxuries). See Frank, "The 5,000-Year World System"; and Gills, "The Cumulation of Accumulation," 81–114. Compare this to the world system model of Immanuel Wallerstein and Samir Amin. Their capitalist world system essentially reinvents modernity (introducing a sixteenth-century Europe-centered capitalism with a global reach), not premodernity. Pre-sixteenth-century China for them was a "tributary empire" (exemplified by the Han empire), whose logic of exchange was governed by politics, not economics. See also Abu-Lughod, "Discontinuities and Persistence." On the Silk Road, see Hansen, *The Silk Road*; Woods, *The Silk Road*; Beckwith, *Empires of the Silk Road*; and Mair, *The Tarim Mummies*.

18. See Moretti's analysis of, and influential appropriation of, the reading practices of world-systems theorists such as Immanuel Wallerstein and Fernand Braudel. See Moretti, "Conjectures on World Literature," and Palumbo-Liu, *Immanuel Wallerstein and the Problem of the World System*.

form, and affect, and not just of empirical record. Debates carried out through innovations in genre and metaphor made the politics of representation part of the history of contact. A map of the Silk Road (see figure 0.1) thus should also incorporate the imaginary maps of Sima Xiangru's *fu* (figure 2.1), the "Tribute of Yu" (figure 0.2), and Emperor Wu (in his conflation of the West with immortality).

This Silk Road "subjunctive" appears in the what-ifs of *qingzhong* economics, with its dream of dominating an economically connected world by harnessing a surplus of single female industrial weavers. The subjunctive also appears in the dialogical absence of *qingzhong* economics, as in the absenting of any consideration of the Han silk market from Ban Zhao's account of the assiduously unproductive wife. This "Silk Road imaginary" is as important as the Silk Road archaeology that examines its material traces. Both analytical approaches to the Silk Road militate against civilizational comparisons that retroactively parcel up antiquity into discrete textual-historical bodies (e.g., China, Europe, India).

Thus, the aspects of Han imperialism, Chinese literary style, and the economic imagination described in these pages do not anticipate or allegorize modern China—any more than they anticipate or allegorize modern Europe or the United States. If these themes speak in any way to our current era of globalization it is not because of some second-century BCE revolution in capital and data, but rather because some twenty-first-century antiquarians (for reasons that will and should come under scrutiny) have come to question dominant visions and ideals of great civilizations.

Appendix:
Numismatic Research on the Han Dynasty Lead Ingots with Blundered Greek (or Foreign) Inscription

Since 1913, over sixty articles have been published—largely in China, but also abroad—about the lead ingots with "foreign," "barbarous Greek," or, more recently, "Middle Indo-Aryan" inscription (see figures 5.8, 5.9, 5.10, and 5.11).[1] Most of the discussion has concerned the interpretation of the inscription and, more recently, whether or not the ingot can be identified as one of the three coins of the *baijin sanpin* 白金三品 currency issued by the Han dynasty Emperor Wu between 119 and 115 BCE. Chapter 5 examined the historical controversies over Emperor Wu's "silver" *baijin* currency, especially in the context of the *Guanzi*'s expansionist *qingzhong* economics and competing approaches to monetary inscriptions. As pointed out in that chapter, the objects discussed below have not yet been absolutely identified as the *baijin*. Much of the most recent work in China, Europe, and the United States has, however, identified them as such. The facts that Han dynasty counterfeiting of the *baijin* was widespread (and lead a common substitute); that Han dynasty people buried themselves with both real money and afterlife money (which was often made in non-precious materials, including lead); and that some of the *baijin* samples come from burial contexts all complicate analysis. Furthermore, numismatists warn that the recent counterfeiting of coins (and other ancient objects) includes *baijin* samples. For this reason, the aim of this appendix is to review the numismatic evidence and, in contrast to earlier accounts, to clarify for future studies which samples come from provenanced archaeological contexts.

Excavation Data

Prior to 1965, an estimated nine to eleven of these ingots, without reliable provenance, were collected privately or by museums.[2] Since 1965, over three hundred similar ingots

---

1. Thierry, *Monnaies chinoises*, 31–32, Huang Xiquan, "Baijin sanpin zhuan wen," and especially Whaley, "A Middle Indo-Aryan Inscription," provide the most useful summaries and analyses of scholarship to date. Research for this book was largely compiled before Whaley's was published, and this analysis differs from his synthesis.

2. See Zheng Wenzhuo, "Lading jin pan," on the ingot in his family possession for nearly a century; Houo-Ming-Tse, *Preuves des antiquités*, 573 and 575, on one ingot reportedly found near Hezhou 河州 in Gansu; Cai Jixiang, "Han xiyu da Qin guo," on two ingots in his possession (one

have been unearthed across Gansu, Shaanxi, and Anhui provinces. However there is still not enough reliable information about the archaeological contexts of these excavated ingots to establish their date or function. Only one ingot is known to have been found in an independently datable tomb, namely a Later Han tomb in Lu'an 六安, Anhui Province, that was excavated by a team from the Wanxi Museum 皖西博物馆 in 1988.[3] There are three other excavations with fairly detailed reports of archeological context, but without sufficient data for conclusive dating: a) the 1965 discovery of thirteen ingots stacked in an upside-down jar in what is thought to be a cellar in the Han ruins of Xichazhai 西查寨, Shaanxi Province;[4] b) the 1973 discovery in Fufeng 扶风 County, Shaanxi, of two ingots in a layer of earth that also contained Han pottery shards and Han *wuzhu* coins;[5] and c) the 1976 discovery in Lingtai 灵台, Gansu Province, of approximately 274 stacked ingots in a tunnel of tiles buried underground (see figures 5.8 and 5.9).[6] There are many additional reports of other ingots found from 1965 to the present, but whose circumstances of discovery are generally limited to information about their location: Lixian 礼县, Gansu (5); Lingtai 灵台, Gansu, 1979 (10); Xihe 西河, Gansu (2); Linxia 临夏, Gansu (1); Xi'an 西安, Shaanxi (1); the Changxingzhen 长兴镇 and Baoji region, Shaanxi (3); Xianyang 咸阳, Shaanxi (1); Lu'an 六安, Anhui, 1986 (2) and 1994 (1).[7] Many museums and collectors in China and abroad possess fur-

---

lead ingot reportedly excavated in Shouzhou 寿州, Anhui, and one bronze ingot obtained in Beijing). See also Maenchen-Helfen, "A Parthian Coin legend," regarding an ingot purchased by Mrs. William Mayer in 1930s Peking that might be Zheng's piece; another allegedly from Luoyang purchased by the Royal Ontario Museum, Toronto; and another whose photograph Baron Stael-Holstein once showed Paul Pelliot (Maenchen-Helfen suggests these might be copies of Zheng's ingot). In addition see Zuo Ming, "Wai guo ming wen," on four ingots stored in the China Historical Museum 中国历史博物馆: one donated by Paul Houo-Ming-Tse 霍明志 (probably the one in his 1930 catalog); one from Luo Bozhao 罗伯昭 allegedly excavated in Changsha 长沙, Hunan; and two ingots without provenance from Zhou Deyun 周德蕴. The Shanghai Museum also has two unpublished ingots that were received in the 1930s. It is unclear where the Zheng, Mayer, and Stael-Holstein pieces are now, and whether any actually became part of the museum collections listed here (hence the confusion over the number of ingots collected prior to 1965).

3. Li Yong, "Anhui Lu'an Han mu chutu qian bing" and "Anhui Lu'an shi Han mu de qingli." Li Yong was part of the Wanxi Museum team who oversaw in person the excavation of the Lu'an tomb and wooden coffin in which a bronze wine vessel, a bronze tripod, and two bronze ladles were found along with the ingot. The Lu'an region has been a fruitful site for discoveries of Han tombs and Li reported that the tomb was from the Later Han period (though exact details of the dating methodology are not given).

4. An Zhimin, "Jin ban yu jin bing." See the subsequent report published by the Archaeological Research Institute Data Office, "Xi'an Han cheng gu zhi," for the results of chemical tests on all thirteen ingots and on the lid of the Xichazhai sample. The cellar had apparently been previously robbed.

5. Luo Xizhang, "Fufeng Jiangyuan faxian."

6. Liu Dezhe, "Gansu Lingtai faxian." For these excavations and several of those mentioned below, the reported finding of *wuzhu* or other Han coins at the same site is not sufficient evidence for dating. See Wang, *Money on the Silk Road,* 10.

7. See Huang Xiquan, "Baijin sanpin zhuan wen ji" for a summary of information about most of these ingots, including information about the conditions of their discovery. (The ingots were submitted to museums by road workers, farmers, and non-specialists). Of the five Lixian ingots,

ther unpublished samples of unclear provenance that were purchased in coin markets in recent decades.

Li Yong 李勇, of the Wanxi Museum team, reported in 1986 that, at Lu'an, farmers found alongside two such ingots with dragons and "foreign inscription," a square ingot with an inscribed horse design, and two oval ingots with an inscribed tortoise shell pattern.[8] These are pictured in figures 5.10 and 5.11. This was separate from the above-mentioned Lu'an tomb finding. There are other informal reports on the finding of two types of ingot (oval and square) at Changxingzhen (Baoji).[9] Mainly as a result of Li Yong's reports of the Lu'an findings, many numismatists have identified these three ingots or coins (the round ingot with foreign inscription and dragon design, the square ingot with horse design, the oval ingot with carapace design) as the *baijin sanpin* currency described in the Han dynasty *Shiji* and *Hanshu*. The three types have not yet, however, been found together at a single, scientifically excavated site. Thus the excavation data so far are compatible with the hypothesis that these three types of ingots are the Former Han *baijin sanpin* (or are copies of it), but do not prove this hypothesis.[10] Our most reliable report about the ingot with "foreign inscription," from Lu'an (1988), only records that the lead ingot with foreign inscription had a funerary function during the Later Han period. The burial context of the ingots leads to further possibilities that the excavated objects are imitation money or amulets, possibly related to the original "real" currency.

Numismatic Data

The (selective) chemical tests on ingots from the four most reliably recorded excavations have verified that they are made mainly of lead, with unspecified proportions of

---

two were found in Yechi 爷池村 in 1971; and three in Yazui 鸭嘴村 in 1976. The ten Lingtai ingots were found in 1979, three years after the large Lingtai hoard listed above, and later given to the Changwu County Museum 长武博物馆 in Shaanxi. The Xi'an ingot was found in the ruins of the Han city of Chang'an.

8. See Li Yong, "Lu'an faxian." See Wang Bin, "Dui Anhui faxian," on the 1994 purchase of an additional set allegedly from Lu'an.

9. There are two articles in *Kaogu yu wenwu* 1994.5 that introduce the finds in Baoji (including the Changxingzhen find). Zhang Liying, "Tan dui baijin san pin," discusses five ingots (one round, three square, and one oval) that were unearthed with *sizhu banliang* coins in Changxingzhen (Mei county, Baoji city) in October 1990. There are no details of the archaeological context. Hu Cheng, "Baijin san pin de guan jian," mentions five ingots (two round, two square, and one oval) shown to him by a man who found them in an unknown location near Baoji also along with *sizhu banliang* coins in late 1990. The hypothesis that the lead ingot with foreign inscription was the round dragon coin of the *baijin sanpin* was first proposed prior to these finds, in 1990. For a list of other excavated horse and tortoise coins (without the so-called dragon ingot), and for further bibliography, see Huang Xiquan, "Baijin sanpin zhuan wen." One sample of two horse ingots was apparently found in a Han tomb in Jiangsu in 1994.

10. For example, Dai Zhiqiang, "Gudai Zhongguo qianbi," and Liu Sen, "Baijin sanpin lun," maintain that there is insufficient information to say whether or not they are the *baijin sanpin*. Scholars who have recently maintained the foreign production of the ingot include Kang Liushuo, "Guanyu Xila wen," and Qian Boquan, "Gansu chutu de xila wen qian bing."

tin and of (unnamed) other elements. The Xichazhai lead ingots tested positive for silver. The few, but more detailed, chemical tests from other samples have yielded comparable results, although the types of other elements and the proportions vary.[11] There remains some confusion about the material composition of the pre-1965 ingots, several of which were reported to be made of "bronze," but which were never scientifically tested. Similar lead and clay ingots without the foreign inscription have also been found.[12] The individual weights of the excavated ingots from the four most reliable reports range from 91 g (Lu'an) to 144 g (Xichazhai). The published weights of the other ingots are within this range, and some scholars have considered the weight of these ingots in terms of gold ingots that served as Han currency, especially across frontiers.[13] In their size (about 5.5 cm in diameter and 0.4–1.2 cm thick) and in their saucer-like shape, they somewhat resemble one-*jin* Han dynasty gold currency ingots. There is some agreement that the obverse of these ingots depicts a coiled dragon.[14] The two square stamps (0.5 cm) punched near the center of the reverse of each ingot seem to be identical in form but they vary slightly in position and orientation across samples. (One might note that small stamps also appear on excavated gold ingots).[15] What appears to be an identical stamp is present on the excavated horse and tortoise ingots. Li Yong's recent interpretation of the character in each stamp as 少 (*shao*), an abbreviation of 少府 (*shaofu*), the imperial bureau that included the privy treasury, has been widely, but not universally, accepted.[16] There is no consensus on the circular inscription on the reverse, discussed below.

Documentary Evidence

Drawings of dragon, horse, and tortoise ingots, without the foreign inscription, survive in eighteenth-century Chinese and European texts (figures 5.12 and 5.13).[17] Numisma-

---

11. Luo Xizhang, "Handai wai wen qian bing."

12. Huang Xiquan, "Baijin sanpin zhuan wen" has a table of excavated ingots that includes many of these. The Xichazhai hoard included one lead ingot (of a similar shape to the other thirteen) that was used as a lid to the jar in which this group of ingots was found. This lead ingot (no. 1) lacked the circular inscription and was of a different chemical composition to the others.

13. The average weight of the thirteen ingots from Xichazhai was 136 g; the two ingots at Fufeng weighed 120 g and 127 g, respectively; and the 274 Lingtai ingots averaged 116 g in weight. There is no more detailed information on the individual Lingtai ingots except that their weights ranged between 110 g and 118 g. In this appendix, the calculated average for the Xichzhai hoard excludes the fourteenth ingot without circular inscription that was used as a lid (and was considerably heavier than the other ingots). See also Thierry, *Monnaies Chinoises*, 31–32; Scheidel, "Monetary Systems," 148.

14. Whaley argues it is a serpent and elephant.

15. See, for example, Lin, *The Search for Immortality*, 120.

16. Li Yong, "Waiwen qian bing kao." The majority of articles in *Shaanxi qianbi yanjiu*, which includes over twenty articles on the lead ingots and the *baijin sanpin*, accept this interpretation of the stamp. See the articles by Jiang Baolian 姜宝莲 and Yuan Lin 袁林, Wang Bin 汪斌 and Xie Shaoshi 谢少石 in particular. For a repudiation of this interpretation see the article of Kang Liushuo, "Guan yu Xila wai wen" in the same volume.

17. Qianlong, *Qian lu*, 1: 52–53; "Du Halde, *A Description of the Empire of China*, vol. 1, between pages 332 and 333. There are drawings in texts dating back to the Song Dynasty that I have not yet found.

tists have pointed out that they look as if they were reconstructed from the parallel *Shiji* and *Hanshu* descriptions of the *baijin sanpin*. Comparisons between the excavated lead ingots and the Han dynasty descriptions have been numerous but not conclusive. The *Shiji* and *Hanshu* tell us the shape (round), the inscribed design (dragon), the weight (eight *liang*, approximately 125 g),[18] and the composition (silver and tin).[19] The surface shape and obverse design of the excavated ingots are compatible with this description. The weight is also compatible, but less conclusively so, given the 91–144 g range of the excavated ingots. The shape, design, and projected weights of the excavated square horse and oval tortoise ingots are also compatible with the records.[20] The primarily lead composition of the excavated ingots does not, however, match the description. Although tin was found in most samples, and trace silver in some, no silver was reported in the tested ingots from the four most reliably recorded sites. Because the use of *baijin sanpin* as legal tender was abolished by 115 BCE (because of widespread counterfeiting), scholars have argued that the lead samples may be counterfeits or funerary coinage based on the *baijin sanpin*.[21] Neither the size and the cross-sectional ingot-shape, nor the foreign inscription and two punched stamps on the reverse are mentioned in the records. Proponents of the *baijin sanpin* hypothesis have noted, however, that the historical records do mention the role of Emperor Wu's *shaofu* in the production of the *baijin sanpin*.[22]

---

18. Eight *liang* was equivalent to half of one *jin*. The Former Han *jin* has been approximated to 245 g in Loewe, *The Ch'in and Han Empires*, xxxviii.

19. *Shiji* 30.1427: "其一曰重八兩，圜之，其文龍." It goes on: "名曰「白選」，直三千" (i.e., they were called *bai xuan* and were worth 3,000 cash). For the same passage see *Hanshu* 24b.1164. There are also descriptions of the so-called horse and tortoise coins, and of an associated auspicious white deer hide square that had cash value (400,000) but was used by nobility when paying tribute at court.

20. The historical records do not give precise weights for the horse and tortoise coins, but do give cash values (500 and 300 cash, respectively). On the premise that weight and cash value correspond, scholars have argued that the recorded weights of these two other ingots correspond to those expected of the *baijin sanpin*. See Zhao Xiaoming, "Xi Han baijin sanpin." On the tortoise design and inscription see Huang Xiquan, "Baijin sanpin zhuan wen."

21. The Han-dynasty 錢律 (Statute on coins) excavated along with other legal statutes dating from 186 BCE in tomb no. 247 at Zhangjiashan 张家山, Hubei province, suggests lead was used for counterfeiting, at least in the early Han dynasty: "錢徑十分寸八以上，雖缺鑠，文章頗可智(知)，而非殊折及鉛錢也，皆為行錢" (All coins over eight-tenths of a *cun* [approx. 18.5 mm] in diameter, even if they are eroded, [as long as] their inscriptions are somewhat recognizable, and if they are not broken or lead money, may circulate as coins.") See *Zhangjiashan hanmu zhujian*, 159. The *Shiji* (30.1427, 30.1434, and 18.953), *Hanshu* (6.178, 24b.1168, and 90.3654), and Wang Liqi, *Yantielun*, 57, emphasize that the widespread illegal minting of the *baijin sanpin* led to its abolition. Some scholars have also argued that the original *baijin sanpin* were largely made of lead—and that either our interpretation of the text is incorrect, or that Sima Qian was incorrect in his original description in the *Shiji*. See Zhao Xiaoming, "Xi Han baijin sanpin xiang guan wenti" for comparisons with the composition of Han mirrors.

22. *Shiji* 30.1425, *Hanshu* 24b.1163.

The Inscription

The least understood element in these ingots remains the circular inscription. It is not mentioned in the historical descriptions of the *baijin sanpin*, nor is it found on the horse or tortoise ingots. However, these accounts do say that the dragon ingots were called *bai xuan* 白選 or 白撰, an unattested phrase that the scholar Mark Whaley suggests refers to the foreign writing on the ingots.[23] Nor have convincing prototypes been found. It is unclear which ingots may have been cast from the same mold. The scholar An Zhimin suggested the thirteen ingots from the same Xichazhai site were not cast from the same mold.[24] However photographs and rubbings from both the pre-1961 collections and post-1961 excavations show a strikingly similar sequence of graphs or signs around most of the ingots. The published rubbing of the 1988 Lu'an tomb ingot unfortunately is not clear enough to verify this sequence. A few scholars have also suggested Chinese origins of the graphs.[25] The numismatist Joe Cribb has argued that their style resembles coinage of Indo-Scythian and Kushan kingdoms of Northwest India and Bactria, rather than that on Parthian coins.[26] Some scholars have read the inscription on the other ingots as a blundered and possibly inverted Greek inscription common on Asian Hellenistic coins beginning ΒΑΣΙΛΕΩΣ ΒΑΣΙΛΕΩΝ (*basileōs basileōn*, meaning "[coin of . . .] King of Kings").[27] The numismatists François Thierry and Dang Shunmin, who both accept that these ingots are the *baijin*, suggest that the most likely template for these ingots was money, familiar to the Han dynasty, of Indo-Greek kings like Apollodotus I (c. 180–160 BCE), Antimachus II (ca. 165–155 BCE), Eucratides I (170–145 BCE), and their successors.[28] Mark Whaley, who also identifies the ingot with the *baijin*, hypothesizes a Middle Indo-Aryan Brāhmī inscription: "Jagaṭhera the Hero (=the Buddha) offers ten creepers (=ten forms of grace), Offering stability, Dissolving Impurity."[29] A conclusive analysis of the inscription and the identity of the ingots may depend on future archaeological discoveries.

---

23. See Whaley, "A Middle Indo-Aryan Inscription" for a thoughtful discussion (though it does not include the *Hanshu* 24B.1164 variant 白撰 or the *Suoyin* comment to *Shiji* 30.1427).

24. An Zhimin, "Jin ban yu jin bing." Michael Alram, "Lead ingots with barbarous Greek inscription," presents two of the ingots from the Lingtai 1976 hoard as being cast from the same mold. Note that the published photograph in the catalog is inverted and it has been re-inverted for figure 5.9. (Alram confirmed this inversion in an e-mail message to the author, July 2, 2007.) A typological and epigraphical analysis of the ingots across samples might yield information on the relation between different molds, of the kind presented in François Thierry, "On the Tang coins collected by Pelliot in Chinese Turkestan (1906–1909)," especially 153–57.

25. See, for example, Zhou Yanling, "Xi Han qian bing ming wen"; Zhao Xiaoming, "Xi Han baijin sanpin xiang guan wenti"; Shi Xiaoqun "Long wen qian bing tan xi."

26. Joe Cribb, "Chinese Lead Ingots with Barbarous Greek Inscriptions"; Dang Shunmin, "Wai wen qian bing xin tan."

27. Many scholars have taken as a point of departure O. Maenchen-Helfen's 1952 reconstruction of the inscription.

28. Thierry, *Monnaies Chinoises*, 31–32.

29. Whaley, "Middle Indo-Aryan Inscription."

Bibliography

Abu-Lughod, Janet. "Discontinuities and Persistence. One World System or a Succession of Systems?" In Frank and Gills, *The World System,* 278–91.

Adorno, Theodor. "Commitment." In *Aesthetics and Politics* by Theodor Adorno, Walter Benjamin, Ernst Bloch, Bertolt Brecht, and Georg Lukács. Afterword by Fredric Jameson. Translated by Francis McDonagh. London: Verso, 1992.

Alcock, Susan E., Terence N. D'Altroy, Kathleen D. Morrison, and Carla N. Sinopoli, eds. *Empires: Perspectives from Archaeology and History.* Cambridge: Cambridge University Press, 2001.

Allan, Sarah. *The Shape of the Turtle: Myth, Art, and Cosmos in Early China.* Albany, NY: State University of New York Press, 1991.

Allen, Joseph R. "Postface: A Literary History of the *Shi jing.*" In Allen, *The Book of Songs,* 336–84.

———, ed. *The Book of Songs.* Edited with Additional Translations and Postface. Translated by Arthur Waley. New York: Grove Press, 2000.

Alram, Michael. "Lead Ingots with Barbarous Greek Inscription." In Juliano and Lerner, *Monks and Merchants,* 37.

An Zhimin 安志敏. "Jin ban yu jin bing—Chu Han jin bi ji qi you guan wenti" 金版与金饼 – 楚汉金币及其有关问题. *Kaogu xuebao* 考古学报 (1973.2): 81–82.

Appadurai, Arjun. "Introduction: Commodities and the Politics of Value." In *The Social Life of Things: Commodities in Cultural Perspective,* edited by Arjun Appadurai, 3–63. Cambridge: Cambridge University Press, 1986.

Aristotle. *The Nicomachean Ethics.* London: Heinemann, 1956.

———. *The Politics.* London: Heinemann, 1932.

Arrighi, Giovanni. *Adam Smith in Beijing: Lineages of the Twenty-First Century.* New York: Verso, 2007.

Bagley, Robert, ed. *Ancient Sichuan: Treasures from a Lost Civilization.* Princeton: Princeton University Press, 2001.

Bai Shangnu 白尚恕, ed. *Jiu zhang suan shu zhu shi* 九章算術注釋. Beijing: Kexue, 1983.

Bai Yulin 白玉林. *Shiji jie du* 史記解讀. Beijing: Hualing, 2006.

Ban Gu 班固. *Hanshu* 漢書. Beijing: Zhonghua shuju, 1962.

Bang, Peter. "Commanding and Consuming the World: Empire, Tribute and Trade in Roman and Chinese History." In *Rome and China: Comparative Perspectives on Ancient*

World Empires, edited by Walter Scheidel, 100–120. Oxford & New York: Oxford University Press, 2009.

Barber, E. J. W. *Prehistoric Textiles: The Development of Cloth in the Neolithic and Bronze Ages with Special Reference to the Aegean.* Princeton: Princeton University Press, 1991.

Barbieri-Low, Anthony J. *Artisans in Early Imperial China.* Seattle: University of Washington Press, 2007.

———. "Craftsman's Literacy: Uses of Writing by Male and Female Artisans in Qin and Han China." In Li and Branner, *Writing and Literacy*, 370–99.

Barfield, Thomas J. *The Perilous Frontier: Nomadic Empires and China.* Cambridge, MA: Blackwell, 1989.

———. "The Shadow Empires: Imperial State Formation along the Chinese-Nomad Frontier." In Alcock, *Empires*, 10–41.

Baxter, William H., [III]. *A Handbook of Old Chinese Phonology.* Trends in Linguistics 64. Berlin: Mouton de Gruyter, 1992.

Beckwith, Christopher I. *Empires of the Silk Road: A History of Central Eurasia from the Bronze Age to the Present.* Princeton: Princeton University Press, 2009.

Beecroft, Alexander. *Authorship and Cultural Identity in Early Greece and China: Patterns of Literary Circulation.* Cambridge: Cambridge University Press, 2010.

Behr, Wolfgang. "'To Translate' Is 'to Exchange' 譯者言易也—Linguistic Diversity and the Terms for Translation in Ancient China." In *Mapping Meanings: The Field of New Learning in Late Qing China*, edited by Michael Lackner and Natascha Vittinghoff, 173–209. Leiden: Brill, 2004.

Beningson, Susan L. "The Spiritual Geography of Han Dynasty Tombs." In Beningson and Liu, *Providing for the Afterlife*, 1–16.

Beningson, Susan L., and Cary L. Liu. *Providing for the Afterlife: "Brilliant Artifacts" from Shandong.* With contributions from Annette L. Juliano, Zhixin Sun, and David A. Graff; edited by J. May Lee Barrett. New York: China Institute Gallery, 2005.

Bernal, Martin. *Black Athena: The Afroasiatic Roots of Classical Civilization.* Vol. 1, *The Fabrication of Ancient Greece, 1785–1985.* London: Free Association Books, 1987.

Bhabha, Homi K. *The Location of Culture.* London: Routledge, 1994.

Bielenstein, Hans. *The Bureaucracy of Han Times.* Cambridge: Cambridge University Press, 1980.

Bielenstein, Hans, and Nathan Sivin. "Further Comments on the Use of Statistics in the Study of Han Dynasty Portents." *Journal of the American Oriental Society* 97, no. 2 (April–June 1977): 185–87.

Birrell, Anne. *Popular Songs and Ballads of Han China.* Honolulu: University of Hawai'i Press, 1993.

Bloch, Maurice, and Jonathan Parry, eds. *Money and the Morality of Exchange.* Cambridge: Cambridge University Press, 1989.

Bohannan, Paul. "The Impact of Money on an African Subsistence Economy." *Journal of Economic History* 19 (1959): 491–503.

Boltz, William G. "The Composite Nature of Early Chinese Texts." In Kern, *Text and Ritual*, 50–78.

———. *The Origin and Development of the Chinese Writing System.* New Haven: American Oriental Society, 2003.

Bottéro, Françoise. "Cang Jie and the Invention of Writing." In *Studies in Chinese Language and Culture*, edited by C. Anderl and H. Eifring, 135–55. Oslo: Hermes Academic Publishing.

Bourdieu, Pierre. *Language and Symbolic Power*. Cambridge, MA: Harvard University Press, 1991.

———. *The Logic of Practice*. Translated by Richard Nice. Cambridge: Polity, 1990.

Bray, Francesca. *Agriculture*. Vol. 6, Part 2 in *Science and Civilisation in China*, edited by Joseph Needham. Cambridge: Cambridge University Press, 1984.

———. *Technology and Gender: Fabrics of Power in Late Imperial China*. Berkeley: University of California Press, 1997.

———. "Toward a Critical History of Non-Western Technology." In *China and Historical Capitalism: Genealogies of Sinological Knowledge*, edited by Timothy Brook and Gregory Blue, 158–209. Cambridge: Cambridge University Press, 1999.

Breckenridge, Carol, Sheldon Pollock, Homi K. Bhabha, and Dipesh Chakrabarty, eds. *Cosmopolitanism*. Durham: Duke University Press, 2002.

Brindley, Erica. "Barbarians or Not? Ethnicity and Changing Conceptions of the Ancient Yue (Viet) Peoples ca. 400–50 BC." *Asia Major* 16, no. 1 (2003): 1–32.

———. *Music, Cosmology, and the Politics of Harmony in Early China*. Albany: State University of New York Press, 2012.

Brook, Timothy. "Capitalism and the Writing of Modern History in China." In *China and Historical Capitalism: Genealogies of Sinological Knowledge*, edited by Timothy Brook and Gregory Blue, 110–57. Cambridge: Cambridge University Press, 1999.

———. "Weber, Mencius, and the History of Chinese Capitalism." *Asian Perspective* 19, no. 1 (1995): 79–98.

Brooks, A. Taeko. "Evolution of the bà 霸 'Hegemon' Theory." *Warring States Papers* 1 (2010): 220–26.

Brooks, E. Bruce, and A. Taeko Brooks. *The Original Analects: Sayings of Confucius and His Successors*. New York: Columbia University Press, 1998.

Brown, Bill. "The Matter of Materialism: Literary Mediations." In *Material Powers: Cultural Studies, History and the Material Turn*, edited by Tony Bennett and Patrick Joyce, 60–78. London: Routledge, 2010.

———. "Thing Theory." In *Things*, edited by Bill Brown, 1–22. Chicago: University of Chicago Press, 2004.

Brown, Miranda. *The Politics of Mourning in Early China*. Albany: State University of New York Press, 2007.

———. "Mothers and Sons in Warring States and Han China, 453 B.C.–A.D. 220." *Nan Nü: Men, Women and Gender in Early and Imperial China* 5.2 (2003): 137–69.

Brown, Miranda, and Rafe de Crespigny. "Adoption in Han China." *Journal of the Economic and Social History of the Orient* 52, no. 2 (2009): 229–66.

Bulag, Uradyn E. *The Mongols at China's Edge: History and the Politics of National Unity*. Lanham: Rowman and Littlefield, 2002.

Burkert, Walter. *The Orientalizing Revolution: Near Eastern Influence on Greek Culture in the Early Archaic Age*. Translated by Walter Burkert and Margaret E. Pinder. Cambridge, MA: Harvard University Press, 1992.

Butler, Judith. *Antigone's Claim: Kinship between Life and Death*. New York: Columbia University Press, 2000.

————. *Excitable Speech: A Politics of the Performative.* New York: Routledge, 1997.

————. *Gender Trouble: Feminism and the Subversion of Identity.* London: Routledge, 1990.

Cai Jixiang 蔡季襄. "Han xiyu da Qin guo niao ti jin kao" 漢西域大秦國裊蹄金考. *Quanbi* 泉幣 19 (1943): 1–6.

Cai, Zong-qi. *Configurations of Comparative Poetics. Three Perspectives on Western and Chinese Literary Criticism.* Honolulu: University of Hawai'i Press, 2002.

————, ed. *Chinese Aesthetics: The Ordering of Literature, the Arts, and the Universe in the Six Dynasties.* Honolulu: University of Hawai'i Press, 2004.

Cao Shenggao 曹胜高. *Han fu yu Handai zhidu: yi ducheng, jiaolie, liyi wei li* 汉赋与汉代制度 – 以都城, 校猎, 礼仪为例. Beijing: Beijing daxue, 2006.

Carson, Anne. *Economy of the Unlost.* Princeton: Princeton University Press, 1999.

Carsten, Janet. "Cooking Money: Gender and the Symbolic Transformation of Means of Exchange in a Malay Fishing Community." In Bloch and Parry, *Money and the Morality of Exchange*, 117–41.

Chang, Chun-shu. *The Rise of the Chinese Empire.* Vol. 1, *Nation, State, and Imperialism in Early China, ca. 1600 B.C.–A.D. 8.* Ann Arbor: University of Michigan Press, 2007.

————. *The Rise of Chinese Empire.* Vol. 2, *Frontier, Immigration, and Empire in Han China, 130 B.C.–A.D. 157.* Ann Arbor: University of Michigan Press, 2007.

Chang, James. "History of Chinese Economic Thought." *History of Political Economy* 19, no. 3 (1987): 481–502.

Chang, K. C. "Ancient China and Its Anthropological Significance." In *Archaeological Thought in America*, edited by C. C. Lamberg-Karlovsky, 155–66. Cambridge: Cambridge University Press, 1989.

Chang, K. C., et al. *The Formation of Chinese Civilization: An Archaeological Perspective.* Edited by Sarah Allan. New Haven: Yale University Press, 2005.

Chavannes, Édouard. *Les Mémoires Historiques de Se-ma Ts'ien.* 5 vols. 1895–1905. Reprint. Paris: Librairie d'Amérique et d'Orient, 1967–69.

Chemla, Karine. "Documenting a Process of Abstraction in the Mathematics of Ancient China." In *Studies in Chinese Language and Culture—Festschrift in Honor of Christoph Harbsmeier on the Occasion of His 60th Birthday*, edited by Christoph Anderl and Halvor Eifring, 169–94. Oslo: Hermes Academic Publishing and Bookshop, 2006.

————. "Usage of the Terms 'Likewise' and 'Like' in Texts for Algorithms. Algorithmic Analogies in Ancient China." In *Analogien in Naturwissenschaft und Medizin*, edited by Klaus Hentschel, 329–57. Halle: Leopoldina, 2010.

Chemla, Karine, and Guo Shuchun, trans. *Les Neuf Chapitres: Le Classique Mathématique de la Chine Ancienne et Ses Commentaires: Édition Critique Bilingue.* Paris: Dunod, 2005.

Chen, Duxiu. "On Literary Revolution." In *Modern Chinese Literary Thought: Writings on Literature 1893–1945*, edited by Kirk A. Denton, 123–45. Stanford: Stanford University Press, 1996.

Chen Huan-chang. *The Economic Principles of Confucius and His School.* 1911. Reprint, Changsha: Yue Lu Press, 2005.

Chen Huan-chang 陈焕章. *Kongmen licai xue* 孔门理财学. Beijing: Zhonghua shuju, 2010.

Chen, Jack Wei. *The Poetics of Sovereignty: On Emperor Taizong of the Tang Dynasty* Cambridge, MA: Harvard University Asia Center, 2010.

———. "Sovereignty, Coinage, and Kinship." *Positions: East Asia Cultures Critique* 21, no. 3 (2013): 637–58.

Chen Jianming, ed. *Noble Tombs at Mawangdui: Art and Life of the Changsha Kingdom, Third Century BCE to First Century CE.* Changsha: Yuelu Publishing House, 2008.

Chen Liping 陈丽平. *Liu Xiang "Lie nü zhuan" yan jiu* 刘向《列女传》研究. Beijing: Zhongguo shehui kexue, 2010.

Chen Mengjia 陈夢家. "Zhan guo du liang heng shi lüe shuo" 战国度量衡略说. *Kaogu* 考古 (1964.6): 312–14.

Chen, Yu-shih. "The Historical Template of Pan Chao's 'Nü Chieh.'" *T'oung pao* 82 (1996): 229–57.

Chen Zhenyu 陈振裕. "Jiangling Fenghuangshan yi liu ba hao Han mu" 江陵凤凰山 一六八号汉墓. *Kaogu xuebao* 考古学报 (1993.4): 455–513.

Chen Zhi 陈直. "Han Jin ren dui Shiji de chuanbo ji qi pingjia" 汉晋人对史记的传播 及其评价. In *Sima Qian yu Shiji lunji* 司馬遷與史記論集, 215–42. Xi'an: Shaanxi renmin, 1982.

———. *Hanshu xin zheng* 漢書新証. Tianjin: Tianjin renmin, 1979.

———. *Juyan Han jian yan jiu* 居延汉简研究. Beijing: Zhonghua shuju, 2009.

———. *Liang Han jingji shiliao luncong* 兩漢經濟史料論叢. Beijing: Zhonghua shuju, 2008.

———. *Shiji xin zheng* 史記新証. Tianjin: Tianjin renmin, 1979.

Chi Wanxing 池万兴. *Sima Qian minzu sixiang chan shi* 司馬遷民族思想闡釋. Xi'an: Renmin jiaoyu, 1995.

Chin, Tamara T. "Antiquarian as Ethnographer: Han Ethnicity in Early China Studies." In *Critical Han Studies: The History, Representation, and Identity of China's Majority,* edited by Thomas Mullaney, James Patrick Leibold, Stéphane Gros, and Eric Armand Vanden Bussche, 128–46. Berkeley: University of California Press, 2012.

———. "Defamiliarizing the Foreigner: Sima Qian's Ethnography and Han-Xiongnu Marriage Diplomacy." *Harvard Journal of Asiatic Studies* 70, no. 2 (December 2010): 311–54.

———. "The Invention of the Silk Road, 1877." *Critical Inquiry* 40, no.1 (Autumn 2013): 194–219.

———. "Orienting Mimesis: Marriage and the Book of Songs." *Representations* 94, no. 1 (Spring 2006): 53–79.

Chow, Rey. *The Protestant Ethnic and the Spirit of Capitalism.* New York: Columbia University Press, 2002.

———. "Introduction: On Chineseness as a Theoretical Problem." In *Modern Chinese Literary and Cultural Studies in the Age of Theory: Reimagining a Field,* edited by Rey Chow, 1–25. Durham: Duke University Press, 2000.

Comaroff, Jean. "Ethnography." In *New Dictionary of the History of Ideas: Volume 2,* edited by Maryanne Cline Horowitz, 725–28. Detroit: Charles Scribner's Sons, 2005.

Comaroff, John, and Jean Comaroff. *Ethnography and the Historical Imagination.* Boulder: Westview Press, 1992.

Chu, Julie Y. *Cosmologies of Credit: Transnational Mobility and the Politics of Destination in China.* Durham: Duke University Press, 2010.

Ch'u T'ung-tsu. *Han Social Structure.* Edited by Jack L. Dull. Seattle: University of Washington Press, 1972.

Chunqiu Zuozhuan zhu 春秋左傳注. Annotated by Yang Bojun 楊柏峻. Revised edition. Beijing: Zhonghua shuju, 2000.

Clifford, James. "Introduction: Partial Truths." In *The Poetics and Politics of Ethnography,* edited by James Clifford and George E. Marcus. *Writing Culture,* 1–26. Berkeley: University of California Press, 1986.

Clunas, Craig. *Superfluous Things: Material Culture and Social Status in Early Modern China.* Cambridge: Polity Press, 1991.

Coblin, W. South. "The Finals of Yang Xiong's Language." *The Journal of Chinese Linguistics* 12 (1984): 1–52.

———. "The Rimes of Chang-an in Middle Han Times, Part I: The Late Western Han Period." *Acta Orientalia* 47 (1986): 93–131.

———. "Some Sound Changes in the Western Han Dialect of Shu." *Journal of Chinese Linguistics* 14 (1986): 184–226.

Connery, Christopher Leigh. *The Empire of the Text: Writing and Authority in Early Imperial China.* Lanham: Rowman & Littlefield Publishers, 1998.

Cook, Constance A. *Death in Ancient China: The Tale of One Man's Journey.* Leiden: Brill, 2006.

Cook, Constance A., and John S. Major, eds. *Defining Chu: Image and Reality in Ancient China.* Honolulu: University of Hawai'i Press, 1999.

Couvreur, Seraphin. *Chou King: Texte Chinois avec Double Traduction en Française et en Latin des Annotations et un Vocabulaire.* Sien Hsien: Mission catholique, 1934.

Cribb, Joe. "Chinese Lead Ingots with Barbarous Greek Inscriptions." *Coin Hoards* 4 (1978): 76–78.

———. "An Historical Survey of the Precious Metal Currencies of China." *The Numismatic Chronicle* 139 (1979): 185–203.

———. "The Sino-Kharoshthi Coins of Khotan: Their Attributions and Relevance to Kushan Chronology, Part 1." *Numismatic Chronicle* 144 (1984): 128–52.

———. "The Sino-Kharoshthi Coins of Khotan: Their Attributions and Relevance to Kushan Chronology, Part 2." *Numismatic Chronicle* 145 (1985): 136–49.

Crossley, Pamela Kyle. "Thinking about Ethnicity in Early Modern China." *Late Imperial China* 11, no. 1 (June 1990): 1–35.

Csikszentmihalyi, Mark. *Readings in Han Chinese Thought.* Indianapolis: Hackett, 2006.

———. *Material Virtue: Ethics and the Body in Early China.* Leiden: Brill, 2004.

Csikszentmihalyi, Mark, and Michael Nylan. "Constructing Lineages and Inventing Traditions Through Exemplary Figures in Early China." *T'oung Pao* 89 (2003): 59–99.

Cui Mingde 崔明德. *Liang Han minzu guanxi sixiangshi* 兩汉民族关系思想史. Beijing: Renmin, 2007.

Cullen, Christopher. *Astronomy and Mathematics in Ancient China: The Zhou bi suan jing.* Cambridge: Cambridge University Press, 1996.

———. "Numbers, numeracy and the cosmos." In Nylan and Loewe, *China's Early Empires,* 323–38.

———. "The *Suan shu shu* 筭數書 'Writings on Reckoning.'" *Needham Research Institute Working Papers* 1 (2004).

———. "The *Suan shu shu.* 'Writings on Reckoning': Rewriting the History of Early Chinese Mathematics in the Light of an Excavated Manuscript." *Historia Mathematica* 34 (2007): 10–44.

Curtin, Philip D. *Cross-Cultural Trade in World History.* Cambridge: Cambridge University Press, 1984.

Dai Zhiqiang 戴志强. "Gudai Zhongguo de qianbi" 古代中国的钱币. *Zhongguo qianbi* 中国钱币 (2003.2): 5–12.

Dang Shunmin 党顺民. "Wai wen qian bing xin tan" 外文铅饼新探. *Kaogu yu wenwu* (1994.5): 84–89.

Davydova, A. V. *Ivolginskiĭ arkheologicheskiĭ kompleks.* Sankt-Peterburg: Fond Aziatika, 1995.

De Crespigny, Rafe. *A Biographical Dictionary of Later Han to the Three Kingdoms (23–220 AD).* Leiden: Brill, 2007.

———. *Northern Frontier: The Policies and Strategy of the Later Han Empire.* Canberra: Faculty of Asian Studies, Australian National University, 1984.

De Pee, Christian. *The Writing of Weddings in Middle-Period China: Text and Ritual Practice in the Eighth through Fourteenth Centuries.* Albany: State University of New York Press, 2007.

Declercq, Dominik. *Writing against the State: Political Rhetorics in Third and Fourth Century China.* Leiden: Brill, 1998.

Denecke, Wiebke. *The Dynamics of Masters Literature: Early Chinese Thought from Confucius to Han Feizi.* Cambridge, MA: Harvard University Press, 2010.

Deng, Gang. *The Premodern Chinese Economy: Structural Equilibrium and Capitalist Sterility.* New York: Routledge, 1999.

Denton, Kirk A., ed. *Modern Chinese Literary Thought: Writings on Literature, 1893–1945.* Stanford: Stanford University Press, 1996.

Derrida, Jacques. *Given Time: Counterfeit Money.* Vol. 1. Translated by Peggy Kamuf. Chicago: University of Chicago Press, 1992

Di Cosmo, Nicola. *Ancient China and Its Enemies: The Rise of Nomadic Power in East Asian History.* Cambridge: Cambridge University Press, 2002.

———. "Ancient Inner Asian Nomads: Their Economic Basis and Its Significance in Chinese History." *Journal of Asiatic Studies* 54, no. 4 (1994): 1092–1126.

———. "Ethnography of the Nomads and 'Barbarian' History in Han China." In *Intentional History: Spinning Time in Ancient Greece,* edited by Lin Foxhall, Hans-Joachim Gehrke, and Nino Luraghi, 229–325. Stuttgart: Franz Steiner Verlag, 2010.

———. "Han Frontiers, Towards an Integrated View." *Journal of the American Oriental Society* 129, no. 2 (2009): 199–214.

———, ed. *Military Culture in Imperial China.* Cambridge, MA: Harvard University Press, 2009.

Didi-Huberman, Georges. "The Imaginary Breeze: Remarks on the Air of the Quattrocento." *Journal of Visual Culture* 2, no. 3 (December 2003): 275–89.

Diény, Jean-Pierre. *Aux Origines de la Poésie Classique en Chine. Étude sur la Poésie Lyrique à l'Époque des Han.* Leiden: Brill, 1968.

Ding Bangyou 丁邦友. *Handai wujia xintan* 漢代物價新探. Beijing: Zhongguo shehui kexue, 2007.

Dirlik, Arif. *Revolution and History: The Origins of Marxist Historiography in China, 1919–1937.* Berkeley: University of California Press, 1978.

Dorofeeva-Lichtmann, Vera. "Mapping a 'Spiritual' Landscape: Representing Terrestrial Space in the *Shan hai jing.*" In *Political Frontiers, Ethnic Boundaries, and Human Geographies in Chinese History,* edited by Nicola di Cosmo and Don Wyatt, 35–79. London: RoutledgeCurzon, 2003.

Du Halde, P. J. B. *A Description of the Empire of China and Chinese-Tartary, Together with the Kingdoms of Korea, and Tibet Containing the Geography and History (Natural as well as Civil) of those Countries—from the French of P.J. B Du Halde, Jesuit.* London: E. Cave, 1741.

Dull, Jack. "Marriage and Divorce in Han China: A Glimpse at 'Pre-Confucian' Society." In *Chinese Family Law and Social Change in Historical and Comparative Perspective,* edited by David C. Buxbaum. 23–74. Seattle: University of Washington Press, 1978.

Durrant, Stephen W. *The Cloudy Mirror: Tension and Conflict in the Writings of Sima Qian.* Albany: State University of New York Press, 1995.

Ebrey, Patricia Buckley. *Women and the Family in Chinese History.* New York: Routledge, 2003.

———. "The Economic and Social History of Later Han." In *The Cambridge History of China,* Vol. 1, *The Ch'in and Han Empires, 221 BC–AD 220,* edited by Denis Twitchett and Michael Loewe, 608–48. Cambridge: Cambridge University Press, 1987.

Ekström, Martin. "On the Concept of Correlative Cosmology." *Bulletin of the Museum of Far Eastern Antiquities* 72 (2000): 7–12.

Elliott, Mark C. *The Manchu Way: The Eight Banners and Ethnic Identity in Late Imperial China.* Stanford: Stanford University Press, 2001.

Elman, Benjamin A. *Classicism, Politics, and Kinship: The Ch'ang-Chou School of New Text Confucianism in Late Imperial China.* Berkeley: University of California Press, 1990.

Elvin, Mark. *Pattern of the Chinese Past.* Stanford: Stanford University Press, 1973.

———. *The Retreat of the Elephants: An Environmental History of China.* New Haven: Yale University Press, 2004.

Emura Haruki 江村治樹. *Shunjū Sengoku jidai seidō kahei no seisei to tenkai* 春秋戦国時代青銅貨幣の生成と展開. Tōkyō: Kyūko Shoin, 2011.

Erickson, Susan N. "Images of Mountains: Boshanlu, Hill Jars, and Hu Vessels." In *Re-carving China's Past: Art, Archaeology, and Architecture of the "Wu Family Shrine,"* edited by Cary Y. Liu, Michael Nylan, and Anthony Barbieri-Low, 402–13. New Haven: Yale University Press, 2005.

———. "Money Trees of the Eastern Han Dynasty." *Bulletin of the Museum of Far Eastern Antiquities* 66 (1994): 5–115.

———. " 'Twirling Their Long Sleeves, They Dance Again and Again . . .': Jade Plaque Sleeve Dancers of the Western Han Dynasty." *Ars Orientalis* 24 (1994): 39–63.

Erickson, Susan N., Yi Sŏng-mi, and Michael Nylan. "The Archaeology of Outlying Lands." In Nylan and Loewe, *China's Early Empires,* 135–68.

Fabian, Johannes. *Time and the Other: How Anthropology Makes Its Object.* New York: Columbia University Press, 1983.

Falkenhausen, Lothar von. *Chinese Society in the Age of Confucius (1000–250 BC): The Archaeological Evidence.* Los Angeles: Cotsen Institute of Archaeology, 2006.

————. "The Concept of *wen* in the Ancient Chinese Ancestral Cult." *CLEAR* 18 (1996): 1–22.

————. "Die Seiden mit chinesischen Inschriften." In Schmidt-Colinet, Stauffer, and Al-Ascad, *Die Textilien aus Palmyra*, 58–81.

————. "The E Jun Qi Metal Tallies: Inscribed Texts and Ritual Contexts." In Kern, *Text and Ritual*, 79–123.

————. "Inconsequential Incomprehensions: Some Instances of Chinese Writing in Alien Contexts." *Res* 35 (1999): 42–69.

————. "Notes on the History of the 'Silk Routes.'" In Mair, *Secrets of the Silk Road*, 58–68.

————. Review of *Shunjū Sengoku jidai seidō kahei no seisei to tenkai* 春秋戦国時代青銅貨幣の生成と展開, by Emura Haruki 江村治樹. Forthcoming in *Tōyōshi kenkyū*.

Fan Wenlan 范文澜. *Zhongguo tong shi* 中国通史. Beijing: Renmin, 2008.

————. "Zi Qin Han qi Zhongguo chengwei tongyi guojia de yuanyin" 自秦汉起中国成为统一国家的原因. In Fan Wenlan, *Han minzu*, 1–16.

————, ed. *Han minzu xingcheng wenti taolunji* 漢民族形成問題討論集. Beijing: Xinhua shudian, 1957.

Farmer, J. Michael. *The Talent of Shu: Qiao Zhou and the Intellectual World of Early Medieval Sichuan*. Albany: State University of New York Press, 2007.

Farquhar, Judith B. *Appetites: Food and Sex in Post-Socialist China*. Durham: Duke University Press, 2002.

Fei Xiaotong 费孝通. "'Hanren' kao." In *Zhonghua minzu duoyuan yiti geju* 中华民族多元一体格局, 137–52. Beijing: Zhongyang minzu xueyuan, 1989.

Feng Liangfang 冯良方. *Han fu yu jing xue* 漢賦與經學. Beijing: Zhongguo shehui kexue, 2004.

Finley, M. I. *The Ancient Economy*. Berkeley: University of California Press, 1999.

Fiskesjö, Magnus. "On the 'Raw' and the 'Cooked' Barbarians of Imperial China." *Inner Asia* 1, no. 2 (1999): 139–68.

Fiskesjö, Magnus, and Chen Xingcan. *China before China: Johan Gunnar Andersson, Ding Wenjiang, and the Discovery of China's Prehistory*. Museum of Far Eastern Antiquities Monograph Series 15. Stockholm: Museum of Far Eastern Antiquities, 2004.

Flad, Rowan K., and Pochan Chen. *Ancient Central China: Centers and Peripheries along the Yangzi River*. Case Studies in Early Societies. Cambridge: Cambridge University Press, 2003.

Flynn, Dennis Owen, and Arturo Giráldez. *China and the Birth of Globalization in the 16th Century*. Farnham, Surrey: Ashgate, 2010.

————. "Money and Growth without Development: The Case of Ming China." In *Asia Pacific Dynamism 1550–2000*, edited by H. Kawakatsu and A. J. H. Latham, 199–215. London: Routledge, 2000.

Forsyth, T. D. "On the Buried Cities in the Shifting Sands of the Great Desert of Gobi." *Journal of the Royal Geographical Society* 47 (1877): 1–17.

Foucault, Michel. *Language, Counter-Memory, Practice: Selected Essays and Interviews*. Translated by Donald Bouchard and Sherry Simon. Ithaca, NY: Cornell University Press, 1977.

————. "Nietzsche, Genealogy, History." In *Language, Counter-Memory, Practice*, 139–64.

———. *The Order of Things: An Archaeology of the Human Sciences.* New York: Pantheon Books, 1971.

———. "Politics and the Study of Discourse." In *The Foucault Effect: Studies in Governmentality. With Two Lectures and an Interview with Michel Foucault.* Edited by Graham Burchell, Colin Gordon, and Peter Miller. Chicago: Chicago University Press, 1991.

———. *Security, Territory, Population. Lectures at the Collège de France 1977–1978.* Edited by Michael Senellart. Translated by Graham Burchell. New York: Picador, 2007.

———. "What Is an Author?" In *Language, Counter-Memory, Practice,* 113–38.

Frank, Andre Gunder. *ReOrient: Global Economy in the Asian Age.* Berkeley: University of California Press, 1998.

Frank, Andre Gunder, and Barry K. Gills. "The 5,000 Year World System. An Interdisciplinary Introduction." In Frank and Gills, *The World System,* 3–58.

———, eds. *The World System: Five Hundred Years or Five Thousand?* London: Routledge, 1993.

Frankel, Hans H. "Cai Yan and the Poems Attributed to Her." *Chinese Literature: Essays, Articles, Reviews* 5, no. 1/2 (July 1983): 133–56.

———. *The Flowering Plum and the Palace Lady: Interpretations of Chinese Poetry.* New Haven: Yale University Press, 1976.

Freedgood, Elaine. *The Ideas in Things: Fugitive Meaning in the Victorian Novel.* Chicago: University of Chicago Press, 2006.

Fried, Daniel. "A Never-Stable Word: Zhuangzi's Zhiyan and 'Tipping-Vessel' Irrigation." *Early China* 31 (2007): 145–70.

Fuyang Hanjian zhengli zu 阜阳汉简整理组, ed. "Fuyang Hanjian *Cang jie pian* shiwen" 阜阳汉简仓颉篇释文. *Wenwu* (1983.2): 35–40.

Galambos, Imre. *Orthography of Early Chinese Writing: Evidence from Newly Excavated Manuscripts (490–221 BC).* Budapest Monographs in East Asian Studies. Budapest: Eötvös Loránd University, 2006

Gallagher, Catherine, and Stephen Greenblatt. *Practicing New Historicism.* Chicago: University of Chicago Press, 2000.

Gandhi, Leela. *Affective Communities: Anticolonial Thought, Fin-De-Siècle Radicalism, and the Politics of Friendship.* Durham: Duke University Press, 2006.

———. *The Common Cause: Postcolonial Ethics and the Practice of Democracy, 1900–1955.* Chicago: University of Chicago Press, 2014.

Gansusheng wenwu kaogu yanjiusuo 甘肃省文物考古研究所, ed. *Qin Han jiandu lunwenji* 秦汉简牍论文集. Lanzhou: Gansu renmin, 1989.

Gernet, Jacques. *Buddhism in Chinese Society: An Economic History from the Fifth to Tenth Centuries.* Translated by Franciscus Verellen. New York: Columbia University Press, 1995.

Giele, Enno. "Excavated Manuscripts: Context and Methodology." In Nylan and Loewe, *China's Early Empires,* 114–34.

———. "Translator's Note." In Nienhauser, *The Grand Scribe's Records.* Vol. 9, 305–8.

Gills, Barry K., and Andre Gunder Frank. "The Cumulation of Accumulation." In Frank and Gills, *The World System,* 81–114.

Goldin, Paul Rakita. *After Confucius: Studies in Early Chinese Philosophy.* Honolulu: University of Hawai'i Press, 2005.

———. *The Culture of Sex in Ancient China*. Honolulu: University of Hawai'i Press, 2002.

Gommans, Jos, and Harriet Zurndorfer, eds. *Roots and Routes of Development in China and India: Highlights of Fifty Years of* The Journal of the Economic and Social History of the Orient *(1957–2007)*. Leiden: Brill, 2008.

Gong Kechang 龚克昌. *Han fu yan jiu* 汉赋研究. Jinan: Shandong wen yi, 1984.

———. *Studies on the Han Fu*. Translated and edited by David Knechtges and Stuart Aque. New Haven: American Oriental Society, 1997.

———. ed. *Quan Han fu ping zhu* 全汉赋评注. Shijiazhuang: Huashan wenyi chubanshe, 2003.

Gong Tingwan 龚廷万, ed. *Ba Shu Handai huaxiang ji* 巴蜀汉代画像集. Beijing: Wenwu, 1998.

Goodman, Howard L. *Ts'ao P'i Transcendent: The Political Culture of Dynasty-Founding in China at the End of the Han*. Seattle: Scripta Serica, 1998.

Goux, Jean-Jacques. *The Coiners of Language*. Translated by Jennifer Curtiss Gage. Norman: University of Oklahoma Press, 1994.

———. *Symbolic Economies: After Marx and Freud*. Translated by Jennifer Curtiss Gage. Ithaca: Cornell University Press, 1990.

Graeber, David. *Debt: The First 5,000 Years*. Brooklyn, NY: Melville House, 2011.

Graham, A. C. *Chuang-Tzu: The Inner Chapters*. Indianapolis: Hackett, 2001.

———. *Disputers of the Tao: Philosophical Argument in Ancient China*. La Salle, IL: Open Court, 1989.

———. *Later Mohist Logic, Ethics and Science*. Hong Kong: Chinese University Press, 1978.

Granet, Marcel. *Festivals and Songs of Ancient China*. London: Routledge, 1932.

Greatrex, Roger. "An Early Western Han Synonymicon: The Fuyang Copy of the *Cang jie pian*." In *Outstretched Leaves on His Bamboo Staff: Essays in Honour of Göran Malmqvist on his 70th Birthday*, edited by Joakim Enwall, 97–113. Stockholm: Association of Oriental Studies: 1994.

Gu Jiegang 顧頡剛. *Gu shi bian* 古史辨. 7 vols. Haikou: Hainan, 2003.

———. *Lun Ba Shu yu Zhongyuan de guanxi* 論巴蜀與中原的關係. Chengdu: Sichuan renmin, 1981.

———. "Qin Han tongyi de youlai he Zhanguo ren dui shijie de xiangxiang" 秦汉统一的由来和战国人对于世界的想像. In Gu Jiegang, *Gu shi bian*, 1–6.

Gu Lihua 顾丽华. *Handai funü shenghuo qingtai* 汉代妇女生活情态. Beijing: Shehui kexue wen xian, 2012.

Gu, Ming Dong. *Chinese Theories of Fiction: A Non-Western Narrative System*. Albany: State University of New York Press, 2006.

———. *Sinologism: An Alternative to Orientalism and Postcolonialism*. London: Routledge, 2013.

Guangzhou shi wenhua ju 广州市文化局, ed. *Guangzhou Qin-Han kaogu san da faxian* 广州秦汉考古三大发现. Guangzhou: Guangzhou chubanshe, 1999.

Guo Jianxun 郭建勋. *Cifu wen ti yanjiu* 辞赋文体研究. Beijing: Zhonghua shuju, 2007.

Guo Moruo 郭沫若. *Nuli zhi shidai* 奴隶制時代. Beijing: Renmin, 1954.

———. *Zhongguo gudai shehui yanjiu* 中国古代社会研究. Beijing: Zhongguo huaqiao, 2008.

———. "Chi mi pian de yanjiu" 侈靡篇的研究. *Lishi yanjiu* (1954.3): 27–62.

Guo yu 國語. 21 vols. Shanghai: Shanghai guji, 1978.

Guo Zhanbo. "The Huang-Lao School." Translated by Paul van Els and Katia Chirkova, *Contemporary Chinese Thought* 34.1 (Fall 2002): 19–36.

Hall, David L., and Roger T. Ames. *Thinking from the Han: Self, Truth, and Transcendence in Chinese and Western Culture*. Albany: State University of New York, 1987.

Hamashita, Takeshi. "The Tribute System and Modern Asia." In *Japanese Industrialization and the Asian Economy*, 91–107, edited by A. J. H. Latham and Heita Kawakatsu. New York: Routledge, 1994.

Han Feizi ji jie 韓非子集解. Annotated by Wang Xianshen 王先慎. Beijing: Zhonghua shuju, 2003.

Han Fuzhi 韓復智. *Liang Han de jingji sixiang* 兩漢的經濟思想. Taibei: Taiwan shangwu yin shu guan zong jing xiao, 1969.

Han Kangxin 韩康信. *Sichou zhilu gudai jumin zhongzu renleixue yanjiu* 丝绸之路古代居民种族人类学研究. Urumqi: Xinjiang renmin chubanshe, 1994.

Han Ying 韓嬰. *Han shi wai zhuan ji shi* 韓詩外傳集釋. Beijing: Zhonghua shuju, 1980.

Han Zhaoqi 韓兆琦. *Shiji ti ping* 史記題評. Xi'an: *Shaanxi renmin jiaoyu*, 2000.

Hansen, Valerie. *Negotiating Daily Life in Traditional China: How Ordinary People Used Contracts, 600–1400*. New Haven: Yale University Press, 1995.

———. *The Open Empire: A History of China to 1600*. New York: W. W. Norton, 2000.

———. *The Silk Road: A New History*. Oxford: Oxford University Press, 2012.

Hanshi waizhuan jin zhu jin yi 韓詩外傳今註今譯. Taibei: Taiwan shang wu yin shu guan, 1986.

Hanshu buzhu 漢書補注. Annotated by Wang Xianqian 王先謙. Taibei: Taiwan shang wu yin shu guan, 1968.

Harbsmeier, Christoph. *Language and Logic*. Vol. 7, Part 1 in *Science and Civilisation in China*, edited by Joseph Needham. Cambridge: Cambridge University Press, 1988.

Hardy, Grant. "The Interpretive Function of Shih Chi 14, 'The Table by Years of the Twelve Feudal Lords.'" *Journal of the American Oriental Society* 133, no.1 (1993): 14–24.

———. *Worlds of Bamboo and Bronze: Sima Qian's Conquest of History*. New York: Columbia University Press, 1999.

Harper, Donald. "A Chinese Demonography of the Third Century B.C." *Harvard Journal of Asiatic Studies* 45, no. 2 (December 1985): 459–98.

———. "Contracts with the Spirit World in Han Common Religion: the Xuning Prayer and Sacrifice Documents of AD 79." *Cahiers d'Extrême-Asie* 14 (2004): 227–67.

———. *Early Chinese Medical Literature: The Mawangdui Medical Manuscripts: Translation and Study*. New York: Kegan Paul International, 1998.

———. "Poets and Primates: Wang Yanshou's Poem on the Macaque." *Asia Major* 14, no. 2 (2001): 1–26.

———. "Resurrection in Warring States Popular Religion." In *Taoist Resources* 5 (1994): 13–28.

————. "Wang Yen-shou's Nightmare Poem." *Harvard Journal of Asiatic Studies* 47, no. 1 (June 1987): 239–83.

————. "Warring States Natural Philosophy and Occult Thought." In *The Cambridge History of Ancient China: From the Origins of Civilization to 221 B.C.*, edited by Michael Loewe and Edward L. Shaughnessy, 813–84. Cambridge: Cambridge University Press, 1999.

————. "The Wu Shih Erh Ping Fang: Translation and Prolegomena." PhD diss., University of California, Berkeley, 1982.

Hart, Keith. "Heads or Tails? Two Sides of the Coin." *Man*, New Series 21, no. 4 (December 1986): 637–56.

Hawkes, David. *The Songs of the South: An Ancient Anthology of Poems by Qu Yuan and Other Poets*. London: Penguin, 1985.

He Jiejun 何介钧, ed. *Changsha Mawangdui er, san hao Han mu* 长沙马王堆二、三号汉墓. Beijing: Wenwu, 2004.

————. *Mawangdui Han mu* 马王堆汉墓. Beijing: Wenwu, 1982.

He Lin 何林. "Guanyu 'Chanyu heqin' wa" 关于"单于和亲"瓦. *Baotou wenwu ziliao* 包头文物资料 1 (1986): 74–86.

He Xingwu 贺兴武, Xiang Xinmin 向新民, and Yu Ru 愚如. "Hunan Hengyang shi Fenghuangshan Hanmu fachu jian bao" 湖南衡阳市凤凰山汉墓发掘简报. *Kaogu* (1993.3): 239–47.

He Zhiguo 何志国. *Han Wei yao qian shu chu bu yan jiu* 汉魏摇钱树初步研究. Beijing: Kexue, 2007.

He Zhihua 何志华, Zhu Guofan 朱國藩, and Fan Shanbiao 樊善標, eds. *Gu Lie nü zhuan yu xian Qin liang Han dian ji chongjian ziliao huibian, Da Dai Li ji yu xian Qin liang Han dian ji chongjian ziliao huibian* 古列女傳與先秦兩漢典籍重見資料彙編, 大戴禮記與先秦兩漢典籍重見資料彙編. Hong Kong: Zhongwen daxue, 2004.

Helms, Mary. *Craft and the Kingly Ideal: Art, Trade, and Power*. Austin: University of Texas Press, 1993.

Henderson, John B. *Scripture, Canon, and Commentary: A Comparison of Confucian and Western Exegesis*. Princeton: Princeton University Press, 1991.

Hervouet, Yves. *Le Chapitre 117 du Che-ki: Traduction avec Notes*. Paris: Presses Universitaires de France, 1972.

————. *Un Poète de Cour sur les Han: Sseu-ma Siang-jou*. Paris: Presses Universitaires de France, 1964.

Hevia, James. *Cherishing Men From Afar: Qing Guest Ritual and the Macartney Embassy of 1793*. Durham, NC: Duke University Press, 1995.

Hightower, James Robert. *Han shih wai chuan: Han Ying's Illustrations of the Didactic Application of the Classic of Songs. An Annotated Translation*. Cambridge, Mass.: Harvard University Press, 1952.

Hill, John E. *Through the Jade Gate to Rome: A Study of the Silk Routes during the Later Han Dynasty 1st to 2nd centuries CE: an Annotated Translation of the Chronicle on the "Western Regions" in the Hou Hanshu*. Charleston, South Carolina: BookSurge Publishing, 2009.

Hinsch, Bret. "The Composition of *Lienüzhuan*: Was Liu Xiang the Author or Editor?" *Asia Major* (third series) 20, no. 1: 1–23.

————. "The Criticism of Powerful Women by Western Han Dynasty Portent Experts." *Journal of the Economic and Social History of the Orient* 49, no. 1: 96–121.

————. "Cross-Genre Influence on the Fictional Aspects of Lie nü Narratives." *Journal of Oriental Studies* 41.1 (2006): 41–66.

————. "Myth and the Construction of Foreign Ethnic Identity in Early and Medieval China." *Asian Ethnicity* 5.1 (2004): 81–103.

————. *Passions of the Cut Sleeve: The Male Homosexual Tradition in China*. Berkeley: University of California Press, 1990.

————. "The Textual History of Liu Xiang's *Lienüzhuan*." *Monumenta Serica* 52: 95–112.

————. *Women in Early Imperial China*. Lanham, MD: Rowman & Littlefield, 2002.

————. "Women, Kinship, and Property as Seen in a Han Dynasty Will." *T'oung Pao* 84 (1998): 1–20.

Holmgren, Jennifer. *Marriage, Kinship, and Power in Northern China*. Aldershot, UK: Variorum, 1995.

Honey, David. "The *Han-Shu*, Manuscript Evidence, and the Textual Criticism of the *Shih-chi*: The Case of the 'Hsiung-nu lieh-chuan.'" *CLEAR* 21 (1999): 67–97.

————. "Stripping off Felt and Fur: An Essay on Nomadic Sinification." *Papers on Inner Asia* 21 (1992): 1–39.

Hostetler, Laura. *Qing Colonial Enterprise: Ethnography and Cartography in Early Modern China*. Chicago: University of Chicago Press, 2001.

Hou, Ching-Lang. *Monnaies d'Offrande et la Notion de Trésorerie dans la Religion Chinoise*. Paris: Collège de France, Institut des hautes études chinoises, 1975.

Hou Han shu 後漢書. By Fan Ye 范曄. Beijing: Zhonghua shuju, 1965.

Houo-Ming-Tse, Paul 霍明志. *Preuves des Antiquités*. Peking, 1930.

Hsing I-tien 邢義田. "Handai huaxiang Hu-Han zhanzheng tu de goucheng, leixing yu yiyi" 漢代畫象胡漢戰爭圖的構成、類型與意義. *Guoli Taiwan daxue meishushi yanjiu jikan* 19 (2005): 1–72.

Hsu, Cho-yun. *Han Agriculture: The Formation of Early Chinese Agrarian Economy, 206 BC–AD 220*. Edited by Jack L. Dull. Seattle: University of Washington Press, 1980.

Hsu, Elisabeth. *Pulse Diagnosis in Early Chinese Medicine: The Telling Touch*. Cambridge: Cambridge University Press, 2010.

Hu Cheng 胡诚. "Baijin sanpin zhi guan jian" 白金三品之管见. *Kaogu yu wenwu* (1994.5): 98–100.

Hu Jichuang 胡寄窗. *Chinese Economic Thought before the Seventeenth Century*. Beijing: Foreign Languages Press, 1984.

————. *A Concise History of Chinese Economic Thought*. Beijing: Foreign Languages Press, 2009.

————. *Zhongguo jingji sixiangshi* 中國經濟思想史. Shanghai: Shanghai renmin, 1978.

Hu Pingsheng 胡平生 and Han Ziqiang 韩自强. "Fuyang Han jian 'Cang jie pian'" 阜阳汉简《苍颉篇》*Wenwu* (1983.2): 24–34.

Huainan zi ji shi 淮南子集釋. Annotated by He Ning 何寧. 3 vols. Beijing: Zhonghua shuju, 1998.

Huan Kuan. *Discourses on Salt and Iron: A Debate on State Control of Commerce and Industry in Ancient China. Chapter I–XXVIII*. Translated by Esson M. Gale, with introduction and notes. Taibei, Ch'eng-Wen Pub. Co., 1967.

Huang Jinyan 黄今言. *Qin Han jing ji shi lun kao* 秦汉经济史论考·Beijing: Zhong-guo shehui kexue, 2000.

Huang Peirong 黄沛榮. "Zhou shu yanjiu" 周書研究. PhD diss., Taiwan daxue zhong-guo wenxue yanjiusuo, 1976.

Huang Qingquan 黄清泉. *Xin yi lie nü zhuan* 新譯列女傳. Taibei: Sanmin shuju, 1996.

Huang Shengzhang 黄盛璋. "Guanyu cheng qian heng mo shu wenzi ji xiang guan wenti" 关于称钱衡墨书文字及相关问题. *Wenwu yanjiu* 6 (1990.10): 107–11.

———— "Guanyu Fenghuangshan yiliuba hao Hanmude jige wenti" 关于凤凰 山一六八号汉墓的几个问题. *Kaogu* (1977.1): 43–50.

Huang Xiquan 黄锡全. "Baijin sanpin zhuan wen ji you guan wenti lüe yi" 白金三品篆文及有关问题略议. *Zhongguo qianbi* 中国钱币 (2003.3): 3–12.

"HubeiJiangling Fenghuangshan Yiliubahao Hanmu fajue jianbao" 湖北江陵凤凰山一六八号汉墓发掘简报. *Wenwu* (1974.9): 1–8.

Hubei sheng wenwu kaogu yanjiusuo 湖北省文物考古研究所. *Jiangling Fenghuang-shan Xihan jian du* 江陵凤凰山西汉简牍. Beijing: Zhonghua shuju, 2012.

————. "Jiangling Fenghuangshan yi liu ba hao Han mu" 江陵凤凰山168号汉墓. *Ka-ogu xuebao* (1993.4): 455–512.

Hulsewé, A. F. P. "The Problem of the Authenticity of Shih chi ch. 123, the Memoir on Ta-yüan." *T'oung Pao* 61, no. 1–3 (1975): 83–147.

————. *Remnants of Han Law*. Leiden: Brill, 1955.

————. "Texts in Tombs." *Asiatische Studien* 8 and 9 (1965): 78–79.

Hulsewé, A. F. P., and Michael Loewe. *China in Central Asia: The Early Stage: 125 BC–AD 23. An Annotated Translation of Chapters 61 and 96 of the History of the Former Han Dynasty*. Leiden: Brill, 1979.

Hunan sheng bowuguan 湖南省博物馆. *Changsha Mawangdui yi hao Han mu fajue ji-anbao* 長沙馬王堆一號漢墓發掘簡報. Beijing: Wenwu, 1972.

Huo Hongwei 霍宏伟. "Luoyang dong Han you yishen shou 'yan sheng qian' kao bian" 洛阳东汉有翼神兽"厌胜钱"考辨. *Zhongguo huobi* (2011.1): 17–47.

Idema, W. L., and Beata Grant. *The Red Brush: Writing Women of Imperial China*. Cambridge, MA: Harvard University Asia Center, 2004.

Idema, W. L., and Lloyd Haft. *A Guide to Chinese Literature*. Ann Arbor: Center for Chinese Studies, University of Michigan, 1997.

Jaspers, Karl. "Philosophy and History." In *Basic Philosophical Writings*, edited and translated, by Edith Ehrlich, Leonard H. Ehrlich, and George B. Pepper, 381–95. Athens: Ohio University Press, 1986.

Jia, Jinhua. "An Interpretation of the Term *fu* 賦 in Early Chinese Texts: From Po-etic Form to Poetic Technique and Literary Genre." *CLEAR* 26 (Dec. 2004): 55–76.

"Jian bo shu fa xuan" bian ji zu 《简帛书法选》编辑组. *Mawangdui Han jian. Qian ce* 馬王堆漢簡. 遣策. Beijing: Wenwu, 2000.

Jian Zongwu 簡宗梧. *Han fu shi lun* 漢賦史論. Taibei: Dong da tu shu gong si, 1993.

————. *Han fu yuanliu yu jiazhi zhi shangque* 漢賦源流與價值之商榷. Taibei: Wen shi zhe, 1980.

————. *Sima Xiangru Yang Xiong ji qi fu zhi yanjiu* 司馬相如楊雄及其賦之研究. Tai-bei?: Jian Zongwu, 1976? [reproduced from manuscript copy].

Jiang Baolian 姜宝莲 and Qin Jianming 秦建明, eds. *Han Zhongguan zhu qian yi zhi* 汉鍾官铸钱遗址. Beijing: Zhongguo shehui kexue, 2004.

Jiang Baolian 姜宝莲 and Yuan Lin 袁林. "Handai baijin sanpin zai tan" 汉代白金三品再探. *Shaanxi qianbi yanjiu wenji* 陕西钱币研究文集 10, no. 4 (2003): 24–29.

Jiang Ruoshi 蔣若是. *Qin Han qianbi yanjiu* 秦漢錢幣研究. Beijing: Zhonghua shuju, 1997.

Jin Chunfeng 金春峰. *Han dai si xiang shi* 汉代思想史. Beijing: Zhongguo shehui kexue, 1987.

Jiu Tang shu 舊唐書. Beijing: Zhonghua shuju, 1975.

Jiu zhang suan shu 九章算術. Edited by Qian Baocong 錢寶琮. Beijing: Zhonghua shuju, 1963.

Juliano, Annette L., and Judith A. Lerner, eds. *Monks and Merchants: Silk Road Treasures from Northwest China*. New York: Asia Society, 2001.

Jullien, François. *In Praise of Blandness: Proceeding from Chinese Thought and Aesthetics*. Translated by Paula M. Varsano. New York: Zone Books, 2004.

Kakinuma, Yōhei 柿沼陽平. *Chūgoku kodai kahei keizaishi kenkyū* 中国古代貨幣経済史研究. Tokyo: Kyūko Shoin, 2011.

Kalinowski, Marc. "Divination and Astrology: Received Texts and Excavated Manuscripts." In Nylan and Loewe, *China's Early Empires*, 339–66.

Kang Liushuo 康柳硕. "Guanyu xila wen qian, tong bing de ji dian si kao" 关于希腊文铅，铜饼的几点思考. *Shaanxi qianbi yanjiu wenji* 陕西钱币研究文集 10 (2003.4): 81–84.

Karl, Rebecca E. *Staging the World: Chinese Nationalism at the Turn of the Twentieth Century*. Durham: Duke University Press, 2002.

Karlgren, Bernhard. *The Book of Documents*. Götenborg: Elanders Boktryckeri Aktierbolag, 1950.

———. *Glosses on the Book of Documents*. Bulletin of the Museum of Far Eastern Antiquities, 1970, 39–206.

———. *Grammata Serica Recensa*. Stockholm: Museum of Far Eastern Antiquities, 1972.

Kern, Martin. "The 'Biography of Sima Xiangru' and the Question of the *Fu* in Sima Qian's *Shiji*." *Journal of the American Oriental Society* 123, no. 2 (2003): 303–16.

———. "Early Chinese Literature, Beginnings through Western Han." In *Cambridge History of Chinese Literature*, edited by Stephen Owen and Kang-i Sun Chang, 1–115. Cambridge: Cambridge University Press, 2010.

———. "The Poetry of Han Historiography." *Early Medieval China* 10–11.1 (2004): 23–65.

———. "Ritual, Text, and the Formation of the Canon: Historical Transitions of *wen* in Early China." *T'oung Pao* 87, no. 1–3 (2001): 43–91.

———. *The Stele Inscriptions of Ch'in Shih-huang: Text and Ritual in Early Chinese Imperial Representation*. New Haven: American Oriental Society, 2000.

———. "Western Han Aesthetics and the Genesis of the *Fu*." *Harvard Journal of Asiatic Studies* 63, no. 2 (December 2003): 383–437.

———, ed. *Text and Ritual in Early China*. Seattle: University of Washington Press, 2005.

Keynes, J. Maynard. *The General Theory of Employment, Interest and Money*. New York: Harcourt, Brace & World, 1965.

———. Review of *The Economic Principles of Confucius and his School*, by Chen Huanchang. *The Economic Journal* 22, no. 8 (December 1912): 584–88.

Khayutina, Maria. "Royal Hospitality and Geopolitical Constitution of the Western Zhou Polity." *T'oung Pao* 96, no. 1–3 (2010): 1–73.

Khazanov, Anatoly M. "Nomads in the History of the Sedentary World." In *Nomads in the Sedentary World*, edited by Anatoly M. Khazanov and André Wink, 1–23. Richmond, Surrey: Curzon, 2001.

Kieschnick, John. *The Impact of Buddhism on Chinese Material Culture*. Princeton: Princeton University Press, 2003.

Kinney, Anne Behnke. *Representations of Childhood and Youth in Early China*. Stanford: Stanford University Press, 2004.

Kirby, E. Stuart. *Introduction to the Economic History of China*. London: Allen & Unwin, 1954.

Kleeman, Terry. "Land Contracts and Related Documents." In *Chūgoku no shūkyō, shisō to kagaku*, edited by Makio Ryōkai, 1–34. Tokyo; Kokusho Kankōkai, 1984.

Klein, Esther Sunkyung. "The History of a Historian: Perspectives on the Authorial Roles of Sima Qian." PhD diss., Princeton University, 2010.

Knechtges, David R. *Court Culture and Literature in Early China*. Burlington, VT: Ashgate/Variorum, 2002.

———. *The Han Rhapsody: A Study of the Fu of Yang Hsiung (53 BC–AD 18)*. Cambridge: Cambridge University Press, 1976.

———. *The Han Shu Biography of Yang Xiong (53 BC–AD 18)*. Tempe: Center for Asian Studies, Arizona State University, 1982.

———. " 'Have You Not Seen the Beauty of the Large?': An Inquiry into Early Imperial Chinese Aesthetics." In *Wenxue, wenhua yu shibian*, disanjie guoji Hanxue huiyi lunwenji 文學、文化與世變.第三屆國際漢學會議論文集, 41–66. Taibei: Zhongyang yanjiuyuan Zhongguo wenzhe yanjiusuo, 2002.

———, trans. *Wen xuan, or Selections of Refined Literature*. 3 vols. Princeton: Princeton University Press, 1982–96.

Knechtges, David R., and Jerry Swanson. "Seven Stimuli for the Prince: the Ch'i-fa of Mei Ch'eng." *Monumenta Serica* 29 (1970–71): 99–116.

Knoblock, John. *Xunzi: A Translation and Study of the Complete Works*. Stanford: Stanford University Press, 1994.

Knoblock, John, and Jeffrey Riegel. *Mozi: A Study and Translation of the Ethical and Political Writings*. Berkeley: Institute of East Asian Studies, 2013.

Ko, Dorothy. *Teachers of the Inner Chambers: Women and Culture in Seventeenth-Century China*. Stanford: Stanford University Press, 1994.

Kopytoff, Igor. "The Cultural Biography of Things: Commoditization as Process." In *The Social Life of Things: Commodities in Cultural Perspective*, edited by Arjun Appadurai, 64–91. Cambridge: Cambridge University Press, 1986.

Kroll, J. L. "Toward a Study of the Economic Views of Sang Hung-yang." *Early China* 4 (1978–79): 11–18.

Kroll, Paul. "Literary Criticism and Personal Character in Poetry ca 100–300 CE." In Nylan and Loewe, *China's Early Empires*, 517–33.

Kuhn, Dieter. "Silk Weaving in Ancient China: From Geometric Figures to Patterns of Pictorial Likeness." *Chinese Science* 12 (1995): 77–114.

———. *Textile Technology: Spinning and Reeling.* Vol. 5, Part 9 in *Science and Civilisation in China*, edited by Joseph Needham. Cambridge: Cambridge University Press, 1988.

Kuriyama, Shigehisa. *The Expressiveness of the Body and the Divergence of Greek and Chinese Medicine.* New York: Zone Books, 1999.

Kurke, Leslie. *Coins, Bodies, Games, and Gold: The Politics of Meaning in Archaic Greece.* Princeton: Princeton University Press, 1999.

———. "Money and Mythic History: The Contestation of Transactional Orders in the Fifth Century BC." In *The Ancient Economy*, edited by Walter Scheidel and Sitta von Reden, 88–113. Edinburgh: Edinburgh University Press, 2002.

———. "The Politics of *habrosune* in Archaic Greece." *Classical Antiquity* 11 (1992): 91–120.

Kuzmina, E. E. *The Prehistory of the Silk Road.* Philadelphia: University of Pennsylvania Press, 2008.

Kwong, Hing Foon. *Wang Zhaojun, une Héroïne Chinoise de L'histoire à la Légende.* Paris: Collège de France, 1986.

La Vaissière, Étienne de. *Sogdian Traders: A History.* Translated by James Ward. Leiden: Brill, 2005.

Lagerwey, John, and Marc Kalinowski, eds. *Early Chinese Religion, Part One: Shang through Han (1250 BC–220 AD).* Handbuch der Orientalistik 4.21. Leiden: Brill, 2009.

Lam, Lay Yong, and Ang Tian Se. *Fleeting Footsteps: Tracing the Conception of Arithmetic and Algebra in Ancient China.* Singapore: World Scientific, 1992.

Lattimore, Owen. *Inner Asian Frontiers of China.* 2nd ed. New York: American Geographical Society, 1951.

———. *Studies in Frontier History: Collected Papers, 1928–1958.* Paris: Mouton, 1962

Laufer, Berthold. *Sino-Iranica: Chinese Contributions to the History of Civilization in Ancient Iran, with Special Reference to the History of Cultivated Plants and Products.* Chicago: Field Museum, 1919.

Legge, James. *The Chinese Classics with a Translation, Critical and Exegetical Notes, Prolegomena, and Copious Indexes.* Vol. 3, *The Shoo King or the Book of Historical Documents.* 1895. Reprint, Taibei: SMC Publishing, 1992.

Lévi, Jean. *La Dispute sur le Sel et le Fer.* Translated and annotated by Jean Lévi. Paris: BellesLettres, 2010.

Levy, Dore J. *Chinese Narrative Poetry: The Late Han through T'ang Dynasties*, Durham, NC: Duke University Press, 1988.

———. "Constructing Sequences: Another Look at the Principle of Fu 賦 Enumeration." *Harvard Journal of Asiatic Studies* 46 (December 1986): 471–93.

Lewis, Mark Edward. *The Construction of Space in Early China.* Albany: State University of New York Press, 2006.

———. *The Early Chinese Empires: Qin and Han.* Cambridge, MA: Harvard University Press, 2007.

———. "The *Feng* and *Shan* Sacrifices of Emperor Wu of the Han." In *State and Court Ritual in China*, edited by Joseph P. McDermott, 50–80. Cambridge: University of Cambridge Oriental Publications, 1999.

———. "The Han Abolition of Military Service." In *Warfare in Chinese History*, edited by Hans J. Van de Ven, 33–76. Leiden: Brill, 2000.

———. *Sanctioned Violence in Early China.* Albany: State University of New York Press, 1990.

———. *Writing and Authority in Early China.* Albany: State University of New York Press, 1999.

Li, Feng. *Bureaucracy and the State in Early China: Governing the Western Zhou.* New York: Cambridge University Press, 2008.

———. "Feudalism and Western Zhou China: A Criticism." *Harvard Journal of Asiatic Studies* 63, no. 1 (June 2003): 115–44.

Li, Feng, and David Prager Branner, eds. *Writing and Literacy in Early China: Studies from the Columbia Early China Seminar.* Seattle: University of Washington Press, 2011.

Li ji yi jie 禮記譯解. Beijing: Zhonghua shuju, 2001.

Li Ling 李零. *Bing yi zha li: wo du Sunzi* 兵以詐立: 我读孙子. Beijing: Zhonghua shuju, 2007.

———. *Sang jia gou: wo du Lun Yu* 喪家狗: 我讀論語. Taiyuan: Shanxi renmin, 2007.

———. *Sunzi yizhu* 孫子譯注. Beijing: Zhonghua shuju, 2007.

———, ed. *Li Ling zi xuan ji* 李零自选集. Guilin: Guangxi shifan daxue, 1998.

Li Linna 李林娜. *Nanyue cang zhen* 南越藏珍. Beijing: Zhonghua shuju, 2002.

Li Tiandao 李天道. *Sima Xiangru fu de meixue sixiang yu diyu wenhua xintai* 司马相如赋的美学思想与地域文化心态. Beijing: Zhongguo shehui kexue, 2004.

Li, Wai-yee. "The Idea of Authority in the Shih chi (Records of the Historian)." *Harvard Journal of Asiatic Studies* 54, no. 2 (1994): 345–405.

———. *The Readability of the Past in Early Chinese Historiography.* Cambridge, MA: Harvard University Press, 2007.

Li Xiangfeng 黎翔鳳, ed. *Guanzi jiao zhu* 管子校注. Beijing: Zhonghua shuju, 2004.

Li Xueqin 李学勤. *Zouchu yigu shidai* 走出疑古时代. Changchun: Xinhua shu dian, 2007.

——— and Xing Wen. "New Light on the Early-Han Code: A Reappraisal of the Zhangjiashan Bamboo-Slip Legal Texts." *Asia Major* (third series) 14, no. 1 (2001): 125–46.

Li Yong 李勇. "Anhui Lu'an Han mu chutu qian bing" 安徽六安汉墓出土铅饼. *Zhongguo qianbi* 中国钱币 (1996.4): 44.

———. "Anhui Lu'an shi Han mu de qingli" 安徽六安市汉墓的清理. *Kaogu* (2002.9): 93–95.

———. "Lu'an faxian san mei long, ma, gui xing jin shu qi" 六安发现三枚龙，马，龟形金属器. *Anhui qianbi* 安徽钱币 (1994.1): 17–18.

———. "Waiwen qian bing kao" 外文铅饼考. *Anhui qianbi* (2001.2): 11–14.

———. "Wo guo li nian chutu de waiwen qianbing kaolüe" 我国历年出土的外文铅饼考略. *Anhui qianbi* 4 (1998): 14–15.

Li Yong and Yang Hua 杨华. "Baijin san pin kao" 白金三品考. *Qianbi wen lun te ji* 3 (2006): 241–50.

Li, Yung-Ti. "On the Function of Cowries in Shang and Western Zhou China." *Journal of East Asian Archaeology* 5, no. 1–4 (2003): 1–26.

Li, Zehou. *The Chinese Aesthetic Tradition.* Translated by Maija Bell Samei. Honolulu: University of Hawai'i Press, 2010.

———. *The Path of Beauty: A Study of Chinese Aesthetics.* Translated by Gong Lizeng. Oxford: Oxford University Press, 1994. [Translation of *Mei de licheng* 美的歷程.]

Liang Qichao 梁啓超. "Shiji huozhi liezhuan jin yi" 史記貨殖列傳今義. In *Yin bing shi he ji* 飲冰室合集, 1:35–45. Beijing: Zhonghua shuju, 1996.

———. *Yin bing shi he ji* 飲冰室合集. Beijing: Zhonghua shuju, 1996.

Lie nü zhuan jiao zhu 列女傳校注. By Liu Xiang 劉向. Taibei: Taiwan Zhonghua shuju, 1981.

Lin Gan 林幹. *Xiongnu shi* 匈奴史. Hohhot: Neimenggu renmin, 2007.

Lin, James C. S., ed. *The Search for Immortality: Tomb Treasures of Han China*. New Haven: Yale University Press, 2012.

Lin Meicun 林梅村. *Sichou zhi lu kaogu shi wu jiang* 丝绸之路考古十五讲. Beijing: Beijing daxue, 2006.

———. *Han Tang Xiyu yu Zhongguo wenming* 汉唐西域与中国文明. Beijing: Wenwu, 1998.

Ling Zhilong 凌稚隆, ed. *Shiji pinglin* 史記評林. 1577. Reprint, Tianjin: Tianjin guji chubanshe, 1998.

Liu Chaojian 刘朝谦. *Fu wen ben de yishu yanjiu* 赋文本的艺术研究. Beijing: Zhongguo shehui kexue, 2006.

Liu Dezhen 刘得祯. "Gansu Lingtai faxian wai guo ming wen qian bing" 甘肃灵台发现外国铭文铅饼. *Kaogu* (1977.6): 427–28.

Liu, Lydia H. *The Clash of Empires: The Invention of China in Modern World Making*. Cambridge, MA: Harvard University Press, 2004.

———. *The Freudian Robot: Digital Media and the Future of the Unconscious*. Chicago: University of Chicago Press, 2010.

———. *Translingual Practices: Literature, National Culture, and Translated Modernity—China, 1900–1937*. Stanford: Stanford University Press, 1995.

———, ed. *Tokens of Exchange: The Problem of Exchange in Global Circulations*. Durham: Duke University Press, 1999.

Liu, Lydia H., Rebecca E. Karl, and Dorothy Ko, eds. *The Birth of Chinese Feminism: Essential Texts in Transnational Theory*. New York: Columbia University Press, 2013.

Liu Nanping 刘南平 and Ban Xiuping 班秀萍. *Sima Xiangru kao shi* 司马相如考释. Tianjin: Tianjin guji, 2007.

Liu Sen 刘森. "Baijin sanpin lun" 白金三品论. *Shaanxi qianbi yanjiu wenji* 陕西钱币研究文集 10, no. 4 (2003): 30–40.

Liu Xie 劉勰. *Wenxin diaolong zhu* 文心雕龍注. Beijing: Renmin wenxue, 2001.

Liu, Xinru. *Ancient India and Ancient China: Trade and Religious Exchanges, AD 1–600*. Delhi: Oxford University Press, 1988.

Lloyd, G. E. R., and Nathan Sivin. *The Way and the Word: Science and Medicine in Early China and Greece*. New Haven: Yale University Press, 2002.

Lock, Margaret, and Judith Farquhar, eds. *Beyond the Body Proper: Reading the Anthropology of Material Life*. Durham: Duke University Press, 2007.

Loewe, Michael. "Attempts at Economic Co-ordination during the Western Han Dynasty." In *The Scope of State Power in China*, edited by S. R. Schram, 237–67. New York: St. Martin's Press, 1985.

———. *A Biographical Dictionary of the Qin, Former Han and Xin Periods (221 BC–AD 24)*. Leiden; Boston: Brill, 2000.

———. *Crisis and Conflict in Han China, 104 BC to AD 9*. London: Allen and Unwin, 1974.

————. *Dong Zhongshu. A "Confucian" Heritage and the Chunqiu Fanlu*. Leiden; Boston: Brill, 2011.

————. "The Former Han Dynasty." In *The Cambridge History of China*. Vol. 1, *The Ch'in and Han Empires, 221 BC–AD 220*, edited by Denis Twitchett and Michael Loewe, 103–222. Cambridge: Cambridge University Press, 1987.

————. "Han Administrative Documents: Recent Finds from the Northwest." *T'oung Pao* 72 (1986): 291–314.

————. *The Men Who Governed China: Companion to a Biographical Dictionary of the Qin, Former Han and Xin Periods*. Leiden: Brill, 2004.

————. *Records of Han Administration*. 2 vols. Cambridge: Cambridge University Press, 1967.

————. "Social Distinctions, Groups, and Privileges." In Nylan and Loewe, *China's Early Empires*, 296–307.

————. *Ways to Paradise: The Chinese Quest for Immortality*. London: George Allen & Unwin, 1979.

————, ed. *Early Chinese Texts: A Bibliographical Guide*. Berkeley: Institute of East Asian Studies, University of California, Berkeley, 1993.

Lu, Sheldon Hsiao-peng. *From Historicity to Fictionality: The Chinese Poetics of Narrative*. Stanford: Stanford University Press, 1994.

Lu Xun. *A Brief History of Chinese Fiction*. Honolulu: University Press of the Pacific, 2000.

Lu Zongli 吕宗力. "Qin Han shi qi zhong yuan de 'qun du'" 秦漢時期中原的"群都". *Shi xue yue kan* 9 (2011.9): 38–44.

————. "Han dai 'yao yan' tan tao" 漢代"妖言"探討. *Zhongguo shi yanjiu* 4 (2006): 39–58.

————. "Problems Concerning the Authenticity of *Shih-Chi* 123 Reconsidered." *CLEAR* 17 (1995): 51–68.

Lun heng jiao shi 論衡校釋. By Wang Chong 王充. Beijing: Zhonghua shuju, 1990.

Lunyu yi zhu 論語譯注. Annotated by Yang Bojun. Beijing: Zhonghua shuju, 1992.

Luo Jiaxian 罗家湘. *Yi Zhou shu yan jiu* 逸周书研究. Shanghai: Shanghai guji, 2006.

Luo Xizhang 罗西章. "Fufeng Jiangyuan faxian Handai waiwen qian bing" 扶風姜塬发现汉代外文铅饼. *Kaogu* 考古 (1976.4): 275–76.

————. "Handai wai wen qian bing de zai ren zhi—jian lun baijin san pin" 汉代外文铅饼的再认识—兼论白金三品. *Shaanxi qianbi yanjiu wenji* 陕西钱币研究文集 10, no. 4 (2003): 16–23.

Luo Yuming 骆玉明. *A Concise History of Chinese Literature*. Translated with Annotations by Ye Yang. Leiden: Brill, 2011.

————. *Zhongguo wen xue shi xin zhu* 中国文学史新著. Edited by Zhang Peiheng 章培恒. Shanghai: Fudan da xue, 2011.

Luo Zhufen 罗竹风, ed. *Hanyu Da Cidian* 汉语大词典. Shanghai: Hanyu da cidian, 2001.

Ma Biao 马彪. *Qin-Han haozu shehui yanjiu* 秦汉豪族社会研究. Beijing: Zhongguo shudian, 2002.

Ma Chengyuan 馬承源. *Zhongguo qingtongqi* 中國青銅器. Shanghai: Shanghai guji, 2003.

Ma Daying 马大英. *Handai caizheng shi* 汉代财政史. Beijing: Zhongguo cai zheng jingji, 1983.

Ma Feibai 馬非百, ed. *Guanzi Qingzhong pian xin quan* 管子輕重篇新詮. Beijing: Zhonghua shuju, 2004.

———, ed. *Yantielun jian zhu* 盐鉄论简注. Beijing: Zhonghua shuju, 1984.

Ma Jigao 马积高. *Fu shi* 赋史. Shanghai: Shanghai guji, 1987.

Ma Shubo 马书波 and Wang Yongbo 王永波. "Shandong Changqing Shuangrushan Hanmu linzhi jin kehua fuhao de pan shi" 山东长清双乳山汉墓麟趾金刻划符号的判识. *Kaogu* (2005.1): 52–63.

Maenchen-Helfen, O. "A Parthian Coin-legend on a Chinese Bronze." *Asia Major* 3, no. 1 (1952): 1–6.

Mair, Victor H. "The North(west)ern Peoples and the Recurrent Origins of the 'Chinese' State." In *The Teleology of the Modern Nation State: Japan and China*, edited by Joshua A. Fogel, 46–84. Philadelphia: University of Pennsylvania Press, 2005.

———. *Painting and Performance: Chinese Picture Recitation and Its Indian Genesis*. Honolulu: University of Hawai'i Press, 1988.

———. *T'ang Transformation Texts: A Study of the Buddhist Contribution to the Rise of Vernacular Fiction and Drama in China*. Cambridge, MA: Harvard University Press, 1989.

———, ed. *The Bronze Age and Early Iron Age Peoples of Eastern Central Asia*. Washington, D.C.: Institute for the Study of Man, Inc., in collaboration with the University of Pennsylvania Museum Publications, 1998.

———, ed. *The Columbia History of Chinese Literature*. New York: Columbia University Press, 2001.

———, ed. *Contact and Exchange in the Ancient World*. Honolulu: University of Hawai'i Press, 2006.

Mair, Victor H., Nancy S. Steinhardt, and Paul R. Goldin, eds. *Hawai'i Reader in Traditional Chinese Culture*. Honolulu: University of Hawai'i Press, 2005.

Major, John S., Sarah Queen, Andrew Meyer, and Harold D. Roth, eds. *The Huainanzi: A Guide to the Theory and Practice of Government in Early Han China*. New York: Columbia University Press, 2010.

Makeham, John. *Name and Actuality in Early Chinese Thought*. Albany: State University of New York Press, 1994.

Mallory, J. P., and Victor Mair. *The Tarim Mummies: Ancient China and the Mystery of the Earliest Peoples from the West*. London: Thames and Hudson, 2000.

Mandeville, Bernard. *The Fable of the Bees and Other Writings*. Abridged and edited by E. J. Hundert. Indianapolis: Hackett, 1997.

Mann, Susan. *Precious Records: Women in China's Long Eighteenth Century*. Stanford: Stanford University Press, 1997.

Mao shi zhu shu 毛詩注疏. Taibei: Yi wen yin shu guan, 1965.

Maurer, Bill. "The Anthropology of Money." *Annual Review of Anthropology* 35 (2006): 15–36.

———. *Mutual Life Limited: Islamic Banking, Alternative Currencies, Lateral Reason*. Princeton: Princeton University Press, 2005.

McCormic, Ken. "Sima Qian and Adam Smith." *Pacific Economic Review* 4, no. 1 (February 1999): 85–87.

McNeal, Robin. "Constructing Myth in Modern China." *Journal of Asian Studies* 71, no. 3 (August 2012): 679–704.

———. *Conquer and Govern: Early Chinese Military Texts from the Yi Zhou shu.* Honolulu: University of Hawai'i Press, 2012.

Mengzi yi zhu 孟子译注. Shanghai: Shanghai guji, 1995.

Mianyang bowuguan 绵阳博物馆, ed. *Mianyang Shuangbao Shan Han mu* 绵阳双包山汉墓. Beijing: Wenwu, 2006.

Miao, Ronald C. "Literary Criticism at the End of the Eastern Han." *Literature East and West* 16 (1972): 1016–26.

Milburn, Olivia. "*Gai Lu*: A Translation and Commentary on a Yin-Yang Military Text Excavated from Tomb M 247, Zhangjiashan." *Early China* 33–34 (2010–11): 101–40.

———. "The Book of the Young Master of Accountancy: An Ancient Chinese Economics Text." *Journal of the Economic and Social History of the Orient* 50.1 (2007): 19–40.

Mitchell, W. J. T. *Iconology: Image, Text, Ideology.* Chicago: Chicago University Press, 1986.

———. "Representation" In *Critical Terms for Literary Study,* edited by Frank Lentricchis and Thomas McLaughlin, 11–22. Chicago: Chicago University Press, 1990.

Moretti, Franco. "Conjectures on World Literature." *New Left Review* 1 (January–February 2000): 54–68.

Morris, Ian. "Foreword [to the updated edition]." In Moses I. Finley, *The Ancient Economy,* ix–xxxvi. Berkeley; Los Angeles; London: University of California Press, 1999.

———. *Archaeology as Cultural History: Words and Things in Iron Age Greece.* Malden: Blackwell, 2000.

Mozi jian gu 墨子閒詁. Compiled by Sun Yirang 孫詒讓. Beijing: Zhonghua shuju, 2001.

Mutschler, Fritz-Heiner, and Achim Mittag, eds. *Conceiving the Empire: China and Rome Compared.* New York: Oxford University Press, 2008.

Nakashima Chiaki 中島千秋. *Fu no Seiritsu to Tenkai* 賦の成立と展開. Matsuyama Shi: Seki Yoshiten Insatsusho, 1963.

Nienhauser, William H., Jr. "A Century (1895–1995) of Shih chi 史記 Studies in the West." In *Asian Culture Quarterly* 24, no. 1 (1996): 1–51.

———. "A Note on a Textual Problem in the 'Shih chi' and Some Speculations Concerning the Compilation of the Hereditary Houses." *T'oung Pao* 89 (2003): 39–58.

———. "The Origins of Chinese Fiction." *Monumenta Serica* 38 (1988–89): 191–219.

———. "The Study of the *Shih-chi* (The Grand Scribe's Records) in the People's Republic of China." In *Das Andere China: Festschrift für Wolfgang Bauer zum 65. Geburtstag,* edited by Schmidt-Glintzer, 381–403. Wiesbaden : Harrassowitz Verlag in Kommission, 1995.

———, ed. *The Indiana Companion to Chinese Literature,* Vol. 1. Bloomington: Indiana University Press, 1986.

———, ed. *The Grand Scribe's Records.* Vol. 1, *The Basic Annals of Pre-Han China by Ssu-ma Ch'ien.* Bloomington: Indiana University Press, 1994.

———, ed. *The Grand Scribe's Records.* Vol. 2, *The Basic Annals of Han China by Ssu-ma Ch'ien.* Bloomington: Indiana University Press, 2002.

————, ed. *The Grand Scribe's Records*. Vol. 5, Part 1, *The Hereditary Houses of pre-Han China by Ssu-ma Ch'ien*. Bloomington: Indiana University Press, 2006.

————, ed. *The Grand Scribe's Records*. Vol. 7, *The Memoirs of Pre-Han China by Ssu-ma Ch'ien*. Bloomington: Indiana University Press, 1994.

————, ed. *The Grand Scribe's Records*. Vol. 8, *The Memoirs of Han China, Part I by Ssu-ma Ch'ien*. Bloomington: Indiana University Press, 2008.

————, ed. *The Grand Scribe's Records*. Vol. 9, *The Memoirs of Han China, Part II by Ssu-ma Ch'ien*. Bloomington: Indiana University Press, 2011.

Nishijima, Sadao. "The Economic and Social History of Former Han." In *The Cambridge History of China*. Vol. 1, *The Ch'in and Han Empires, 221 BC–AD 220*, edited by Denis Twitchett and Michael Loewe, 545–607. Cambridge: Cambridge University Press, 1987.

————. "The Formation of the Early Chinese Cotton Industry." In *State and Society in China: Japanese Perspectives on Ming-Qing Social and Economic History*, edited by Linda Grove and Christian Daniels, 17–77. Tokyo: University of Tokyo Press, 1984.

Nylan, Michael. "Administration of the Family (Qihuai bisi)." In Nylan and Loewe, *China's Early Empires*, 266–95.

————. "The Art of Persuasion from 100 BCE to 100 CE." In Nylan and Loewe, *China's Early Empires*, 492–502.

————. "The *chin wen/ku wen* (New text/old text) Controversy in Han." *T'oung pao* 80 (1994): 83–145.

————. *The Five "Confucian" Classics*. New Haven: Yale University Press, 2001.

————. "Han Classicists Writing in Dialogue about Their Own Tradition." *Philosophy East and West* 47.2 (April 1997): 133–88.

————. "Notes on a Case of Illicit Sex from Zhangjiashan: A Translation and Commentary." *Early China* 30 (June 2005): 25–45.

————. "The Rhetoric of 'Empire' in the Classical Era in China." In *Conceiving the Empire: China and Rome Compared*, edited by Fritz-Heiner Mutschler and Achim Mittag, 39–66. Oxford: Oxford University Press, 2008.

————. "Sima Qian: A True Historian?" *Early China* 24 (1998): 1–44.

Nylan, Michael, and Michael Loewe, eds. *China's Early Empires: A Re-appraisal*. Cambridge: Cambridge University Press, 2010.

Ōba, Osamu. "The Ordinances on Fords and Passes Excavated from Han Tomb Number 247, Zhangjiashan." Translated by David Spafford. *Asia Major* (third series) 14, no. 2 (2001): 119–41.

Olberding, Garret P. S. *Dubious Facts: The Evidence of Early Chinese Historiography*. Albany: State University of New York, 2012.

Owen, Stephen. "Hsieh Hui-lien's 'Snow Fu': A Structural Study." *Journal of the American Oriental Society* 94, no. 1 (January–March 1974): 14–23.

————. *The Making of Early Chinese Classical Poetry*. Cambridge, MA: Harvard University Asia Center, 2006.

————, ed. *Readings in Chinese Literary Thought*. Cambridge, MA: Harvard University Press, 1992.

Palumbo-Liu, Bruce Robbins, and Nirvana Tanoukhi, eds. *Immanuel Wallerstein and the Problem of the World: System, Scale, Culture*. Durham: Duke University Press, 2011.

Pan Yinge 潘吟閣. *Shiji huozhi zhuan xin quan* 史記貨殖傳新詮. Shanghai: Shangwu yin shu guan, 1931.

Pearson, Margaret J. *Wang Fu and the Comments of a Recluse*. Tempe, AZ: Center for Asian Studies, Arizona State University, 1989.

Peng Hao 彭浩, ed. *Zhangjiashan Han jian "Suan shu shu" zhu shi* 張家山漢簡《算數書》註釋. Beijing: Kexue, 2001.

Peng Xinwei 彭信威. *A Monetary History of China*. Translated by Edward H. Kaplan. Bellingham, WA: Western Washington, 1994.

———. *Zhongguo Huobi Shi* 中國貨幣史. Shanghai: Shanghai renmin chubanshe, 1958.

Perdue, Peter C. *China Marches West: The Qing Conquest of Central Eurasia*. Cambridge, MA: Harvard University Press, 2005.

Pines, Yuri. "Beasts or Humans: Pre-Imperial Origins of the 'Sino-Barbarian' Dichotomy." In *Mongols, Turks, and Others: Eurasian Nomads and the Sedentary World*, edited by Reuven Amitai and Michal Biran, 59–102. Leiden: Brill, 2005.

———. *Envisioning Eternal Empire: Chinese Political Thought of the Warring States Era*. Honolulu: University of Hawai'i Press, 2009.

———. *Foundations of Confucian Thought. Intellectual Life in the Chunqiu Period, 722–453 B.C.E.* Honolulu: University of Hawai'i Press, 2002.

———. "The Question of Interpretation: Qin History in Light of New Epigraphic Sources." *Early China* 29 (2004): 1–44.

Pirazzoli-t'Serstevens, Michèle. *The Han Dynasty*. New York: Rizzoli International Publications, 1982.

———. "Urbanism." In *China's Early Empires*, edited by Michael Nylan and Michael Loewe, 83–113. Cambridge: Cambridge University Press, 2010.

Plaks, Andrew. *Archetype and Allegory in the Dream of the Red Chamber*. Princeton: Princeton University Press, 1976.

———. *Chinese Narrative: Critical and Theoretical Essays*. Princeton: Princeton University Press, 1977.

Polanyi, Karl. "The Economy as Instituted Process." In Polanyi, Arensberg, and Pearson, *Trade and Market*, 243–70.

———. "Marketless Trading in Hammurabi's Time." In Polanyi, Arensberg, and Pearson, *Trade and Market*, 12–26.

———. "Ports of Trade in Early Societies." In *Primitive, Archaic, and Modern Economies: Essays of Karl Polyani*, edited by George Dalton, 238–60. New York: Anchor Books, 1968.

Polanyi, Karl, Conrad M. Arensberg, and Harry W. Pearson, eds. *Trade and Market in the Early Empires*. Glencoe, IL: The Free Press, 1957.

Pomeranz, Kenneth. *The Great Divergence: Europe, China, and the Making of the Modern World Economy*. Princeton: Princeton University Press, 2000.

Pomeroy, Sarah B. *Xenophon Oeconomicus: A Social and Historical Commentary*. Oxford: Clarendon Press, 1994.

Poo, Mu-chou. *Enemies of Civilization: Attitudes Toward Foreigners in Ancient Mesopotamia, Egypt, and China*. Albany: State University of New York Press, 2005.

———. "Ritual and Ritual Texts in Early China." In Lagerwey and Kalinowski, *Early Chinese Religion*, 281–313.

————. *In Search of Personal Welfare: A View of Ancient Chinese Religion.* Albany: State University of New York Press, 1998.

Poovey, Mary. *Genres of the Credit Economy: Mediating Value in Eighteenth- and Nineteenth-Century Britain.* Chicago: University of Chicago Press, 2008.

Powers, Martin Joseph. *Art and Political Expression in Early China.* New Haven: Yale University Press, 1992.

————. *Pattern and Person: Ornament, Society, and Self in Classical China.* Cambridge, MA: Harvard University Asia Center, 2006.

Průšek, Jaroslav. *Chinese Statelets and the Northern Barbarians in the Period 1400–300 B.C.* Dordrek: Reidel, 1971.

Psarras, Sophia-Karin. "Han and Xiongnu: A Reexamination of Cultural and Political Relations." *Monumenta Serica* 51 (2003): 55–236.

Puett, Michael. *The Ambivalence of Creation: Debates Concerning Innovation and Artifice in Early China.* Stanford: Stanford University Press, 2001.

————. *To Become a God: Cosmology, Sacrifice, and Self-Divinization in Early China.* Cambridge, MA: Harvard University Asia Center, 2002.

Qian Baocong 錢寶琮, ed. *Suanjing shishu* 算經十書, 2 vols. Beijing: Zhonghua shuju, 1963.

Qian Boquan 钱伯泉. "Gansu chutu de xila wen qian bing xin tan" 甘肃出土的希腊文铅饼新探. *Xinjiang qianbi* 新疆钱币 (2007.1): 1–8.

Qian fu lun jian jiao zheng 潛夫論箋校正. By Wang Fu 王符. Beijing: Zhonghua shuju, 1985.

Qianlong (Emperor) 乾隆. "Qian lu" 錢錄. In *Gao Zong chi zhuan* 高宗勅撰. 1:52–53. Shanghai: Shang wu yin shu guan, 1937.

Qiu Xigui 裘锡圭. *Chinese Writing.* Translated by Gilbert Mattos and Jerry Norman. Berkeley: Institute of East Asian Studies, University of California, 2000.

————. "Hubei Jiangling Fenghuangshan shihao Hanmu chutu jiandu kaoshi" 湖北江陵凤凰山十号汉墓出土简牍考释. *Wenwu* (1974.7): 49–62.

Queen, Sarah. *From Chronicle to Canon: The Hermeneutics of the Spring and Autumn Annals According to Tung Chung-shu.* Cambridge: Cambridge University Press, 1996.

Raft, Zeb. "The Beginning of Literati Poetry—Four Poems From 1st Century BCE China." *T'oung Pao* 96 (2010): 74–124.

Raphals, Lisa Ann. "Arguments by Women in Early Chinese Texts." *Nan nü* 3, no. 2 (2001): 157–95.

————. *Knowing Words: Wisdom and Cunning in the Classical Traditions of China and Greece.* Ithaca: Cornell University Press, 1992.

————. *Sharing the Light: Representations of Women and Virtue in Early China.* Albany: SUNY Series in Chinese Philosophy and Culture, 1998.

Rawson, Jessica. "Chu Influences on the Development of Han Bronze Vessels." *Arts Asiatiques* 44 (1989): 84–99.

————. "Cosmological Systems as Sources of Art, Ornament and Design." *Bulletin of the Museum of Far Eastern Antiquities* 72 (2000): 133–89.

————. "The Eternal Palaces of the Western Han: A New View of the Universe." *Artibus Asiae* 59, no. 1–2 (1999): 5–58.

————. "Strange Creatures." *Oriental Art* 44, no. 2 (1998): 44–47.

Ren Jiliang 任继亮. *Guanzi jing ji si xiang yan jiu: qing zhong lun shi hua.* 《管子》经济思想研究: 轻重论史话. Beijing: Zhongguo shehui kexue, 2005.

Ren Naiqiang 任乃強, ed. *Huayang guozhi jiao bu tu zhu* 華陽國志校補圖注. Shanghai: Shanghai guji chubanshe, 1987.

Rhea, Blue. "The Argumentation of the *Shih-Huo Chih*: Chapters of the Han, Wei, and Sui Dynastic Histories." *Harvard Journal of Asiatic Studies* 11, no. 1–2 (June 1948): 1–118.

Richter, Matthias. "Textual Identity and the Role of Literacy in the Transmission of Early Chinese Literature." In Li and Branner, *Writing and Literacy*, 206–36.

Rickett, W. Allyn. *Guanzi: Political, Economic, and Philosophical Essays from Early China; A Study and Translation.* 2 vols. Princeton: Princeton University Press, 1998.

———. "*Kuan–tzu* and the Newly Discovered Texts on Bamboo and Silk." In *Chinese Ideas about Nature and Society: Studies in Honour of Derk Bodde*, edited by Charles Le Blanc and Susan Blader, 237–48. Hong Kong: Hong Kong University Press, 1987.

Riegel, Jeffrey. "Do Not Serve the Dead as You Serve the Living: The *Lüshi Chunqiu* Treatises on Moderation in Burial." *Early China* 20 (1995): 301–30.

———. "Early Chinese Target Magic." *Journal of Chinese Religions* 10 (Fall 1982): 1–18.

———. "Eros, Introversion, and the Beginnings of *Shijing* Commentary." *Harvard Journal of Asiatic Studies* 57, no. 1 (1997): 143–77.

———. "A Passion for the Worthy." *Journal of the American Oriental Society* 128.4 (2008): 709–21.

Riegel, Jeffrey, and John Knoblock. *The Annals of Lü Buwei: A Complete Study and Translation.* Stanford: Stanford University Press, 2000.

Riley, Denise. "Does Sex Have a History?" In *Feminism and History*, edited by Joan Scott, 17–33. Oxford: Oxford University Press, 1996.

Roetz, Heiner. "The Axial Age Theory: A Challenge to Historism or an Explanatory Device of Civilization Analysis? With a Look at the Normative Discourse in Axial Age China." In *The Axial Age and Its Consequences*, edited by Robert N. Bellah and Hans Joas, 248–76. Cambridge, MA: Harvard University Press, 2012.

———. "Worte als Namen: Anmerkungen zu Xunzi und Dong Zhongshu." In *Han-Zeit: Festschrift für Hans Stumpfeldt aus Anlaß seines 65. Geburtstages*, edited by Michael Friedrich, 203–16. Wiesbaden: Harrassowitz Verlag, 2006.

Rossabi, Morris, ed. *China Among Equals: The Middle Kingdom and its Neighbors, 10th–14th Centuries.* Berkeley: University of California Press, 1983.

Rostovsteff, M. *The Social and Economic History of the Hellenistic World.* Vol. 2. Oxford: Clarendon Press, 1941.

Rouzer, Paul. *Articulated Ladies: Gender and the Male Community in Early Chinese Texts.* Cambridge, MA: Harvard University Asia Center, 2001.

Rubin, Gayle. "The Traffic in Women: Notes on the 'Political Economy' of Sex." In *Feminism and History*, edited by Joan Scott, 105–51. Oxford: Oxford University Press, 1996.

Sage, Steven. *Ancient Sichuan and the Unification of China.* Albany: State University of New York Press, 1992.

Sahlins, Marshall. *Stone Age Economics.* London: Routledge, 2004.

Said, Edward. *Orientalism*. New York: Vintage, 1979.

Sanft, Charles. "Paleographic Evidence of Qin Religious Practice from Liye and Zhoujiatai." *Early China* (forthcoming).

Saussure, Ferdinand de. *Course in General Linguistics*. Translated by Wade Baskin. New York: Columbia University Press, 2011.

Saussy, Haun. "Correlative Cosmology and its Histories." *Bulletin of the Museum of Far Eastern Antiquities* 72 (2000): 13–28.

———. *Great Walls of Discourse and Other Adventures in Cultural China*. Cambridge, MA: Harvard University Asia Center, 2001.

———. *The Problem of a Chinese Aesthetic*. Stanford: Stanford University Press, 1993.

Schaab-Hanke, Dorothee. *Der Geschichtsschreiber als Exeget: Facetten der Frühen Chinesischen Historiographie*. Gossenberg: Ostasien, 2010.

Schaberg, David. *A Patterned Past: Form and Thought in Early Chinese Historiography*. Cambridge, MA: Harvard University Asia Center, 2001.

———. "Playing at Critique: Indirect Remonstrance and the Formation of *Shi* Identity." In *Text and Ritual in Early China*, edited by Martin Kern, 194–225. Seattle: University of Washington Press, 2005.

———. "Travel, Geography, and the Imperial Imagination in Fifth-Century Athens and Han China." *Comparative Literature* 51, no. 2 (Spring 1999): 152–91.

Schafer, Edward H. *The Golden Peaches of Samarkand: A Study of T'ang Exotics*. Berkeley: University of California Press, 1963.

Scheidel, Walter. "The Monetary Systems of the Han and Roman Empires." In *Rome and China*, edited by Walter Schiedel, 137–207.

———. *Rome and China: Comparative Perspectives on Ancient World Empires*. New York: Oxford University Press, 2009.

Scheidel, Walter, and Sitta von Reden, eds. *The Ancient Economy*. Edinburgh: Edinburgh University Press, 2002.

Schmidt-Colinet, Andreas, Annemarie Stauffer, and Khaled Al-Ascad, eds. *Textilien aus Palmyra: Neue und alte Funde*. Deutsches Archäologisches Institut, Orient-Abteilung: Damaszener Forschungen 8. Mainz: Philipp von Zabern, 2000.

Schneider, David. *A Critique of the Study of Kinship*. Ann Arbor: University of Michigan Press, 1984.

Schopen, Gregory. *Buddhist Monks and Business Matters: Still More Papers on Monastic Buddhism in India*. Honolulu: University of Hawai'i Press, 2004.

Schuessler, Axel. *Minimal Old Chinese and Later Han Chinese: A Companion to Grammata Serica Recensa*. Honolulu: University of Hawai'i Press, 2009.

Schumpeter, Joseph A. *History of Economic Analysis*. Oxford: Oxford University Press, 1954.

Scott, Joan, ed. *Feminism and History*. Oxford: Oxford University Press, 1996.

Seidel, Anna K. "Buying One's Way to Heaven: The Celestial Treasury in Chinese Religions." *History of Religions* 17, no. 3–4 (1978): 419–31.

———. "Imperial Treasures and Taoist Sacraments: Taoist Roots in the Apocrypha." In Strickmann, 2:291–371.

———. "Traces of Han Religion in Funeral Texts Found in Tombs." In *Dōkyō to shūkyō bunka* 道教と宗教文化, edited by Akizuki Kan'ei 秋月觀英, 21–57. Tokyo: Hirakawa, 1987.

Shaanxi lishi bowuguan 陕西历史博物馆, ed. *Da Tang yibao: Hejiacun jiaocang chutu wenwuzhan* 大唐遺寶：何家村窖藏出土文物展. Xi'an: Shaanxi Renmin, 2010.

Shanghai bowuguan 上海博物馆, ed. *Shanghai bowuguan cang sichou zhilu gudai guojia qianbi* 上海博物馆藏丝绸之路古代国家钱币. Shanghai: Shanghai shuhua, 2006.

Shang jun shu jin zhu jin yi 商君書今註今譯. Taibei: Taiwan shang wu yin shu guan, 1988.

Shang jun shu ping zhu 商君书评注. Beijing: Zhonghua shuju, 1976.

Shanghai guji chubanshe, ed. *Han Wei Liu chao bi ji xiao shuo da guan* 汉魏六朝笔记小说大观. Shanghai: Shanghai guji, 1999.

Shanghai Shi fang zhi kexue yanjiuyuan 上海市纺织科学研究院, ed. *Changsha Mawangdui yi hao Han mu chutu fangzhipin de yanjiu* 长沙马王堆一号汉墓出土纺织品的研究. Beijing: Wenwu, 1980.

Shaughnessy, Edward. *I Ching: The Classic of Changes*. New York: Ballantine Books, 1996.

———. "I Chou shu." In Michael Loewe, *Early Chinese Texts*, 229–33.

———. *Rewriting Early Chinese Texts*. Albany: State University of New York Press, 2006.

Shelach, Gideon. *Prehistoric Societies on the Northern Frontiers of China: Archaeological Perspectives on Identity Formation and Economic Change during the First Millennium* BCE. London: Equinox, 2009.

Shelach, Gideon, and Yuri Pines. "Secondary State Formation and the Development of Local Identity: Change and Continuity in the State of Qin (770–221 B.C.)." In Stark, *Archaeology of Asia*, 202–30.

Shell, Marc. *The Economy of Literature*. Baltimore: Johns Hopkins University Press, 1978.

———. *Money, Language, and Thought: Literary and Philosophical Economies from the Medieval to the Modern Era*. Baltimore: Johns Hopkins University Press, 1982.

Shen, Chen. "Early Urbanization in the Eastern Zhou in China (770–221 B.C.): An Archaeological Overview." *Antiquity* 68, no. 261 (1994): 724–44.

Shen, Kangshen, John N. Crossley, and Anthony W. C. Lun, eds. *The Nine Chapters on the Mathematical Art: Companion and Commentary*. New York: Oxford University Press, 1999.

Shi Shiqi 石世奇 and Zheng Xueyi 郑学益, eds. *Zhongguo gu dai jing ji si xiang shi jiao cheng* 中国古代经济思想史教程. Beijing: Beijing daxue, 2008.

Shi Xiaoqun 師小群 and Dang Shunmin 党顺民. "Long wen qian bing tan xi" 龙文铅饼探析. *Shaanxi qianbi yanjiu wenji* 陕西钱币研究文集 10, no. 4 (2003): 104–7.

Shih, Vincent Yu-chung. *The Literary Mind and the Carving of Dragons by Liu Hsieh: A Study of Thought and Pattern in Chinese Literature*. New York: Columbia University Press, 1959.

Shiji 史記. By Sima Qian 司馬遷. Beijing: Zhonghua shuju, 1959.

Shui jing zhu shu 水經注疏. Annotated by Li Daoyuan 酈道元. Nanjing: Jiangsu guji, 1999.

Shuihudi Qinmu zhujian zhengli xiaozu 睡虎地秦墓竹簡整理小組. *Shuihudi Qin mu zhujian* 睡虎地秦墓竹簡. Beijing: Wenwu, 1978.

Shun, Kwong-loi. *Mencius and Early Chinese Thought*. Stanford: Stanford University Press, 1997.

Sichuan sheng bowuguan 四川省博物馆, cd. *Ba Shu Qingtongqi* 巴蜀青銅器. Chengdu: Chengdu, n.d. [1992?].

Simmel, Georg. *The Philosophy of Money*. London: Routledge, 1978.

Sinor, Denis. "The Myth of Languages and the Language of Myth." In Mair, *The Bronze Age*, 729–66.

Sivin, Nathan. "State, Cosmos, and Body in the Last Three Centuries B.C." *Harvard Journal of Asiatic Studies* 55, no. 1 (June 1995): 5–37.

Slingerland, Edward. *Effortless Action: Wu-wei as Conceptual Metaphor and Spiritual Ideal in Early China*. New York: Oxford University Press, 2003.

———, trans. *Confucius Analects: With Selection from Traditional Commentaries*. Indianapolis: Hackett, 2003.

Smith, Adam. *The Wealth of Nations*. 3 vols. London: Penguin, 1999.

Sommer, Matthew H. *Sex, Law, and Society in Late Imperial China*. Stanford: Stanford University Press, 2000.

Spengler, Joseph J. "Ssu-Ma Ch'ien, Unsuccessful Exponent of Laissez Faire." *Southern Economic Journal* 30, no. 3 (January 1964): 223–43.

Spivak, Gayatri Chakravorty. *An Aesthetic Education in the Era of Globalization*. Cambridge, MA: Harvard University Press, 2012.

———. *Death of a Discipline*. New York: Columbia University Press, 2003.

———. "Scattered Speculations on the Question of Value." *Diacritics* 15, no. 4 (Winter 1985): 73–93.

Spring, Madeline Kay. *Animal Allegories in T'ang China*. New Haven, CT: American Oriental Society, 1993.

Stark, Miriam T., ed. *Archaeology of Asia*. Malden, MA: Blackwell, 2006.

Stein, Aurel. *Ancient Khotan: Detailed Report of Archaeological Explorations in Chinese Turkestan*. New York: Hacker Art Books, 1907.

Sterckx, Roel. *The Animal and the Daemon in Early China*. Albany: State University of New York Press, 2002.

———. "The Economics of Religion in Warring States and Early Imperial China." In Lagerwey and Kalinowski, *Early Chinese Religion*, 839–80.

Strickmann, Michel, ed. *Tantric and Taoist Studies in Honour of R. A. Stein*. 3 vols. Brussels: Institut belge des hautes études chinoises, 1981.

Subrahmanyam, Sanjay. "Connected Histories: Notes towards a Reconfiguration of Early Modern Eurasia." *Modern Asian Studies* 31.3 (1997): 735–62.

Sukhu, Gopal. "Yao, Shun and Prefiguration: The Origins and Ideology of the Han Imperial Genealogy." *Early China* 30 (2005–6): 91–153.

Sun Ji 孙机. *Han dai wu zhi wen hua zi liao tu shuo* 汉代物质文化资料图说. Beijing: Wenwu chubanshe, 1991.

Suzuki Torao 鈴木虎雄. *Fu shi da yao* 賦史大要. Translated by Di ping xian chuban she 地平線出版社. Taibei: Di ping xian, 1963.

Svarverud, Rune. *Methods of the Way: Early Chinese Ethical Thought*. Leiden: Brill, 1998.

Swann, Nancy Lee. *Pan Chao: Foremost Woman Scholar of China, First Century AD; Background, Ancestry, Life, and Writings of the Most Celebrated Chinese Woman of Letters*. New York: The Century Company, 1932.

————, trans. *Food and Money in Ancient China. The Earliest Economic History of China to AD 25, Han shu 24, with Related Texts, Han shu 91 and Shih-chi 129*. Princeton: Princeton University Press, 1950.

Takigawa Kametarō 瀧川龜太郎. *Shiki kaichū kōshō [Shiji huizhu kaozheng]* 史記會注考證. Tokyo: Tōhō Bunka gakuin Tōkyō kenkyūjo, 1932–34.

Tang Guangbin 唐光斌. "Xian Qin zhu zi jingji zhexue sixiang zhi ben mo lun" 先秦诸子经济哲学思想之本末论. *Guizhou cai jing xue yuan xue bao* 贵州财经学院学报 5, no. 118 (2005): 71–74.

Tang Shifu 唐石父. *Zhongguo gu qianbi* 中国古钱币. Shanghai: Shanghai guji, 2001.

Thapar, Romila. *Early India: From the Origins to AD 1300*. Berkeley: University of California Press, 2002.

Thierry, François. *Amulettes de Chine: Catalogue*. Paris: Bibliothèque de France, 2008.

————. *Monnaies chinoises: catalogue*. 2 vols. Paris: Bibliothèque nationale de France, 1997.

————. *Monnaies de Chine*. Paris: Bibliothèque nationale de France, 1992.

————. "On the Tang Coins Collected by Pelliot in Chinese Turkestan (1906–1909)." In *Studies in Silk Road Coins and Culture: Papers in Honour of Professor Ikuo Hirayama on his 65th Birthday*, edited by Katsumi Tanabe, Joe Cribb and Helen Wang, 149–79. Kamakura: Institute of Silk Road Studies, 1997.

————. "The Origins and Development of Chinese Coins." In *Origin, Evolution and Circulation of Coins in the Indian Ocean*, 15–62. Manohar, Sri Lanka, 1998.

Tinios, Ellis. "Emperors, Barbarians and Historians in Early Imperial China" (booklet, School of History, the University of Leeds, n.d.).

————. "Hanshu 94: Memoir on the Hsiung-nu" (booklet, School of History, the University of Leeds, n.d.).

————. "'Loose Rein' in Han Relations with Foreign Peoples." University of Leeds: Leeds East Asia Papers, no. 61 (2000).

————. "Sure Guidance for One's Own Time: Pan Ku and Tsan to Han Shu 94." *Early China* 9–10 (1983–85): 184–203.

Tomashevsky, Boris. "Thematics." In *Russian Formalist Criticism: Four Essays*, translated by L. T. Lemon and M. J. Reis, 62–95. Lincoln: University of Nebraska Press, 1965.

Tseng, Lillian Lan-ying. *Picturing Heaven in Early China*. Cambridge, MA: Harvard University Asia Center, 2011.

————. "Representation and Appropriation: Rethinking the TLV Mirror in Han China." *Early China* 29 (2004): 161–213.

Vainker, Sheila. *Chinese Silk: A Cultural History*. New Brunswick: Rutgers University Press, 2004.

van Els, Paul. "Guest Editor's Introduction." *Contemporary Chinese Thought* 34, no. 1 (Fall 2002): 3–18.

van Ess, Hans. "The Old Text/New Text Controversy: Has the 20th Century Got It Wrong?" *T'oung Pao* 80, no. 1 (1994): 146–70.

————. "Praise and Slander: The Evocation of Empress Lü in the *Shiji* and the *Hanshu*." *Nan Nü* 8, no. 2 (2006): 221–54.

Van Norden, Bryan W., trans. *Mengzi: With Selections from Traditional Commentaries*. Indianapolis: Hackett, 2008.

Vankeerberghen, Griet. "Texts and Authors in the Shiji." In *China's Early Empires: A Re-appraisal,* edited by Michael Nylan and Michael Loewe, 461–79. Cambridge: Cambridge University Press, 2010.

Vissering, W. *On Chinese Currency: Coin and Paper Money.* Leiden: Brill, 1877.

Von Glahn, Richard. *Fountain of Fortune: Money and Monetary Policy in China, 1000–1700.* Berkeley: University of California Press, 1996.

———. Review of *Shunjū Sengoku jidai seidō kahei no seisei to tenkai,* by Emura Haruki. *Journal of Asian Studies* 72, no. 2 (May 2013): 442–45.

Vovin, Alexander. "Did the Xiongnu Speak a Yeniseian Language?" *Central Asiatic Journal* 44.1 (2000): 87–104.

Wagner, Donald B. *Iron and Steel in Ancient China.* Leiden: Brill, 1993.

———. *The State and the Iron Industry in Han China.* Copenhagen, Denmark: NIAS, 1991.

Wang, Aihe. "Correlative Cosmology: From the Structure of Mind to Embodied Practice." *Bulletin of the Museum of Far Eastern Antiquities* 72 (2000): 110–32.

———. *Cosmology and Political Culture in Early China.* Cambridge: Cambridge University Press, 2000.

Wang Baoping 王保平. *Han Yang ling kao gu chen lie guan* 汉阳陵考古陈列馆. Beijing: Wenwu, 2004.

Wang Bin 注斌 and Xie Shaoshi 谢少石. "Dui Anhui faxian baijin sanpin de chu bu ren shi" 对安徽发现白金三品的初步认识. *Shaanxi qianbi yanjiu wenji* 陕西钱币研究文集 10, no. 4 (2003): 55–61.

Wang Binghua 王炳华. *Xiyu kaogu lishi lun ji* 西域考古历史论集. Beijing: Zhongguo renmin daxue, 2008.

Wang Daqing 王大庆. *Ben yu mo: gudai Zhongguo yu gudai Xila jingji sixiang bijiao yanjiu* 本与末: 古代中国与古代希腊经济思想比较研究. Beijing: Shang wu yin shu guan, 2006.

Wang, Eugene. "Crystallizing the 'Bleary Blur': Bronze Mat Weights and the Emergence of New Plastic Thinking in the Western Han Dynasty." In *A Bronze Menagerie: Mat Weights of Early China,* edited by Michelle C. Wang, 65–74. Pittsburgh: University of Pittsburgh Press, 2007.

Wang, Helen. *Money on the Silk Road: The Evidence from Eastern Central Asia to AD 800; Including a Catalogue of the Coins Collected by Aurel Stein.* London: British Museum Press, 2004.

———. "Official Salaries and Local Wages at Juyan, North-West China, First Century BCE to First Century CE." In *Wages and Currency: Global Comparisons from Antiquity to the Twentieth Century,* edited by Jan Lucassen. International and Comparative Social History, 59–76. Bern: Peter Lang, 2007.

Wang, Hui. *The Politics of Imagining Asia.* Edited by Theodore Huters. Cambridge, MA: Harvard University Press, 2011.

Wang Jijie 王纪洁. "Ya sheng qian ji xiangguan wenti lüe lun" 压胜钱及相关问题略论. *Zhongguo qianbi* 中国钱币 (2004.4): 43–47.

Wang Liqi 王利器, ed. *Yantielun jiaozhu* 鹽鐵論校注. Revised and enlarged edition. Tianjin: Tianjin guji, 1983.

Wang Ming-ke 王明珂. *Huaxia bianyuan: lishi jiyi yu zuqun rentong* 华夏边缘：历史记忆与族群认同. Beijing: Shehui kexue wenxian, 2006.

Wang Qinjin 王勤金, Wu Wei 吴炜, Xu Liangyu 徐良玉, and Yin Zhihua 印志华. "Jiangsu yizheng xu pu 101 hao Xi Han mu" 江苏仪征胥浦101号西汉墓. *Wenwu* (1987.1): 1–13.

Wang Rongbao 汪榮寶. *Fa yan yi shu* 法言義疏. Beijing: Zhonghua shuju, 1987.

Wang Tongling 王桐齡. *Zhongguo minzu shi* 中國民族史. Taibei: Hua shi, 1977.

Wang Xuenong 王雪农. "Zhongguo de mingbi yi qian ji qi yan bian guocheng" 中国的冥币瘗钱及其演变过程. *Zhongguo qianbi lunwen ji* 中国钱币论文集 (1998.3): 329–37.

Wang Yongsheng 王永生. *Xinjiang li shi huo bi: dong xi fang huo bi wen hua jiao rong de li shi kao cha* 新疆历史货币：东西方货币文化交融的历史考察. Beijing: Zhonghua shu ju, 2007.

Wang, Zhenping. *Ambassadors from the Islands of the Immortals: China-Japan Relations in the Han-Tang Period*. Honolulu: University of Hawai'i Press, 2005.

Wang, Zhongshu. *Han Civilization*. New Haven: Yale University Press, 1982.

Wang Zhuangmu 王庄穆. *Zhongguo sichou cidian* 中國絲綢辭典. Beijing: Zhongguo kexue jishu, 1996.

Wang Zijin 王子今. *Qin Han shehui shi lun kao* 秦汉社会史论考. Beijing: Shang wu yin shu guan, 2006.

———. "Nan gong gongzhu de hun shi" 南宫公主的婚事. *Du shu* 读书 (2006.3): 127–33.

Warburg, Aby. *The Renewal of Pagan Antiquity*. Translated by David Britt. Los Angeles: Getty Research Insititute for the History of Art and the Humanities, 1999.

Watson, Burton. *Chinese Rhyme Prose: Poems in the Fu Form from the Han and Six Dynasties Periods*. New York: Columbia University Press, 1971.

———. *Early Chinese Literature*. New York: Columbia University Press, 1962.

———. *Ssu-ma Ch'ien: Grand Historian of China*. New York: Columbia University Press, 1958.

———, trans. *Records of the Grand Historian by Sima Qian. Han Dynasty*. 2 vols. Revised edition. New York: Columbia University Press, 1993.

———, trans. *Records of the Grand Historian by Sima Qian. Qin Dynasty*. Revised edition. New York: Columbia University Press, 1993.

Wei Zheng 韦正, Li Huren 李虎仁, and Zou Houben 邹厚本. "Xuzhou Shizishan Xihan mu de fajue yu shouhuo" 江苏徐州市狮子山西汉墓的发掘与收获. *Kaogu* 8 (1998): 673–92.

Wenwu chubanshe 文物出版社, ed. *Lingnan xi Han wenwu baoku: Guangzhou Nanyue wang mu* 嶺南西漢文物寶庫：廣州南越王墓. Beijing: Wenwu, 1994.

Wenxin diaolong zhu 文心雕龍注. By Liu Xie 劉勰. Beijing: Renmin wenxue, 2001.

Wen xuan 文選. Edited by Xiao Tong 蕭統. 6 vols. Shanghai: Shanghai guji, 1986.

Whaley, Mark A. "A Middle Indo-Aryan Inscription from China." *Acta Orientalia Academiae Scientiarum Hung*, 4 (2009): 413–60.

White, Hayden. *Figural Realism: Studies in the Mimesis Effect*. Baltimore: Johns Hopkins Press, 2000.

Whitfield, Susan. *Life Along the Silk Road*. Berkeley: University of California Press, 1999.

Wiener, Annette B. *Inalienable Possessions: The Paradox of Keeping-While-Giving*. Berkeley: University of California Press, 1992.

Wieschöfer, Josef. *Ancient Persia. From 550 BC to 650 AD.* Translated by Azizeh Azodi. London: I. B. Tauris, 1996.

Wilbur, Martin. *Slavery in China during the Former Han Dynasty, 206 BC–AD 25.* New York: Russell and Russell, 1967.

Wilhelm, Hellmut. "The Scholar's Frustration: Notes on a Type of 'Fu.'" In *Chinese Thoughts and Institutions,* edited by John K. Fairbank, 310–19. Chicago: University of Chicago Press, 1957.

Wilkinson, Endymion. *Chinese History: A Manual.* Cambridge, MA: Harvard University Asia Center, 2000.

Williams, Raymond. *Keywords: A Vocabulary of Culture and Society.* New York: Oxford University Press, 1976.

———. "Forms of Fiction in 1848." In *Literature, Politics, and Theory: Papers from the Essex Conference, 1976–84,* edited by Francis Barker, Peter Hulme, Margaret Iversen, and Diana Loxley, 1–16. London: Methuen, 1986.

Wong, R. Bin. *China Transformed: Historical Experience and the Limits of European Experience.* Ithaca: Cornell University Press, 1997.

———. "The Political Economy of Agrarian Empire and Its Modern Legacy." In *China and Historical Capitalism: Genealogies of Sinological Knowledge,* edited by Timothy Brook and Gregory Blue, 210–45. Cambridge: Cambridge University Press, 1999.

Wood, Frances. *The Silk Road: Two Thousand Years in the Heart of Asia.* Berkeley: University of California Press, 2002.

Woodmansee, Martha, and Mark Osteen. *The New Economic Criticism: Studies at the Intersection of Literature and Economics.* New York: Routledge, 1999.

Wu Baosan 巫宝三. *Guanzi jingji sixiang yanjiu* 管子经济思想研究. Beijing: Zhongguo shehui kexue, 1989.

———, ed. *Zhongguo jingji sixiangshi ziliao xuanji; Liang Han bufen* 中国经济思想史资料选辑 两汉部分. Beijing: Zhongguo shehui kexue, 1988.

Wu, Gu. "Reconstructing Yi History from Yi Records." In *Perspectives on the Yi of Southwest China,* edited by Stevan Harrell, 21–34. Berkeley: University of California Press, 2001.

Wu, Hung. *The Art of the Yellow Springs: Understanding Chinese Tombs.* Honolulu: University of Hawai'i Press, 2010.

———. *Monumentality in Early Chinese Art and Architecture.* Stanford: Stanford University Press, 1995.

———. "A Sanpan Shan Chariot Ornament and the *Xiangrui* Design in Western Han Art." *Archives of Asian Art* 37 (1984): 38–59.

———. "On Tomb Figurines: The Beginning of a Visual Tradition." In *Body and Face in Chinese Visual Culture,* edited by Wu Hung and Katherine R. Tsiang, 13–47. Cambridge, MA: Harvard University Press, 2005.

———. *The Wu Liang Shrine: The Ideology of Early Chinese Pictorial Art.* Stanford: Stanford University Press, 1989.

Xia Lu 夏路. *Shanxi sheng bowuguan guan cang wenwu jinghua* 山西省博物馆馆藏文物精华. Taiyuan: Shanxi renmin, 1999.

Xi'an wenwu baohu xiufu zhongxin 西安文物保护修复中心, comp. and ed. *Han Zhongguan zhu qian yi zhi* 汉钟官铸钱遗址. Beijing: Kexue, 2004.

Xiao Tong. *Wen Xuan, or, Selections of Refined Literature.* Translated, with Annotations and Introduction, by David R. Knechtges. 3 vols. Princeton: Princeton University Press, 1982–96.

Xie Guihua 谢桂华, Li Junming 李均明, and Zhu Guozhao 朱国炤, eds. *Juyan Han jian shi wen he jiao* 居延汉简释文合校. Beijing: Wenwu, 1987.

Xijing za ji jiao zhu 西京雜記校注. Shanghai: Shanghai guji, 1991.

Xin shu 新書. By Jia Yi 賈誼. Taibei: Taiwan zhonghua shuju, 1981.

Xing Jianguo 邢建國. "Zhongguo jingji sixiang shi shang ben mo guan de yan bian" 中国经济思想史上本末观的演变. *Anhui shifan daxue bao* 24 (1996.1): 42–49.

Xu Fuguan 徐復觀. *Liang Han si xiang shi* 兩漢思想史. Hong Kong: Xianggang Zhong wen da xue, 1975.

Xu Gan 徐幹. *Balanced Discourses. A Bilingual Edition.* English translation by John Makeham. New Haven: Yale University Press, 2002.

Xu, Jay. "Sichuan before the Warring States Period." In *Ancient Sichuan: Treasures from a Lost Civilization*, edited by Robert Bagley, 21–27. Princeton: Princeton University Press, 2001.

Xu Limin 徐力民. "Lun zongjiao yu woguo gudai de yan sheng qian—jian tan zongjiao huobi jingji de yingxiang" 论宗教与我国古代的厌胜钱—兼谈宗教对货币经济的影响. *Zhongyuan wenwu* 中原文物 (1988.3): 76–81.

Xu Shen 許慎. *Shuo wen jie zi xin bian* 説文解字新編. Edited by Feng Siyu 馮思禹. Hong Kong: Youwen shuju, 1966.

Xunzi ji shi 荀子集釋. Taibei: Taiwan xue sheng shu ju, 1979.

Xuzhou bowuguan 徐州博物馆, ed. *Da Han Chu wang: Xuzhou Xi Han Chu wang lingmu wenwu jicui* 大漢楚王: 徐州西汉楚王陵墓文物辑萃. Beijing: Zhongguo shehui kexue, 2005.

———. "Xuzhou Beidongshan Xihan mu fajue jianbao" 徐州北洞山徐州北洞山, *Wenwu* 2 (1988): 2–18.

Yang Jiping 杨际平. "Fenghuangshan shi hao Han mu ju 'suan' pai yi wenshu yanjiu" 凤凰山十号汉墓据"算"派役文书研究. *Lishi yanjiu* (2009.6): 51–62.

Yang, Lien-sheng 楊聯陞. "The Concept of *pao* as a Basis for Social Relations in China." In *Excursions in Sinology*, 3–26. Cambridge, MA: Harvard University Press, 1969.

———. "Economic Justification for Spending—An Uncommon Idea in Traditional China." *Harvard Journal of Asiatic Studies* 20, no. 1–2 (June 1957): 36–52.

———. *Money and Credit in China. A Short History.* Cambridge, MA: Harvard University Press, 1952.

———. *Studies in Chinese Institutional History.* Cambridge, MA: Harvard University Press, 1961.

———. *Zhongguo wenhua zhong "bao," "bao," "bao" zhi yiyi* 中國文化中「報」、「保」、「包」之意義. Hong Kong: Zhongwen daxue, 1987.

Yang Shuda 杨树达. *Han dai hun sang li su kao* 汉代婚丧礼俗考. 1933. Reprint, Shanghai: Shanghai guji, 2000.

———. *Yantielun yao shi* 鹽鐵論要釋. Beijing: Kexue, 1957.

Yang Xiong. *Exemplary Figures.* Translated and Introduced by Michael Nylan. Seattle: University of Washington Press, 2013.

Yantielun jian zhu 盐铁论简注. Annotated by Ma Feibai 马非百. Beijing: Zhonghua shuju, 1984.

Yates, Robin D. S. "Cosmos, Central Authority, and Communities in the Early Chinese Empire." In Alcock, *Empires*, 351–68.

———. *Five Lost Classics: Tao, Huang-Lao, and Yin-Yang in Han China*. Toronto: Random House, 1997.

———. "Slavery in Early China: A Socio-Cultural Approach." *Journal of East Asian Archaeology* 3, no. 1–2 (2001): 283–331.

———. "Social Status in the Ch'in: Evidence from the Yün-meng Legal Documents. Part One: Commoners." *Harvard Journal of Asiatic Studies* 47, no. 1 (1987): 197–237.

——— "Soldiers, Scribes, and Women: Literacy among the Lower Orders in Early China." In Li and Branner, *Writing and Literacy in Early China*, 339–69.

Ye Shichang 叶世昌. *Gudai Zhongguo jingji sixiang shi* 古代中国经济思想史. Shanghai: Fudan daxue, 2003.

Yee, Cordell. "Cartography in China." In *The History of Cartography*. Vol. 2, Book 2. *Cartography in the Traditional East and Southeast Asian Societies*, edited by J. B. Harley and David Woodward, 35–202. Chicago: University of Chicago Press, 1994.

Yin Qing 殷晴. *Sichou zhilu yu Xiyu jingji: shi er shiji qian Xinjiang kai fa shi gao* 丝绸之路与西域经济: 十二世纪前新疆开发史稿. Beijing: Zhonghua shu ju, 2007.

Young, Iris. "House and Home: Variations on a Theme." In *Motherhood and Space: Configurations of the Maternal Through Politics, Home, and the Body*, edited by Sarah Hardy and Caroline Weidmer, 115–47. New York: Palgrave Macmillan, 2005.

Young, Leslie. "The Tao of Markets: Sima Qian and the Invisible Hand." *Pacific Economic Review* 1.2 (September 1996): 137–45.

Young, Robert J. C. *Postcolonialism: An Historical Introduction*. London: Routledge, 2001.

Yu, Pauline. *The Reading of Imagery in the Chinese Poetic Tradition*. Princeton, NJ: Princeton University Press, 1987.

Yü Ying-shih 余英時. *Zhongguo jin shi zong jiao lun li yu shang ren jing shen* 中國近世宗教倫理與商人精神. Taibei: Lian jing chu ban shi ye gong si, 1987.

———. "Business Culture and Chinese Traditions—Toward a Study of the Evolution of Merchant Culture in Chinese History." In *Dynamic Hong Kong: Business and Culture*, edited by Wang Gungwu and Wong Siu-lun, 1–84. Hong Kong: Centre of Asian Studies, University of Hong Kong, 1997.

———. "Han Foreign Relations." In *The Cambridge History of China*. Vol. 1, *The Ch'in and Han Empires, 221 BC–AD 220*, edited by Denis Twitchett and Michael Loewe, 377–462. Cambridge: Cambridge University Press, 1987.

———. *Trade and Expansion in Han China: A Study in the Structure of Sino-Barbarian Economic Relations*. Berkeley: University of California Press, 1967.

Yuxi diqu xingzheng gongshu 玉溪地區行政公署, ed. *Yunnan Lijia Shan qingtongqi: fu, Yuxi Diqu wenwu jingpin* 雲南李家山青銅器—附玉溪地區文物精品. Kunming: Yunnan renmin, 1995.

Zeitlin, Judith. *Historian of the Strange: Pu Songling and the Chinese Classical Tale*. Stanford: Stanford University Press, 1993.

Zhang Dainian. *Key Concepts in Chinese Philosophy*. Translated and edited by Edmund Ryden. New Haven: Yale University Press, 2002.

Zhang Dake 張大可. *Shiji yanjiu jicheng* 史記研究集成. Beijing: Hua wen, 2005.

Zhang Liying 张立英. "Tan dui 'baijin san pin' de ren zhi" 谈对"白金三品"的认知. *Kaogu yu wenwu* (1994.5): 90–92.

Zhang Longxi. *Allegoresis: Reading Canonical Literature East and West.* Ithaca: Cornell University Press, 2005.

———. *The Tao and the Logos: Literary Hermeneutics, East and West.* Durham: Duke University Press, 1992.

Zhang Wenyu 张闻玉. *Yi zhou shu quan yi* 逸周书全译. Guiyang: Guizhou renmin, 2000.

Zhang Xinke 张新科. *Shiji xue gailun* 史记学概论. Beijing: Shang wu yin shu guan, 2003.

Zhang Zengqi 張增祺, ed. *Dianguo qingtong yishu* 滇國青銅藝術. Kunming: Yunnan renmin, 2000.

Zhang Zhengming 張正明. "Heqin tong lun" 和亲通论. In *Minzu shi lun cong* 民族史论丛, edited by Zhongguo shehui kexue yuan minzu yanjiusuo, 3–24. Beijing: Zhonghua shuju, 1986.

Zhangjiashan Hanmu zhujian [er si qi hao mu] 张家山汉墓竹简 [二四七号墓]. Beijing: Wenwu, 2001.

Zhao Feng 赵丰. *Zhongguo sichou tongshi* 中国絲綢通史. Suzhou: Suzhou daxue, 2005.

Zhao, Henry Y. H. "Historiography and Fiction in Chinese Culture." In *The Novel.* Vol. 1, *History, Geography, and Culture*, edited by Franco Moretti, 69–93. Princeton: Princeton University Press, 2006.

Zhao Shouzheng 赵守正. *Guanzi jingji sixiang yanjiu* 管子经济思想研究. Shanghai: Shanghai guji, 1989.

Zhao Xiaoming 赵晓明. "Xi Han baijin sanpin xiang guan wenti de shen tao" 西汉白金三品相关问题的深讨. *Shaanxi qianbi yanjiu wenji* 陕西钱币研究文集 10, no. 4 (2003): 41–54.

Zheng Shubin 郑曙斌. "Qiance de kaogu faxian yu wenxian quanshi" 遣策的考古发现与文献诠释. *Nanfang wenwu* 2005, no. 2: 28–34.

Zheng Wenzhuo 鄭文焯. "Lading jin pan" 臘丁金槃. *Shenzhou da guan* 神州大觀 2 (1913): n.p.

Zheng, Yen. "Barbarian Images in Han Period Art." *Orientations* (June 1998): 50–59.

Zhongguo ke xue yuan kaogu yanjiu suo 中国科学院考古研究所, ed. *Changsha Mawangdui yi hao Han mu* 長沙馬王堆一號漢墓. Beijing: Wenwu, 1973.

Zhongguo Qin Han shi yanjiuhui 中國秦汉史研究会, ed. *Nanyue guo shi ji yantaohui lunwen xuanji* 南越国史迹研讨会论文选集. Beijing: Wenwu, 2005.

Zhongguo shehui kexue yuan kaogu yanjiusuo 中国社会科学院考古研究所. *Mancheng Han mu fa jue* 滿城汉墓发掘报告. Beijing: Wenwu, 1980.

Zhou Rong 周容. *Shi xue tong lun* 史學通論. Shanghai: Kai ming, 1933.

Zhou Shirong 周世荣. "Xi Han Changsha guo huobi xin tan" 西汉长沙国货币新探. *Zhongguo huobi lunwen ji* (1998. 3): 185–93.

Zhou Yanling 周延龄. "Xi Han qian bing ming wen kao xi" 西汉铅饼铭文考析. *Shaanxi qianbi yanjiu wenji* 陕西钱币研究文集 10, no. 4 (2003): 75–80.

Zhou, Yiqun. *Festivals, Feasts, and Gender Relations in Ancient China and Greece.* Cambridge: Cambridge University Press, 2010.

Zhuangzi ji shi 莊子集釋. Beijing: Zhonghua shuju, 1995.

Zhuangzi jin zhu jin yi 莊子今注今譯. Annotated by Chen Guying 陳鼓應. Beijing: Zhonghua shuju, 1983.

Zong Fan 踪凡. *Hanfu yanjiu shilun* 汉赋研究史论. Beijing: Beijing daxue, 2007.

Zufferey, Nicolas. "Traces of the Silk Road in Han-Dynasty Iconography: Questions and Hypotheses." In *The Journey of Maps and Images on the Silk Road*, edited by Philippe Forêt and Andreas Kaplony, 9–28. Leiden: Brill, 2008.

Zuo Ming 作铭. "Waiguo zi ming wen de Handai(?) qian bing" 外国字铭文的汉代(?) 铜饼. *Kaogu* (1961.5): 50–54.

Index

Harvard-Yenching Institute Monograph Series
(titles now in print)

Harvard-Yenching Institute Monograph Series

Harvard-Yenching Institute Monograph Series